TEACHER'S MANUAL

FOR THE

TEN BASIC STEPS TOWARD CHRISTIAN MATURITY

TEACHER'S MANUAL

FOR THE

TEN BASIC STEPS
TOWARD CHRISTIAN MATURITY

William R. Bright

Editor

CAMPUS CRUSADE FOR CHRIST, INTERNATIONAL

Arrowhead Springs, San Bernardino, California

1965

Printed in the
United States of America

First Printing 1965

Second Printing 1966

Third Printing 1967

Fourth Printing 1968

Fifth Printing 1970

Sixth Printing 1971

Seventh Printing 1972

Eighth Printing 1972

A WORD OF INSTRUCTION TO THE INSTRUCTOR

from

Bill Bright

Would you like to know how to teach the Bible? *You can!*

This *Teacher's Manual* for the *Ten Basic Steps Toward Christian Maturity* has been designed and written to enable even a new Christian to lead and teach Bible study groups.

Nearly every major doctrine of the Christian faith has been carefully considered and clearly presented so that any person sincerely seeking spiritual truth will be generously rewarded by even a casual reading of these pages.

The *Ten Basic Steps Toward Christian Maturity,* together with this *Teacher's Manual,* are the product of necessity. As the ministry of Campus Crusade for Christ expanded rapidly to scores of campuses across America, thousands of students committed their lives to Christ — as many as four or five hundred on a single campus. Individual follow-up of all new converts soon became an impossibility. Who was to help them grow in their new-found faith?

A Bible study series designed for new Christians was desperately needed, a study which would stimulate individuals and groups alike to explore the depths and the riches of God's word. Though several excellent studies were available, there was nothing which we felt met the particular need of the college student.

In 1955, several members of our staff were assigned to assist me in the preparation of materials which we hoped would stimulate both Christian growth and evangelism on the part of the new believer. The contribution by campus staff members was especially significant because of their constant contact with students, introducing them to Christ and meeting regularly with them to assist them in their Christian growth.

Thus, the *Ten Basic Steps Toward Christian Maturity* — a study in "Follow-up Evangelism" — was the fruit of our combined labor. After several revisions and many printings, this Bible study series is used by hundreds of churches and other Christian groups across America, in many countries and in several languages.

The unusual popularity of this Bible study series posed an additional problem — a *Teacher's Manual* was needed. No longer could one staff member teach all of the many Bible study groups organized on a single campus. Also, many other groups were now requesting use of these materials. As the Campus Crusade for Christ ministry expanded to new campuses and many additional workers joined our staff, I found it necessary to be away from my ministry on the campus at U.C.L.A. where the work was first launched. My wife, Vonette, was recruited to substitute. In order to properly supervise the many Bible studies on the campus, she found it necessary to appoint a leader for each Bible study group. Each week Vonette prepared lesson plans and met with all the leaders to teach them the material they would teach their individual Bible study groups.

This was the beginning of the *Teacher's Manual* for the *Ten Basic Steps.* Since that modest beginning, many other members of the staff have contributed generously to the present volume which you hold in your hands. On occasion, for example, I have found myself involved in research and writing sessions which involved several of our staff, all seminary graduates, several with advanced degrees, one with his doctorate in theology. More important, all of them are actively engaged in "winning men, building men and sending men" for Christ on the college campus.

Written originally with the college student in mind, the *Ten Basic Steps Toward Christian Maturity* have proved equally effective with adults and youth. In addition to churches and home Bible study groups, the *Steps* are used by chaplains of prisons, chaplains of the military and by many high school student groups.

Although thousands of hours have been invested in writing these materials, we are still confident that they can be improved. You can be of great assistance by advising us of any suggestions which you may have, or of corrections in reference or in content which should be made.

This *Teacher's Manual* and the *Ten Basic Steps Toward Christian Maturity* have been prepared with the prayer that this study will encourage multiplied thousands of students and adults around the world to become true disciples of the Lord Jesus Christ.

BILL BRIGHT

Founder and President

Campus Crusade for Christ, Int'l.

TABLE OF CONTENTS

TEACHER'S MANUAL

for the

TEN BASIC STEPS TOWARD

CHRISTIAN MATURITY

INTRODUCTION

I. THE VALUE OF THE TEN BASIC STEPS:

College students usually study a little of everything, but all too often give minimum or no time to a study of the Bible. Yet the Bible undoubtedly has had a more profound effect on history than any other book. It has played a major role in the founding and molding of western culture. The daily life of every American would be vastly different if the Bible had never been written. No college education can be considered complete without at least a general knowledge of the Bible, and no person can be considered well-educated who is ignorant of its teachings.

The Ten Basic Steps are designed to give you an efficient means for systematic study of the Christian faith as taught in the Bible. The result of this study should be two-fold in your life. First, it should communicate knowledge. Without a knowledge of at least some Biblical teaching no person can become a Christian, and no Christian can live the Christian life. A great many people reject Christianity and a great many Christians live miserable, defeated, frustrated lives for no reason except that of sheer ignorance. The Psalmist said, "The entrance of Thy Words giveth light " (Psa. 119:130), and Jesus taught that "The truth shall make you free" (John 8:32). Second, it should communicate power to your life. Hebrews 4:12 says that "The Word of God is quick and powerful, and sharper than any two-edged sword, piercing even to the dividing asunder of soul and spirit, and of the joints and marrow, and is a discerner of the thoughts and intents of the heart." The Bible differs from all other books in that it is a living book, and through it the life and power of God are communicated to the life of an individual. Men and women by the thousands, including Augustine, Luther, Wesley and many others have changed history because God used the Bible to change them.

Even as your group begins to study the Ten Basic Steps, a change should come over them. Also some should receive Christ. There should

1

be more consistent living, more love, more devotion to Christ, more patience, more desire to spread the Christian message and at the same time a decrease in pride, jealousy, gossip, harsh words, sloppy living, etc.

In this study several things will be emphasized. You will notice an emphasis on the distinctiveness of Christianity. For example, no religion makes provision for the breach between God and man. Christianity calls this breach sin, and provides for it not in what man can do for God, as all religions attempt to do, but in what God has done for man in sending His Son, Jesus Christ, to die on the cross. You will also notice an emphasis on the distinctive claims of Christ. Many people feel that Christ was only a good moral teacher, but this study will make clear that He claimed to be no less than deity, and is either the true God or else a liar and impostor. Also, you will notice an emphasis on the abundant life God has for every Christian through the power of the Holy Spirit. Many students have had their lives utterly transformed through a proper understanding of the abundant life God has for them and the doctrine of the filling of the Holy Spirit (see Step 3, The Christian and the Holy Spirit).

II. MOTIVATION FOR STUDYING THE TEN BASIC STEPS:

A. The *Ten Basic Steps Toward Christian Maturity* are designed specifically to help the Christian in the following ways:

1. To give him a general knowledge of the Bible.

2. To provide him with a systematic plan of study.

3. To acquaint him with the major doctrines of the Christian faith.

4. To help him with problems that are facing college students.

B. This study is good for the older Christian because it:

1. Gives tools with which he can help another find Christ or help another grow in his faith.

2. Helps him establish a systematic devotional and study plan.

C. This study is good for the new Christian because it:

1. Aids his growth.

2. Increases his familiarity with the Bible.

3. Teaches him the basic doctrines of his Christian faith.

4. Answers problems of his life from Scripture.

2

D. This study is good for the non-Christian because it:

1. Helps him to understand the Bible.

2. Presents the claims and Person of Christ.

3. Shows him clearly how to become a Christian and live the Christian life.

E. These *Ten Basic Steps* can be used in two different ways: Individual follow-up sessions and group Bible studies. You may use either of the following procedures:

1. A summary study completing one Step at each session.

2. A more detailed study completing one Lesson at each session.

(Note to teacher: Both of these types of lesson plans are available.)

III. SUMMARY OF THE TEN BASIC STEPS:

This course of study is designed to give you a broad survey of Christianity. You will meet its central figure, Jesus Christ, and you will study its authoritative literature, the Holy Bible. You will learn of the nature, privileges and responsibilities of the Christian way of life, and you will discover the secret of its power to transform men and give them a continually abundant life.

A. The Uniqueness of Jesus.

This Introductory Step to the Ten Basic Steps Toward Christian Maturity presents the Person of Jesus Christ. It explains who He is, His earthly life, His death, resurrection and continuing ministry in the lives of all believers. A special emphasis is given to the importance of the Church of Jesus Christ.

B. The Christian Adventure.

Step One deals with various facets of the Christian walk, i.e., the Christian's certainty, the Christ-controlled life, principles of growth, the Christian's authority and the importance of the Church to the believer.

C. The Christian and the Abundant Life.

Step Two describes the Christian way of life—what it is, and how it works out practically. It discusses problems of sin and temptation and the warfare of life. It points the way to Christian victory and the abundant life.

D. The Christian and the Holy Spirit.

Step Three is a discussion of the Holy Spirit, who is the third member of the Godhead, or Trinity. This lesson teaches us who the Holy Spirit is and how He works in the lives of individuals. It shows us how we may have Him working in our own lives and what the results will be. It teaches us how we may have His power continually energizing us.

E. The Christian and Prayer.

Step Four introduces us to prayer—communion with God. It gives us suggestions regarding a time of meditation. It discusses the purpose, privileges, procedures and promises in prayer, and the power to be derived from it.

F. The Christian and His Bible.

In Step Five we turn to an analysis of the Bible itself. We learn of its composition, authority, central theme and character, and its power to help us. We also will learn methods of studying it and the soul food to be derived from such a study.

G. The Christian and Obedience.

Step Six teaches us what the Bible says about obedience. It discusses such matters as finding and doing God's will, security, personal purity, fears, use of the tongue and the problems of insincerity.

H. The Christian and Witnessing.

Step Seven deals with the subject of sharing Christianity with others. We will see how Jesus did it and its relationship to the word of God, prayer and the Holy Spirit. We will also learn of the value and place of the personal testimony.

I. The Christian and Stewardship.

Stewardship is discussed in Step Eight. This subject speaks of God's claim upon every individual in everything that makes up his life. It discusses consecration of the spiritual and physical aspects of one's life, as well as all of the material things that he possesses. The nature and responsibilities of the Christian steward are defined.

J. Highlights of the Old Testament.

Step Nine is a brief survey of the highlights of the Old Testament. It discusses the history of Israel, through whom God revealed

Himself to the world. It tells of the creation and fall of man, the promise of the Messiah (God's deliverer), Abraham (father of the Jews), Joshua and deliverance, David and forgiveness, Elijah and the power of the Holy Spirit, and Jeremiah, the prophet of God.

K. Highlights of the New Testament.

The Tenth, and final, Step gives us highlights of the New Testament. It reviews each of the New Testament books and gives a brief survey of its contents.

These lessons, of course, are not intended as a complete development of Christian beliefs. However, a careful study of the material will give you, with God's help, a sufficient understanding of how you may know and appropriate God's plan for your life. If fully appropriated, the spiritual truths contained in this study will assure you of the full and abundant life which Jesus promised in John 10:10.

IV. MEMORIZATION:

The memory verses have been provided to help you in your walk with Christ. As you study, you will find that by "binding certain truths on the table of your heart" you will be enabled to meet each and every situation as it arises. Psa. 119:9, "Wherewithal shall a young man cleanse his way? By taking heed thereto according to Thy Word."

It is suggested that you learn each verse in connection with the corresponding lesson by writing it out. Retain the verses, reviewing daily, and then as you begin the second step, start memorizing these seven verses in the same way. When you have finished the second Basic Step, continue with the third Step, writing out each verse. Remember, a regular review and systematic method are essential in our daily walk. Cards for memorization can be obtained from any bookstore or printshop, or they can be made by cutting down filing cards.

The importance of memorizing as a means of study cannot be overemphasized. The Lord has commanded that we learn His word. Proverbs 7:1-3 says, "My son, keep my words, and lay up my commandments with thee. Keep my commandments and live; and my law as the apple of thine eye. Bind them upon thy fingers, write them upon the table of thine heart."

As you memorize, you will experience some of the joy, victory and power which the memorized word gives to the CHRISTian's walk.

Strive diligently to finish the *Ten Basic Steps,* and later, as you develop your own Bible study, continue to have a systematic method of memorization of God's word.

V. ROLE OF THE TEACHER:

The purpose of the teacher is not to be an "answer checker," but to supplement the student's own study. *The teacher should not monopolize the time.* The teacher should be prepared to answer the student's questions and to bring out the deeper things from the word of God which the student may have missed. He should stimulate the student's thinking and challenge him to dig deeper for more knowledge than is required. The teacher should be able to show the student how to apply the new knowledge which he has acquired to his life, for real learning does not take place until there is a change in one's thinking, attitudes or actions. The Master Teacher is our Lord Jesus Christ. He knows the needs of every pupil. Allow Him first to be your teacher; then, yielding to Him, let Him teach your students through you.

VI. HOW TO ORGANIZE A BIBLE STUDY CLASS:

Organizing a class to study the *Ten Basic Steps* should be done only after prayer for God's leading and blessing. Classes may vary in size from just one person to several. Generally, you will approach students with whom some previous contact has been made, though announcement may be made concerning the Bible class to others in your dormitory, fraternity or other living group as the case may be. Often those to whom you have witnessed but who have not yet accepted Christ will be interested. New Christians and others who need follow-up are also likely prospects. Choose the ones you think would be best to start with, pray about each one individually and then see each one personally. After you have made the contacts you may choose a definite meeting place and time. If the study is in your room at school or your living-room at home be sure it is neat, attractive in appearance and well-ventilated. Choose a place where you will be free from interruptions. If several days elapse between the contact and the first Bible study, remind those involved by announcement, phone or card. If you have had no experience teaching one of these classes, and feel unsure of yourself, you might ask an experienced teacher to take the first one or two classes, and observe the methods he uses. On some campuses in the past some students have chosen not to teach a study in their own houses and therefore have arranged to exchange houses with another student. This method might appeal to you.

In selling students on the idea of a Bible study, it is important to avoid pressuring them. At the same time, however, you must avoid a negative or apologetic attitude. The best way to promote interested enthusiasm is to be interested and enthusiastic about it yourself. Here is a suggested approach to a student.

"John, when we've talked before, you've expressed an interest in knowing more about Christianity and the Bible. I wish you'd take a look at this book for a minute (Show him the Introductory Step, "The Uniqueness of Jesus"). This really has been a tremendous help to me in learning more about the Bible in a short time. (Show him Lesson One, and the outline of the Ten Steps in the back.) John, I think this could be a real help to both of us if we could study it together." Or, "John, we're starting a class of several who are eager to study the Bible, and we feel that if we did it together we would all benefit. Why don't you join us? etc . . ."

With patience and prayer, you will be led to those whom God would have in your class.

VII. HOW TO LEAD A GROUP BIBLE STUDY:

These lessons are presented in such a way that they can be used with groups of Christians, non-Christians or mixed groups. Each Lesson Plan contains directional material for conducting the lesson. Subject matter is to be found in the corresponding lesson in the *Ten Basic Steps Toward Christian Maturity*. A Lesson Amplification follows each lesson to provide background material and additional information for discussion.

For those who have had very little background in the study of the Bible, there are few ways of getting into the Scriptures as effective as the *group* method. In a group the new student is encouraged immediately to participate, to say something himself. This sharpens his desire to learn for he realizes that he is not only receiving, but is giving to others.

The group method gives each individual an opportunity for expression. *This is important for building leaders.* Each group should have as one of its chief goals the producing of leaders for other groups. If one person dominates the discussion and does not allow others to participate, this *leadership-training* goal is frustrated.

A. Basic principles of group Bible study:

1. The purpose of a Bible study should be:

   a. To learn of Christ.

   b. To encourage holy living.

   c. To provide an opportunity for evangelistic outreach.

2. All Bible studies should be evangelistic in emphasis, to introduce non-Christians to Christ.

3. It is a *Bible study,* not a general discussion time. The whole point is to learn the contents of the Bible and to increase in the knowledge of Christ. The leader should see to it that the discussion stays centered on definite passages from the Scripture.

4. The discussion should follow the definite outline of study as set forth by the lesson plan.

5. There may be certain groups geared to specific needs, although following the same curriculum as the others; there may be a special group for working people; a special group for new Christians; a special group for more advanced students, etc.

6. The group leader is not a lecturer, but a *discussion leader.* He should not dominate the discussion, but should lead it, draw it out. However, he should be well prepared to suggest ideas, give background material, offer suggestions and ask questions to keep the conversation rolling when it lags. If another member is saying something to the point and productive, the discussion leader should *not* be anxious to insert his own thoughts, although he should guide, clarify and summarize.

7. The group leader should never leave the group once it has started. If materials have to be secured or extra chairs are needed, he should appoint someone else to get them.

8. When there are several groups meeting in the same room, care should be taken not to place them so close together that they disturb each other. The group leader should sit facing the other groups so that as much as possible his people are not distracted by things happening outside their circle.

9. The leader should know everyone in his group by name and refer to them often by their names. He should see to it that new people are introduced before the discussion begins.

10. Visitors should be contacted during the week after their visit and invited back.

11. Ideally, no group should be over ten people. It may be less. If more than ten, intimacy is lost. It is best to sit in a circle.

12. For larger groups such as church Bible study, two sessions are suggested: the first led by the pastor for twenty minutes or so to introduce and provide background for the study; the second session led by several trained discussion leaders of smaller groups.

B. How to keep the discussion moving clearly, not too fast (shallow) or too slow (tedious):

1. Ask the group to read the passage to be discussed, each one taking a verse.

2. Ask one member to summarize the passage in his own words before any questions are asked about it.

3. When going over the study questions, *ask specific people to answer them*. This will keep everyone on his toes. However, care should be given to avoid embarrassing participants. When you ask a question of a group member, *be sure he is going to answer it aptly*. If he stumbles, help him along and *make him think he did answer it,* at least in part. *Compliment* him on his answer. A person should not be allowed to feel that he has failed. This is especially true of new members of your group study.

4. Restate the question in different words, from another point of view.

5. The leader should have several parallel passages worked out for each study passage and for each question. If everybody looks blank at the first question and no one has anything to say, suggest that one of them look up a parallel passage which you give him.

   a. Have him read the passage.

   b. "What similarity do you see between this passage and the one we have been studying?"

   c. "What light does this new passage throw upon the original question?"

6. After one person has made a point, ask others if they agree. Have them state their reasons. Often a great deal can be learned by disagreeing over a passage. Bring in other members and get their opinion. At the end of the discussion have someone summarize the points that have been made. It is sometimes best for the leader to do this.

7. Apply the passage personally. "What significance does this have for us today?" "What does this mean to you?" "How does (or will) it affect your life?"

8. There should be some who have been doing extra studying of the lessons. Have them briefly share their results. Be sure to commend them for their effort.

9. Encourage others individually (apart from the group, in private conversation) to work on some of the "further study projects." Offer to help them and look over their work.

9

10. Questions that stimulate discussion:

    a. What do you think this passage means?

    b. Can you think of any parallel passages in the Bible with the same idea?

    c. What can we learn from this passage about God, Christ, ourselves, our responsibility, our relationships to others, etc.

    d. Has this passage ever meant something special to you? If so, why? (Be sure the statement is correct and in keeping with the passage.)

11. "What don't you understand about this passage?" Be sure that all unusual words are clearly defined. Have a different translation read (Responsibility of leader).

12. Keep the discussion relevant and personal.

13. Keep the discussion non-argumentative.

14. Use brainstorming and buzz groups for variety and stimulation in your discussion group.

C. Characteristics of good questions:

1. Questions should be brief and simple. The pupil should be able to grasp the meaning quickly.

2. Questions should be clear, with only one possible interpretation as to what is meant. This demands great care in the choice of words and phrasing of sentences.

3. Questions should provoke thought, testing judgment, not merely the memory.

4. Questions should never suggest the answer.

5. Questions should not offer the student a choice between two possible answers contained in the question because such do not compel the student to think, but rather to guess.

6. Questions should not be stated in the words of the text, pamphlet or notes being used. This encourages verbatim memory of content and discourages thoughtful assimilation of ideas.

7. Questions should be adapted to the knowledge and experience of the pupil with special attention being given to the quickest and slowest in the class and an opportunity for answering given to each.

8. Questions should prepare the person for further study, starting a train of associated ideas.

9. Questions should be logical and interrelated.

10. Questions should fulfill an essential purpose and not merely be asked for the sake of asking.

11. Questions should be asked in a conversational, spontaneous way, as if personally addressed to each of the group before one is selected to answer.

D. Technique of Questioning:

1. Questions should be asked in an informal way, implying that the student is able to answer.

2. Questions should be distributed so that all have an opportunity to learn as nearly equally as possible. This should not involve a purely mechanical distribution, e.g. alphabetically, seating order, etc.

3. Strike a balance between volunteers and stimulating shy people.

4. A person should be allowed sufficient time to answer. Do not be impatient. A too rapid placing of questions with insufficient time to answer them will distract rather than develop the thinking skill.

5. The answer should not be suggested by word, or hint, or inflection of the voice, or in any other way.

6. The leader should systematize and integrate his questioning process to provide a unity and coherence which will lead the class through the material in an organized way.

7. Usually, neither answers nor questions should be repeated. If the leader is at fault, the question must be repeated. Otherwise people will become inattentive.

8. When a person says that he is not able to answer a question, the leader should normally assume that this is true. Don't prod.

9. The question should evidence adaptability to the material and to the immediate situation.

10. Care should be taken not to ask too many questions, especially in a deliberate way.

11. Sometimes the leader should not answer or give agreement, but move ahead to clarifying information in the lesson.

Much of the above material has been edited from suggestions received from Mrs. Frank Renwick, a well-known Bible teacher.

THE UNIQUENESS OF JESUS

INTRODUCTORY STEP

OBJECTIVE: To establish and to be assured of our position in Christ.

I.   OPEN WITH PRAYER.

II. MEMORY VERSE: John 1:12.

III. MOTIVATION: In what ways do men seek happiness? List some of them. Are these really satisfying? Why not? Look up John 4:13-14.

IV. BIBLE STUDY:

A. Ask for questions from those who have completed the study.

Quickly look over each lesson. In the event the Introductory Step is not completed, take key questions from each lesson for them to complete.

B. Discussion:

1. Why was Jesus sent (two reasons)?

2. Why was Christ's coming necessary?

3. What is sin (Romans 8:7)?

4. What is the result of sin (Romans 3:23 and 6:23)?

5. What did Jesus say of Himself?

6. Why did Christ die?

7. What does His resurrection tell us about Jesus Christ (Romans 1:4)?

8. Is it possible to reach God through living a good life?

9. What does it mean to have Christ dwelling within us?

10. Can we be sure that we have a personal relationship with Jesus Christ? How?

(Romans 3:23; 6:23; Ephesians 2:8-9; John 14:6; Revelation 3:20; John 1:12; I John 5:11-13. Use circles and quotes from God's Plan.)

11. What is the church?

12. Why is it important that we be a part of the church?

V.   PARALLEL PASSAGES:

A. Trinity (Genesis 1:26. "Let *us* make man in *our* image").

B. Prophecy (Isaiah 9:6. Written 700 years before Christ's coming, tells how He will come).

C. Why Christ came (Hebrews 1:1-3).

D. Christ's authority (Matthew 7:29; John 12:49-50).

E. Lamb sacrifice (Exodus 12).

F. Lamb of God (John 1:29; Romans 5:10).

G. Christ is coming again (John 14:3; Mark 13:32; Matthew 24:36).

H. Christ, a free gift (Romans 5:18).

I. God's direction (Proverbs 3:5-6, Psalm 37:23).

J. Attitude when we take communion (I Corinthians 11:28-33).

VI.   SUMMARY:

God has a plan for our lives. God did not plan for man to live a negative, miserable, defeated existence. The Bible tells us that God meant for man to live life to the fullest, a life of abundant living. Jesus said, "I am come that they might have life and that they might have it more abundantly."

Every man is seeking happiness. The Bible says that there is only one way to know true happiness and this is through God's plan in a personal relationship with Jesus Christ.
Do you know Him as your Saviour? Would you like to know Him?

VII.   CLOSE IN PRAYER:

As we close in prayer, if you are not sure that Christ is in your heart, won't you ask Him to come in? (Repeat Revelation 3:20; John 1:12.) You might repeat after me, "Lord Jesus, I ask you to come into my heart, to take over my life, to forgive my sins and to show me your plan for my life."

"If you have done this, where is Christ right now? (Give assurance.) As you leave the room tonight, won't you come and tell me that you have made this decision?" (You might have them sign a piece of paper or make an appointment for further discussion.)

WHO IS JESUS CHRIST?

LESSON ONE   INTRODUCTORY STEP

OBJECTIVE: To present Jesus Christ as the Son of God, all that He claimed to be, and to enable students to recognize Him as the Son of God.

I.   OPEN WITH PRAYER: Leader or someone appointed to pray.

II.   MEMORY VERSE: John 14:6.

III. MOTIVATION: Give each student a sheet of paper and ask him to to answer this question: "Who do you think Jesus Christ is, and why?" After each one has written briefly, allow him to keep his paper. Do not read papers aloud. At the conclusion of the lesson, summarize by pointing out who the Bible says Jesus Christ is. Ask each person to compare his answer with the Biblical answer.

IV.   BIBLE STUDY:

A. Jesus Christ and fulfilled prophecy.

   1. Power of prophecy.

   2. 300 O. T. prophecies about Christ fulfilled in the N. T.

   3. Examples of fulfilled prophecy.

B. What Jesus Christ said concerning Himself.

   1. He claimed to be the Son of God.

   2. He referred to God as "My Father."

   3. He claimed Deity and offered proof by His miracles.

   4. He claimed His mission was to reveal the Father (Illustration of the devout Hindu).

   5. He claimed to be the only way to God.

   6. T.B.S. questions.

C. What others said concerning Christ.

   1. New Testament personalities.

   2. Historians.

3. Testimonies of great men.

    a. Tertullian.

    b. Napoleon.

    c. Rousseau.

    d. C. S. Lewis.

4. Testimony of discussion leader (2 minutes).

5. Discussion of corresponding questions in T.B.S.

D. Why Jesus Christ is of vital importance to us today.

E. How to know Christ personally.

V.   PARALLEL PASSAGES:

A. Trinity—Gen. 1:26.

B. Christ's coming—Gen. 3:15.

C. Manner of Coming—Isa. 9:6.

D. Spoke to men—Heb. 1:1-3.

E. Christ, the Light of the world—John 9:5.

F. Christ, the Resurrection and the Life—John 11:25.

VI.   SUMMARY:

A. Invite Christ into your life now.

B. Two words to remember: subordinate, expendable.

C. By accepting Christ as Saviour and crowning Him as Lord you can personally experience that He is all He claimed to be.

D. Why is Jesus Christ of vital importance to us today?

E. How can we know Christ personally?

VII. CLOSE IN PRAYER:

Give opportunity for those present to silently invite Christ into their lives. Then, you close in audible prayer, giving thanks that we can trust the Word of Christ, and thanking Him for answering the prayers of those present.

WHO IS JESUS CHRIST?

LESSON ONE   INTRODUCTORY STEP

INTRODUCTION:

Jesus Christ, the divine Son of God, is one with the Father (John 10:30), eternally existing (John 8:56-58). In order to free men from condemnation for their sin, He took upon Himself the form of man, becoming totally human, while yet totally divine (Philippians 2:6-7).

1. His *humanity* is illustrated by the fact of His birth of a human mother, His natural human growth and development (Luke 2:40), His physical emotions, His need for sleep, His hunger and His thirst.

2. His *deity* is pointed out by the name "Immanuel" (God with us) (Matthew 1:23), by His witness to Himself (John 5:17-19; 10:30-33) and by the witness of the writing apostles.

He came into the world through the means of birth of the virgin Mary, conceived of the Holy Spirit (Matthew 1:18-25; Luke 1:26-36). Throughout His life upon earth as a man, Jesus Christ withstood all temptation to sin (Matthew 4; Hebrews 4:15) and lived His life here completely without sin (II Corinthians 5:21—"Him who knew no sin . . ."). While He was upon the earth, Jesus performed many miracles: healing the sick, raising the dead, restoring sight to the blind, and others (Matthew 8:1-16,23,24; 9:1-8,27-33).

At the close of His short, earthly ministry, Jesus willingly submitted Himself to the shame and pain of death by crucifixion in order to die for the sins of the world, ". . . that we might become the righteousness of God in Him" (II Corinthians 5:21). Dead and buried for three days, He arose (Matthew 28; I Corinthians 15:4-20), and appeared to His disciples and others.

After forty days (Acts 1:3) Jesus ascended into heaven, where He is today at the right hand of the Father (Romans 8:34), as our great eternal High Priest, interceding for us before the Father (Hebrews chapters 5 and 7; particularly 7:25—"Wherefore also He is able to save to the uttermost them that draw near unto God through Him, seeing He ever liveth to make intercession for them").

I. JESUS CHRIST AND FULFILLED PROPHECY:

A. T.B.S. par. 1, 2, 3. Expanded study on this subject will be found in Step Five, Lesson Two. (It is suggested you leave this for future study.)

B. Fulfilled prophecy.

Prophecy	O. T. Prediction	N. T. Fulfillment
The town of His birth is named.	Micah 5:2	Matthew 2:1-6 John 7:42
Born of a virgin	Isaiah 7:14	Matthew 1:23
The exact amount paid for His betrayal and several related details	Zechariah 11:12	Matthew 27:9-10
He would be scourged and spit upon.	Isaiah 50:6	Matthew 26:67
He would be given gall and vinegar.	Psalm 69:21	Matthew 27:34, 48
His Resurrection	Psalm 16:8-10	Acts 2:22-28; 13:34-35
He will come again in glory to judge the nations	Psalm 50:3-5 Ezekiel 21:27 Zechariah 14:1-7 Luke 1:31-33 Philippians 2:10-11	To be fulfilled

II. WHAT JESUS CHRIST SAID CONCERNING HIMSELF:

A. Jesus claims to be the Son of God in the following references:

1. Matthew 11:27; Luke 10:22.

2. Matthew 21:37-38 (Read verses 33-46, to see that in this parable Jesus is presenting Himself as the Son.)

Questions you can use:

a. Whom do the servants represent? Ans: prophets or messengers of God.

b. Whom do the tenants of the vineyard represent? Ans: Those who reject God's message. In the parable, the tenants more specifically represent those who so violently reacted that they beat, killed and stoned the prophets or messengers of God.

c. To whom does the son in the parable refer? Ans: Jesus Christ, Himself.

d. Did the listeners understand the parable (verses 45 and 46)? Ans: Yes.

B. Jesus speaks of God as "my Father" in the following references: Matthew 7:21; 10:32,33; 11:27; 12:50; 15:13; 16:17; 18:10,19,35; 20:23; 25:34; 26:29,39,42,53; Luke 2:49; 22:29; 24:49.

C. *Christ Himself claimed deity.* He claimed to have all authority on earth and in heaven (Matthew 28:18). He claimed power to forgive sins (Matthew 9:6). He allowed Himself to be worshipped as God (Matthew 14:33 and John 20:25-28). He said He was from heaven (John 5:17-18). He claimed He should have the same reverence which God has (John 5:23). He said He would raise all humans from the grave and judge them (John 5:27-29). He said He would give everlasting life to all who trust in Him (John 6:47). He said He never failed to please God and never sinned (John 8:46). He said He was eternal (John 8:58). He said He would come again to earth a second time (John 14:1-3).

To prove His claims, He preached sermons which have never been equalled (Matthew, Chapters 5-7) and performed miracles, such as feeding 5,000 people with five loaves of bread, walking on water, controlling the wind and forces of nature, healing the desperately sick, giving life to a man who had been dead four days and finally rising from the dead Himself. His early followers, who were in a better position than we are to judge His claims, surrendered their own lives to Jesus Christ as Saviour and Lord.

D. Jesus Christ claimed that He came into the world to reveal the Father.

The story is told of a devout member of a Hindu sect who was confronted with the claims of Christ. To him all life was sacred—a cow, an insect, a cobra. Yet, he could not grasp the Christian concept that God actually visited this planet in the flesh in the person of Jesus of Nazareth, as we are told in John 1:14. One day as he walked through the fields wrestling in his mind with this concept of God, he observed also an ant hill with thousands of ants in evidence. He observed that the ant hill was in the path of a farmer plowing the field. Gripped with a concern that you and I would feel for hundreds of people trapped in a burning building, he wanted to warn them of their impending destruction. But how? He could shout to them, but they would not hear. He could write in the sand, but they would be unable to read. How then could he communicate with them? Then, the realization came. If only he were an ant, he could warn them before it was too late. Now, he understood the Christian concept. God became a man—Jesus Christ—in order to communicate His love and forgiveness to us.

E. In John 14:6 (memory verse) and Matt. 11:27 Jesus Christ states that He is the only way to God. Peter later (Acts 4:12) states, "Neither is there salvation in any other: for there is none other name under heaven given among men, whereby we must be saved."

F. Discussion of students' answers concerning who they think Christ is.

III. WHAT OTHERS SAID CONCERNING JESUS CHRIST:

A. New Testament personalities.

1. Peter: Matt. 16:15-17 (". . . Christ, the Son of the living God ").

2. Thomas: John 20:25-28 (". . . My Lord and my God ").

3. John the Baptist: John 1:29-36 (". . . Behold the Lamb of God . . .").

4. Philip: John 1:45 (". . . Him, of whom Moses in the law, and also the prophets wrote, Jesus of Nazareth . . .").

5. Nathaniel: John 1:49 (". . . the Son of God, the King of Israel ").

6. Martha: John 11:27 (". . . The Christ, the Son of God, which should come into the world ").

7. The Centurion: Matt. 27:54 (". . . Son of God"). Note that these men were not disciples, but independent observers.

B. Historians.

1. Encyclopedia Britannica considers Jesus Christ of such importance that it devotes 20,000 words to Him.

2. H. G. Wells, though he denies much concerning Jesus Christ, is nevertheless compelled to devote more than ten pages to Him in his two-volume set, *Outline of History*.

3. Arnold Toynbee gives more space to Jesus Christ in his well-known writings than he gives to any other person.

C. Testimonies of great men.

1. *Tertullian* (A.D. 155-200) — in his book *Apology*, which was a defense of Christianity addressed to the Roman Government, mentions the exchange of correspondence between Pontius Pilate and Caesar: "Tiberius accordingly, in whose days the Christian name made its entry into the world, having himself

received intelligence from Palestine of events which had clearly shown the truth of Christ's divinity, brought the matter before the senate, with his own decision in favor of Christ. The senate, because it had not given the approval itself, rejected his proposal. Caesar held to his opinion, threatening wrath against all the accusers of the Christians."

2. *Napoleon*—On the lonely isle of St. Helena the exiled emperor was once discussing Christ with General Bertrand, a faithful officer who had followed him into banishment and who did not believe in the deity of Jesus. Napoleon said, "I know men, and I tell you that Jesus Christ is not a man. Superficial minds see a resemblance between Christ and the founders of empires and the gods of other religions. That resemblance does not exist. There is between Christianity and whatever other religions the distance of infinity . . . Everything in Christ astonishes me. His spirit overawes me, and His will confounds me. Between Him and whoever else in the world, there is no possible term of comparison. He is truly a being by Himself. His ideas and sentiments, the truth which He announces, His manner of convincing are not explained either by human organization or by the nature of things . . . The nearer I approach, the more carefully I examine, everything is above me—everything remains grand, of a grandeur which over-powers. His religion is a revelation from an intelligence which certainly is not that of man . . . One can absolutely find nowhere, but in Him alone, the imitation or the example of His life . . . I search in vain in history to find the similar to Jesus Christ or anything which can approach the gospel. Neither history, nor humanity, nor the ages, nor nature offer me anything with which I am able to compare it or to explain it. Here everything is extraordinary."

3. *Rousseau*—"Yes, if the life and death of Socrates were those of a sage, the life and death of Jesus are those of a God."

4. *C. S. Lewis*—Concerning the *unlikelihood* that Jesus' followers were of the type who would have been easily convinced concerning His person, or willingly exaggerated, this professor at Oxford says, "What are we to do about reconciling the two contradictory phenomena? One attempt consists in saying that the Man did not really say these things, but, that His followers exaggerated the story, and so the legend grew up that He had said them. This is difficult because His followers were all Jews; that is, they belonged to that Nation which of all others was most convinced that there was only one God—that there could not possibly be another. It is very odd that 'this horrible invention about a religious leader' should grow up among the one people in the whole earth least likely to make such a mistake. On the

contrary, we get the impression that none of His immediate followers or even of the New Testament writers embraced the doctrine at all easily."

D. Testimony of discussion leader.

In presenting your testimony try to follow the theme of the subject. Example of outline:

1. Your examination of the evidence regarding Christ.

2. Your personal testing of His claims by:

a. inviting Him into your life.

b. making Him your Lord and Master.

Keep your testimony to two minutes. If you cannot in complete honesty say you have made Christ your Lord and Master, it is best that you not give a testimony at all.

IV. WHY JESUS CHRIST IS OF VITAL IMPORTANCE TO US TODAY:

It is interesting to consider that Jesus Christ claimed to be God. He claimed to be the author of a new way of life. Interestingly enough wherever this message has gone, new life, new hope and purpose for living have resulted. Either Jesus of Nazareth was who He claimed to be, the Son of God, the Saviour of mankind, or He was the greatest impostor the world has ever known. If His claims were false, a lie has accomplished more good than the truth ever has.

Does it not make sense that this person who is regarded as the greatest teacher, the greatest example and the greatest leader the world has ever known would be, as He Himself claimed to be and as the Bible tells us, the one person who could bridge this chasm between God and man?

You remember in Romans 6:23, we read, "The wages of sin is death, but the gift of God is eternal life through Jesus Christ our Lord." As you study the religions and philosophies of the world, you will find no provision for man's sin, apart from the sacrificial death of Christ. The Bible says that without the shedding of blood there is no remission (or forgiveness) of sin.

Jesus said, "I am the Way, the Truth, and the Life: no man cometh unto the Father, but by me" (John 14:6). Let me show you what Jesus said to a man who came to Him for counsel. They talked even as we are talking. Let us turn to the third chapter of John and read the first six verses. Here, would you mind reading it? But before you read, let me explain who Nicodemus was.

He was a man of the Pharisees, a ruler of the Jews, one of the great religious leaders of his day. We find that as far as the law was concerned, Nicodemus was above reproach. He was moral and ethical. He was so eager to please God that he prayed seven times a day. He went to the synagogue to worship God three times a day. Yet, Nicodemus approached Jesus by saying, ". . . Rabbi, we know that thou art a teacher come from God: for no man can do these miracles that thou doest, except God be with him. Jesus answered and said unto him, Verily, verily, I say unto thee, Except a man be born again, he cannot see the kingdom of God. Nicodemus saith unto him, How can a man be born when he is old? can he enter the second time into his mother's womb, and be born? Jesus answered, Verily, verily, I say unto thee, Except a man be born of water and of the Spirit, he cannot enter into the kingdom of God. That which is born of the flesh is flesh; and that which is born of the Spirit is spirit" (John 3:2-6).

Take for example a caterpillar crawling in the dust, an ugly, hairy worm. One day this worm weaves about its body a cocoon. Out of this cocoon there emerges a butterfly. We do not understand fully what has taken place. We know only that where once a worm has crawled in the dust, now a butterfly soars in the heavens. So it is in the life of a Christian. Where once we lived on the lowest level, we now dwell on the highest plane, experiencing a full and abundant life.

God is Spirit and we cannot communicate with Him until we become a spiritual creature. (This is what takes place when Jesus takes residence in our life.) Before Jesus comes into our lives, we cannot hear God's voice. We know nothing of His plan for our lives. The word of God is a dull, uninteresting book and we have no desire to be with others who love and follow Christ. But when Christ comes into our lives, we are changed. We love to be with Christians; we love to read the word of God; we want our lives to count for Him. You might compare it with television. Suppose, for the sake of illustration, we are sitting in this room and we know that there are a number of television programs available to us. We are looking and yet we cannot see the images or hear the voices. What is needed? An instrument, a television set. The moment we move the television set into the room and turn the dial, we can hear the voices and see the images. So it is when Christ comes into our lives. He is our divine instrument, plugging us into God, making known God's will and love for our lives.

Christ is either all He claimed to be or He is a liar, an impostor, and in a moral universe, a lie then has done more good than truth.

C. S. Lewis: "On the one side clear, definite, moral teaching. On the other, claims, which, if not true, are those of a megalomaniac, compared with whom Hitler was the most sane and humble of men. There is no half-way house, and there is no parallel in other religions. If you had gone to Buddha and asked him, 'Are you the son of Bramah?', he would have said, 'My son, you are still in the vale of illusion.' If you had gone to Socrates and asked, 'Are you Zeus?', he would have laughed at you. If you had gone to Mohammed and asked, 'Are you Allah?', he would first have rent his clothes and then cut your head off. If you had asked Confucius, 'Are you Heaven?' I think he would have probably replied, 'Remarks which are not in accordance with nature are in bad taste.' The idea of a great moral teacher saying what Christ said is out of the question. In my opinion, the only person who can say that sort of thing is either God or a complete lunatic suffering from that form of delusion which undermines the whole mind of man . . ."

V.   HOW TO KNOW CHRIST PERSONALLY:

The Bible tells us that "God so loved the world that He gave His only begotten Son that whosoever believeth on Him should not perish but have everlasting life" (John 3:16). In other words, the great chasm between God and man cannot be bridged by man's effort but only by God's effort through His son, Jesus Christ. Religion and philosophy have been defined as man's attempt to find God. Christianity has been defined as God's only means of reaching man.

In Revelation 3:20 we hear Him speak, "Behold, I stand at the door and knock; if any man hear my voice, and open the door, I will come in to him, and sup with him and he with me." The door refers to the heart—your will, your intellect and your emotions. Christ is knocking and He is saying,"I have come that you might have life and have it more abundantly." "I have come to forgive your sins. I have come to bring peace and purpose to life."

Our lives are filled with many activities such as studies, finances, athletics, social life, business and home life with no real purpose or meaning. Jesus wants to come into your life and make harmony out of discord, meaning and purpose where now there is something lacking. He wants to forgive your sins and bridge the chasm between you and God. He does not want to come into your life as a guest, but He wants to be in control of your life.

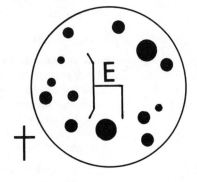

There is a throne in each heart. All these years your ego has been on the throne. Now Christ waits for you to invite Him to be on the throne. You must step down and relinquish the authority of your life to Him.

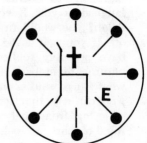

I think you can see from this simple diagram how, when Christ becomes the Lord of your life, He also becomes the Lord of every activity of your life, which as you can see, makes for a harmonious life. (Read Romans 10:9 emphasizing the Lordship of Christ.) (Taken from 'God's Plan' by William R. Bright.)

For additional information see Step Seven: (Four Spiritual Laws).

VI. SUMMARY:

A. Invite Christ into your life today (II Cor. 6:2b—"Now is the day of salvation").

1. Though the Lord is "not willing that any should perish," (II Peter 3:9), He will not force His way into your life. He comes only by personal invitation. Just deciding to do something now is not enough. All decisions are valueless until accompanied with action.

Accepting the historical person called Jesus Christ is only giving mental assent to His humanity. Even giving Him credit for being the Son of God is not sufficient. You must "BELIEVE" in the true scriptural sense of "trust, cling to, rely on" Him as the ONLY "bridge" to span the chasm between you and God. Place your life in His hand. He is the "Great Physician" who is able to remake you into a "new creation" (II Cor. 5:17), open a new dimension for "abundant living" (Jn. 10:10) and give you His life which is everlasting (Jn. 3:16).

2. How to believe:

a. It is possible to believe something is true with our mind and yet not fully trust it with our heart. You may look at a long swinging foot bridge that spans a deep ravine. At first examination you say, "I believe it will hold my weight if I walk across." Yet, it is only by actually walking out on the bridge, trusting it completely with your life, that you express, "I believe on this bridge to hold me without falling."

b. You can believe in your physician's ability to perform a successful operation. Yet, it is only by lying down on his operating table with your very life in his hands that you express true belief: "I believe on my physician's ability to keep me alive."

c. In the same sense you must trust Jesus Christ with your salvation. You can recognize the facts concerning His life and acknowledge that His claims are true. Yet you need a personal encounter with Him—you must meet Him, you must respond by inviting Him into your heart and life to forgive your sin, give you eternal life and provide the power and resources to live for Him.

B. Two words to remember. Add these words to your spiritual vocabulary. Meditate on their significance to your life with Christ.

1. *Subordinate:* Dictionary definition: "Placed in a lower *rank*. Inferior in order, importance, position. Involving dependence. Submissive to authority. Consider as of less value or importance. To make subservient." Subordinate yourself to Christ as Lord *daily,* and as often as He brings this word into your thinking, tell the Lord you want everything (will, intellect, affection, desires, plans etc.) in your life to be in *subordination* to His will.

2. *Expendable:* Dictionary definition: "Capable of being expended. Military use: Normally used up or consumed in service." *Daily* tell Christ that you desire to be completely *expendable* for His purposes and plan for your life.

C. Christ must be met and known personally to be appreciated as all He claimed to be.

THE EARTHLY LIFE OF JESUS CHRIST

LESSON TWO   INTRODUCTORY STEP

OBJECTIVE: To present Jesus Christ as the greatest Person who has
ever lived—with the objective of leading to the conclusion
that His moral character, teaching and influence upon history demonstrate who He is: God Himself.

I.   OPEN WITH PRAYER.

II.   MEMORY VERSE: John 1:12 (All quote verse together).

III. MOTIVATION: Say to the group, "Each of us has heard these
statements occasionally: 'Yes, Jesus was a great leader, but there
have been many other good teachers, as well. I don't see why the
teachings of Jesus are necessarily any more important than those of
other great men.'" Give each student a sheet of paper and pencil and
have him write his answer to this statement. After each has written
briefly, have papers passed in. Then discuss briefly, allowing students
to express their answers.

Alternate: Have each student write what he considers the two or three
top qualifications of a great teacher. Then discuss.

1. Moral character (no sin).

2. Authority (credentials) (John 12:49-50).

3. Able to back up what he says (Jesus predicted His own death, resurrection and other future events; performed miracles).

4. Teaching to have beneficial effect upon humanity.

5. Teaching trustworthy.

6. Teachings demand a verdict (John 12:48).

IV.   BIBLE STUDY:

A. The entrance of Jesus Christ into the world.

1. Reason(s) for Jesus' entrance into the world (Hebrews 1:1-3).

2. Where He was before He came into the world (John 17:5).
Discuss students' answers from the T.B.S., Lesson Two.

26

3. Circumstances surrounding His birth (Matthew 1:18-23). Discuss students' answers from the T.B.S., Lesson Two.

B. The character of Jesus Christ.

   1. New Testament documentation.

      a. Mark 1:40-42 (". . . moved with pity . . .").

      b. Luke 23:33-34 (". . . Father forgive them . . .").

      c. John 2:13-17 (". . .zeal for Thy house . . .").

      d. John 13:1-5 (". . . began to wash the disciples' feet . . .").

   2. Testimony of historians and writers.

      a. William H. Lecky.

         1) Quote from lesson amplification (". . . an ideal character . . .").

         2) Quote from the T.B.S., Lesson Two (". . . highest pattern of virtue . . .").

      b. William E. Channing (". . . calmness and self-possession . . .").

C. Jesus Christ as a teacher.

   1. Content of His teaching.

      a. The new birth (John 3:1-8).

      b. Jesus' claims.

      c. Jesus' demands.

   2. Method and content of His teaching (Matthew 7:7-11).

   3. Authority of His teaching.

      a. Matthew 7:29 (". . . one who had authority . . .").

      b. John 12:49-50 (". . . the Father who sent Me . . .").

   4. Trustworthiness of Jesus' teaching.

      a. Discussion.

      b. Testimony of well-known men.

         1) John Stuart Mill (". . . personal originality . . .").

         2) Philip Schaff ("controls the destinies of the civilized world . . .").

D. Impact of Jesus Christ on history.
Statements of historians and other well-known men.

    1. W. H. Griffith Thomas (". . . greatest influence in the world today . . .").

    2. James Russell Lowell (". . . Saviour alone has given hope of eternal life . . .").

    3. Caleb Cushing (". . . levels upward . . .").

    4. George Romanes (". . . unparalleled by any other movement in history").

    5. Kenneth Scott Latourette (". . . millions of individuals have been transformed . . .").

    6. John Richard Green (". . . whole temper of England changed . . .").

    7. Hilaire Belloc (". . . astounding influence on England . . .").

    8. Rufus Choate (". . . Constitution is in the New Testament . . .").

    9. Ernst Haeckel (". . . ennobling influence . . .").

V.   PARALLEL PASSAGES: See the Lesson Amplification.

VI.   SUMMARY:

A. "The Influence of One Life" (". . . centerpiece of the human race . . .").

B. Vernon Grounds (". . . changes the hearts and character of men . . .").

C. Jesus Christ can change your life.

VII. CLOSE IN PRAYER: "Ask Christ to come into your life, to guide and empower you. He will. Your life can be one of purpose and fulfillment."

THE EARTHLY LIFE OF JESUS CHRIST

LESSON TWO   INTRODUCTORY STEP

INTRODUCTION: THE INCOMPARABLE CHRIST.

"More than nineteen hundred years ago there was a Man born contrary to the laws of life. This Man lived in poverty and was reared in obscurity. He did not travel extensively. Only once did He cross the boundary of the country in which He lived; that was during His exile in childhood. He possessed neither wealth nor influence. His relatives were inconspicuous and had neither training nor formal education. In infancy He startled a king; in childhood He puzzled doctors; in manhood He ruled the course of nature, walked upon the billows as if pavements, and hushed the sea to sleep. He healed the multitudes without medicine and made no charge for His service. He never wrote a book, yet all the libraries of the country could not hold the books that have been written about Him. He never wrote a song, and yet He has furnished the theme for more songs than all the songwriters combined. He never founded a college, but all the schools put together cannot boast of having as many students. He never marshaled an army, nor drafted a soldier, nor fired a gun; and yet no leader ever had more volunteers who have, under His orders, made more rebels stack arms and surrender without a shot fired. He never practiced medicine, and yet He has healed more broken hearts than all the doctors far and near. Every seventh day the wheels of commerce cease their turning and multitudes wend their way to worshiping assemblies to pay homage and respect to Him. The names of the past proud statesmen of Greece and Rome have come and gone. The names of the past scientists, philosophers, and theologians have come and gone, but the name of this Man abounds more and more. Though time has spread nineteen hundred years between the people of this generation and the scene of His crucifixion, yet He still lives. Herod could not destroy Him and the grave could not hold Him. He stands forth upon the highest pinnacle of heavenly glory, proclaimed of God, acknowledged by angels, adored by saints, and feared by devils, as the living, personal Christ, our Lord and Saviour."

—Author Unknown

I.   ENTRANCE OF JESUS CHRIST INTO THE WORLD:

A. Reasons for Jesus' entrance into the world (Hebrews 1:1-3).

B. Discuss first two questions in the T.B.S., Lesson Two.

II. CHARACTER OF JESUS CHRIST:

A. Discuss questions 1-4 in corresponding section of T.B.S.

B. Testimony of historians and writers.

    1. William H. Lecky, one of the most noted historians of Great Britain: "It was reserved for Christianity to present to the world an ideal character which through all the changes of eighteen centuries has inspired the hearts of men with an impassioned love; has shown itself capable of acting on all ages, nations, temperaments and conditions; has not only the highest pattern of virtue, but the strongest incentive to its practice." Quote in the T.B.S., Lesson Two.

    2. American author, William Channing: "The charge of self-deluding fanaticism is the last to be fastened on Jesus. Where can we find traces of it in His history? Do we detect them in the calm authority of His precepts; in the mild, practical, beneficent spirit of His religion; in the sublime truths of religion; or in the good sense, the knowledge of human nature which He always discloses in His estimate and treatment of the different classes of men with whom He acted? . . . The truth is that remarkable as was the character of Jesus, it was distinguished by nothing more than by calmness and self-possession."

III. JESUS CHRIST AS A TEACHER:

A. Content of His Teaching.

    1. The new birth (John 3:1-8). In His conference with the religious leader Nicodemus, Jesus clearly points out the absolute necessity of spiritual birth before one can qualify to enter the kingdom of God. He explains that just as one enters the world as a physical human being through physical birth, one can become a spiritual being (child of God, John 1:12) only through a spiritual birth.

    2. Jesus' claims.

        a. ". . . I am the Light of the world . . ." (John 8:12; 9:5).

        b. "I am the good Shepherd . . . who lays down His life for the sheep" (John 10:11).

        c. "Before Abraham was, I am" (John 8:58).

        d. I am your Master and Lord (John 13:13-14).

        e. "I am the Vine, you are the branches"(John 15:1ff).

        f. I came, not to destroy, but to fulfill (Matthew 5:17). (He here refers to prophecy and the Old Testament.)

g. He claimed to forgive sin (Mark 2:1-12).

h. He read from Isaiah 61, the great prophecy of the Messiah, and laid the scroll down with the statement, "This day has this Scripture been fulfilled."

i. "I am the resurrection, and the life: he that believeth in me, though he were dead, yet shall he live: and whosoever liveth and believeth in me shall never die . . ." (John 11:25-26).

j. "I am the Way, the Truth, and the Life: no man cometh unto the Father, but by Me" (John 14:6).

Regarding the claims and demands of Jesus, *Professor Archibald M. Hunter of Aberdeen University* says, "Then what manner of man is this who knows that by His dying He will inaugurate this new and blessed order of relations between God and men. No mortal man makes such a claim, or we know him to be mad. We are driven back on the words of the wise old 'Rabbi' Duncan: 'Christ either deceived mankind by conscious fraud, or he was himself deluded, or He was divine. There is no getting out of this trilemma.' (Colloquia Peripatetica, 109). Christians have never been in any doubt which of the propositions is true" *(The Work and Words of Jesus,* pp. 89-90).

3. Jesus' demands. These are not simply for ethical obedience; they are for utter self-committal to Himself. They represent the "totalitarian" claim of Jesus.

a. "Everyone who shall confess me before men, him will I also confess before my Father who is in Heaven" (Matthew 10:32; Luke 12:8; Mark 8:38).

"Could any language say more clearly than this that fidelity to Jesus is that on which a man's final destiny depends?" (A. M. Hunter, p. 88).

b. "He that receiveth you, receiveth me; and he that receiveth me receiveth Him that sent me" (Matthew 10:40; Luke 10: 16; Mark 9:37). Here is One who knows His cause to be the cause of God.

c. "He that loveth father or mother more than Me, is not worthy of Me; and he that loveth son or daughter more than Me is not worthy of Me; and he that doth not take up his cross and follow Me, is not worthy of Me" (Matthew 10:37*f,* Luke 14:26*f,* Mark 8:34).

d. "Follow Me" (Matthew 9:9; 10:38; 16:24; 8:22).

e. "Learn of Me" (Matthew 11:29).

f. "Come to Me" (Matthew 11:28; Luke 9:23).

g. "Forsake all and follow Me" (Luke 14:33; Matthew 19:28). (See also Mark 1:18; Luke 5:11.)

h. "Believe on the Lord Jesus Christ, and thou shalt be saved . . ." (Acts 16:31). His demand for faith in Himself is as insistent as Paul's words to the Philippian jailer.

B. Method and Content of His Teaching. (See question 1 under "Jesus Christ as a Teacher" in the T.B.S., Lesson Two.)

C. Authority of His Teaching. (Discuss questions 2 and 3 under "Jesus Christ as a Teacher" in the T.B.S., Lesson Two.)

D. Trustworthiness of Jesus' Teaching.

1. Ask group to give three reasons why they feel they can trust Jesus' teaching (question 4, "Jesus Christ as a Teacher" in the T.B.S., Lesson Two).

2. Quote the testimony of the following well-known men:

a. *John Stuart Mill*, one of the keenest philosophers of modern times: "About the life and sayings of Jesus there is a stamp of personal originality combined with profundity of insight, which must place the prophet of Nazareth, even in the estimation of those who have no belief in his inspiration, in the very first rank of the men of sublime genius of whom our species can boast. When this pre-eminent genius is combined with the qualities of probably the greatest moral reformer, and martyr to that mission, who ever existed upon earth, religion cannot be said to have made a bad choice in picking on this man as the ideal representative and guide of humanity; nor, even now would it be easy, even for an unbeliever, to find a better translation of the rule of virtue from the abstract into concrete, than to endeavor so to live that Christ would approve our life."

b. *Philip Schaff*, well-known historian, and author of *The History of the Christian Church:* "Jesus of Nazareth, without money and arms, conquered more millions than Alexander, Caesar, Mohammed and Napoleon; without science and learning, He shed more light on things human and divine, than all the philosophers and scholars combined; without the eloquence of the school, He spoke words of life such as were never spoken before, nor since, and produced effects which lie beyond the reach of orator or poet. Without writing a single line, He has set more pens in motion and furnished themes for more sermons, orations, discussions, works of art, learned volumes, and sweet songs of praise than the whole army of great men of ancient and modern times. Born in a manger and crucified as a malefactor, He now controls the destinies of the civilized world and rules a spiritual empire which embraces one-third of the inhabitants of the globe."

IV. THE IMPACT OF JESUS CHRIST ON HISTORY:

A. Statements of Historians and Other Well-Known Men.

1. The British scholar *W. H. Griffith Thomas* said, "The testimony to the present work of Jesus Christ is no less real than it has been in the past. In the case of all the other great names of the world's history, the inevitable and invariable experience has been that the particular man is first a power, then only a name, and last of all a mere memory. Of Jesus Christ the exact opposite is true. He died on a cross of shame, His name gradually became more and more powerful, and He is the greatest influence in the world today. There is, as has been well said, a fifth Gospel being written—the work of Jesus Christ in the hearts and lives of men and nations.

"The present social status of men, women, and children is so familiar to us that we sometimes fail to realize what it was before Christ came. In the Roman world the father had absolute right over his children to sell, to enslave, to kill them. It is Christianity that has made these atrocities impossible. Woman was the living chattel of her husband, as she is still in some parts of the world. It is through Christianity that she has obtained a new status, and now in Christian countries 'Home' receives its true and full meaning. The slavery of the Roman Empire was one of its most deep-seated features, and the power of master over slave was as absolute as it was often exercised with cruelty and ferocity. But Christianity proclaimed the universality and brotherhood of all men in Christ, and thereby struck at the root of slavery, and wherever the Gospel of Christ has had its way, slavery has been compelled to disappear."

2. *James Russell Lowell,* a noted writer of the 19th century, suggests that when the keen scrutiny of skeptics "has found a place on this planet, ten miles square, where a decent man can live in decency, comfort, and security, supporting and educating his children unspoiled and unpolluted, a place where age is reverenced, infancy respected, womanhood honoured, and human life held in due regard, on this globe where the Gospel of Christ has not gone and cleared the way and laid the foundations, and made decency and security possible, it will then be in order for the skeptical *literati* to move thither, and then ventilate their views. But so long as these men are very dependent on the religion which they discard for every privilege they enjoy, they may well hesitate a little before they seek to rob a Christian of

his hope and humanity of its faith in that Saviour who alone has given to men that hope of eternal life which makes life tolerable and society possible, and robs death of its terrors and the grave of its gloom."

3. *Caleb Cushing,* statesman and former Attorney General of the United States, suggests: "The Christian religion levels upward, elevating all men to the same high standard of sanctity, faith and spiritual promise on earth as in heaven. Just so is it, that, wherever Christianity is taught, it inevitably dignifies and exalts the female character."

4. *George Romanes,* the British physicist, made this statement: "It is on all sides worth considering (blatant ignorance or base vulgarity alone excepted) that the revolution effected by Christianity in human life is immeasurable and unparalleled by any other movement in history.

"But not only is Christianity thus so immeasurably in advance of all other religions. It is no less so of every other system of thought that has ever been promulgated in regard to all that is moral and spiritual. Whether it be true or false, it is certain that neither philosophy, science, nor poetry has ever produced results in thought, conduct, or beauty in any degree to be compared with it.

"Only to a man wholly destitute of spiritual perception can it be that Christianity should fail to appear the greatest exhibition of the beautiful, the sublime, and of all else that appeals to our spiritual nature, which has ever been known upon our earth."

5. *Kenneth Scott Latourette,* director of the department of religion in Yale's graduate school, historian, and author of a set of well-known works, *Expansion of Christianity,* comments: "Measured by its fruits in the human race, that short life has been the most influential ever lived on this planet. As we have been at pains to point out, the impress of that life, far from fading with the passing centuries, has deepened. Through Him millions of individuals have been transformed and have begun to live the kind of life which He exemplified. Gauged by the consequences which have followed, the birth, life, death and resurrection of Jesus have been the most important events in the history of man. Measured by His influence, Jesus is central in the human story."

6. *John Richard Green,* English historian, and author of the *Short History of the English People,* notes: "England became the people of a book, and that book was the Bible. It was, as yet, the one English book which was familiar to every Englishman. It was read in churches, it was read at home, and everywhere its words, as they fell on ears which custom had not deadened to their force and beauty, kindled a startling enthusiasm . . .

Elizabeth might silence or tune the pulpits, but it was impossible for her to silence or tune the great preachers of justice and mercy and truth, who spoke from the book which the Lord again opened to the people. . . . The effect of the Bible in this way was simply amazing. The whole temper of the nation was changed. A new conception of life and of man superseded the old. A new moral and religious impulse spread through every class. . . . Theology rules there, said Grotius of England, only ten years after Elizabeth's death. The whole nation, in fact, became a church."

7. The historian, *Hilaire Belloc,* has said: "The astounding strength of Biblical influence on England, the depth to which it has penetrated the English mind, the universality of its effect and the extraordinary persistence of it in our own generation, when all the old religious basis of it is disappearing, proceeds from a special factor which only those to whom the English language is native can understand. This factor was the power of the Word."

8. A friend of *Rufus Choate* in looking over the large library of that outstanding lawyer and United States Senator, remarked banteringly, "Seven editions of the New Testament and not a copy of the Constitution!" To which Choate replied, "Ah, my friend, you forget that the Constitution of my country is in them all."

9. This is no exaggeration—think about this: What is the origin of *Lincoln's* imperishable phrase, "Government of the people, by the people, and for the people?" That phrase, which is the essence of democracy, comes from the introduction to Wycliffe's Bible, the first English Version of the Holy Scripture. Here is the preface to that pioneer translation: "The Bible will make possible a Government of people, by people, and for people."

10. *Ernst Haekel,* the noted German scientist and philosopher who was an untiring protagonist of atheistic rationalism, admitted the world-transforming power of the Bible when he said: "Beyond all doubt the present degree of human culture owes, in great part, its perfection to the propagation of the Christian system of morals and its ennobling influence."

V. SUMMARY:

A. "The Influence of One Life." "Here is a man who was born in an obscure village, the child of a peasant woman. He grew up in another village. He worked in a carpenter shop until He was thirty, and then for three years He was an itinerant preacher. He never wrote a book. He never held an office. He never owned a home. He never had a family. He never went to college. He never put His feet inside a big city. He never traveled two hundred miles from the place where He was born. He never did one of the things that usually accompany greatness. He had no credentials but Himself.

"While still a young man, the tide of popular opinion turned against Him. His friends ran away. One of them denied Him. He was turned over to His enemies. He went through the mockery of a trial. He was nailed upon a cross between two thieves. His executioners gambled for the only piece of property He had on earth while He was dying, and that was His coat. When He was dead He was taken down and laid in a borrowed grave through the pity of a friend.

"Nineteen wide centuries have come and gone, and today He is the centerpiece of the human race and the leader of the column of progress.

"I am far within the mark when I say that all the armies that ever marched, and all the navies that were ever built, and all the parliaments that ever sat, and all the kings that ever reigned, put together have not affected the life of man upon this earth as has that one solitary life."

B. "The Bible possesses a world-transforming power because it possesses a life-transforming power. The Bible is able to change nations and customs only because, to begin with, it is able to change the hearts and characters of men" *(Vernon Grounds,* President of Denver Conservative Baptist Theological Seminary).

C. Throughout the pages of history, Jesus Christ transformed lives. Today He is continuing to provide spiritual reality—fellowship with God—to those who receive Him as Saviour and Lord.

If you have never asked Jesus Christ to come into your life, to take the throne of your heart and life, do it now. In Revelation 3:20, Jesus Himself is speaking. He says, "Behold, I stand at the door (of your heart and life) and knock: if any man hear My voice, and open the door (inviting Him to come in) I will come in . . ." Ask Him to come in—to save you from sin, to empower you to live the kind of life He wants you to live, to enrich your life with His presence, power, peace, and pardon. Ask Him to guide you continually.

He will answer our prayer. I John 5:14-15 tells us that if we ask anything according to His will, He hears and answers. Verses 11 and 12 tell us that when Christ comes into our life, we then have eternal life, our sin is forgiven and we now have access to God in prayer. We become a child of God (John 1:12). With Christ in our life, we have peace with God. Jesus Christ within provides power to live and experience the "abundant life" of which He spoke (John 10:10b). He can now direct us in a life of purpose and fulfillment.

LESSON PLAN

THE DEATH OF JESUS CHRIST

LESSON THREE

INTRODUCTORY STEP

OBJECTIVE: To demonstrate the significance of Christ's death and to bring the student to realize the importance of receiving Christ as Saviour and Lord. It is only because of the death of Christ on the cross that our sin can be forgiven; we can be reconciled to God; and we can have eternal life.

I.   OPEN WITH PRAYER.

II.   MEMORY VERSE: Romans 5:8 (Check with each other).

III.   MOTIVATION: Ask the group, "Have you ever heard this: 'I believe that Jesus was a martyr—public opinion turned against Him, and He died for His cause. I don't understand how this has anything to do with me personally in my search for purpose and meaning in life.'"

IV.   BIBLE STUDY:

A. *Need for the Death of Christ.*

See the Introductory Step, Lesson Three, for discussion questions, and explanation of physical and spiritual death.

B. *Result of the Death of Christ* (Introductory Step questions).

1. Christ's moral character (II Corinthians 5:21).

2. Christ's attitude toward His death (Hebrews 12:2).

3. Christ's teaching concerning His death.

4. Christ's reason for dying.

C. *True Significance of the Death of Christ.*

1. Reconciliation.

2. Propitiation.

3. Redemption.

4. Sacrifice.

5. Atonement.

6. Christ, the Redeemer.

7. Justification.

V. PARALLEL PASSAGES: See the Lesson Amplification.

VI. SUMMARY:

Apart from Jesus Christ, it is impossible for man to know God. By His death on the cross, Christ became your substitute, taking upon Himself the death penalty for your sin. This can become effective for you right now, if you receive Jesus Christ as your personal Saviour. Ask Him to forgive your sin, come into your life, and guide you to live for Him. If you already know Christ as personal Saviour, pause now to ask His guidance in sharing these truths with those who do not know Him.

VII. CLOSE IN PRAYER: Give opportunity for those who wish to silently receive Christ as Saviour, or pray for guidance.

LESSON AMPLIFICATION

THE DEATH OF JESUS CHRIST

LESSON THREE   INTRODUCTORY STEP

INTRODUCTION:

The 22nd Psalm was written hundreds of years before the cross, yet it contains amazingly detailed prophecy of what happened at the cross. Christ desired that no one miss the point that this was a prophecy of the cross; therefore, at the end of the three hours of darkness at the crucifixion, when God had turned His back upon His Son, Christ cried out in the Hebrew language the verse of this Psalm: "My God, My God, why hast thou forsaken me?" (See Matthew 27:45-49; Mark 15:33-37). This searching question of Christ has mystified many. Some have even gone so far as to suggest that this is Christ's final admission that His life and claims had been a hoax. Such a suggestion demonstrates either a lack of scholarship in failure to investigate the facts or an intentional distortion of the Scripture to keep from personally facing the claims of Christ.

Christ does three things in quoting the first verse of Psalm 22: (1) He points us to the awful fact that He was forsaken of the Father on the Cross. Christ had enjoyed fellowship with the Father from eternity past. He had lived a life as man that was well pleasing to the Father. He had no sins of His own to die for. Yet on the cross He took upon Himself the sin of the world, and as a result He was cut off from fellowship with God the Father. His cry is an admission of this agony of soul. (2) By pointing to Psalm 22, Christ points us to the explanation of His cry, as found in verse three of the Psalm. This verse gives the answer to why God had forsaken Christ on the cross: "But thou art holy, O thou that inhabitest the praises of Israel." In other words, God in His holiness cannot have fellowship with sin, thus he had to turn His back upon His beloved Son, who at this point in time took upon Himself the sin of the world. Because God is holy, Christ, bearing our sins, was forsaken on the cross. (3) A third reason why Christ quoted Psalm 22 was to point to this prophecy of His death. He wanted us to realize that his death on the cross was not just a tragic event in history, but that it was the climactic event in God's dealing with sin. It was an event completely foreknown of God and planned according to His purpose (I Peter 1:18-19). As one reads the first part of Psalm 22, he is aware of a description of events that were fulfilled on the cross.

Examples of exact details fulfilled:

v. 1 ....Matt. 27:46 Word of Christ, "Why hast thou forsaken me?"

v. 7 ....Matt. 27:39 Scorned and derided by the mob.

v. 8 ....Matt. 27:43 "Let God deliver him": words of scoffers.

v. 16 ....Matt. 27:35 Christ's hands and feet pierced.

v. 18 ....Matt. 27:35; Mark 15:24; Luke 23:34; John 19:24
Soldiers cast lots and divided his garments.

What more fitting way for Christ to point to the awful price in dying for our sins, and yet to give clear testimony of his faith in God's purpose as well, than to say, "My God, My God, why hast Thou forsaken me," thus pointing to Psalm 22.

I. NEED FOR THE DEATH OF CHRIST:

See the T.B.S. for discussion questions and explanation of physical and spiritual death.

II. RESULT OF THE DEATH OF CHRIST:

See Introductory Step for discussion questions on points 1, 2 and 4.

A. Christ's moral character.

1. II Corinthians 5:21 (". . . knew no sin . . .").

2. Acts 10:38 (". . . went about doing good . . .").

3. Matthew 27:24 (testimony of Pilate: "This righteous man's blood . . .").

4. John 8:46 (words of Jesus: "Which of you convicts me of sin?").

5. Hebrews 4:15 (tempted without sinning).

6. Hebrews 9:14 ("without blemish . . .").

7. I Peter 1:19 ("without blemish or spot").

8. I Peter 2:21-22 (". . . no sin, no guile . . .").

B. Voluntary submission was Christ's attitude toward His death.

1. John 10:11 ("lays down his life for the sheep").

2. John 10:15 ("lay down my life for the sheep").

3. John 10:17-18 ("I have power to lay it down, and I have power to take it again . . .").

C. His teaching concerning His death.

1. Before His death.

a. Mark 2:19-20 (bridegroom taken away).

b. Mark 8:31-32 (suffer, be rejected, be killed, rise again after three days).

c. Mark 9:31 (be killed, rise again in three days).

d. Mark 10:32, 34 (details on death, rise again in three days).

e. Mark 10:38 (the "cup" and prediction regarding James and John).

f. Mark 10:45 (give His life as ransom for man).

g. Mark 14:21 (Son of Man goes as it is written of Him, also reference to betrayal, yet future).

h. Mark 14:22-25 (Last Supper: reference to body broken, blood poured out for man).

i. Mark 14:32-50 (Gethsemane).

j. Mark 15:34 (cry from the cross).

k. Luke 17:24, 25 (reference to His death in context of teaching concerning His Second Coming—first death, then demonstration of His power and glory).

l. Luke 13:32-34 (reply to Herod).

m. Luke 22:15 (at the Last Supper).

n. Luke 22:28-30 (at the Last Supper).

o. Luke 22:37 (at the Last Supper).

2. Following His resurrection.

a. Luke 24:25-27 (reviews with disciples the prophecies regarding His death and resurrection).

b. Luke 24:44-48 (reviews prophecies regarding His death and resurrection).

D. Christ's reason for dying.

1. I Corinthians 5:7 ("Christ, our paschal lamb, has been sacrificed").

2. Romans 5:6-11 (". . . for the ungodly . . . reconciled to God by the death of His Son").

3. Romans 5:15-19 (". . . leads to acquittal . . . many will be made righteous").

4. Hebrews 2:9, 17 (". . . expiation for the sins of the people").

5. Hebrews 9:14, 22 (". . . . purify . . . forgiveness of sins").

6. I John 2:2 ("expiation [propitiation] for our sins").

III. TRUE SIGNIFICANCE OF THE DEATH OF CHRIST:

Some of the most important and yet least understood questions of the Christian faith are: "Why did Christ have to die in my place?" "What is the significance of Christ's physical death to me?" "Why couldn't God redeem man without Christ's physical death in his place?"

The answers to these questions make up the very heart of the Gospel. They must be understood before a person can really experience personally the great liberating power of Christ's death.

God has chosen to reveal these answers in certain WORDS which carry systematic concepts of these truths. The following study will be developed around these "great key WORDS" which explain the true meaning and significance of Christ's death.

Being Himself JUST, God cannot be expected to justify any but those who have kept His law—yet there are none who have kept His law.

Keep in mind that to be "justified" means to be acquitted of guilt, resulting in the elimination of condemnation. The result is restoration to fellowship with God and eternal life.

Words which explain the meaning of Christ's death:

1. Reconciliation (II Corinthians 5:13-21).

2. Propitiation (Isaiah 53:5-6).

3. Redemption (Galatians 3:13).

4. Sacrifice (John 1:29).

5. Atonement (Psalms 78:38).

6. Christ, the Redeemer (Galatians 3:13; Ephesians 1:7).

7. Justification (Romans 5:1).

A. Reconciliation.

1. *Definition:* The root meaning of this word in the original Greek means "to change a person from enmity to friendship." The theological meaning applies only to man, who is said to be born at enmity with God. This enmity is caused by the sense of guilt which man has because of the barrier which he has erected between himself and God through sin. Therefore, reconciliation is that aspect of Christ's death on the cross which removed the barrier of man's sin and its consequences and thus took away guilt which was the cause for enmity against God.

This great act of Christ on the cross has removed every possible barrier which could exist between a holy God and sinful man. Reconciliation is available to all men, no matter how sinful.

Reconciliation is *sufficient* for ALL MEN, but only *effective* for those who *accept* this reconciliation personally by faith.

2. *Scriptures:* Main passage II Corinthians 5:14-21. Other key passages—Romans 5:6-11; Colossians 1:20-22.

3. *Illustration of Reconciliation:* Because God in His eternal knowledge has always known as a divine certainty that Christ would die in man's place and provide reconciliation, He has always had an attitude of love and acceptance toward men who would come to Him by faith.

The story of the "Prodigal Son" in Luke 15:11-32 illustrates reconciliation well. Note: (1) the father's attitude of love and acceptance never changed throughout. He didn't have to be reconciled when his son returned to him. (2) The son deliberately chose to go his own independent way. For some time his guilt and pride kept him from being reconciled to his father, and he chose to eat husks with the hogs. When he did go to his father, he was accepted immediately because there were no barriers against him in his father's heart.

B. Propitiation: The Godward Aspect of the Cross.

1. *Definition:* Propitiation means *"satisfaction"* in modern day terminology. This is the most important aspect of the cross because it deals with the very character of God. God will not compromise His attributes of righteousness and justice which were outraged by man's deliberate violation of God's will. God's attribute of love motivated Him to provide a way whereby He could bring man back into fellowship with Himself *without compromising* His attributes of absolute righteousness and justice. God's holy character demanded that man's sin be paid for. Man, who is born a sinner, could not do this because he had no true righteousness (Isaiah 64:6), while God is absolute righteousness. Therefore, God Himself came into the world in the person of Jesus Christ. Jesus Christ was born without sin and never committed an act of sin. Possessing the righteousness of God, He qualified and was willing to bear all of the holy wrath of God which was due the human race. In so doing He *"satisfied"* the just demands of God's holy character against the human race thus setting God's love free to pour out upon the human race in what the Bible calls GRACE. This is "propitiation."

2. *Scriptures:* Main passage is Romans 3:21-27. Other Scriptures are I John 4:10; 2:2.

C. Redemption: (See F., *Christ, The Redeemer*).

1. *Definition:* There are three Greek words which are translated

"redeem." The first means "to buy"; the second, "to buy out," and therefore remove from sale; and the third, "to ransom in order to set free."

Now all men are born sinners and are therefore in the slave market of sin, so to speak. When the Bible speaks of redemption, it means that Christ, the only free man who ever lived (because He was sinless), paid the ransom price of His own blood in order to purchase sinners out of the slave market of sin and set them free to become sons of God.

In other words, every person is born into the slave market of sin (John 8:34). In the slave market, however, there is no means of self-liberation or rescue (Ephesians 2:8-9). Only by the price of death can one be freed from the slave market of sin (Romans 6:23). There is no slave who can redeem himself, nor any other slave. Only a free man, one without sin, is able to purchase any slave out of the slave market. There is only *one* free (sinless) man who has ever lived. He is Jesus Christ (Hebrews 4:15; II Corinthians 5:21). By paying the ransom price of His shed blood, He purchased man out of the slave market of sin and set him free to become a son of God (Galatians 3:13; I Timothy 2:5-6; I Peter 1:18-19; Galatians 4:4-5). Christ has made this provision of redemption on the cross, but in order for one to be released from the slave market of sin, he must accept the provision which has been made. This he does by receiving God's Son (Ephesians 1:5).

2. *Scripture:* John 8:32-36; Galatians 3:13; Colossians 1:14; I Timothy 2:5-6; I Peter 1:18-19; Romans 3:24; Ephesians 1:7; Hebrews 9:12.

3. *General Old Testament usage of the term.*

   a. Original meaning of the Hebrew word *gaal.* "To demand back, to extricate" (Genesis 48:16).

   b. Other general meanings.

      1) To buy back or redeem property, such as a field or farm sold (Leviticus 25:25; Ruth 4:4, 6).

      2) A thing consecrated to God (Leviticus 27:13, 15, 19, 20, 31).

      3) Spoken of a slave (Leviticus 25:48-49).

4. *Usage in reference to God.*

   a. God redeeming Israel out of Egypt, with outstretched arm (Exodus 6:6; 15:13).

   b. God redeeming Israel out of bondage of the Babylonians, and other foreign peoples (Isaiah 43:1; 44:22; 48:20; 49:7).

c. God redeeming individuals, as "kinsman redeemer." The principle of redemption of property involved the repayment of a debt or an exchange of property (Leviticus 25 and 27). A provision was made for cases in which the individual was unable to make payment and had no property to exchange. In this case, the nearest of kin was responsible for the "redemption" of the property (or slave, etc). Leviticus 25:25; Ruth 3:12-13; 4:1-9; Jeremiah 32:7-8).

In respect to his sin, man is a debtor. He is unable to "redeem" or "buy back" himself, so God acts as the kinsman redeemer, redeeming the individual to Himself, from wrath upon sin, to eternal life (Isaiah 35:9; 41:14; 43:1, 14; Psalm 103:4; 107:2). See Proverbs 23:10-11.

1) Speech of Job (19:25).

2) Crying out of the Psalmist (Psalm 19:14; 69:18), for the redemption of his soul.

d. Further definitive usages:

1) The avenging of the blood of the slain (to require the penalty of bloodshed) (Numbers 35:19; Deuteronomy 19:6; Joshua 20:3; II Samuel 14:11; Isaiah 63:4).

2) Deliverance from captivity (Isaiah 63:9, 16).

3) *Padah,* "to spare"; "deliver, ransom, rescue."

a) Redemption of the first-born, precluded from being offered as sacrifice (Exodus 13:13, 15; Numbers 18:16-17). In the case of sacrifices, a set price was to be paid for their deliverance or freedom (Exodus 21:30).

b) Deliverance of a servant from slavery (Exodus 21:8).

c) Rescue from death (I Samuel 14:45).

d) Redemption of the soul (Psalm 31:5; 34:22; 49:7-8, 15; 130:7-8).

e) ". . . The Lord, who redeemed Abraham . . ." (Isaiah 29:22).

4) *Yasha,* "to save, help, preserve, rescue, defend, deliver."

a) Deliverance from bondage or tribulations (Exodus 14:30; Isaiah 43:3; I Samuel 10:19).

b) Deliverance from the enemies (Numbers 10:9; Deuteronomy 20:4).

c) Saving care over poor and helpless individuals who need and claim God's protection (Job 5:15; 22:9; Psalm 76:9; 72:4, 13; 34:18; Proverbs 28:18).

5. *Principles upon which redemption from sin rests.*

   a. God's purposes.

      1) Merciful disposition of God (Psalm 109:26).

      2) Integrity and honor of God (Isaiah 37:35).

      3) God's own name's sake (Isaiah 43:11; 45:22).

   b. Mode or extent of redemption.

      1) Connection with righteousness (Psalm 24:5).

      2) Connection with truth (Psalm 25:5).

      3) Hearing of prayer (Psalm 69:13).

      4) Forgiveness of sins (Psalm 79:9).

6. *Conclusions.*

   a. In actuating redemption, God in His grace acts as the "kinsman redeemer" of the repentant sinner, freeing him from the bondage of the power and penalty of sin.

   b. The Old Testament words translated with the sense of "redemption" vividly portray the picture of a sinner who is spiritually bankrupt, unable to redeem himself.

   c. God's act of redemption is truly a rescue from an enemy, as well as an act of protection of men who are in dire need of God's intervening hand.

   d. Perhaps a present day illustration of the "kinsman redeemer" would be the one who co-signs a note, thereby making himself liable for the responsibility of its payment in the event of inability on the part of the first signer.

   e. In the sense of "buying back," God acts to buy the sinner back from bondage in sin.

D. Sacrifice. The sacrifices in the Old Testament: How they pointed forward in time to the sacrifice of Jesus Christ on the cross.

The sacrifices of the Old Testament serve as perfect symbols pointing to and being completely fulfilled in the death of Christ. All the prophecies regarding specific details and events in the life, death and resurrection of Jesus Christ were perfectly fulfilled. The perfect accuracy of the Bible is thus demonstrated. This could not be true if the Bible were not the inspired word of God. The Bible was spoken by God through the mouths of His prophets. See Acts 2:18, 21.

1. Origin of the sacrifice.

   a. *Divine origin.* Based upon the account of Genesis 4:4 and following, a faith in the true God is presupposed on the part of Abel and is confirmed by Hebrews 11:4.

   b. Theories based upon the erroneous idea that man himself originated the idea of sacrifice.

      1) Gift theory, which teaches that men began to offer gifts to God in order to establish good relations.

      2) Magic theory, which teaches that the purpose of the sacrifice was either to entice a demon from the offerer into the sacrificed animal or to obtain the good will of Deity by the act of shedding blood. These ideas maye have been true of heathen sacrifices.

      3) Expiatory or atoning theory, in which the sacrifice was a substitution for the sin of the offerer.

      4) Sacramental communion theory, which teaches that men believed that the eating of certain animals enabled them to partake of their god with resulting increased strength and moral qualities.

      5) Homage theory, which teaches that the sacrifice was a sort of acted prayer.

      6) Table-bond theory, which teaches that men believed that by sharing in fellowship of a banquet, they were knit into closer fellowship with one another and their god.

These ideas may have a part in heathen sacrifices but certainly are not the essence of the Old Testament concept of sacrifices.

2. The meaning of Old Testament sacrifices.

   a. General.

      1) *Korban*—"thing brought near (Leviticus 2:4-5, 7, 12-13; 3:1, 7:14, 29, 38; 22:18; Numbers 18:9; 31:50).

      2) *Nagash*—"approach, draw near" applied to offerings presented (Amos 5:25; Malachi 1:7-8, 11, 13; 3:3; see also Jeremiah 30:21).

   b. Specific.

      1) *'Olah*—"burnt-offering (Genesis 8:20; 22:2-13; Job 1:5; 42:8; Exodus 24:5; Psalm 51:19; 66:15; Isaiah 57:6; 66:3;

Ezekiel 43:18, 24; Amos 5:22).

Calil—"that which is complete," is used of the whole burnt-offering (Leviticus 6:22-23; Deuteronomy 33:10; I Samuel 7:9; Psalm 51:19).

2) *Minchah*—"meat-offering, the meat signifying food, rather than flesh." The general idea is that of a gift to God (Genesis 4:3-5; Leviticus 2:1; Isaiah 66:20; Jeremiah 41:5; Zephaniah 3:10; Malachi 3:3-4). Translated "gift" (Psalm 45:12), sacrifice, oblation at other times. Regarded as a token of gratitude, and thanksgiving to God. An acknowledgment that God Himself is the giver of all good gifts (Psalm 20:3).

3) *Zevach*—"slay, kill," to slay an animal (Deuteronomy 12:15, 21; I Samuel 28:24; II Chronicles 18:2; Ezekiel 34:3). Used in connection with a sacred feast in which the animal was slain and the family partook of the flesh, thus entering into communion with God.

c. Significance of particular offerings.

1) *Pasach*—Passover feast, commemorated the episode in Egypt (Exodus 12) where the death angel passed over the houses with blood on the doorposts. Application of the parallel to Christ is found in I Corinthians 5:7.

2) *Shelem*—Peace-offering, indicated right relations with God and expressed gratitude and obligation (Leviticus 3:1-17; Psalm 50:14; 56:12; 76:11; 116:14; Isaiah 19:21; Jonah 2:9; Nahum 1:15).

3) *Chattath*—Sin-offering, was an expiatory sacrifice for the purpose of cleansing, purging—an offering for sin (Leviticus 6:26; 9:15; Psalm 51:7. Described in Exodus 29; Leviticus 4).

4) *Asham*—Trepass offering, described in Leviticus chapters 5 and 6. Expiating and restitution for particular types of sin were expressed.

5) *Tenuphah*—Wave-offering and *Terumah*—Heave-offering, were parts of the peace-offering (Exodus 29:24-28; Leviticus 7:30-34).

3. Conclusions.

a. Sacrifices were divinely instituted for the instruction of the people of Israel.

b. In many ways, the sacrifices were object lessons, teaching the sinful condition of the people and showing them that God had provided a way by which they could be reconciled to Him.

c. The principle of substitution was thus illustrated before the people as early as the time of Abel (Genesis 4:4).

d. Sacrifices were improperly used by many, however, for they conceived of them as substitutes for righteousness or appeasements in themselves. Faith was absent and thus God said ". . . I despise your feasts, and I will take no delight in your solemn assemblies" (Amos 5:21).

e. When misused, sacrifices and offerings are an abomination to God. "Bring no more vain oblations; incense is an abomination unto me . . ." (Isaiah 1:13). (See also Isaiah 29:13 and Amos 5:25.)

f. Sacrifices were intended to point to the Coming One, who would fulfill all sacrifices so that ". . . there is no more sacrifice for sin. . ."

g. The sacrifice of Christ and His relationship to Israelite sacrifice: Hebrews 10:4 and Romans 3:25 explain how Christ's death profited Moses, Joshua, David, etc. What was it? The word Atonement (AV) in Hebrew is the word "to cover." The Jew spoke of covering.

Read Exodus 12:1-13 and relate the similarities of the following to the sacrifice of Christ:

Lamb	(Ans. Male, Slain.)
Application of the Blood	(Ans. Salvation decision by us.)
Passing Over of Death Angel	(Ans. Forgiveness.)
Meal together as family	(Ans. Christian Fellowship.)
Pharaoh	(Ans. Satan.)
Slavery in Egypt	(Ans. Slave to sin.)
Egypt	(Ans. World.)

Read Isaiah 53:7 and Luke 23:9. What is the item that is fulfilled? (Ans. Christ, as lamb, is mute.)

E. Atonement.

1. Usage of the term "atonement" in the Old Testament:

a. To cover, thus to pardon sin (Psalm 65:4; 78:38; Jeremiah 18:23; II Chronicles 30:18; Ezekiel 16:63; Deuteronomy 21:8).

b. To obtain forgiveness, to expiate an offense (Daniel 9:24; Ezekiel 45:20).

c. To free an offender from charge (Exodus 30:10; Leviticus 4:20; 16:6, 11, 24).

d. Forgiveness, through God's compassion (Psalm 78:38).

e. Removal of the guilt or of the punishment which follows from guilt (Psalm 79:9; Proverbs 16:6 [Jeremiah 18:23 for contrast]; Isaiah 6:7; 22:14; 27:9; see also Isaiah 28:18).

f. Sin treated as non-existent (disannulled) (Isaiah 28:18).

g. Pacification of God (Ezekiel 16:62; Psalm 65:3)—Also to be noted that this pacification originates with God only, not from man.

h. Reconciliation, often mistaken as the result of atonement, is similar to atonement (Daniel 9:24; Ezekiel 45:15, 17, 20).

i. Idea of costliness is presented as an element in atonement in several usages:

1) Satisfaction (Numbers 35:31-32).

2) Bribe (I Samuel 12:3; Amos 5:12).

3) Sum of money (Exodus 21:30).

4) Ransom (Exodus 30:12; Job 33:24; 36:18; Psalm 49:7; Proverbs 6:35; 13:8; 21:18; Isaiah 43:3).

2. Procedure of the Day of Atonement.

a. Frequency—once a year (Exodus 30:10).

1) To begin on the tenth day of the seventh month (Leviticus 23:26).

2) Aaron was to make an atonement on the horns of the altar at this time, with the blood of the sin offering (Exodus 30:10).

b. Procedure:

1) Necessary items for the ceremony (Leviticus 16).

a) For the priest himself.

(1) Young bullock as sin-offering (16:6, 11, 14-15, 27).

(2) Ram for burnt offering (16:24).

(3) Sacred garments (16:23-32).

(4) A bath (16:24).

b) For the congregation.

    (1) Two he-goats as sin-offering (16:7, 15-22, 25, 27, 32-33).

    (2) Ram as a burnt offering (16:24).

2) Sequence of activity.

a) Bullock is killed as sin-offering for the priest and his household.

b) Lots were cast upon the two kids which were sin-offerings for the congregation—one killed and the other sent away into the desert.

c) Burning coal from the altar and two handfuls of beaten incense placed behind the veil, in the Holy of Holies.

d) Resulting cloud of incense protected Aaron.

e) Aaron then entered the Holy of Holies with the blood of the slain bullock and sprinkled the blood first on the front side of the mercy-seat and then upon the ground before the mercy-seat.

f) Act of atonement for the congregation was then made when he slew the goat and brought its blood into the Holy of Holies and sprinkled as before.

g) Atonement acts in the Holy Place followed.

h) Atonement for the altar of burnt offering.

i) Live goat covered with the blood of the slain goat and sent away into the wilderness.

j) Aaron laid aside his linen garments, bathed, put on the regular garb of the High Priest, came forth out of the Holy Place.

k) Offering of his burnt offering, then that of the congregation.

l) Aaron burned the fat of the sin offering.

3. Conclusions.

a. The day of atonement was of major significance, requiring spiritual preparation on the part of the people who were to "afflict their souls."

b. It was necessary that first the priest be atoned for, before he could be a representative of the people before God.

c. This day and the events which transpired, prefigured that day when Christ, our High Priest, entered heaven itself to intercede for us before God.

d. As "Without the shedding of blood there is no remission for sins," the high priest was instructed to use blood in the ceremony of making atonement for himself and for the congregation.

e. The ground of appeal for atonement or forgiveness is not the the goodness or any merit of the individual but the nature of God Himself.

f. The means through which atonement is granted is through the grace and mercy of God. (Numbers 14:15-20; Isaiah 48: 9-11). Likewise, this atonement can be withheld. (I Samuel 3:14).

F. Christ the Redeemer.

1. The need for a Redeemer.

a. God required a holy, righteous life.

1) The people were commanded to keep His statutes and commandments (Deuteronomy 4:40).

2) They were to walk in the way which God had appointed (Deuteronomy 5:33).

3) God required personal communion with Himself on the part of His people (Deuteronomy 4:29).

4) The people were commanded to love God with all of their mind, heart and strength (Deuteronomy 6:5).

b. The Bible liberally attests to the fact that man has at no time obeyed the commands of God. Because of this fact, God provided the plan of redemption and Himself became the Redeemer of mankind in the Person of His Son.

2. The Person of the Redeemer.

a. God (Isaiah 43:10-11; 49:26; 64:8-9; Psalm 78:35).

1) Prophecies of regathering of His people (Jeremiah 31:7-8; Ezekiel 34:22; Zechariah 8:8).

2) Promise of the rebuilding of cities of Judah (Psalm 69:35).

3) Innumerable other prophecies are within the Old Testament, promising future aspects of God's redeeming work.

b. A distinct Person, sent from God. (Isaiah 44:6).

    1) Prophesied throughout the Old Testament and looked for as the Messiah. (Genesis 3:15; Job 19:25).

    2) The Son of God and coming King (Zechariah 6:13).

3. Prophecies concerning His Person and Coming.

  a. His Person.

    1) Seed of the woman (Genesis 3:15).

    2) Seed of David (II Samuel 7:12-16; Jeremiah 23:5).

    3) Virgin Birth (Isaiah 7:14).

    4) Divinity.

      a) His name is to be Immanuel or "God with us" (Isaiah 7:14).

      b) His name is also to be Wonderful Counsellor, Mighty God, Everlasting Father, and Prince of Peace (Isaiah 9:6).

    5) Priestly office.

      a) A priest after the order of Melchizedek (Psalm 110:4).

      b) A priest upon His throne (Zechariah 6:12-13).

    6) Kingship, the ruler of all, eternally (Isaiah 9:7; Daniel 7:14; Psalm 72:8).

    7) Prophetic office (Deuteronomy 18:15).

4. Conclusions.

  a. Prophecies concerning the Redeemer, or Messiah, are numerous and unmistakably clear in many cases.

  b. God Himself became the "kinsman redeemer" in the Person of His Son, Jesus Christ.

  c. Apart from this act on the part of God, man would be without hope, mired in his sinful state and unable to redeem himself.

G. Justification:

Man cannot in any sense earn favor in the sight of God, but can approach God only through Christ, in faith and repentance for sin. Even this would not be possible, except through the great plan of redemption which God instituted (Romans 6:23; John 3). Salvation is the gift of God and not of works, lest any man should boast

(Eph. 2:9). The expression of God's love was given upon the cross of Christ, as recorded in Romans 5:8. "Much more now that we are reconciled, shall we be saved by His life" (Romans 5:10). Christ was the fulfillment of the Law, as well as the end of all sacrifices, for after he had offered one sacrifice for sins *forever,* "He sat down at the right hand of God . . ." (Hebrews 10:12). Grace is the gift of God and so justification by faith (because of grace) is also the free gift of God. Justification signifies position, in a legal sense. The idea is that the justified individual is declared righteous. His position is "in Christ," and is secured because of the sacrifice of Christ (Titus 3:5-7).

IV. SUMMARY:

A. Read John 3:18.

    1. What two fates are described here? (condemned [judged]—or not condemned).

    2. What is the only reason that one is condemned?

    3. (Thought question, not to be answered orally): According to what the Bible says in John 3:18, are you condemned or not condemned?

B. According to I John 5:11-12, how does one obtain eternal life?

C. The apostle Paul emphasizes many times in his writings the fact that Jesus Christ is the one Mediator between God and man, by the blood of His cross (Colossians 1:20; I Corinthians 2:2), removing the sin barrier between God and man.

D. Peter shows that Jesus is the one way to God (Acts 4:12; I Peter 1:2, 18-19; 2:21, 24; 3:18).

E. See also the following references:

    1. Ephesians 2:16, 18 (". . . through Him we have access to the Father").

    2. I Timothy 2:5 (". . . one mediator . . . Christ Jesus").

F. Read Romans 1:13-20. "His nature has been clearly perceived in (nature) the things which have been made." Why can God rightfully punish anyone who glorified Him not as God?

G. Read Romans 1:22-32.
How what mental, physical and social problems have resulted from man's choice to "go his own independent way?"

THE RESURRECTION OF JESUS CHRIST

LESSON FOUR   INTRODUCTORY STEP

OBJECTIVE: To present some of the evidence regarding the historical fact that Jesus Christ rose from the dead. To discuss the importance of this event, as it relates to our personal lives.

I. OPEN WITH PRAYER.

II. MEMORY VERSE: I Corinthians 15:3-4. Students check each other.

III. MOTIVATION: "Each spring, Easter comes around, reminding each one of us of the resurrection of Jesus Christ, three days after His death. How do you know if Jesus actually did rise from the dead? Write down as many items of evidence as you can." (Optional: Have members of the group name them, and you, or a designated person, write them down.)

IV. BIBLE STUDY:

A. Veracity of the resurrection of Jesus Christ.

Quote Thomas Arnold, from conclusion of lesson in the T.B.S.

B. Six proofs that Jesus actually rose from the dead.

1. Foretold by Jesus, the Son of God.

a. Matthew 16:21, ". . . and on the third day be raised."

b. Discuss questions in Lesson Four in Introductory Step.

2. Empty tomb.

a. Discuss questions in the T.B.S.

3. Appearances of Jesus to His disciples.

a. List of appearances, over a period of six weeks.

b. Discuss questions in the T.B.S.

4. Beginning of the Christian Church.

   a. "Without this fact the church could never have been formed" (Philip Schaff).

   b. Over half of Peter's sermon deals with the Resurrection (W. J. Sparrow-Simpson) (Acts 2:14-36).

   c. Discuss questions in the T.B.S.

   d. "The Resurrection . . . proclaimed Him to be the Son of God with power" (Dr. H. D. A. Major).

5. Transformation of the disciples.

   a. Peter.

   b. Other disciples.

   c. Note that the disciples were not expecting a resurrection.

      (1) The women.

      (2) Thomas.

   d. "If their testimony was not true there was no possible motive for its fabrication" (Simon Greenleaf).

   e. "We have evidence, . . ." (Encyclopedia Brittanica).

6. Testimony and transformation of the Apostle Paul.

   a. Paul's experience.

   b. Paul's testimony.

   c. ". . . established beyond the possibility of doubt" (Robert H. Kennett).

C. *Testimony of other well-known men, in support of the resurrection of Christ.*

   1. "Our faith is based on the resurrection . . ." (William Lyon Phelps).

   2. ". . . as sure as historical evidence could make it" (Professor Edwin Gordon Selwyn).

   3. "Such evidence . . . has never been broken down" (John Singleton Copley [Lord Lynhurst]).

4. "Some of the outstanding thinkers of every age have boldly confessed the same faith" (Dr. Wilbur Smith).

V. PARALLEL PASSAGES: See the Lesson Amplification.

VI. SUMMARY: Results of the resurrection.

A. Romans 1:4.

B. Ephesians 1:19-20.

C. Philippians 3:21.

D. Refer to conclusion in Lesson Amplification.

VII. CLOSE IN PRAYER: Give opportunity for those present to silently pray, asking Christ to become their personal Saviour. Encourage those who already know Christ as Saviour to give Him pre-eminence in their lives, asking Him in silent prayer to take control.

THE RESURRECTION OF JESUS CHRIST

LESSON FOUR   INTRODUCTORY STEP

INTRODUCTION:

The resurrection of Jesus Christ has come under the most careful scrutiny of men, from New Testament times to the present day. Legal minds have examined the evidence, historians have examined the facts and the testimonies of those who reported the event, and others have written books concerning the relevance of the resurrection.

Historians, men trained in the laws of evidence, and others have affirmed that the resurrection of Jesus Christ is an extremely well-established historical fact. To those who know Christ as personal Saviour and Lord, the resurrection is vital and central in importance. There are several converging lines of evidence in support of the resurrection, each of considerable weight, and demanding consideration. In this lesson we shall deal with six.

I.   VERACITY OF THE RESURRECTION OF JESUS CHRIST:
      Quote Thomas Arnold, from conclusion of lesson four in the Introductory Step to the T.B.S.

II.   SIX PROOFS THAT JESUS ACTUALLY ROSE FROM THE DEAD:

      A. First proof: *The resurrection was foretold by Jesus Christ, the Son of God.*

         1. Discuss Matthew 16:21.

         2. Discuss questions in the T.B.S.

      B. Second proof: *The resurrection is the only reasonable explanation for His empty tomb.* Discuss the precautions taken by both Jesus' friends and His enemies, to insure that His body would not be stolen (Mark 15:46 and Matthew 27:62-66, questions in the T.B.S.)

      C. Third proof: *The resurrection is the only reasonable explanation for the appearances of Jesus Christ to His disciples.*

         1. Appearances of Jesus Christ, between the morning of His resurrection and His ascension forty days later:

            a. To certain women as they returned from the sepulchre, after having seen the angel who told them Christ had arisen (Matt. 28:1-10).

58

b. To Mary Magdalene at the sepulchre, probably upon her second visit to it that morning (John 20:11-18; Mark 16:9-11).

c. To the Apostle Peter, before the evening of the day of the resurrection, but under circumstances of which we have no details (Luke 24:34; I Corinthians 15:5).

d. To the two disciples, Cleopas and another, on the way to Emmaus on Sunday afternoon (Mark 16:12-13; Luke 24:13-35).

e. To the ten apostles (Thomas being absent) together with others whose names are not given, assembled together on Sunday evening at their evening meal (Mark 16:14-18; Luke 24:36-40; John 20:19-23; I Corinthians 15:5).

f. One week later, to all the eleven apostles, probably in the same place as the preceding appearance (John 20:26-28).

g. To several of the disciples at the Sea of Galilee, while they were fishing. (The exact time is undesignated (John 21:1-23).

h. To the apostles, and over five hundred others, at once, on an appointed mountain in Galilee (Matthew 28:16-20; I Corinthians 15:6).

i. To James, under circumstances of which we have no details (I Corinthians 15:7).

j. To the apostles at Jerusalem, immediately before the ascension from the Mount of Olives (Mark 16:19; Luke 24:50-52; Acts 1:3-8).

2. Discuss questions in the T.B.S.

D. Fourth proof: *The resurrection is the only reasonable explanation for the beginning of the Christian Church.*

1. "Without this fact the church could never have been formed." "The Christian church rests on the resurrection of its Founder. Without this fact the church could never have been born, or if born, it would soon have died a natural death. The miracle of the resurrection and the existence of Christianity are so closely connected that they must stand or fall together. If Christ was raised from the dead, then all His other miracles are sure, and our faith is not vain. It was only His resurrection that made His death available for our atonement, justification and salvation; without the resurrection, His death would be the grave of our sins. A gospel of a dead Saviour would be a contradiction and a wretched delusion. This is the reasoning of St. Paul, and its force is irresistible.

"The resurrection of Christ is therefore emphatically a test question upon which depends the truth or falsehood of the Christian religion. It is either the greatest miracle or the greatest delusion which history records.

"Historical questions are not like mathematical problems. No argument in favor of the resurrection will avail to these critics who start with the philosophical assumption that miracles are impossible, and still less with those who deny not only the resurrection of the body, but even the immortality of the soul. But facts are stubborn and if a critical hypothesis can be proved to be psychologically and historically impossible, the results are fatal to the philosophy which underlies the critical hypothesis. It is not the business of the historian to construct a history from preconceived notions and to adjust it to his own liking, but to reproduce it from the best evidence and to let it speak for itself" (Philip Schaff, *History of the Christian Church*, Vol. I, p. 172-73).

2. Over half of Peter's sermon deals with the Resurrection.

"Acts 2:14-36. Twelve of the twenty-three verses, or over half of the first sermon, deals with the Resurrection of Jesus Christ. The first sermon of the divinely established church, the one delivered by the Apostle Peter on the day of Pentecost, is 'wholly and entirely founded on the Resurrection.' Not merely is the Resurrection its principal theme, but if that doctrine were removed there would be no doctrine left. For the Resurrection is propounded as being: (1) the explanation of Jesus' death; (2) prophetically anticipated as the Messianic experience; (3) apostolically witnessed; (4) the cause of the outpouring of the Spirit, and thus accounting for religious phenomena inexplicable; and (5) certifying the Messianic and Kingly position of Jesus of Nazareth. Thus the whole series of arguments and conclusions depends for stability entirely upon the Resurrection. Without the Resurrection, the Messianic and Kingly position of Jesus could not be convincingly established. Without it the new outpouring of the Spirit would continue a mystery unexplained. Without it the substance of the apostolic witness would have disappeared. All that would be left of this instruction would be the Messianic exposition of Psalm 26; and that, only as a future experience of a Messiah who had not yet appeared. The Divine Approval of Jesus as certified by His works would also remain: but apparently as an approval extended only to His Life; a life ending like that of any other prophet whom the nation refused to tolerate any longer. Thus the first Christian sermon is founded on the position of Jesus as determined by His Resurrection" (W. J. Sparrow-Simpson, *The Resurrection and Modern Thought*, London 1911, pp. 230-231).

3. Discuss questions in the T.B.S.

4. "The Resurrection . . . proclaimed Him to be the Son of God with power."

> Dr. H. D. A. Major, Principal of Ripon Hall at Oxford, editor of the *Modern Churchman*, made this statement: "Had the crucifixion of Jesus ended His disciples' experience of Him, it is hard to see how the Christian church could have come into existence. That church was founded on faith in the Messiahship of Jesus. A crucified messiah was no messiah at all. He was one rejected by Judaism and accursed of God. It was the Resurrection of Jesus, as St. Paul declares in Romans 1:4, which proclaimed him to be the Son of God with power" (*Mission and Message of Jesus.* New York, 1938, p. 213).

E. Fifth proof: *The resurrection is the only reasonable explanation for the transformation of the disciples.* They had seen their leader arrested and crucified, and feared for their own lives.

1. Peter denied three times that he even knew Jesus Christ (Matthew 26:69-75). After he saw the resurrected Christ, Peter was now willing to stand up before crowds (the very crowds who had put Christ to death) to proclaim the resurrection (Acts 2:14-37).

2. The disciples went into hiding in an upper room, "for fear of the Jews." After seeing and talking with Jesus for approximately six weeks, they went out to "turn the world upside down," fearlessly proclaiming Jesus Christ (Acts 8:4; 17:6; 3:12-26; 4:1-20, 31, 33).

3. It is important to note that the disciples were not expecting Jesus to rise from the dead (Luke 24:11, 41).

   a. The women's intention to embalm a corpse shows that they did not expect him to rise from the dead (Mark 16:1-4).

   b. Thomas was skeptical to the end. Only when Jesus Christ stood before him, asking Thomas to put his fingers in the nailprints and to inspect the wound in His side—only then was Thomas convinced (John 20:24-28).

4. "If their testimony were not true, there was no possible motive for its fabrication."

"We next turn to an American authority in jurisprudence: Simon Greenleaf (1783-1853), the famous Royall Professor of Law at Harvard University, who succeeded Justice Joseph Story as the Dane Professor of Law in the same university, upon Story's death in 1846. It is recognized that 'To the efforts of Story and Greenleaf is to be ascribed the rise of the Harvard Law School to its eminent position among the legal schools of the United States.' (H. W. H. Knott, in *Dictionary of American Biography, Vol. VII*, New York, 1937, p. 584).

"Greenleaf's famous work, A Treatise on the Law of Evidence, the first volume of which appeared in 1842, was 'regarded as the foremost American authority,' passing through edition after edition, is still considered the greatest single authority on evidence in the entire literature of legal procedure. Greenleaf, trained in weighing evidence, while still professor of law at Harvard, wrote in 1846, a volume that immediately took its place as one of the most significant works on the truthfulness of the Christian religion of his day: *An examination of the Testimony of the Four Evangelists by the Rules of Evidence Administered in Courts of Justice*. The author devotes a number of pages to the consideration of the value of the testimony of the Apostles to the resurrection of Christ. The one who wrote the following discussion of evidences was the one who, by his legal works, was quoted thousands of times in the great court battles of our country, for three-quarters of a century" (Wilbur M. Smith, *Therefore Stand*, p. 423ff.).

Concerning Jesus Christ and His Resurrection, Greenleaf wrote the following:

"The great truths which the apostles declared were that Christ had risen from the dead, and that only through repentance from sin, and faith in Him, could men hope for salvation. This doctrine they asserted with one voice, everywhere, not only under the greatest discouragements, but in the face of the most appalling terrors that can be presented to the mind of man. Their master had recently perished as a malefactor, by the sentence of a public tribunal. His religion sought to overthrow the teachings of His disciples. The interests and passions of all the rulers and great men in the world were against them. The fashion of the world was against them. Propagating this new faith, even in the most inoffensive and peaceful manner, they could expect nothing but contempt, opposition, revilings, bitter persecutions, stripes, imprisonments, torments, and deaths. Yet this faith they zealously did propagate; and all these miseries they endured undismayed, nay rejoicing. As one after another was put to a miserable death, the survivors only prosecuted their work with increased vigor and resolution. The annals of military warfare afford scarcely an example of the like heroic constancy, patience, and unflinching courage. They had every possible motive to review carefully the grounds of their faith, and the evidences of the great facts and truths which they asserted; and these motives were pressed upon their attention with the most melancholy and terrific frequency. *It was therefore impossible that they could have persisted in affirming the truths they have narrated, had not Jesus actually risen from the dead, and had they not known this fact as certainly as they knew any other fact.* If it were morally possible for them to have been deceived in this matter, every human motive operated to lead them to discover and avow their error. To have persisted in so gross a falsehood, after it was known to them, was not only to encounter, for life, all the evils which man could inflict, from without, but to endure also the pangs of inward conscience, no expectation of honor or esteem among men, no hope of happiness in this life, or in the world to come.

"Such conduct in the apostles would moreover have been utterly irreconcilable with the fact that they possessed the ordinary constitution of our common nature. Yet their lives do show them to have been men like all others of our race; swayed by the same motives, animated by the same fears, and subject to the same passions, temptations, and infirmities, as ourselves. And their writings show them to have been men of vigorous understandings. If then their testimony was not true, there was no possible motive for its fabrication" (Simon Greenleaf, *The Testimony of the Evangelists Examined by the Rules of Evidence Administered in Courts of Justice,* New York, 1874, pp. 28-31.).

5. "We have evidence . . ."

"We have evidence that a very few weeks after the event Jesus Christ's followers, who had scattered in dismay, were reunited at Jerusalem, men and women to the number of about 120, feeling themselves to be bound together in a religious society through a common conviction, a common expectation and a common attitude toward Jesus. They were fully persuaded that He was alive, and that He had been seen by individuals and by groups of His followers. They were eagerly expecting that He would quite shortly return as the Messiah of their race, the Son of God, with power, and they adopted an attitude toward Him which, though still undefined, was an attitude of religious faith. The strength and the sincerity of their conviction were tested by persecution and proved by their steadfastness. The religious quality of their attitude to Jesus was evidenced by devotion, self-sacrifice and a sense of obligation to Him which swept away the last barrier of selfishness and they had a message concerning this same Jesus which they proceeded to proclaim with enthusiasm and amazing success. The Christ became a fact of history" *(Encyclopedia Britannica, 1956, p. 15.)*.

F. Sixth proof: *The witness of the Apostle Paul, and the transformation of his life, can only be reasonably explained because of the resurrection.*

    1. Paul was born a Roman citizen and studied under the scholar Gamaliel. He became educated in Greek, Aramaic, Hebrew and the Law. Paul, under his earlier name Saul, was devoting his energies and time to the self-appointed task of seizing or killing those who proclaimed Jesus Christ as the promised Messiah and resurrected Lord. Acts 9 relates his meeting with Christ; and Acts chapters 22 and 26 record Paul's account as he testified before a crowd, and before King Agrippa.

    2. In I Corinthians 15, where Paul is proving the resurrection of Christians, he presents the resurrection of Jesus Christ as primary evidence, giving a list of the various appearances of Christ. Note that he includes the appearance of Christ to himself. The transformation of his life from that of one who hated Jesus Christ and His followers, to that of one who dedicated his life to follow and serve Jesus Christ, was due to one thing—the fact of the death and resurrection of the One whom Paul now knew —Jesus Christ (II Corinthians 5:14-15).

    3. ". . . established beyond the possibility of doubt."

        "Within a very few years of the time of the crucifixion of Jesus, the evidence for the resurrection of Jesus was, in the mind of at least one man of education, absolutely irrefutable."

        "Surely common sense requires us to believe that that for which he so suffered was in his eyes established beyond the possibility of doubt."

        (Both statements are by Robert H. Kennett, quoted in the *International Standard Bible Encyclopedia*, Vol. IV, p. 2568.).

III. THE TESTIMONY OF OTHER WELL-KNOWN MEN, IN SUP-
PORT OF THE RESURRECTION OF CHRIST:

A. "Our faith is based on the resurrection . . ."

Dr. William Lyon Phelps was, for more than forty years,
Yale's distinguished professor of English literature, author
of some twenty volumes of literary studies and public orator
of Yale. He has said many worthwhile things about the
word of God and given a definite confession of his faith in
Jesus Christ as the Son of God.

"In the whole story of Jesus Christ, the most important
event is the resurrection. Christian faith depends on this.
It is encouraging to know that it is explicitly given by all
four evangelists and told also by Paul. The names of those
who saw Him after His Triumph over death are recorded;
and it may be said that the historical evidence for the resurrection is stronger than for any other miracle anywhere
narrated . . . Our faith in God, in Christ, in life itself is
based on the resurrection; for as Paul said, if Christ be not
risen from the dead then is our preaching vain, and your
faith is also vain" *(Human Nature and the Gospel*, p.131-
132.).

B. ". . . as sure as historical evidence could make it."

Professor Edwin Gordon Selwyn in his able apologetic work
of a few years ago, *The Approach to Christianity,* said, "The
fact that Christ rose from the dead on the third day in full
continuity of body and soul, and passed into a mode of
new relationships with those who knew Him on earth—that
fact seems as secure as historical evidence could make it"
(The Approach to Christianity, London, 1925, p. 199.).

C. "Such evidence has never been broken down . . ."

"At the time Greenleaf did his most important work, another
great legal authority in Great Britain was also expressing,
though not as fully, his faith in the resurrection of Christ.
We refer to *John Singleton Copley,* better known as *Lord
Lyndhurst* (1772-1863), recognized as one of the greatest
legal minds in British history, the Solicitor-General of the
British government in 1819, attorney-general of Great Britain in 1824, three times High Chancellor of England, and
elected in 1846; High Steward of the University of Cambridge, thus holding in one lifetime the highest offices which
a judge in Great Britain could ever have conferred upon
him. When Chancellor Lyndhurst died, a document was
found in his desk, among his private papers, giving an ex-

tended account of his own Christian faith; and in this precious, previously unknown record, he wrote: 'I know pretty well what evidence is; and I tell you, such evidence as that for the Resurrection has never broken down yet' " (Wilbur M. Smith, *Therefore Stand*, p. 425.).

D. "Some of the outstanding thinkers of every age have boldly confessed the same faith."

"These are not rare expressions of faith in the Resurrection. On the contrary some of the outstanding thinkers of every age have boldly confessed the same faith. The greatest man in the first century of the Christian era is the one who went everywhere throughout the Roman Empire testifying to the truth of a resurrection, the Apostle Paul. The greatest man in the fourth century was St. Augustine, and he never wearied of referring to the bodily Resurrection of the Lord. The man who is recognized as probably the greatest intellect of modern times, Sir Isaac Newton, believed in the Resurrection of Christ. Those men who laid the foundations of our famous American colleges and universities all believed strongly in the Resurrection of Christ, as can easily be seen by even the most superficial reading of their writings, as for instance, Increase Mather, President of Harvard; Timothy Dwight, President of Yale; Nathan Lord, President of Dartmouth; Edward Hitchcock, President of Amherst; Mark Hopkins, President of Williams College; John Witherspoon, President of Princeton. No man has to be ashamed of being found in the company of such men" (Wilbur M. Smith, *Therefore Stand*, p. 430-431.).

IV. SUMMARY: Discuss questions in concluding section of Introductory Step of the T.B.S. dealing with the following material on the results of the resurrection.

A. Romans 1:4 (demonstrates that He was the divine Son of God).

B. Ephesians 1:19-20 (shows up what power He has available on our behalf).

C. Philippians 3:21 (indicates how He will one day change our bodies to be like His resurrected body).

D. He is the same today (Hebrews 13:8) and so will transform your life.

E. Receive Him now, as your Saviour and Lord.

V. CLOSE IN PRAYER.

JESUS CHRIST LIVING IN THE CHRISTIAN

LESSON FIVE   INTRODUCTORY STEP

OBJECTIVE: To demonstrate that the Christian cannot live the Christian life by his own power and resources; to show that Christ alone can make a life of victory and power a reality in the life of a Christian; and to explain the importance of absolute surrender to Christ, in order to experience the abundant life.

I.   OPEN WITH PRAYER.

II. MEMORY VERSE: Revelation 3:20 (Have the group quote in unison).

III. MOTIVATION: Read Introduction in the Lesson Amplification to the group.

IV. BIBLE STUDY:

   A. Need for Jesus Christ to live in the Christian.

      1. Christ indwells all Christians (Romans 8:8-9).

      2. "Christ Himself is the very life content of the Christian life" (W. Ian Thomas).

      3. ". . . only Christ's life wins . . ." (Charles G. Trumbull).

      4. Discuss questions in Lesson Five.

      5. "One gift to meet our need—His Son Jesus Christ" (Watchman Nee).

   B. Fact that Jesus Christ lives in the Christian.

      1. "His resources are our resources" (William Culbertson).

      2. Discuss questions 1-5 in this section, in Lesson Five.

      3. Scriptures which teach the fact of Christ living within.

C. Jesus Christ at home within the Christian.

    1. Christ must be truly at home in your heart.

    2. You must live in conscious dependence upon Him.

        a. Relate everything to Christ's adequacy.

        b. Live in conscious dependence upon Him.

    3. Christ will provide all needed resources. Discuss questions from concluding section of Lesson Five.

V.   PARALLEL PASSAGES: See the Lesson Amplification.

VI.   SUMMARY:

A. "Christ within is the only place where Christian experience can begin" (Andrew Murray).

B. "Christ alone can supply the power to live a Christian life" (Major Ian Thomas).

C. How to submit to Christ:

    1. Surrender absolutely to Christ.

    2. Believe that God has set you free from the law of sin.

VII. CLOSE IN PRAYER: Invite those present to pray silently, surrendering their lives totally to God, believing the fact that He has set them free from the law of sin. Invite non-Christians present to receive Christ into their lives, to save and guide them in an abundant life with Him. Then close in verbal prayer.

JESUS CHRIST LIVING IN THE CHRISTIAN

LESSON FIVE   **INTRODUCTORY STEP**

INTRODUCTION:

"The great difference between present-day Christianity and that of which we read in these letters is that to us it is primarily a performance, to them it was a real experience. We are apt to reduce the Christian religion to a code, or at best a rule of heart and life. To these men it is quite plainly the invasion of their lives by a new quality of life altogether. *They do not hesitate to describe this as Christ 'living in' them.* Mere moral reformation will hardly explain the transformation and the exuberant vitality of these men's lives— even if we could prove a motive for such reformation, and certainly the world around offered little encouragement to the early Christians. We are practically driven to accept their own explanation, which is that their little human lives had, through Christ, been linked up with the very Life of God" (*Letters to Young Churches, J. B. Phillips,* Mac-Millan Company, p. xiv.).

I. NEED FOR JESUS CHRIST TO LIVE IN THE CHRISTIAN:

A. *Christ indwells all Christians.* Discuss this according to Romans 8:8-9.

B. "Christ Himself is the very life content of the Christian life."

"There is something which makes Christianity more than a religion, more than an ethic, and more than the idle dream of the sentimental idealist. It is something which makes it relevant to each one of us right now as a contemporary experience. It is the fact that Christ HIMSELF is the very life content of the Christian faith. It is He who makes it 'tick.' 'Faithful is he that calleth you, who also will do it' (I Thess. 5:24). The One who calls you is the one who does that to which He calls you. 'For it is God which worketh in you, both to will and to do of His good pleasure' (Phil. 2:13). He is Himself the very dynamic of all His demands.

"Christ did not die simply that you might be saved from a bad conscience, or even to remove the stain of past failure, but to 'clear the decks' for divine action. You have been told that Christ died to save you. This is gloriously true

69

in a very limited though vital sense. In Romans 5:10 we read, 'If, when we were enemies, we were reconciled to God by the death of his Son, much more, being reconciled, we shall be saved by his life.' The Lord Jesus Christ therefore ministers to you in two distinct ways—He reconciles you to God by His death, and He delivers you from sin's power daily by His resurrected life in you."

(Major W. Ian Thomas)

C. "Only Christ's life wins."

"There is only one life that wins; and that is the life of Jesus Christ. Every man may have that life; every man may live that life. I do not mean that every man may be Christ-like; I mean something very much better than that. I do not mean that a man may always have Christ's help; I mean something very much better than help. I do not mean that a man may have power from Christ; I mean something very much better than power. And I do not mean that a man shall be merely saved from his sins and kept from sinning; I mean something better than even that victory.

"Jesus Christ does not want be our helper; He wants to be our life. He does not want us to work for Him. He wants us to let Him do His work through us, using us as we use a pencil to write with—better still, using us as one of the fingers on His hand. When our life is not only Christ's but *Christ,* our life will be a winning life; for He cannot fail. And a winning life is a fruit-bearing life, a serving life. It is after all only a small part of life, and a wholly negative part, to overcome; we must also bear fruit in character and service if Christ is our life. And we shall—because Christ is our life. 'He cannot deny himself'; He 'came not to be ministered unto, but to minister.' An utterly new kind of service will be ours now, as we let Christ serve others through us, using us. And this fruit-bearing and service, habitual and constant, must all be by faith in Him; our works are the RESULT of His life in us; not the condition or the secret or the cause of the Life."

(Charles Trumbull)

D. Discuss questions in corresponding section in Step Five.

E. "Christ's life must be reproduced in us."

" 'I thank God through Jesus Christ!' That exclamation of Paul's is fundamentally the same as his other words in Galatians 2:20 which we have taken as the key to our study: 'I live; and yet no longer I, but Christ.' We saw how prominent is the word 'I' throughout his argument in Romans 7, culminating in the agonized cry: 'O wretched man that I am!' Then follows the shout of deliverance: 'Thank God . . . Jesus Christ!' and it is clear that the discovery Paul has made is this, that the life we live is the life of Christ alone. We think of the Christian life as a 'changed life' but it is not that. God offers us an 'exchanged life', a 'substituted life', and Christ is our Substitute within. 'I live; and yet no longer I, but Christ liveth in me.' This life is not something which we ourselves have to produce. It is Christ's own life reproduced in us. How many Christians believe in 'reproduction' in this sense, as something more than regeneration? Regeneration means that the life of Christ is planted in us by the Holy Spirit at our new birth. 'Reproduction' goes further: it means that that new life grows and becomes manifest progressively in us, until the very likeness of Christ begins to be reproduced in our lives. That is what Paul means when he speaks of his travail for the Galatians 'until Christ be formed in you' (Gal. 4:9).

"Let me illustrate with another story. I once arrived in America in the home of a saved couple who requested me to pray for them. I inquired the cause of the trouble. 'Oh, Mr. Nee, we have been in a bad way lately,' they confessed. 'We are so easily irritated by the children, and during the past few weeks we have both lost our tempers several times a day. We are really dishonoring the Lord. Will you ask Him to give us patience?' 'That is the one thing I cannot do,' I said. 'What do you mean?' they asked. 'I mean that one thing is certain,' I answered, 'and that is that God is not going to answer your prayer.' At that they said in amazement, 'Do you mean to tell us we have gone so far that God is not willing to hear us when we ask Him to make us patient?' 'No, I do not mean quite that, but I would like to ask you if you have ever prayed in this respect. You have. But did God answer? No! Do you know why? Because you have no need of patience.' Then the eyes of the wife blazed up. She said, 'What do you mean? We do not need patience, and yet we get irritated the whole day long! What do you mean?' 'It is not patience you have need of,' I answered, 'it is Christ.'

"God will not give me humility or patience or holiness or love as separate gifts of His grace. He is not a retailer dispensing grace to us in doses, measuring out some patience to the impatient, some love to the unloving, some meekness to the proud, in quantities that we take and work on as a kind of capital. He has given only one gift to meet all our need—His Son Jesus Christ, and as I look to Him to live out His life in me, He will be humble and patient and loving and everything else I need—in my stead. Remember the word in the first Epistle of John: 'God gave unto us eternal life, and this life is in his Son. He that hath the Son hath life; and he that hath not the Son of God hath not the life' (I John 5:11-12). The life of God is not given us as a separate item; the life of God is given us in the Son. It is 'eternal life in Christ Jesus our Lord' (Rom. 6:23). Our relation to the Son is our relationship to the life.

"It is a blessed thing to discover the difference between Christian graces and Christ: to know the difference between meekness and Christ, between patience and Christ, between love and Christ. Remember again what is said in I Corinthians 1:30: 'Christ Jesus . . . was made unto us wisdom from God, and righteousness and sanctification, and redemption.' The common conception of sanctification is that every item of the life should be holy; but that is not holiness, it is the fruit of holiness. Holiness is Christ. It is the Lord Jesus being made over in us. So you can put in anything there: love, humility, power, self-control. Today there is a call for patience: He is our patience! Tomorrow the call may be for purity: He is our purity! He is the answer to every need. That is why Paul speaks of 'the fruit of the Spirit' as one (Gal. 5:22) and not of 'fruits' as separate items. God has given us His Holy Spirit, and when love is needed the fruit of the Spirit is love; when joy is needed the fruit of the Spirit is joy. It is always true. It does not matter what your personal deficiency, or whether it is a hundred and one different things, God has one sufficient answer—His Son Jesus Christ, and He is the answer to every human need."

(Watchman Nee, *The Normal Christian Life,* pp. 169-172.)

II. FACT THAT JESUS CHRIST LIVES IN THE CHRISTIAN:

A. "His resources are our resources."

"Here is the great principle of life which sets forth the potential of all Christian living; namely, Christ lives in the believer. His resources are our resources. His power is most surely at our disposal."

(William Culbertson)

B. Discuss questions in corresponding section of the T.B.S.

C. Additional Scriptures which teach this fact and explain the purpose for which Christ lives within:

1. Colossians 1:27 (relationship to eternal life).

2. John 14:20-23 (Jesus introduces the fact).

3. Matthew 28:20 (fact of His presence and empowerment).

4. I John 3:24 (fact is communicated by the Spirit).

5. I John 4:13,15-16 (relationship between God and man through Christ).

6. I John 5:11-12 ("He that has not the Son, has not (eternal) life").

7. II Corinthians 13:5 ("Know ye not . . . how that Jesus Christ is in you?").

> "In the last night Christ put it clearly to His disciples, that the Spirit would teach them: 'In that day ye shall know that I am in the Father, and ye in Me, and I *in you*.' First of all *Ye in me*. Through the power of God all we who believe were crucified with Christ, and raised again with Him. And as a result: *Christ is in us*. But this knowledge does not come easily. Through faith in God's Word the Christian accepts it, and the Holy Spirit will lead us into all truth. Take time this very day to realize and appropriate this blessing in prayer."
>
> (Andrew Murray)

8. Galatians 2:20 ("I have been crucified with Christ: yet I live; and yet no longer I, but Christ liveth in me").

> " 'I live and yet no longer I.' Having actually participated in the death of Christ he could say: 'No longer do I live.' My life has been yielded to death upon the Cross of Christ. By faith I see my life under sentence of death. It is still mine, in my flesh wherein no good thing dwells, but I am free in Christ, so that I no longer serve in sin, as long as I abide in Christ. 'Christ liveth in me' is the true secret of a Christlike life. Christ was not only crucified for me. He does not live in heaven to intercede for me. No! *Christ liveth in me.* He Himself said that even as His Father dwelt and worked in Him, even so He dwells and works in us. He is truly the life in us by which we live."
>
> (Andrew Murray)

9. John 7:38-39 ("He that believeth on Me, from within him shall flow rivers of living water. This spake He of the Spirit, which they that believe on Him were to receive").

"Each Person of the blessed Trinity gives honor to the Other. The Father seeks the honor of the Son and the Son seeks the honor of the Spirit, and the Spirit honors the Son. So in our text we hear Christ calling us to *believe in Him,* confident that the Holy Spirit will work powerfully in us according to the measure of our faith in Christ. On the other hand Christ says, 'The Spirit shall not speak from Himself; but what things soever He shall hear, these shall He speak. He shall glorify Me: for He shall take of Mine, and shall declare it unto you' (John 16:13-14). Here we learn the important lesson that we must not expect the Holy Spirit always to give us tokens of His Presence. He will ever seek to fix our attention upon Christ. The surest way to be filled with the Spirit is whole-heartedly to occupy ourselves by faith with Christ. We may rely upon the Holy Spirit to enable us to do this.

"Begin every morning in God's Presence, and there commit yourself to Christ to accomplish His work in you. Thank the Father for the gift of the Holy Spirit, who enables you to abide in the love and the obedience of the Lord Jesus. Believe firmly that the Triune God works in your heart and has His hidden heaven there, which will be revealed to you as your heart is wholly given to His Son and Spirit. 'Through Christ we have access to the Father through the Spirit.' Learn this important lesson. The stronger your faith in Christ the more freely will the Spirit flow from you. The more you believe in the ever-abiding Spirit the more surely you will know the Christ dwells and works within."

(Andrew Murray)

10. Colossians 3:3-4 ("For you have died, and your life is hid with Christ in God . . . Christ who is our life").

"Only God's Spirit can enable the believer to grasp and appropriate the truth that he was actually crucified and died with Christ. The new life he receives in Christ through the Spirit is life out of death. In Christ as the Lamb in the midst of the throne, the power of that life is shown as a crucified life in each one who has received it. The Holy Spirit gives me the assurance that I died with Christ, and the power of His death works in me. And of Christ's life: 'Your life is hid with Christ in God.' This is what Christ said in the last night: 'Ye shall know that I am in the Father and ye in Me'—with Him in the Father. My life is safely hid with Christ in God, and from there I, each day, by faith, receive it anew through the working of the Holy Spirit.

"Is this not the reason why so many of God's children make so little progress? They do not know that the life of Christ who died on the cross and now lives in heaven is truly *their* life hid in God. Christ and the Holy Spirit will grant to each humble believing child of God to receive this new life. O Spirit of God, let me rely upon Thee to make this true in my life!"

(Andrew Murray)

III. JESUS CHRIST AT HOME IN THE CHRISTIAN:

A. Christ must be truly at home in your heart. Discuss Ephesians 3:17. When you invited Jesus Christ to come into your life as Saviour and Lord, He heard and answered your prayer. When He came in, you were then born spiritually (John 3:3,6), becoming a child of God (John 1:12). However, the New Testament teaches that now Christ must be allowed to direct and guide your life. Ephesians 3:17 expresses the prayer that "Christ may dwell in your hearts through faith." The word *dwell* literally means, "to be at home." Christ, who lives within your heart, desires to be at home—not just a tenant.

William Culbertson expresses it thus: "I need not tell you that it is possible to live in a place and not be at home. It does not take very much spiritual insight to understand that this which is contrary to the will of God, that which we know from the Word of God is opposed to God's will, will grieve our Lord. How could He be at home in a heart that grieves Him?"

Ephesians 3:17 is translated thus in the *Amplified New Testament:* "May Christ through your faith (actually) dwell—settle down, abide, make His permanent home in your hearts." Kenneth Wuest translates it, ". . . settle down and feel completely at home in your hearts."

Galatians 4:19 demonstrates the objective of Christ's dwelling: ". . . until Christ be formed (completely and permanently formed—molded) in you." (See the *Amplified New Testament.)* The goal is that we become "conformed to the image of His Son" (Romans 8:29) and reach the "the stature of the fulness of Christ" (Ephesians 4:13).

How can this be accomplished? Jesus Himself gives the solution in John 15:1-5. Here, Jesus illustrates our total dependence upon Him, by comparing us as branches of which He is the Vine. In verse 4 He states that none of us can "bear fruit" unless we abide in (continue in vital union with) Him. In verse 5, He plainly states, "Without Me, you can do *nothing.*"

B. Live in conscious dependence upon Christ.

1. " 'Because I live, ye shall live also' (John 14:19).

"Christ says here, 'I live, and ye shall live also.' The disciples were to receive from Him not the life He then had, but the resurrection life in the power of its victory over death, and of His exaltation to the right hand of God. He would from thenceforth ever dwell in them; a new, a heavenly, an eternal life; the life of Jesus Himself should fill them. And this promise is to all who will accept it in faith.

"Alas, how many there are who are content with the beginnings of the Christian life, but never long to have it in its fulness, the more abundant life! They do not believe in it; they are not ready for the sacrifice implied in being wholly filled with the life of Jesus. Child of God, the message comes again to you: 'The things that are impossible with men are possible with God.' I pray you, do take time, and let Christ's wonderful promise take possession of your heart. Be content with nothing less than a full salvation, Christ living in you, and you living in Christ. Be assured that it is meant for everyone who will take time to listen to Christ's promises, and will believe that the Almighty power of God will work in him the mighty wonder of His grace—Christ dwelling in the heart by faith."

(Andrew Murray)

2. " 'Christ liveth in me' (Gal. 2:20).

" 'Christ is our life' (Col. 3:4).

"It has often been said of the missionary, that unless he lives out the Christ life on an entirely different level from that on which other men live, he misses the deepest secret of power and success in his work. When Christ sent His disciples forth, it was with the command: 'Tarry till ye be endued with power from on high.' 'Wait, and ye shall receive the power of the Holy Ghost, and be my witnesses to the ends of the earth.' *Many a missionary has felt that it is not learning and not zeal, and not the willingness for self-sacrifice in Christ's service, but the secret experience of the life hid with Christ in God, that enables him to meet and overcome every difficulty.*

"Everything depends upon the life with God in Christ being right. It was so with Christ, with the disciples, with Paul. It is the simplicity and intensity of our life in Christ Jesus, and of the life of Christ Jesus in us, that sustains a man in the daily drudgery of work, that makes him conqueror over self and everything that could hinder the Christ-life, and gives the victory over the powers of evil and over the hearts from which the evil spirits have to be cast out. The life is everything. It was so in Christ Jesus. It must be so in His servants. It can be so, because Christ Himself will live in us. When He spoke the word, 'Lo, I am with you always,' He meant nothing less than this: 'Every day and all the day I am with you, the secret of your life, your joy, and your strength.' Oh, to learn what hidden treasures are contained in the blessed words we love to repeat: 'Lo, I am with you all the days.' "

(Andrew Murray)

C. Christ will provide all needed resources to realize victory in your life. Discuss questions from last section of Introductory Step, Lesson Five.

IV. SUMMARY: Christ within is the only place where Christian experience can begin. Submit now to Christ. If you have never invited Him into your heart as Saviour, do it now. If He has already come into your life, tell Him now that you want Him to guide and empower you, to be completely at home in your heart.

A. Christian experience begins with Christ.

"Christ within is the only place where Christian experience can begin. Many say they believe in Christ. They do believe in the Christ of history—the Christ of Bethlehem, Galilee and Judea, and Calvary—but it is only an *historical faith*, just as we believe any fact of history. I believe that Caesar lived and wrought, but all that I believe of him has never affected or changed my life a particle; he is still back yonder in history. So it is with historical faith in Christ. He remains outside of me, and apart from me—merely an historical personage.

"But when I believe *on* Him, with a *saving faith*, he more than saves me; He moves into my life and becomes a part of me. This is the beginning of Christian experience. There is no substitute. Do you know this personal Christ? Has He come in? And coming in, has He opened this fountain of the experience of Himself in your nature? 'Whosoever drinketh of the water that I shall give him shall never thirst; but the water that I shall give him shall be *in him* a well of water springing up into everlasting life' (John 4:14). 'He that believeth on Me, as the Scripture hath said, from *within him* shall flow rivers of living water' (John 7:38, RV).

"In salvation He imparts His life to us—we who were 'dead in trespasses and sins'; now we live in Him (See Philippians 1:21). But by His indwelling presence He im-

77

parts Himself to us; now He lives in us. And that for practical purposes, He becomes the root of our living, and we say with Paul, 'It is no longer I that live, but Christ that liveth in me' (Gal. 2:20, RV). Life finds a new center, takes on a new purpose in its outgoings. It views everything from a new focal-point. 'For to me to live is Christ' (Phil. 1:21).

"That is Christian experience realized. How is it with you? Do these words of Paul falter upon your lips for lack of reality? Let Christ be to you both the Source of life and the Center of life's living and you too will soon express your spiritual biography in these selfsame words.

" 'That life which I now live in the flesh I live in faith, the faith which is in the Son of God, who loved me, and gave Himself for me' (Gal. 2:20). These words are St. Paul's reply to the objection: 'If you say, "Christ lives in me," where does your will come in?' If Christ does actually live in you, and holds Himself responsible for your life, what remains for you to do?

"Christ's own words to His disciples best explain this. Even as the Father dwelt in Him, and worked His work in Him, so our Lord dwells in us and works His work in us. The Son expressed the Father. We are to express Christ. The Father worked in the Son, and the Son worked out what the Father had wrought in Him. Christ works in us and enables us to carry on His work. This is His gift to us.

"The only attitude that becomes us is one of trust, strengthening our faith in the assurance that 'He loved me and gave Himself for me.' He and I are eternally inseparably one. 'He lives in me.' This is almost too great to grasp or to believe, and yet it is God's truth. The child of God needs time for meditation and adoration, so that the Spirit of God may reveal to Him how completely He will fill our being accomplishing the work in us. Oh, the depth of the riches of the wisdom and the knowledge of God! How unsearchable are His judgments, and His ways past finding out! Oh, the depth of the love of God in Christ! Let us sacrifice all, that we may know, and trust and honor His love."

(Andrew Murray)

B. Christ alone can supply the power to live a Christian life.

"How ridiculous it would be to buy a car with a powerful engine under the hood, and then to spend the rest of your days pushing it! Thwarted and exhausted, you would wish to discard it as a useless thing! When God redeemed you through the precious blood of His dear Son, He placed, in the language of my illustration, a powerful engine under the hood—nothing less than the resurrection life of God the Son, made over to you in the person of God the Holy Spirit. Then stop pushing! Step in and switch on, and expose every hill of circumstance, of opportunity, of temptation, or perplexity—no matter how threatening—to the divine energy that is unfailingly available.

"With what magnificent confidence you may step out into the future when once you have consented to die to your own self-effort and to make yourself available as a redeemed sinner to all that God has made available to you in His risen Son!

"To be IN CHRIST—that is redemption; but for Christ to be IN YOU—that is sanctification! To be IN CHRIST— that makes you fit for heaven; but for Christ to be IN YOU —that makes you fit for earth! To be IN CHRIST—that changes your destination; but for Christ to be IN YOU— that changes your destiny! The one makes heaven your home—the other makes this world His workshop.

"I may wish to return to my home in England, and I stand in New York. But ever since I was born I have been bound to this earth by a law that I have never been able to break —the law of gravity. I am told, however, that there is another law, a higher law, the law of aero-dynamics, and if only I will be willing to commit myself in total trust to this new law, then this new law will set me free from the old law. By faith I step into the plane, I sit back in the REST of faith, and as those mighty engines roar into life, I discover that the new law of aero-dynamics sets me free from the law of gravity.

"So long as I maintain by faith that position of total dependence, I do not have to *try to be free* from the law of gravity—I am being SET FREE by the operation of a new and a higher law. Of course, if I am stupid enough, way out across the Atlantic, I may decide that the cabin of the plane is too stuffy, and step out through the emergency window— but the moment I discard my position of faith in the new and higher law that is setting me free, I discover that the down-drag is still fully in operation, and I am caught again by the law of gravity and plunged into the water! I must maintain my attitude of *dependence* if I am to remain airborne!

"So you too are called upon by God to WALK by faith, to WALK in the Spirit, resting the whole weight of your personality upon the living Christ who is in you; and as by faith you walk in the Spirit, so God declares you will not fulfill the lusts of the flesh. You will be liberated, emancipated, set free from the down-drag of that inbred wickedness, which Christ alone can overcome. You will be made more than conqueror through 'Christ, who is our life' (Col. 3:4).

"I wonder how it is with you? Have you ever put your trust in the Lord Jesus as your Redeemer? Have you been reconciled to God by the death of His Son? I wonder, if reconciled, whether you are at this moment being saved by His life? Have you learned to step out of every situation and relate it wholly to WHAT HE IS IN YOU, and by faith say 'Thank You?' "

(Major W. Ian Thomas)

C. How to submit to Christ.

"The conditions of thus receiving Christ as the fulness of the life are simply two—after, of course, our personal acceptance of Christ as our Saviour—through His shed blood and death as our Substitute and Sin-Bearer—from the guilt and consequences of our sin.

1. "Surrender absolutely and unconditionally to Christ as Master of all that we are and all that we have, telling God that we are now ready to have His whole will done in our entire life, at every point, no matter what it costs.

2. "Believe that God has set us wholly free from the law of sin (Rom. 8:2)—not WILL do this, but HAS done it. Upon this second step, the quiet act of faith, all now depends. Faith must believe God in entire absence of any feeling or evidence. For God's word is safer, better and surer than any evidence of His word. We are to say, in blind, cold faith if need be, 'I KNOW that my Lord Jesus IS meeting ALL my needs NOW (even my need of faith), because His grace is sufficient for ME.'

"And remember that Christ Himself is better than any of His blessings; better than the power, or the victory, or the service, that He grants. Christ creates spiritual power; but Christ is better than that power. He is God's best; He is God; and we may have this best; we may have Christ, yielding to Him in such completeness and abandonment of self that it is no longer we that live, but Christ liveth in us. Will you thus take Him?"

(Charles Trumbull)

LESSON PLAN

THE CHURCH OF JESUS CHRIST

LESSON SIX   INTRODUCTORY STEP

OBJECTIVE: To present to the student what the church is—universal and local—and to demonstrate the purpose for which it exists.

I. OPEN WITH PRAYER.

II. MEMORY VERSE: Hebrews 10:25.

III. MOTIVATION: "Have you ever considered the changes that have taken place in those parts of the world where the Christian message has gone? Let us illustrate by considering four maps of the world. On the first, consider the areas where there is a short life expectancy, low sanitary conditions, low literacy, few or no hospitals, no women's suffrage, little concern for children and where very little value is placed upon human life. On the second map, consider the areas where the Christian message has not penetrated, has not been taken or has not been welcomed and received. As you compare the maps, you will observe that the same areas of the world have been pictured. Now, on the third map picture in your mind those areas of the world where a higher standard of living exists, where a greater value is placed on human life, where schools, hospitals and other similar institutions abound for the benefit of all. Finally, picture a fourth map where the Gospel of Jesus Christ has gone, been received and practiced. You will find that maps three and four are identical. Where the message of Jesus Christ, His love for man, His death and resurrection has gone, new life, new hope and purpose for living have resulted. This is the importance of Christianity and the establishment of the Church. In this lesson, we shall see what the Church really is, what it represents and why it exists."

IV. BIBLE STUDY: The Bible describes the church in two senses: First, the *universal* church, which includes all who know Christ as personal Saviour. Second, the *local* church, which is an individual group of Christians who gather for worship, instruction and mutual encouragement.

A. *The Universal Church:*

   1. Description and definition.

   2. How one becomes a member.

3. Relationship between Christ and His church.

   a. How illustrated in the New Testament.

   b. Discuss question 1, Introductory Step.

   c. Priesthood of believers.

4. Unity of the body (church).

   a. Fact of unity.
      Discuss question 2, Introductory Step.

   b. Exhortation to unity.

5. Relationship between the members.

   a. Discuss question 3, Introductory Step.

   b. Gifts or abilities of members.

B. *The Local Church: Discuss questions in the T.B.S. where appropriate.*

   1. Description and definition.

   2. Importance of participation in church.
      Discuss question 1, Introductory Step.

   3. The Lord's Supper.

   4. Baptism.

   5. Purposes of the local church.

V. PARALLEL PASSAGES:

A. Christ's body (Ephesians 5:25-32; Romans 12:5; I Corinthians 12:27-28).

B. Attitude toward communion (I Corinthians 11:28-33).

C. Unity (I Corinthians 12:13).

VI. SUMMARY:

A. Relationship between the Church and Christ's future return.

B. Spiritual qualities which are expected in believers.

C. Suggestions to more meaningful Church worship.

VII. CLOSE IN PRAYER.

THE CHURCH OF JESUS CHRIST

LESSON SIX   INTRODUCTORY STEP

INTRODUCTION:

The Bible describes the church in two ways: First, the universal church, which includes all who know Christ as personal Saviour (Acts 2:47). Second, the *local* church, which is an indvidual group of Christians who gather regularly for worship, instruction, Bible study and mutual encouragement (I Corinthians 1:2; Galatians 1:2; I Thessalonians 1:1 etc.).

I.   THE UNIVERSAL CHURCH:

A. Description and Definition.

The basic New Testament word which is used in reference to the Church is a moderately common one, appearing at least 135 times in our New Testament. The word is *soma*. Translated "body," the word at times refers to the body of men or animals, a dead body or corpse; a living body; the glorified body which Christ now has in Heaven; flesh, the instrument of the soul; or celestial bodies. Again, it can at times refer to a slave, or to an object which casts a shadow. A final usage, and that to which we are to turn our attention, however, is that which refers to a "number (large or small) of people closely united into one society, or family, as it were; a society, an ethical, mystical body; so is the New Testament view of the Church."

Paul, in writing to the church at Corinth, tells the members that they are God's building, with Jesus Christ as the foundation which was first laid (I Corinthians 3:9-11). In the Epistle to the Ephesians (2:19-21) Paul further pursues this thought in stating to the Ephesian Christians that they are "Fellow Citizens with the saints, and of the household of God." The apostles and prophets have laid the foundation, with Jesus Christ as the cornerstone.

B. How one becomes a member of the true (universal) Church.

When you receive Jesus Christ into your heart and life, giving over your life to Him as your personal Saviour, you become a child of God (John 1:12, I John 5:11-12), and automatically become a member of the *universal Church*. This is explained as being baptized into the body of Christ (I Corinthians 12:12-13), which is the church (Colossians 1:24).

C. Relationship between Christ and His Church.

In the Epistle to the Ephesians, we read that our Lord Jesus Christ has had everything put beneath His feet, and that He is head over all things to the Church. The Church is here stated to be His body, and His fullness. The headship of Christ is again stated in Ephesians 4:15-16, where He is described as the one from whom the whole body grows as a unit, unto maturity. This is seen again in Colossians 2:19.

A parallel is drawn, in Ephesians 5, between Christ as the Head of the Church and Saviour of the body; and the husband as head of the wife. Here, we read that the Church is subject to Christ, who loved the Church and gave Himself for it in order that He might cleanse it so it might be holy and without blemish. In the sense that we are members of His body, we are also members of His flesh and bones. As such, we are the visible manisfestation of His life upon the earth—this presents a great challenge to us, the Body of Christ, to ". . . so walk ye in Him . . ." worthy of the vocation whereunto we are called.

Jesus' words concerning this relationship are found in the Gospel of John, chapter 15. It is here, in what is perhaps the last opportunity of Jesus to formally teach his disciples, that He tells them of the relationship between Himself and them as that of a vine and branches. Several times in this chapter we see His words, "I am the vine . . . ye are the branches . . . abide in me. . . ." He warns that no one can bear fruit unless he continues to abide in Him. Jesus Christ is the vine, the giver of life. A branch not receiving this life withers and dies.

In the illustration of the vine and branches we can see that all of the branches abiding in the vine are thus united with one another. Similarly, if we are in Christ, we are united into one body —the body of Christ—with Christ as the Head.

1. Illustrations of the relationship between Christ and the members of His Church:

   a. Vine and branches (John 15), emphasizing sustenance and growth.

   b. Shepherd and sheep (John 10), emphasizing protection and care.

   c. Chief cornerstone and building (Ephesians 2:20-22; I Peter 2:5), emphasizing growth.

   d. Head and body (I Corinthians 12:12-13; Colossians 1:24), emphasizing headship and unity.

e. Bridegroom and bride (Ephesians 5:23-30), emphasizing headship of Christ.

2. Discuss question 1, Introductory Step.

3. *Priesthood of Believers.*

Every individual is invited to make his requests known unto God, through the one mediator, Christ Jesus (I Timothy 2:5; Hebrews 8:1— "We have such a high priest"; Ephesians 2:18). The New Testament teaches that the local church ought to have leaders, in the person of evangelists, pastors, and teachers; *not* to in any sense *mediate between* the other members and God, but ". . . for the perfecting of the saints, unto the work of ministering, unto the building up of the body of Christ" (Ephesians 4:11-16).

D. Unity of the body (Church).

1. Fact of unity. Discuss question 2, in the T.B.S.

"There is one body . . .," writes Paul to the Ephesians, (Chapter 4) even as there is one Lord, one Spirit, one faith, one baptism, one God and Father of all. To list the "one body" together with these other great truths places the utmost emphasis upon the fact of the importance of the one body, ". . . fitly joined together." Stress is evident in the epistle to the Colossians (3:15) where Paul states that the Church was "Called in one body," and exhorts the recipients to be thankful.

In Romans 12:4-5 Paul makes the reader clearly aware of the unity which exists among the members of the Body of Christ. Here, it is clearly stated that "We, being many, are one Body in Christ, and every one members one of another."

The word "communion," found in I Corinthians 10:6, means "the act of a thing used in common," (Young's Concordance); "fellowship, association, community, joint participation" (Thayer). In using this term, Paul speaks of the communion of the blood and of the body of Christ, or the blood and body of Christ which we share in joint participation in association. He reiterates the truth that we are all one bread, one body—"for we are all partakers of that one bread—the Body of Christ" (I Corinthians 10:17).

Jesus' emphasis on unity is found primarily in the Gospel of John, chapters ten and seventeen. Here is found His instruction to the hearers concerning the Good Shepherd and His sheep. After describing the characteristics of a good shepherd, He reveals that He is the Good Shepherd, who is about to lay down His life for His sheep, including other sheep not of the fold at the time. They will also hear His voice, however, and "There shall be one fold and one shepherd."

Before Jesus was arrested in the Garden of Gethsemane, He prayed to the Father on behalf of his disciples that they might be sanctified unto the truth. This prayer, on the authority of Jesus' own words, included all who were yet to believe on Him (John 17:20). His prayer also was, that they might all be *one* —a unity—"As thou, Father, art in Me, and I in Thee, that they also may be *one* in us; that the world may believe that Thou hast sent me" (John 17:21). Jesus' prayer was that the believers in Him may be one, even as He and the Father are one.

2. Exhortation to unity.

Following the presentations of the fact that the Body of Christ is a unity, Paul and Peter exhort the members to exhibit the outward evidence of this unity.

Paul exhorts the Roman Christians to live in harmony with one another, that together with *one* voice they may glorify the God and Father of our Lord Jesus Christ (Romans 12:16 and 15:5-7). To the Corinthians he appeals that there be no dissensions, but that they be *united* in mind and judgment (I Corinthians 1:10), to live in peace and agreement with one another (II Corinthians 13:11). To the Ephesians, Paul asks for *unity* of the Spirit in the bond of peace—that they will live lives worthy of their calling (Ephesians 4:3). The Philippians are asked to complete Paul's joy by being of the *same* mind, having the *same* love and standing firm in *one* Spirit (Philippians 1:27 and 2:2).

Peter exhorts the dispersed Christians to have ". . . *unity* of spirit, sympathy, love of the brethren, a tender heart and a humble mind" (I Peter 3:8).

E. Relationship between the members.

1. Discuss question 3, in the T.B.S.

The apostle Paul exhorts the recipients of his Epistle to the Romans to present their bodies as a living sacrifice to God (Romans 12:1), remembering that they are all members of one Body (Romans 12:5). He then elaborates upon the analogy of the body, in emphasizing that the members do not all have the same office, responsibilities or gifts. Some are gifted through grace to prophesy, some to minister, some to teach, some to exhort. Paul exhorts each to apply all diligence in faithfully fulfilling his task.

In the first Epistle to the Corinthians, chapter 12, Paul brings greater emphasis upon this aspect. After stating that we are all baptized into one body, and have all been made to drink of the One Spirit, he begins to show that differences exist between the members, in function and characteristics. Paul points out that this is as it should be, for ". . . if they were all one member, then where were the body?" (I Corinthians 12:19). He draws comparison for the purpose of illustration by enumerating parts of a human body—the foot, the hand, the eye, the ear, the head. We then are made to see that the body needs each of these members in order to function properly. In fact, he says, some of the members which appear to be the most feeble are also essential to the body's well-being.

One point should be particularly emphasized here in regard to honor, suffering and the mutual care of the members for one another: Scripture states expressly that there should be no division or jealousy in the body—if one member suffers, all of the other members suffer with it, and if one member is honored, all of the other members rejoice with the honored member.

No member of the body can say to another, "I do not need you," for God has arranged the body in such a way that all the members are interdependent. The parts of the body which seem the least worthy of notice often have the most important functions. The least beautiful members are given another form of beauty because of their importance, while the outwardly beautiful members are sometimes of less essence. While writing this, the writer is reminded of the old story of the deer who was proud of his long, beautiful antlers, but ashamed of his long, thin legs. The story shows that his values were misplaced, for when attacked by wolves the deer was swiftly carried out of danger until his antlers caught in the overhanging branches of a tree, and he was ultimately caught and killed by the wolves.

The members are to be "fitly joined together and compacted" according to the effectual working of every part according to its assignment, maturing to its edification in love" (Ephesians 4:16).

2. Gifts or abilities of the members.

As each member of our physical body has a particular function, so each member of the Body of Christ also has an individual ability, or "gift" for which he is responsible (I Peter 4:10). Gifts enumerated by Paul in the First Epistle to the Corinthians include those of the ability to teach, the ability to be a helper, to govern, to speak with wisdom and to speak with knowledge. If a member has been "gifted" in more than one area, he will be held the more responsible. Paul points out that all do not have the same gifts, since they are given according to the sovereign discretion of the Holy Spirit (Hebrews 2:4 and I Corinthians 12:11). Rather, he exhorts all to seek "higher gifts"—to experience and communicate the fruit of the Spirit, which is available to all—especially that of *love* (I Corinthians 13). See also Galatians 5:22-23.

II. THE LOCAL CHURCH: Discuss questions in Introductory Step where appropriate.

   A. Description and definition.

   The Church, the mightiest body of fellowship ever to exist upon the earth, is composed of members around the world—that is, every individual who is regenerated by the Holy Spirit, redeemed by the blood of Christ (Ephesians 1:22-23; 5:24-25; Colossians 1:18), including those of all ages, in heaven or upon the earth. It is this company which is known as the Body or Bride of Christ.

   Within this great company, however, there are included a great number of local churches, and we are using the term in a slightly different and more limited sense, in referring to specific groups of fellowship among believers. The apostle Paul made many such references to churches in specific geographic locations. (Romans 16:1; I Corinthians 1:2; Galatians 1:2, 22; I Thessalonians 1:1, and others). The Book of Revelation speaks specifically to seven churches in Asia (chapters 2 and 3).

   It is important to note that the term "church" means "an assembly of called-out ones." Believers are "called-out ones" and should gather together for instruction and worship. (The local church is *not* an edifice or building. The term, *church,* refers to people.)

   The significance of the local church is made obvious in the fact recorded again and again throughout the Book of Acts that everywhere Paul went, local assemblies of believers were established.

   B. The importance of participation in church: Discuss question 1 in the T.B.S.

   1. What would a community be like without a church? Would you like to live in a community without a church? (Get answers). My own answer would be "No," but if I were in one without a church, I would do everything possible to gather believers and find a place in which to worship as a group.

   2. Why should church attendance not be neglected? (Hebrews 10:25 was written to show the need of Christian fellowship and exhortation.) Hebrews 10:25 is a command of God. If we violate this, are we sinning ? (Yes.) Why?

It is important for us to realize the real reason for joining a church. Many people are spiritually blind and join a church, believing this is the means of their salvation. Some join a church for social prestige or for many other reasons. Joining a church does not make one a Christian. We become Christians only by the grace of God through Jesus Christ, and by saving faith in Him. However, when we are true believers and Christ is our Saviour and Lord, *we need the church for a number of reasons.* What would you say these reasons are?

(a) For fellowship with God's children. (Dr. Henry Brandt, a Christian psychologist, has said that we need each other very much, for others see us as we are; we need each other because we choose to go our own way, to justify our action and to defend ourselves. We need others who see us as we often do not see ourselves, and who can, in Christian love, help us to see ourselves as others see us, and help us to become strong where we are weak.)

(b) For our own spiritual help and growth. I John 5:16. "Confess your faults one to another, and exhort one another to good works."

(c) In remembrance of the Saviour and His death, resurrection and ascension.

(d) To follow Christ's command.

Some people say that they can be Christians and not attend church. That is true, but one cannot be a *dedicated* Christian and not take time to worship God with others.

Example: A group of logs burn brightly when they are burning together—take one aside and its flame goes out. This illustration can be applied to our Christian lives.

Some give the excuse that there are so many hypocrites in the church. Actually the church is not an organization of perfect individuals, but a group of individuals who desire to be like Christ. Some are more advanced than others, etc. The church is like a hospital. It helps in making repairs in our spiritual growth. Would you call Peter a hypocrite when he said, "All may deny Christ but I won't?" His heart's desire was to be loyal to the end, but he failed. Christ forgave him and gave him the power to be loyal and to become a great preacher of the Gospel.

Because one becomes a Christian does not mean that he is perfect. When the caterpillar becomes a butterfly he is no longer made to crawl in the dust. He may light there for a time but he does not stay. For the one that truly knows Christ as his personal Saviour, the "old life" does not satisfy. He may slip for a time but soon he confesses and "soars in the heavens" again.

C. The Lord's Supper was instituted by our Lord Jesus Christ at the feast of the Passover, on the night preceding His arrest and trial (Matthew 26:19-29). The significance of the bread and wine is as follows: the *bread* symbolized the body of the Lord, given in death, the sacrifice for all sin. The *wine* symbolized the blood of Christ, shed ". . . for many, unto remission of sins" (Matthew 26:28).

The fellowship of the Lord's Supper is a commemoration event, looking back upon Calvary, and looking ahead with joy and anticipation to the return of the Lord. (I Corinthians 11:26 ". . . ye do show the Lord's death till He come.")

D. Baptism as an ordinance of the church was instituted by the Lord, both by commandment and by example (Mark 1:9; Matthew 28:19 and others).

The significance of baptism is correctly interpreted only when we keep in mind that one must be a regenerated believer before he can truly partake of the ordinance. Baptism then symbolizes the cleansing from sin which has taken place, by the figure of death, burial and resurrection into newness of life (Romans 6:3-8).

Baptism is both a *testimony*, or confession of faith (an outward confirmation of the fact that we are new creatures), and a step of *obedience* to Christ (Galatians 3:27; Matthew 28:19).

E. The purposes of a local church are:

1. To glorify Christ (as part of the universal church) (cf. Ephesians 3:20-21).

2. To instruct believers so that they are equipped to minister to believers and non-believers (II Timothy 4:2). As a place of instruction, the local church's importance is observed in the fact that many epistles were written to local churches (Ephesians 4:12).

3. To witness of Christ (Acts 1:8; 13:1-4; Revelation 1:20; John 15:16).

III. SUMMARY:

A. Relationship between the Church and Christ's future return.

Do we know when He will return? There is much speculation and always has been as to when Christ will come again. Mark 13:32 and Matthew 24:36 tell us, "But of that day and that hour knoweth no man, no, not the angels which are in heaven, neither the Son, but the Father." Mark 13:33 "Take ye heed, watch and pray; for ye know not when the time is."

Though the Bible does not tell us when Christ will return, it gives us sign posts by which we can tell whether or not His coming is near. In I Timothy 4:1 it says, "Some shall depart from the faith." In other words, some who say they are Christians will turn aside to false doctrines. This is unfortunately true in Christendom today. In II Timothy 3:1 it says, "Perilous times shall come for men shall be lovers of their own selves, covetous, boasters, proud, blasphemers, disobedient to parents, unthankful, unholy," etc. Though this has always been true to a certain extent, in the last days sin is to increase greatly. This also seems true today. The last two world wars and the threat of a third one indicate the world is getting worse. Jesus confirms this in Matthew 24:6-7 when He says there will be "wars and rumours of wars . . . For nation shall rise up against nation and kingdom against kingdom . . ." There are many other indications, such as the return of Israel to Palestine, the great increase of knowledge (Daniel 12:4), the uniting of a major part of the world under atheistic communism, etc. God's time clock may be running out. The end of our civilization may be near. In light of this, every Christian should be looking forward to His coming and his prayer should be, "Come, Lord Jesus" (Revelation 22:20).

B. Spiritual qualities which are expected in believers in Jesus Christ (Hebrews 10:22-25. See also Hebrews 11:8).

1. Draw near to God.

2. Strengthen our faith, and hold fast without wavering.

3. Declare our faith.

4. Be of help to others (Verse 24—see the *Amplified New Testament*).

5. Assemble ourselves together, as believers.

6. Encourage one another.

C. Some suggestions that will make your Church worship more meaningful. It is interesting to note the difference in the attitudes of an individual toward church and what he gains from it now as compared to his attitudes before knowing Christ as Saviour. What was meaningless before, now takes on real meaning.

1. Bow for silent prayer before the service begins. Pray for your-

self, the minister, those taking part and those worshiping, asking that Christ will be very real to them, and that those who do not know Christ may come to know and trust Him.

2. Take your Bible to church with you. Underline portions that are made especially meaningful by the sermon.

3. Meditate upon the words of the hymns.

4. Take notes on the sermon. Review them later in the day, and apply what you learned to your daily living.

D. Note to teacher.

1. Encourage students to participate in the ministry of a local church. Encourage them to go to the pastor and offer their services.

2. Encourage those who now know Christ to become members of a local church since they are already members of the universal church.

3. Caution new converts to avoid criticism of other Christians, churches and pastors who appear to be less zealous than they. "Judge not," is a command of God.

THE CHRISTIAN ADVENTURE

STEP ONE

OBJECTIVE: To ground the new convert in some of the most basic doctrines and areas of Christian living.

I. OPEN WITH PRAYER.

II. MEMORY VERSE: I John 5:11-12.

III. MOTIVATION:

Ask the class, "What do you think are some of the things you really need to know and be certain of before you can successfully live the Christian life?" Get several answers, then mention what you consider the most important areas, drawing them from the subject of each lesson.

IV. BIBLE STUDY:

Use the lesson "Checkout" (Lesson 7). Go over each question with the group and supplement your answers from the material in the teacher's manual for each lesson. The questions refer to the following lessons:

Question 1—Lesson 1.
Question 2—Lesson 3 ("SOLUTION TO CARNALITY").
Question 3—Lesson 3 ("THE SPIRITUAL, OR CHRIST-
                    CONTROLLED, CHRISTIAN").
Question 4—Lesson 4.
Question 5—Lesson 5.
Question 6—Lesson 5.
Question 7—Lesson 6.
Question 8—All the lessons.

V. PARALLEL PASSAGES:

See the various lessons.

VI. SUMMARY:

Encourage the class to commit themselves totally to Jesus Christ. Use the quotation from Jim Elliot found at the end of Lesson 3.

VII. CLOSE IN PRAYER.

LESSON PLAN

THE CHRISTIAN'S CERTAINTY

LESSON ONE   STEP ONE

OBJECTIVE: To assure the new Christian that Christ has given him
eternal life and now lives in his heart.

I.   OPEN WITH PRAYER.

II. MEMORY VERSE: I John 5:13. Ask two different class members
     to quote the verse from memory or explain what
     the verse means to them personally.

III. MOTIVATION:

     Ask the class, "If someone told you he thought he had accepted Christ
     and had become a Christian, but was not really sure of it, what would
     you tell him?" Try to get some different answers and allow a few
     minutes of discussion. Do NOT give any answer yourself at this time
     (See the Lesson Amplification).

IV. BIBLE STUDY:

     Assign question 1 to one of the class. After he has answered, supple-
     ment and promote discussion with further questions, insights, and il-
     lustrations from Lesson Amplification material. Then ask another to
     answer question 2 and follow the same procedure until you have
     covered all questions under the first two sections ("Christian Cer-
     tainty" and "New Life"). Be careful that no one monopolizes the
     session. Undoubtedly the discussion time will be longer on some ques-
     tions than others, as some are more important.

V.   PARALLEL PASSAGES:

     A. Christian Certainty: John 3:18,36; 14:6; Acts 4:12; I John 5:11-12;
        Romans 10:13; Isaiah 1:18.

     B. New Life: John 4:13-14; 6:35,47; 10:10; 17:2; Romans 6:20-23.

VI. SUMMARY:

     A. Re-introduce the question with which you opened the meeting and
        make sure the class now understands the correct answer.

     B. Ask them, "Now that you are certain you have eternal life, what
        should be the practical results?" (See the Lesson Amplification.)

VII. CLOSE IN PRAYER.

THE CHRISTIAN'S CERTAINTY

LESSON ONE   STEP ONE

INTRODUCTION:

Your opening question and the resulting discussion should stimulate thinking but not necessarily supply answers, as this will be accomplished during the Bible study. Guide the discussion and keep it going but do not give your own answer to the opening question until the Bible study. To keep discussion from ending prematurely you may interject further questions. For example, if someone replies to the opening question, "I would show him what the Bible says," ask the individual to name specific verses. Do not correct wrong answers at this time, but use them to stimulate group thinking further by asking if other class members have different opinions.

I.   CHRISTIAN CERTAINTY:

   A. Question 1—Ask the class, "What does it mean to receive Christ?" It means "the same thing that it means to receive a gift someone offers us—we put forth our hand and take the proffered gift."—Donald Grey Barnhouse. Cf. Romans 6:23, "The *gift* of God is eternal life through Jesus Christ our Lord." "To believe on His name" is an expression which means "to have faith in all that He is." By deciding to have personal faith in Jesus Christ we become Christians.

   B. Question 2 — John 1:13 talks about the family of God. Ask the class, "Isn't everyone God's child?" The answer is "no." Everyone is a creature of God, but only those who have received His Son are members of His family.

      ILLUSTRATION: A carpenter once said to a minister, "I believe that God created all men, therefore all men must be His children."

      The minister replied, "Have you ever made a table?"

      "Why of course," said the carpenter, "scores of them."

      "Do you believe the tables are your children because you made them?"

      "Oh, no," said the carpenter.

      "Why not?" said the minister.

      "Well, because they don't have my life in them."

      "Exactly," said the minister—"do you have God's life in you?"

This is what it means to be God's child—you must have God's life in you, and this comes only by receiving Christ.

C. Question 3 — Phillips translates John 5:24, "I solemnly assure you that the man who hears what I have to say and believes in the One who has sent Me, has eternal life. He does not have to face judgment; he has already passed from death into life." Ask the class two questions: (1) When do you get eternal (everlasting) life? (2) What is eternal life? According to this verse we receive eternal life *when we believe*. Christianity is not "pie in the sky when I die"; it brings new life here and now. Eternal life "is not reserved to be entered on in the blessed future, but is a present possession . . . heaven is not different in kind and circumstance from the Christian life on earth, but differs mainly in degree and circumstance"—ALEXANDER MACLAREN. But what is eternal life? It is not endless existence, for all men, Christian or non-Christian, have this according to Matthew 25:46. It is a rich, abundant, full life, centered about God and in vital contact with Him, which no non-Christian has (cf. John 10:10). Does everyone in the class have this eternal life?

D. Question 4 — Phillips again has a good translation of these verses, "And He personally bore our sins in His own body on the cross, so that we might be dead to sin and be alive to all that is good. It was the suffering that He bore which has healed you. You had wandered away like so many sheep, but now you have returned to the shepherd and guardian of your souls."

ILLUSTRATION: Suppose you get a traffic ticket for speeding, but when you show up in court your own father is the judge. Because you are his son, would it be fair for him to fine everyone else who has a ticket, but excuse you? Of course not. Suppose, then, he fines you thirty dollars or thirty days in jail. Since you do not have the thirty dollars, you must spend thirty days in jail. But because he loves you, your father steps down off the judge's bench, and holds out thirty dollars. Justice is satisfied, yet you go free. The only condition is that you accept your father's payment. Similarly, we have violated God's laws and justice demands the penalty be paid. But because of His love for us, God has paid it for us in the person of His Son. We must accept this payment to be forgiven.

E. Question 5-6 — The background for these verses is the shepherd life in Biblical countries. After watering and resting his sheep, the shepherd calls them to go to another feeding ground. "At the first sound of his call, which is usually a peculiar gutteral sound, hard to imitate, the flock follow off. . . . Even should two shepherds call their flocks at the same time and the sheep be intermingled, they never mistake their own master's voice. . . ." Note that John 10;28-30 teaches that a Christian can *never* be lost. He may sin and lose his fellowship, or communication with God, but he can never lose his salvation.

ILLUSTRATION: You are always the son (or daughter) of your mother and father—this never changes. Yet you may argue with your parents and not even be on speaking terms. You would still be their child, but you would have no fellowship with them. We are *always* God's children, if we are Christians; but we may lose our fellowship with Him.

F. Question 7 — This verse assures the Christian beyond a doubt that he has eternal life. It is impossible to have Christ and not have eternal life. Note: (1) The assurance of eternal life is based on your acceptance of God's gift, His only begotten Son, and on your trust in God's promise, not feelings or experiences. You may feel discouraged and distant from God, but if you have received Christ this cannot affect your possession of eternal life.

ILLUSTRATION: The Pacific Ocean exists regardless of whether we see it or experience it. The fog may shroud it from view so that those who live nearby cannot even see it—yet it is just as much there as any other day, because it is an unchanging fact. Eternal life is also an unchanging fact regardless of whether we can feel it.

(2) There are only two classes of human beings—those who have Christ and eternal life and those who do not. There is *no neutral class*. Ask the class how many kinds of men there are in I John 5:12.

ILLUSTRATION: Everyone in the world is either an American citizen or he is not. There is no in between class. Regardless of whether you live in Canada, right next to the border, or in Australia, thousands of miles away, you are not an American citizen unless you were born one or have become naturalized. Regardless of how much one admires Christ or would like to believe in Him, he is just as much a non-Christian as the most hardened atheist until he accepts Christ.

G. Question 8 — Alexander Maclaren says concerning Revelation 3:20, "Who knocks? The exalted Christ. What is the door? This closed heart of man. What does He desire? Entrance. What are His knockings and His voice? . . . whatsoever sways our hearts to yield to Him and enthrone Him."

The Abingdon Bible Commentary states: "How courteous for the Lord of the world to *stand at the door* not presuming to enter until he is invited. 'God is always courteous' said Francis of Assisi, 'and does not invade the privacy of the human soul.' He who hearkens and opens will find Christ both guest and host, yes, and a feast too (John 6:54). The common meal is the symbol to the Oriental for confidence and affection. . . ."

Ask the class what you have to do to keep Christ from coming in. The answer is *nothing*. He only comes in when we act and open the door.

ILLUSTRATION: When someone knocks at the door of your room or home, you can do one of three things—(1) Open the door and invite him in; (2) Ignore him in the hope he will go away; (3) Tell him to go away. Which response have you made to Christ?

II. NEW LIFE:

A. Question 1 — Ask the class what it means to be born again. Note: (1) It does not mean that we "turn over a new leaf," for it is a far more radical change than that. (2) It applies to good as well as bad. Nicodemus, to whom Jesus spoke these words, was a Pharisee, a ruler of the Jews, one of the great religious leaders of his day. He was moral and ethical, prayed seven times a day and worshipped at the synagogue three times a day.

Birth gives life. A new birth means that a new life must be given to us. This new life is the eternal life which comes when we receive Christ.

ILLUSTRATION: A caterpillar crawling in the dust is an ugly, hairy worm. But one day this worm weaves about its body a cocoon. Out of this cocoon emerges a beautiful butterfly. We do not understand fully what has taken place. We realize only that where once a worm has crawled in the dust, now a butterfly soars in the heavens. So it is in the life of a Christian. Where once we lived on the lowest level as sinful egocentric man, we now dwell on the highest plane, experiencing a full and abundant life as children of God. An individual becomes a Christian through spiritual birth.

NOTE: For illustrations of how many collegians and others have found new life, consult issues of the COLLEGIATE CHALLENGE magazine, a Campus Crusade publication.

B. Questions 2-3 — The four verses listed in Question 2 describe some of the results of accepting Christ. According to these passages we have: (1) *Forgiveness* (Ephesians 1:7). All of our disobedience to God is eternally forgiven. Christianity alone offers a solution to the guilt problem. (2) *Peace* (Romans 5:1). According to the Bible, the very best non-Christians are at war with God. Peace comes only through accepting Christ. When the United States was at war with Japan there was no friendly contact, little communication, only active hostility between the two. This was not changed until the peace treaty was signed in Tokyo Bay. Similarly, all non-Christians, whether they know it or not, are at war with God and have no hope for communication or friendship with Him until they make peace through Christ. (3) *Righteousness* (Romans 3:22). This is not the personal righteousness of every-day life, but the righteousness of God ascribed to us when we accept Christ. God has ascribed to us Christ's righteousness and ascribed to Christ our sins, as He suffered on the cross. (4) *Christ in you* (Colossians 1:27b). Though God forgives us, makes peace with us and clothes us with Christ's righteousness, this would do us little good in this life unless Christ came to live in our hearts. Because He is in our hearts, we have a new strength from Him, and are able to keep His commandments.

III. SUMMARY:

What is the result of being sure we have accepted Christ and knowing He has given us eternal life? Basically, it is that we are now set free from fear and doubt and we can begin to enjoy God and the life of purpose and meaning He has for us. The Christian who does not have assurance looks at God fearfully, never knowing whether the Father has received him or not. He usually is defeated and miserable. But the Christian who has assurance can be joyful because he belongs to God, and instead of always regarding Him with fear, he will learn to love Him and serve Him.

ILLUSTRATION: Suppose that when you were a child you had never been sure that you were really a member of your family, and felt that if you were bad in any way they might put you out of the family. How much love and joy would you have experienced and demonstrated? Discuss.

THE PERSON OF JESUS CHRIST

LESSON TWO   STEP ONE

OBJECTIVE: To show who Jesus Christ is by examining the Biblical evidence concerning Him.

I.   OPEN WITH PRAYER.

II. MEMORY VERSE: John 1:18. Students should check each other briefly in pairs. Then have one student explain the meaning to the entire class.

III. MOTIVATION: Ask the class "Who do you think Jesus Christ is, and why do you think so?" Allow a few minutes for discussion, then proceed into the Bible study.

IV. BIBLE STUDY:

Because of the length of the lesson, go over only the following questions:

    I.   The Claims of Christ—A 1, 2, 3, 4.

    II.   Contemporary Opinions about Christ—A 1, B 2, 5.

    III. The Deity of Christ—C 2, 3.

    VI.   The Resurrection of Christ—4, 5.

    VII. The Future Bodily Return of Christ to this Earth—1, 2.

Have various members of the class answer each question, as in Lesson One. Supplement the class contributions with Lesson Amplication material.

V.   PARALLEL PASSAGES:

A. The claims of Christ:

    1. The Son of God: Matthew 11:27 (Luke 10:22).

    2. Came from heaven: John 5:17-18.

    3. Claimed He should have the same reverence which God has: John 5:23.

    4. Never failed to please God, and never sinned: John 8:45.

100

B. Contemporary opinions about Christ.

    1. Philip: John 1:45.

    2. Nathaniel: John 1:49.

    3. Centurion and soldiers: Matthew 27:54.

C. The deity of Christ.

    1. John 1:14; Colossians 2:9; Hebrews 1:3; John 1:12.

    2. Lord: Philippians 2:11; I Timothy 6:14-15; Ephesians 1:20-21.

    3. Son of God: Hebrews 1:1-2; I John 4:9,15.

    4. Messiah: Matthew 1:23; John 1:41.

D. The compassion of Christ.

    1. Matthew 20:30-34.

    2. Mark 1:41.

    3. Luke 19:41.

E. The death of Christ.

    1. I Corinthians 15:3.

    2. II Corinthians 5:14-15.

    3. I John 3:16.

    4. Ephesians 1:7.

F. The resurrection of Christ.

    1. Acts 2:24, 32-33.

    2. Romans 1:4.

    3. Ephesians 1:20.

G. The future bodily return of Christ to this earth.

    1. Matthew 24:27.

    2. Acts 1:11.

    3. Revelation 1:7.

VI. SUMMARY: Close with this question, "If Jesus Christ is who He claimed to be, the Son of God, what are some of the differences it should make in our lives?"

VII. CLOSE IN PRAYER.

THE PERSON OF JESUS CHRIST

LESSON TWO   STEP ONE

INTRODUCTION:

Make sure the class members state reasons for what they believe about Jesus. If they are all Christians, you can suggest they list as many proofs as they can think of for His deity.

I.   THE CLAIMS OF CHRIST:

Stress to the class how stupendous Jesus' claims really are:

A. He claims to be God's Son, who sits at His right hand, and shall one day return to the earth in great power—Mark 14:61-62.

B. He claims that He and God are the same—John 10:30; 14:9. Note in John 10:31-32 the crowd attempts to kill Him for this claim. They understood what He was saying perfectly.

C. He claims to be the most powerful authority in the whole universe (not just in the world)—Matthew 28:18.

D. He claims to be the only way to God the Father (Note that He says He is *the* way, not *a* way)—John 14:6.

Jesus also makes many other similar claims to these. These claims must be true or false. If true, we should worship and serve Him all of our lives. If false, we can come to one of two conclusions about Jesus: (1) He knew these claims were false, which makes Him one of the world's greatest impostors and liars. (2) He did not know they were false, which makes Him insane. If your roommate made just one of the claims listed above, and really believed it, his family and friends would quickly see that he was put in a mental institution.
C. S. Lewis, Professor at Oxford University and a former agnostic, confirms the facts mentioned above when he says:

"A man who was merely man and said the sort of things Jesus said wouldn't be a great moral teacher. He'd either be a lunatic— on a level with the man who says he's a poached egg—or else he'd be the Devil of Hell. You must make your choice. Either this man was, and is, the Son of God, or else a mad-man or something worse. You can shut Him up for a fool, you can spit at and kill Him as a demon; or you can fall at His feet and call Him Lord and God. But don't let us come with any patronizing nonsense about His being a great human teacher. He hasn't left that open to us."

Ask the class, "Which of these three choices—liar, lunatic, or Son of God—seems most logical to you? Why?" The obvious answer is that Jesus is the Son of God. How is it that the greatest moral example ever known, admired by Christian and non-Christian alike, could be that of an unprincipled deceiver? And why should He and His followers die for what they knew was a lie? Or how is it that the sanest, most well-balanced figure ever known, whose teachings serve as a basis for mental health, could himself be a psychopath? Those who deny the deity of Christ are faced with these insuperable difficulties.

II. CONTEMPORARY OPINIONS ABOUT CHRIST:

A. Pilate, who allowed Him to be crucified, said He was a "righteous person."

B. Peter, who lived with Him day and night for the better part of three years, stated, "He did no sin."

C. Thomas, who was skeptical and unbelieving, acknowledged Him as "My Lord and my God."

D. Regardless of whether they believed in Him, those who had the best opportunity to observe Him admitted openly that there was something absolutely unique about Jesus. And this has been the consensus of many of the greatest leaders and thinkers in history. Napoleon, for example, as he neared the end of his life acknowledged:

"I know men; and I tell you that Jesus Christ is not a man. Superficial minds see a resemblance between Christ and the founders of empires, and the gods of other religions. That resemblance does not exist. . . . Between Him and whoever else there is in the world there is no possible term of comparison. He is truly a Being by Himself. . . .

"Alexander, Caesar, Charlemagne and myself founded empires. But on what did we rest the creations of our genius? Upon force. Jesus Christ alone founded His empire upon love; and at this hour, millions of men would die for Him."

III. THE RESURRECTION OF CHRIST:*

Ask the class, "What is the significance of so many different appearances of the risen Christ to so many different people?" The answer is that it is one of the strongest confirmations that Christ actually did rise from the dead. Certainly the abundance of witnesses destroys any theory that this was a vision or hallucination.

Floyd E. Hamilton states: "Now it is perfectly possible for one man to have an hallucination, and two men might have the same hallucination by a singular coincidence, but that eleven men of intelligence, whose characters and writings indicate their sanity in other respects, or that five hundred men in a body should have the *same* hallucination and at the *same* time, stretches the law of probability to the breaking point!"

In I Corinthians 15:12-26 Paul shows that Christianity stands or falls with the resurrection of Jesus Christ:

(1) The Christian faith is in vain if Christ be not risen (v. 14).

(2) The leaders of the early church, including Paul himself, are liars and Christianity a hoax (v. 15).

(3) The Christian believer individually is unforgiven and his faith is in vain (v. 17).

(4) The Christian has no hope of a future life, and the many trials which the early church and Christians through the ages endured are therefore to no avail (v. 19).

Many have attempted to explain away the resurrection by various theories, but with no real success. Some of these theories include:

A. The *swoon theory*—Jesus never actually died, but only fainted and was removed from the cross still alive. Afterwards when he revived, his followers thought He was resurrected. The objections to this are (a) Jesus could never have moved the stone or escaped from the guards in His weakened condition. (b) The soldiers judged He was dead and pierced his side to make sure, and blood and water, a sign of death, flowed out.

B. *The vision theory and the hallucination theory*—Jesus' followers saw an hallucination or a vision of Him because of their disturbed mental condition at this time. See the quote by Hamilton, above, for a refutation of this. This theory also fails to explain why Jesus' enemies did not produce His body when the disciples began to preach the resurrection. It would have soon ended the Christian movement.

* See Lesson 4 in the Teacher's Manual for the *Introduction to the Ten Basic Steps* for a detailed treatment of the resurrection.

C. *The stolen body theory*—Jesus' body was stolen by either His followers or His enemies. This theory quickly falls apart when we realize (a) His enemies had no reason to steal the body, since they did not want to give credence to a belief in His resurrection. And even if they had stolen the body they would have produced it when His disciples began to preach resurrection. (b) His friends were too weak and scattered to steal the body if they wished, since Roman soldiers guarded the tomb. And if they had stolen the body they would not have preached His resurrection at the risk of their lives when there was nothing to gain and they knew it was a lie. Men are not in the habit of sacrificing their lives, which many of these early Christians did, for what they know is a deception.

We can only conclude that Paul in I Corinthians 15 is expressing that he and the other early Christians were willing to stake their lives on the resurrection for the simple reason that they had actually seen it.

We conclude, therefore, that in I Corinthians 15 Paul believes in Christ's resurrection because he had actually seen it (v. 7-8), and for the same reason the leaders of the early church fearlessly preached it. The resurrection really happened!

IV. THE FUTURE BODILY RETURN OF CHRIST TO THIS EARTH:

The Bible specifically prophesies a second coming of Christ to earth, though even devout Christians disagree over details concerning this great event. Use the following material to give the class clearer understanding of major aspects of the second coming.

A. The Second Coming of Christ will be physical and visible.

Ask the class, "What does it mean in Acts 1:11 when it says Christ will return 'in like manner as ye have seen Him go?' " Answer: How did Christ go into heaven? He went physically and visibly. Therefore, He will return the same way. Cf. Revelation 1:7, "every eye shall see Him." Old and New Testament writers frequently speak of such a coming of Christ (cf. Daniel 7:14; Titus 2:13), and Jesus Christ himself repeatedly refers to this kind of second coming (Mark 13:24-27; Matthew 24:37). Therefore, unless the Bible is mistaken, Jesus Christ Himself deluded, and Christianity a hoax, He will certainly come again physically and visibly.

B. The second coming of Christ will be in sharp contrast to the first coming of Christ.

At his first coming Christ entered human history humbly and obscurely, being virgin born into the poor Jewish family of Joseph and Mary. He imposed human limitations on Himself such as need for food and rest, and concluded His earthly sojourn by allowing the world He came to save to crucify Him. But at His second coming He will suddenly descend out of heaven with great power and glory (Mark 13:24-27), conquer His enemies and assume rulership of the world (Matt. 25:31-32). Human history is not wandering on aimlessly, it is heading inescapably toward this goal.

C. The second coming of Christ will be preceded by certain signs.

1. Critical world conditions. Christ specifically states world conditions will worsen before He comes (Matt. 24:6-8; cf. II Timothy 3:1-5), which jibes with historical trends in the twentieth century. All hopes that mankind will eventually solve its problems or reform itself are doomed to failure. Christians should attempt to reform evils in society wherever possible, but their main task is to call men to Christ out of a world headed toward destruction.

ILLUSTRATION: D. L. Moody, the famous evangelist, once stated, "God has not told me to reform the whole world. The world is like a sinking ship which cannot be kept from going down. But God has given me a life boat and said, 'Moody, save everyone off that ship you can.' Our chief task is to save everyone we can."

2. The catching up of the church to meet Christ in the air. I Thessalonians 4:13-18 describes what is known as the "rapture" of the church. At this great event all believers are suddenly caught up out of the world to meet the Lord in the air. Some devout scholars feel this will take place before Christ comes to earth, others feel it will take place at the same time. Though the Bible does not clearly indicate when this will happen, without doubt it will be one of the most marvelous acts God has ever performed. I Corinthians 15:51-56 indicates that at this time believers will receive new physical bodies which will be perfect and glorious. "As the believer then passes into a condition of glory, his body must be altered for the new conditions . . . it becomes a 'spiritual' body belonging to the realm of the spirit. . . ." INTERNATIONAL STANDARD BIBLE ENCYCLOPEDIA.

3. The Great Tribulation. Mark 13:14-23, Revelation 6-18, and other passages describe the last seven years of history before Christ comes again—a period known as "The Great Tribulation." At this time calamity and evil will sweep over the world in an unprecedented manner. A great world leader known as the Anti-Christ, who will outdistance all cruelties perpetrated

by any before him, will come to power. At the end of this period Christ will return to earth to deliver His people and set up His kingdom. If the rapture occurs before Christ's return, Christians living then will not have to go through the Great Tribulation.

D. The second coming of Christ should motivate us to live for Him.

   1. We are warned to watch and to be ready. "Take ye heed, watch and pray; for ye know not when the time is" (Mark 13:33).

   2. We must be extremely careful to maintain a worthy character. The hope of His coming should motivate us to holy living (see I John 3:1-3).

   3. We are to carry out the terms of the Great Commission (Matt. 28:18-20). We must do our utmost to see that the world is evangelized.

ILLUSTRATION: During the fall of every year, hurricanes frequently strike the Southeast and Texas gulf coasts of the United States. Many hours before the hurricane strikes, the weather bureau issues warnings to areas likely to be devastated. As the storm approaches, tides and wind begin to rise and the weather grows more ominous. During this time people board up windows, move boats, store food and water and make every preparation for the winds, rain and high tides. Only a fool would not prepare for the storm because so many signs of its approach are apparent. In the same way, the signs of our age and the increasing world problems indicate that Christ's coming is drawing nigh. In light of this the Christian who refuses to prepare for Christ's coming is unbelievably foolish.

LESSON PLAN

THE CHRIST-CONTROLLED LIFE

LESSON THREE   STEP ONE

OBJECTIVE: To demonstrate that the Christian life is maintained by the
power and life of the indwelling Christ and not by the individual's own efforts.

I.   OPEN WITH PRAYER.

II. MEMORY VERSE: Philippians 4:13. Ask two or three to quote the
verse.

III. MOTIVATION: Ask the class, "What do we mean when we talk
about Jesus Christ controlling our lives?" After a
few minutes of discussion ask, "How can we make
certain He is controlling our lives?"

IV. BIBLE STUDY:

A. The non-Christian or Natural man.

1. Have the class answer question 1, then ask "What does it mean
when it says the natural man does not receive the things of the
Spirit of God?" Ask if they know some particularly good illustration of this. You might supply some from your own witnessing
experiences.

2. Have the class answer question 3, then ask further who "the
prince of the power of the air" is. Does this mean Satan controls
the lives of *all* non-Christians, or just the worst non-Christians?

3. Have the class answer questions 4-6.

B. The Spiritual, or Christ-controlled, Christian.

1. Have the class answer questions 1-4.

2. Dwell especially on question 1. Why does Paul use the term
"fruit" to describe these characteristics (see the Lesson Amplification material)?

3. Emphasize what is involved in the Christ-controlled life.

C. The Carnal Christian and solution to Carnality.

Go over most of the questions in these two sections with the class, using Lesson Amplification material to supplement and illustrate answers.

V.   PARALLEL PASSAGES:

A. The non-Christian, or Natural man: Romans 3:9-20; Titus 3:3; John 5:19.

B. The Spiritual, or Christ-Controlled, Christian: John 15:1-7; the Book of Acts; Ephesians 3:16-19; Colossians 1:10-11.

C. The Carnal Christian: Romans 7:15, 17-18, 21, 24; 8:7; I Corinthians 3:1-7.

VI. SUMMARY:

A. Read quotation from the Lesson Amplification material.

B. Briefly challenge the class to a total surrender to Jesus Christ.

VII. CLOSE IN PRAYER.

THE CHRIST-CONTROLLED LIFE

LESSON THREE   STEP ONE

INTRODUCTION:

Make sure the class thinks through on what is involved in the Christ-contolled life. Some additional questions you might use to stimulate thinking:
"Is the Christ-controlled life a perfect life?" "If Christ controlled every area
of my life, would I lose my individual personality?—In other words, should
all Christians be stereotyped?"

I.   THE CARNAL MAN:

   A. Question 1 — Note that the non-Christian can intellectually un-
      derstand the Bible, but until he becomes converted he cannot
      respond to its truth. "Not that the natural faculty of discerning
      is lost, but evil inclinations and wicked principles render the man
      unwilling to enter the mind of God, in spiritual matters of His
      Kingdom, and to yield to their force and power. It is the quickening
      beams (of light) of the Spirit of truth and holiness that must help
      the mind to discern their excellency, and to come to so thorough
      a conviction of their truth as heartily to receive and embrace
      them."— MATTHEW HENRY.

      ILLUSTRATION: Bertrand Russell, the great philosopher, is not
      only descendent from one of England's most distinguished families,
      but also is a versatile and brilliant scholar, the author of many im-
      portant works and a winner of the 1950 Nobel Prize for literature.
      Yet he has been consistently antagonistic toward Christianity and
      much that it stands for. One of his works is entitled *Why I am not
      a Christian.* He obviously is capable of intellectually understand-
      ing the Bible, but not of receiving its truth.

   B. Question 3 — Note that *every* man without Christ is under
      Satan's dominion. The phrase "prince of the power of the air" is a
      description of Satan. The Greek word for "air" here means "the
      lower denser atmosphere." "The kingdom of Satan is in this lower
      atmosphere where we human beings are, in order that that sinister
      being, filled with a bitter hatred of God and the human race, might
      with his demons, prey upon humanity. . . . The unsaved order
      their behavior according to his dictates and those of his demons."
      —KENNETH WUEST.

      How then can we explain that some non-Christians have much

higher standards than others, if all are under Satan's control? "For in all ages there have been some persons, who, from the mere dictates of nature, have devoted their whole lives to the pursuit of virtue. . . . These examples, then, seem to teach us that we should not consider human nature to be totally corrupted. . . . But here we ought to remember, that amidst this corruption of nature there is some room for Divine grace, not to purify it, but to internally restrain its operations. For should the Lord permit the minds of all men to give up the reins to every lawless passion, there certainly would not be an individual in the world, whose actions would not evince all the crimes for which Paul condemns human nature in general. . . . if the Lord should suffer the human passions to go to all lengths to which they are inclined. . . . there is no river, though ever so rapid and violent, that would overflow its boundaries with such impetuosity."—JOHN CALVIN.

ILLUSTRATION: An enormous variety of life exists in the ocean, from microscopic creatures to huge whales. Some live near the shore or the surface, others in the very depths. But all these creatures have this in common—they are aquatic and can only exist permanently in the ocean. So there are many different kinds of non-Christians—some very good, some very bad, some in between. But all have this in common—they are self-centered and sinful before God. Only if a fish could be remade from within could it live on land, and only if God remakes us within by the new birth can we please Him.

C. Questions 4-6 — Note in question 5 the meanings of some of the thirteen sins:

"Adulteries"—a Greek word for sexual impurity of *any* kind. We derive our word "pornographic" from this term.

"Coveteousness"—means extreme greed, the longing to have more than you need.

"Lasciviousness"—complete lack of restraint, allowing all of your lower desires to rule you, especially in the area of sex.

"Evil eye"—an oriental phrase meaning "envy." Jealousy of another because of his abilities; desire to have what belongs to others.

"Blasphemy"—speaking against God *or* fellow human beings. Includes all gossip.

"Foolishness"—without sense, acting without thinking; for example, living as if God did not exist.

Matthew Henry comments on John 3:36, "As God offers and conveys good things to us by the testimony of Jesus Christ, whose

word is the vehicle of divine favors, so we receive and partake of
those favors by believing the testimony, and entertaining the testimony as true and good; this way of receiving fitly answers that
way of giving. We have here the sum of the gospel which is to be
preached to every creature. . . . He that believeth not the Son is
undone. . . . They cannot be happy in this world nor that to come.
. . . God's wrath for his daily actual transgressions lights and lies
upon him. Old scores lie undischarged, and new ones are added—
something is done every day to fill the measure, and nothing to
empty it."

II. THE SPIRITUAL, OR CHRIST-CONTROLLED CHRISTIAN:

A. Question 1 — Wuest says this about Galatians 5:22-23: "The
choice of (the word) 'fruit' here instead of 'works' is due probably
to the conception of the Christian experience as the product of a
new and divine life implanted in the saint. . . . The word 'fruit' is
singular, which fact serves to show that all of the elements of character spoken of in these verses are a unity, making for a well-
rounded and complete Christian life."

Note the individual elements of the fruit:

1. "Love"—The divine love which only God can give and which
exceeds normal human love.

2. "Joy"—Happiness.

3. "Peace"—The tranquility of mind which comes from a right
relationship with God; freedom from anxiety.

4. "Longsuffering"—Patient endurance under wrong or ill-treat-
ment without anger or thought of revenge.

5. "Gentleness"—A better translation is "kindness."

6. "Goodness"—Moral uprightness.

7. "Faith"—Modern translations render this "faithfulness." Trustworthiness, dependability.

8. "Meekness"—Concerning this word W. E. Vine says, "The
meaning . . . is not readily expressed in English,
for the terms meekness, mildness, commonly used,
suggest weakness . . . whereas the Greek word
does nothing of the kind . . . meekness is the opposite to self-assertiveness and self-interest; it is
equanimity of spirit that is neither elated nor
cast down, simply because it is not occupied with
self at all."

9. "Temperance"—The Greek word means "self-control." The word thus refers to a mastery of one's own desires or impulses. Christians who lose control of themselves in any area—sex, money, studies, etc.—are not spiritual Christians.

B. Question 2 — Galatians 2:20 is a key verse of Scripture on the Christian life, for it clearly explains that the Christ-controlled life is Christ living through the Christian. "Instead of attempting to live his life in obedience to a set of rules in the form of the legal enactments of the Mosaic law, Paul now yields to the indwelling Holy Spirit and cooperates with Him in the production of a life pleasing to God"—KENNETH WUEST.

"Faith connects you so intimately with Christ, that He and you become as it were one person. As such you may boldly say, 'I am now one with Christ. Therefore Christ's righteousness, victory, and life are mine.' On the other hand, Christ may say: 'I am that big sinner. His sins and his death are Mine, because he is joined to Me, and I to him' "—MARTIN LUTHER.

Note that the Christ-contolled life does not mean our individual personality is abolished. Christ expresses Himself through *me*—my own personality with its peculiarities—though He may knock off some rough edges in the process. Paul was a logical thinker before conversion and God used this element so that he could write logical treatises like the Epistle to the Romans. John thought more mystically, on the other hand, and God used this element in his personality to write the Gospel of John. God did not totally change their personalities, but He used their personalities as His instrument.

ILLUSTRATION: Several different artists could paint exactly the same scene, yet no two paintings would be identical. They might all reproduce the scene with reasonable faithfulness, but each product would reflect some characteristics of the artist through whom the scene was communicated to the canvas. So Christ is communicated to the world in different ways through each different personality in whom He lives.

C. Question 3 — Alexander Maclaren comments on Philippians 4:13: "This inward impartation of strength is the true and only condition of that self-sufficingness which Paul has just been claiming. Stoicism breaks down because it tries to make men apart from God sufficient for themselves, which no man is. To stand alone without Him is to be weak. Circumstances will always be too strong for me, and sins will be too strong. A godless life has a weakness at the heart of its loneliness, but Christ and I are always in the majority, and in the face of all foes, be they ever so many and strong, we can confidently say, 'They that be with us are more than they that be with them.' "

D. Question 4 — I Corinthians 2:14-16. "The man whose mind is illuminated by the Spirit of God, and shares the thoughts of Christ, has a criterion by which he can test every principle of conduct. Insofar as he conforms to the mind of Christ he is beyond natural man's assessment. The mere humanist is no more competent in the spiritual sphere than one who is tone-deaf is capable of criticizing music, or a man who is color-blind is qualified to discuss a painting"—ABINGDON BIBLE COMMENTARY.

"The spiritual man . . . is qualified to sift, to examine, to decide rightly, because he has the eyes of his heart enlightened (Eph. 1:18) and is no longer blinded by the god of this world (Satan) . . . Men of intellectual gifts who are ignorant of the things of Christ talk learnedly and patronizingly about things of which they are grossly ignorant. The spiritual man is superior to all this false knowledge. . . . Men will pass judgment on him, but the spiritual man refuses to accept the decision of his ignorant judges"—A. T. ROBERTSON.

This is the difference that the indwelling Holy Spirit can make in one's life.

III. THE CARNAL CHRISTIAN AND THE SOLUTION TO CARNALITY:

A. The Carnal Christian.

1. Question 1 — Ask the class, "What is a carnal Christian?" Ruth Paxson's definition: "The carnal man has accepted Christ as his Saviour but he has little or no apprehension of a life of complete surrender to, and of full appropriation of, Jesus Christ as his Lord and his life. Christ has *a* place in his heart but not *the* place of supremacy and pre-eminence. . . . He attempts to live in two spheres, the heavenly and the earthly—and he fails in both." The carnal man is undoubtedly a Christian, for Paul calls the carnal church members at Corinth "brethren" in verse 1, a term he never applies to unbelievers. But the life of the carnal Christian is inconsistent and unhappy.

2. Question 2 — Galatians 5:19-20 lists practices which result from letting our old sinful nature rule us instead of Jesus Christ.

a. *Sins in the realm of sex (v. 19).*

(1) Fornication — Any kind of sexual impurity.

(2) Uncleanness — Extreme immorality, "dirty" jokes; "dirty" thoughts.

(3) Lasciviousness — Open indecency.

114

b. *Sins in the realm of religion (v. 20).*

   (1) Idolatry—Allowing something else, family, a friend, good grades, a job, etc. to become more important than God; also false religion.

   (2) Witchcraft—Sorcery, use of magic—common in the ancient world. It includes such modern day phenomena as astrology, fortune telling, conducting seances, etc.

c. *Sins in the realm of personal relationship (v. 20-21).*

   (1) Hatred—The opposite of love. Hostility toward fellow students, professors, etc.

   (2) Variance—Quarreling, fighting.

   (3) Emulations—Jealousy.

   (4) Wrath—Passionate outbursts of anger—losing one's temper.

   (5) Strife—Factiousness—inability to get along with others.

   (6) Seditions—Divisions—one group against another.

   (7) Heresies—"Self-willed opinions" which lead to division.

   (8) Envyings—Desiring to take away from another what is his.

d. *Sins in the realm of self-control (v. 21).*

   (1) Drunkenness—A problem in that time as today.

   (2) Revellings—Drunken, lewd parties; orgies.

3. Question 3 — The "carnal mind", i.e., our self-centered ego, is opposed to God and could not be subject to Him even if it wanted to. Our own ego naturally "rebels against His authority, thwarts His design, opposes His interest, spits in His face"— MATTHEW HENRY.

   ILLUSTRATION: Several years ago a story in a national magazine described a couple who "adopted" two wolves. They discovered the two wolves, still young and small, while making a movie of caribou in Alaska. They took them to their home, raised them, gave them the kindest treatment and for a while the wolves behaved just like friendly dogs. Finally, however, the wolves turned on their masters, who barely escaped with their lives, and then fled to join a wild wolf pack. No matter how kind was their treatment, the nature of the wolves was such that sooner or later they were bound to behave like other wolves. The wolf-nature could not be educated out of them. Similarly, our sinful nature always stays the same—no amount of education, refinement, culture, kindness, psychiatric treatment or anything else can take away its selfishness and proneness toward sin. This is why Jesus Christ, not we ourselves, must live in our bodies. We cannot improve the flesh. Our old nature, which is antagonistic to God, according to Romans 8:7-8, has been crucified, according to Galatians 2:20 and Romans 6:6,11.

B. The Solution to Carnality.

Note the three steps to spirituality here:

1. Confession (Questions 1-2) — I John 1:9. We must confess all *known* sins. "The word confess is *homologeo,* from *homos,* 'the same,' and *lego* 'to say,' thus 'to say the same thing as another,' or to 'agree with another.' Confession of sin . . . means therefore to say the same thing that God does about that sin, to agree with God as to all the implications of that sin as it relates to the Christian who commits it and to a holy God against whom it is committed"—KENNETH WUEST. When we confess, however, God is faithful and just to forgive and cleanse from all unrighteousness. The first part of this verse should never be read without looking at the last part. God openly and freely forgives us because Christ has died for us.

2. Surrender (Question 3) — What is "surrender"? Surrender is "the definite, deliberate, voluntary transference of the undivided possession, control and use of the whole being, spirit, soul and body from self to Christ, to whom it rightfully belongs by creation and by purchase. . . . It is not in order to be His, but because we are His, that we yield up our lives. . . . The question is not, 'Do I belong to God?' but 'Have I yielded to God that which already belongs to Him?' "—JAMES MC-CONKEY.

   ILLUSTRATION: Two cars are driving down a highway. One is an ambulance on an errand of mercy, saving a life by speeding someone to needed medical help. The other car is a late model sedan, but it swerves recklessly around the curves and finally, attempting to pass another car, it is engaged in a head-on collision which takes several lives. What is the fundamental difference between these two cars and their behaviour. The motor? The type of body? No. There is one main difference—who is in the driver's seat. One was a man on an errand of mercy, the other a drunken driver. The basic difference between the defeated, half-hearted, ineffective Christian and the happy, fruitful, effective Christian is simply this—who is in control. Self controls the ineffective Christian; Christ controls the effective Christian.

3. Faith (Questions 4-6) — Some Christians surrender to Christ but fail to experience victory. Why? Lack of faith. "Surrender opens the door; faith believes that Christ enters, fills, abides." What are the elements of faith?

   a. *Knowledge*—"Faith is not ignorance; it is not closing one's eyes to the facts. Faith is never afraid to look truth squarely in the face. Man is not saved by knowledge, but he cannot be saved without it"—LINDSELL AND WOODBRIDGE. We have a knowledge that God will take over control of our lives because it is His will (I John 5:14-15).

b. *Intellectual acceptance of the fact.* We must give a rational assent to the truth to be believed.

c. *Personal appropriation.* "Mental assent is not enough. The will must be exercised and a decision must be made"— LINDSELL AND WOODBRIDGE. We must believe that Christ will take control of our lives.

ILLUSTRATION: Three factors are involved in becoming a Christian, as in marriage: the intellect, the emotions and the will. (1) Intellectually, we must know the other person—what he looks like, how he acts, etc. (2) Emotionally, we must agree that he would be a good husband for us, that it would be best for us to marry. But this still does not cause us to be married. (3) We must be willing to take a step of faith. We must have sufficient trust in the other person to commit ourselves, our wills, to him in a marriage ceremony. Only after this third step is taken are we married, and only after we commit ourselves to Christ in faith, believing He will control our lives, do we experience His control.

IV. SUMMARY:

The diary of Jim Elliot, one of five missionaries murdered by the Auca Indians in 1955 in an Ecuadorian jungle, contained these words:

> "I walked out to the hill just now. It is exalting, delicious, to stand embraced by the shadows of a friendly tree with the wind tugging at your coattail and the heavens hailing to your heart, to gaze and glory and give oneself to God— what more could a man ask? Oh, the fullness, pleasure, sheer excitement of knowing God on earth! I care not if I raise my voice again for Him, if only I may love Him, please Him. Mayhap in mercy He shall give me a host of spiritual children that I may lead them through the vast star fields to explore His delicacies whose finger ends set them to burning. . . .

> "O Jesus, Master and Center and End of all, how long before that Glory is Thine which has so long waited Thee? Now there is no thought of Thee among men; then there shall be thought for nothing else. Now other men are praised; then none shall care for any other's merits. Hasten, hasten, Glory of Heaven, take Thy crown, subdue Thy Kingdom, enthrall Thy creatures."

THE FIVE PRINCIPLES OF GROWTH

LESSON FOUR   STEP ONE

OBJECTIVE: To teach the class the principles most essential to growth in the Christian life so that they may begin to practice them.

I.   OPEN WITH PRAYER.

II. MOTIVATION:

Read the following excerpt to the class:

"I do not consider myself to have 'arrived', spiritually, nor do I consider myself already perfect. But I keep on, grasping ever more firmly that purpose for which Christ grasped me. . . . But I do concentrate on this: I leave the past behind and . . . go straight for the goal—my reward the honor of being called by God in Christ."

Ask the class who wrote this. If they know, ask them if they have any idea how long he had been a Christian when he wrote it. The excerpt is from Philippians 3:12-14 in the Phillips translation. These verses were written by Paul, probably the greatest Christian of all time, *at least 25 years* after his conversion! If he still needed to grow, how much more do we. The way we grow is by practicing what is set forth in this lesson.

III. BIBLE STUDY:

Go over the first three questions under each principle of growth, supplementing when necessary from the Lesson Amplification material.

A. The Bible—Matt. 22:29; Romans 15:4; II Timothy 3:16-17; I Peter 1:25; Psalm 119:30.

B. Prayer—I Chronicles 16:11; Daniel 6:10; Luke 18:1; Psalm 55:17.

C. Fellowship with other Christians—Matthew 18:20; II Corinthians 6:14; Galatians 6:2; Proverbs 13:20.

D. Witnessing for Christ—Matthew 4:19; Acts 5:20; 18:9-10; Psalm 107:2.

E. Obedience—Matthew 12:50; John 7:17; Romans 14:12-13; I John 2:6.

V. SUMMARY:

"God, give us men who have learned to walk with Christ a step at a time, a moment at a time, and who never faint! Men who cannot be overcome because they walk hand in hand, lockstep with the Lord of Glory. This is the answer to the spendid frontier that challenges Christians at the mid-twentieth century"—RICHARD C. HALVERSON.

VI. CLOSE IN PRAYER.

THE FIVE PRINCIPLES OF GROWTH

LESSON FOUR   STEP ONE

I. PRINCIPLE ONE: WE MUST READ THE BIBLE:

A. Ask the class, "Why is it necessary to study the Bible in order to grow?"

The answer is that the Bible, being the word of God, does the following for us:

1. It causes our faith to grow. Romans 10:17 tells us faith comes from hearing the word of God. You may pray all you want for more faith, but you will only get it by reading God's word. (See the quotation below by D. L. Moody.)

2. It convicts us of sin. Hebrews 4:12-13 shows that the word of God reveals our inmost self to us. Without this correcting influence, we soon wander astray.

3. It helps keep us from committing sin. Psalms 119:11 teaches that the word of God holds us back from sins we might otherwise commit.

4. It gives us a standard by which we can guide our lives. II Timothy 3:16-17 emphasizes that the Bible is inspired by God and therefore practical in everyday life. It gives guidance in the difficult areas of life—studies, social life, family life, etc.

B. Questions 1-2—These verses compare the Bible to physical food. Concerning I Peter 2:2, Matthew Henry remarks:
"The manner in which they are to desire this sincere milk of the word is stated thus: *As newborn babes.* He puts them in mind of of their regeneration. A new life requires suitable food. They, being newly born (spiritually), must desire the milk of the word. Infants desire common milk, and their desires toward it are fervent and frequent, arising from an impatient sense of hunger. Such must a Christian's desire be for the word of God. Strong desires and affections for the word of God are a sure evidence of a person's being born again. The word of God, rightly used, does not leave a man as it finds him, but improves him and makes him better."

C. Question 3—Phillips translates II Timothy 2:15-16, "For yourself, concentrate on winning God's approval, on being a workman with nothing to be ashamed of, and who knows how to use the word to best advantage." Matthew Henry comments on this verse saying that those who teach the word "must be workmen; they have work to do, and they must take pains in it. Workmen that are unskillful or unfaithful, or lazy, have need to be ashamed; but those who mind their business, and keep to their work, are workmen that need not be ashamed. And what is their work? It is rightly to divide the Word of Truth. Not to invent a new gospel, but rightly to divide the gospel that is committed to their trust." Notable sayings about the Bible:

1. "It is impossible rightly to govern the world without God and the Bible"—GEORGE WASHINGTON.

2. "I am profitably engaged in reading the Bible. Take all of this book upon reason that you can and the balance by faith, and you will live and die a better man"—ABRAHAM LINCOLN.

3. "The vigor of our spiritual life will be in exact proportion to the place held by the Bible in our life and thoughts . . . I have read the Bible through one hundred times and always with increasing delight. Each time it seems like a new book to me. Great has been the blessing from consecutive, diligent, daily study. I look upon it as a lost day when I have not had a good time over the Word of God"—GEORGE MUELLER.

4. "I prayed for faith, and thought that some day faith would come down and strike me like lightning. But faith did not seem to come. One day I read in the tenth chapter of Romans, 'Now faith cometh by hearing, and hearing by the Word of God.' I had closed my Bible and prayed for faith. I now opened my Bible and began to study, and faith has been growing ever since" —D. L. MOODY.

II. PRINCIPLE TWO: WE MUST PRAY:

A. Question 1 — Jesus commanded His disciples to "watch and pray." The word "watch" means to "be wide awake," "alert." "Watchfulness and prayer are inseparable. The one discerns dangers, the other arms against them. . . . The eye that sees clearly the facts of life will turn upwards from its scanning of the snares and traps, and will not look in vain. These two are the indispensable conditions of victorious encountering of temptation. Fortified by them we shall not 'enter into' it, though we encounter it. The outward trial will remain, but its power to lead us astray will vanish"—ALEXANDER MACLAREN.

B. Questions 2-3 — A major cause of Peter's failure was prayerlessness. Ask the class, "Why do you think Peter failed to pray?" The answer is that apparently he did not feel sufficient need of it.

He would rather sleep. When physically exhausted, sleep is undoubtedly more important than prayer, but at this crisis moment Peter should have prayed. A further look at the chapter reveals why Peter felt so little need of prayer and why he failed so tragically. Matthew 26:33, 35 shows that Peter had too much confidence in himself. On these verses Matthew Henry says:

"He fancied himself better armed against temptation than anyone else, and this was his weakness and folly. . . . It argues a great degree of self-conceit and self-confidence, to think ourselves either safe from the temptations, or free from the corruptions, that are common to men. We should rather say, if it be possible that others may be offended, there is danger that I may be so. But it is common for those who think too well of themselves, easily to admit suspicions of others."

To be effective in prayer, we must not feel self-confident like Peter, but helpless before God. Dr. O. Hallesby states concerning the necessity of recognizing our own weakness:

"Helplessness in prayer resembles in a striking way the condition of a person who is lame or sick of the palsy. At first it is painful, almost unbearable, to be so helpless that one cannot hold a spoon to his mouth or chase a fly from his face. . . . But notice this same person after he has become resigned to his illness and reconciled to his helplessness. He is just as helpless as he was before, but his helplessness no longer causes him any pain or anxiety. . . . When he quietly and humbly asks for help, he does so as though he were apologizing for doing so. Notice, look how grateful he is for the least bit of assistance that he receives. . . . All his thinking and all his planning have been conditioned by his helplessness. He is, of course, dependent in all things upon those who care for him. We notice, too, that this feeling of dependence develops into a peculiar bond of sympathy between him and them. . . . Thus our helplessness should make us attached to God and makes us more strongly dependent upon Him than words can describe. Recall to mind the words of Jesus, 'Without me ye can do nothing' (John 15:5). In one single line He tells us here what it takes us a whole lifetime to learn, and even when we reach the portals of death, we have not learned it fully."

C. Notable Sayings About Prayer:

1. "The words *pray* and *prayer* are used at least 25 times in connection with the Lord in the brief record of His life in the four Gospels. John 17 is one of several examples of Jesus in prayer. Prayer took much of the time and strength of Jesus. One who does not spend much time in prayer cannot properly be called a follower of Jesus Christ"—R. A. TORREY.

2. "I never prayed sincerely for anything but it came, at some time . . . somehow, in some shape"—ADONIRAM JUDSON.

III. PRINCIPLE THREE: WE MUST FELLOWSHIP WITH OTHER CHRISTIANS:

Fellowship means more than mere friendship. The Greek word for fellowship is *koinonia,* which means "sharing in common." We desperately need to share our Christian experience with others who believe and likewise allow them to share with us. The church, where we can meet other Christians and hear the word of God preached, is God's appointed place for Christians to meet in fellowship, though meetings on campus, in homes, etc., are also extremely helpful.

Ask the class, "In what ways can we profit from spending time with other Christians?" Some suggested answers:

1. Profit from others' experience.

2. Mutual encouragement.

3. Opportunity for group prayer. God especially honors united prayer (Matt. 18:19).

4. Learning what others have discovered in the Bible.

5. Planning and teamwork for reaching others with the message of Christ.

A. Question 1—"It is the will of Christ that his followers should assemble together, sometimes more privately for conference and prayer, and in public for hearing and joining in all the ordinances of . . . worship. . . . The communion of the saints is a great help and privilege, and a good means of steadiness and perseverance; hereby their hearts and hands are mutually strengthened"— MATTHEW HENRY.

B. Question 2—Phillips translates Hebrews 10:24-26: "And let us think of one another and how we can encourage each other to love and do good deeds. And let us not hold aloof from our church meetings, as some do. Let us do all we can to help one another's faith, and this the more earnestly as we see the final day drawing ever nearer." Christians are not to just assemble for no purpose. They are to encourage and strengthen one another in the faith. They are to encourage a corporate morale, much like the members of an athletic team encourage each other and promote a group morale. Lindsell and Woodbridge state further about the necesssity of being connected with a local church:

"No matter what reasons he adduces, no Christian can afford to overlook the truth that every believer must engage in corporate

123

worship. Every true follower of Christ should be identified in some way with the Christian community. The church needs men, but more than this, men need the church. Even if the church is not what it ought to be, we are not to bypass the church; we are to purify it and bring it back to the place which God intended for it."

ILLUSTRATION: Think of some group you belong to—a fraternity or sorority, an athletic team, a political club of some kind, etc. Now suppose the members of this group never came together at any time and most of them did not even know each other. All business was transacted by mail. How much would this group mean to its members? How much enthusiasm would they have for it? How much good would it do them? Very little. So Christians, as long as they wish to be independent of each other, have little to do with each other, and never come together in a group, can accomplish nothing. If the early Christians had not come together for mutual encouragement and common worship, Christianity never could have survived and we would not know Christ today!

C. Question 3 — Acts 2:42 pictures the Christian church right after it came into being. Its four characteristics were: (1) Adherence to the apostles' doctrines, which are now contained for us in the New Testament. We should, if at all possible, select a church where the Bible is explained and preached. Next time you listen to a sermon, notice whether the minister really preaches the Bible, or merely expresses his own opinions. (2) Fellowship— this indicates the Christians regularly met together for fellowship and mutual encouragement. "It has become very difficult for Christian people to talk of things of Christ to each other. They meet together in ordinary life, and they talk of everything except the deepest things of their spiritual life"—G. CAMPBELL MORGAN. (3) Breaking of bread, which was the communion service. Since Christians had no church buildings then, this was done in homes. Usually they ate a meal also, which was known as the "love feast." It was a time of very close fellowship. (4) Prayers— "Systematic, definite, positive praying, not as individuals only, but in connection with one another."

Note in verse 43 the effect such a new society had upon the outside world. These early Christians had a closeness, a fellowship, a vitality which many churches lack today. Do you think that the practices of the church in verse 42 had anything to do with its effectiveness? If so, what?

ILLUSTRATION: In contrast to the closeness of the early Christians, A. B. Bruce has compared many churches today to a restaurant, "Where all kinds of people meet for a short space, sit down together . . . then part, neither knowing or caring anything about each other."

IV. PRINCIPLE FOUR: WE MUST WITNESS FOR CHRIST:

A. What is witnessing? It has been aptly described as, "One beggar telling another where to get bread." Ask the class to name as many reasons as possible why we should witness. Some suggested answers:

1. Jesus Christ commanded it—Matthew 28:18-20.

2. Non-Christians cannot be saved unless someone witnesses to them—Romans 10:17.

3. Our own Christian experience will become more vital—John 4:27-34.

4. God has prepared a large number who are ready to accept Christ—John 4:35.

5. Jesus Christ will be with us as we do it—Matthew 28:20.

B. Question 3—In Romans 1:14-16 Paul states his three great "I am's."

1. " 'I am a debtor'—The Greek word for debtor means 'one bound by obligation or duty.' Every servant of Jesus Christ, who has received the truth for himself, has received it as a steward, and is, as such, indebted to God, from whom he got the trust, and to the men for whom he got it. The only limit to the obligation is, as Paul says in the context, 'as much as in me is.' Capacity, determined by facilities, opportunities and circumstances, prescribes the kind and degree of the work to be done in discharge of the obligation; but the obligation is universal. We are not at liberty to choose whether we shall do our part in spreading the name of Jesus Christ. It is a debt that we owe to God and to men"—ALEXANDER MACLAREN. The Greeks Paul refers to here were those versed in Greek language and culture — hence the cultured and civilized in society. The barbarians were not necessarily savages, they were merely those not associated with Greek culture—generally the more ignorant and backward. The wise were the morally wise—hence those who were moral. The foolish were those who were of low morals. So in this verse Paul makes clear that our obligation is to all kinds of

people, cultured and crude, good and bad—we have a universal debt. Are you willing to witness to only certain groups of people but not to others?

2. "I am ready"—The Greek word for ready is literally "of a forward mind," hence, willing and eager. Paul did not witness out of sheer duty; he was eager to so serve His Lord. God should not have to force us to witness. cf. II Corinthians 5:14.

3. "I am not ashamed"—There was a great deal in the gospel which might tempt Paul to be ashamed, for it centered about a man who was crucified. It had little appeal to the scholars of the day, and its followers were persecuted and despised. But Paul was not ashamed because the Gospel was "the power of God unto salvation." Rome was a city which had a vast empire and great military might—hence, power was a keynote there. James Denney notes, "The conception of the gospel as a force pervades the Epistles . . . its proof, so to speak, is dynamical, not logical. It is demonstrated, not by argument, but by what it does; and looking to what it can do, Paul is proud to preach it anywhere."

C. Some helpful suggestions in witnessing:

1. Combine aggressiveness with tact. People will not always come to you. Often you must go to them and make your own openings for presenting the gospel. But *always* use love and tact. Irreparable damage can be done by those who witness in an offensive manner. If you are driving people away rather than winning them, you should change your methods.

2. Make use of a good plan of presentation, such as "The Four Spiritual Laws" which can be obtained from Campus Crusade. This will make your witnessing more organized, concise and effective.

3. Avoid arguments. They never win people and usually drive them away. If the person wants to argue don't feel obliged to continue witnessing.

4. Expect people to trust Christ. In John 15:5, 8, Jesus promises us much fruit if we follow Him. In Matthew 9:37-38, He says the harvest is great and the laborers few. Multitudes are waiting to hear the gospel, so you need have no fear in approaching people. If some do not accept, do not be discouraged, because sooner or later others will.

ILLUSTRATION:Share with the class one of your own witnessing experiences.

V. PRINCIPLE FIVE: WE MUST OBEY GOD:

A. Question 1 — Reasons why we should obey God:

1. Because we love Him—John 14:21.

2. Because we are not our own—I Corinthians 6:20.

3. Because God has given us the power to obey Him—Philippians 4:13.

4. Because His commandments are not burdensome—I John 5:3.

5. Because we can not possibly benefit in the long run by disobedience—Job 9:4; Galatians 6:7-8.

B. Question 2 — Serving two masters, Matthew 6:24. Here is the example of Paul the apostle. Before his conversion he was convinced Christianity was a fraud and a heresy so he went to all ends to stamp it out. After his conversion, when he realized his mistake, he began to serve God with all his heart. He was either for or against Christianity, but he never made the mistake of trying to be neutral. We should make the same choice. Either we should make Jesus Christ Lord of our lives, obey Him in all things, and seek His will for our lives, or we should renounce Christ entirely, do all we can to tear down the Christian faith, and in no way identify ourselves with it. Revelation 3:16 says God counts lukewarmness and neutrality a greater sin toward Christ than active opposition to Him! Matthew Henry further comments on Matthew 6:24:

"Our Lord Jesus here exposes . . . those . . . who think to divide between God and the world, to have a treasure on earth and a treasure in heaven too, to please God and to please men too . . . No, says Christ, it will not do . . . While two masters go together a servant may follow them both; but when they part, you will see to which he belongs; he cannot love, and observe, and cleave to both as he should. . . .

"Mammon is a Syriac word that signifies gain (or money) . . . He does not say we must not or we should not, but we cannot serve God and mammon. . . . God says, 'My son, give me thy heart.' Mammon says, 'No, give it me.' God says, 'Be content with such things as ye have.' Mammon says, 'Grasp all that ever thou canst. . . . Money, money; by fair means or foul, money.' God says 'Defraud not, never lie, be honest and just in thy dealings.' Mammon says, 'Cheat thy own father, if thou canst gain by it.' God says, 'Be charitable.' Mammon says, 'Hold thy own, this giving undoes all.' . . . Thus inconsistent are the commands of God and Mammon, so that we *cannot serve* both . . . choose this day whom ye will serve, and abide by your choice."

C. Question 3—This verse stresses that we must have a complete love for God. "Our love of God must be a sincere love, and not in word and tongue only, as theirs is who say they love Him, but their hearts are not with Him. It must be a strong love, we must love Him in the most intense degree. . . . It must be a singular and superlative love, we must love Him more than anything else; this way the stream of our affections must entirely run. . . . All our love is too little to bestow upon Him, and therefore all the powers of the soul must be engaged for Him, and carried out toward Him. This is the first and great commandment"—MATTHEW HENRY.

ILLUSTRATION OF OBEDIENCE: "I never saw anybody try to walk on both sides of the street but a drunken man; he tried it, and it was a very awkward work indeed; but I have seen many people in a moral point of view try to walk on both sides of the street, and I thought there was some kind of intoxication in them, or else they would have given it up as a very foolish thing. Now, if I thought this world and the pleasures thereof worth my seeking, I would seek them and go after them, and I would not pretend to be Christian , but if Christ be Christ, and if God be God, let us give our whole hearts to Him. . . ."—CHARLES HADDON SPURGEON.

"If Christ be God, and died for me, there is nothing too great that I can do for Him"—C. T. Studd, missionary to Africa, who gave up fame, fortune and family to be spent for God on a primitive continent.

LESSON PLAN

THE CHRISTIAN'S AUTHORITY

LESSON FIVE   STEP ONE

OBJECTIVE: To demonstrate the dependability and authority of the
Bible, and the importance of studying it and applying it
to our lives.

I.   OPEN WITH PRAYER.

II.   MEMORY VERSE: I Thessalonians 2:13.

III. MOTIVATION:

A biographer of General Douglas MacArthur records that one evening before a major battle in the Pacific, feeling uneasy, he picked up
his Bible and read until he felt at peace, then went to bed and slept
soundly, even though the battle the next day would play a major part
in the course of World War II. Why the Bible? Why not Shakespeare,
some great novel, some discourse on philosophy—why the Bible? The
Bible has always done for man what no other book could do. It has
always brought peace, happiness, comfort and power when nothing
else could. Why? We will discuss some of the reasons why the Bible
has such power, and suggest some of the best ways to study it in this
lesson.

IV.   BIBLE STUDY:

A. Biblical Claims of Authority—Go over all questions briefly, supplementing from Lesson Amplification material.

B. Purpose of Bible Study—Go over question 3.

C. Preparations for Bible study—Go over briefly.

D. Procedure for Bible study—Go over the procedure, then have the
class take two sheets of paper (preferably 8½ x 11). Make two
columns lengthwise on one sheet. Over the first column write "ob-

servation;" over the second, "interpretation." On the other sheet write "application." Now have the class divide into groups and spend twenty minutes or so studying Luke 19:1-10, recording their findings on their papers. Then come together and share results.

V. PARALLEL PASSAGES:

A. Old Testament claims of authority: Exodus 32:16; 34:27,32; Isaiah 59:21; Jeremiah 30:2; 36:1.

B. Jesus Christ's claim of authority: Matthew 7:23ff; Mark 13:31; John 7:16; 12:48-49.

C. Paul's view of Scripture: Acts 28:25ff; Ephesians 6:17; II Timothy 3:16.

D. Peter's view of Scripture: Acts 1:16; II Peter 1:20-21.

E. Results of Bible Study: John 15:3,7; Romans 15:4; I Peter 2:2-3.

VI. SUMMARY:

See the Lesson Amplification material and illustration of Richard Woike.

VII. CLOSE IN PRAYER.

THE CHRISTIAN'S AUTHORITY

LESSON FIVE   STEP ONE

I.   BIBLICAL CLAIMS OF AUTHORITY:

A. Question 1 — Why has the Bible met man's basic need? Because it is an authoritative message from God. Since it is from God, who knows the human heart as no one else can, it naturally meets the needs of the human heart as nothing else can. Isaiah, Jeremiah and Ezekiel, in the passages cited, acknowledge that the messages they spoke came from God. Carl F. H. Henry states concerning the Old Testament prophets:

"Both in speech and writing they are marked off by their unswerving assurance that they were spokesmen for the living God. They believed that the truths they uttered about the Most High and His works and will, and the commands and exhortations they voiced in His name, derived their origin from Him and carried His authority. The constantly repeated formula, 'thus saith the Lord,' is so characteristic of the prophets as to leave no doubt that they considered themselves chosen agents of the divine self-communication."

B. Question 2 — New Testament writers likewise viewed Scripture as being inspired of God. At this time, of course, the main Scriptures in existence were the Old Testament, so the New Testament writers mainly claim inspiration for the Old Testament. But even toward their own writings

"They extended the traditional claim of divine inspiration. Jesus their Lord had not only validated the conception of a unique and authoritative corpus of sacred writings, but spoke of a further ministry of teaching by the Spirit (John 14:26; 16:13). The apostles assert confidently that they thus speak by the Spirit (I Peter 1:12). They ascribe both the form and matter of their teaching to Him (I Corinthians 2:13). They not only assume a divine authority (I Thessalonians 4:2,15; II Thessalonians 3:6,12), but they make acceptance of their written commands a test of spiritual obedience (I Corinthians 14:37)"—CARL F. H. HENRY.

Thus the Biblical writers viewed their message as coming from God. Either they were deluded or the Bible is from God. But the

131

Bible, acknowledged as the greatest and most influential book of all time, does not give evidence of being the product of deluded men. The power of this book rather is evidence that it comes from God.

ILLUSTRATION: Suppose you suddenly became ill. Your younger brother, a high school student, says that he thinks it is indigestion and you shouldn't worry about it. Your older brother, however, who has just graduated with honors from medical school, looks at you, diagnoses the illness as appendicitis, and wants to rush you to the hospital. Whose word would you take—the high school student's or the medical school graduate's? You would take the latter, of course, because he is an authority in his field and should know what he is talking about. In areas of the spiritual life, and any other area it discusses, the Bible is an authority. You can confidently trust its word. Will you believe it, or the prejudiced suggestions of some non-Christian college professor, or spiritually ignorant fellow student? Will you follow the expert advice of the Bible or the unqualified counsel of those around you?

II.   PURPOSE OF BIBLE STUDY:

A. Question 3 — Phillips translates James 1:22-25:

"Don't, I beg you, only hear the message, but put it into practice; otherwise you are merely deluding yourselves. The man who simply hears and does nothing about it is like a man catching the reflection of his own face in a mirror. He sees himself, it is true, but he goes on with whatever he was doing without the slightest recollection of what sort of person J e saw in the mirror. But the man who looks into the perfect mirror of God's law, the law of liberty, and makes a habit of so doing, is not the man who sees and forgets. He puts that law into practice and he wins true happiness."

One who hears and studies God's word without doing anything about it is like a man who looks in a mirror, sees that his face is dirty and unshaven, yet goes away without washing and shaving it.

"The great aim of education is not knowledge but action."

—Herbert Spencer

ILLUSTRATION: A minister once visited Sing Sing prison. One of the convicts said to him, "I want you to know that I didn't come in here like all these others did. I came in a Christian." The only reply the minister could make was, "I am very sorry that being a Christian didn't keep you out of here."

"It is only when we obey God's laws that we can be quite sure that we really know Him. The man who claims to know God but does not obey His laws is not only a liar but lives in self-delusion. In practice, the more a man learns to obey God's laws, the more truly and fully does he express his love for Him. Obedience is the test of whether we really live 'in God' or not"—I John 2:4-6 (Phillips translation).

III. PREPARATIONS FOR BIBLE STUDY:

Discuss one or two questions briefly.

IV. PROCEDURE FOR BIBLE STUDY:

A sample inductive study of Luke 19:1-10:

OBSERVATION	INTERPRETATION
Vv. 1-2 — Zacchaeus was *chief* among the publicans and *very* rich.	Publicans were tax collectors. They were often cruel and dishonest. Zacchaeus had probably been unscrupulous and dishonest in acquiring his riches.
Vv. 3-4—Zacchaeus *ran* ahead of the crowd and climbed a sycamore tree to see Jesus.	He must have been extremely anxious to see Jesus to go to so much trouble. His behaviour is even more remarkable considering his wealth and high position.
Vv. 5-6—Jesus sees Zacchaeus and invites Himself to stay at his house. Zacchaeus responds by receiving Jesus *joyfully*.	Jesus had evidently observed Zacchaeus' behaviour and detected a hungry soul, thus He had no reservations about inviting Himself to stay with Zacchaeus.
Vv. 7 — The c r o w d murmurs against Jesus because He stayed with a man of bad reputation rather than with one of the religious rulers.	The crowd must have been very self-righteous. They should have been overjoyed that such a man as Zacchaeus would be interested in Jesus.
Vv. 8-9—Zacchaeus now publicly announces that he will give half of his fortune to the poor, which was probably quite a bit, and offers to restore *four* times as much as he may have cheated any individual. Jesus responds by announcing that *this day* Zacchaeus had acquired salvation, and that he was a true descendant of Abraham.	Zacchaeus offers proof of a conversion experience. Before this time money had probably been his god, but he gives up what he considers most dear for something worth much more. Jesus' response shows how willing God is to forget past sins when we give evidence of true repentance.

| V. 10—Jesus states that He came specifically to save the lost. | This is apparently the whole point of the story. Zacchaeus was lost, and now is found. The crowd was also lost, but did not know it, and hence remained lost. |

APPLICATION
(through first seven verses)

Vv. 1-4: (1) Among even the least likely classes there are those ready to receive God. Perhaps I have friends who are outwardly sinful and godless, but *inwardly* are as anxious as Zacchaeus to know Christ. I should make a list of some of these and witness to them. (2) God responds immediately to a seeking heart. Zacchaeus did not have to wait to find salvation. I do not have to wait to find God in my daily experience either. Even though I have sinned in the past, if my heart is open to Him now, I can actually experience and know Him *now*.

Vv. 5-6: (1) Jesus knows who will respond to Him and who will not—if I am led by Him, I will come in contact with hungry souls just as He did. (2) Jesus was bold in inviting Himself to stay with Zacchaeus. If I meet one who is hungry for God, I can be bold with him too. Am I asking Jesus to lead me to those who are hungry for Him? When He does, am I bold with them?

V. 7: (1) How easy it is to be snobbish. Do I purposely steer clear of others just because they don't measure up to my standards? Am I willing to take time out to be friends with Joe, or Mary, whom no one else seems to like? They might be another Zacchaeus. (2) How easy it is to be self-righteous. Zacchaeus *knew* he needed Jesus—the crowd did not. Do I feel I am pretty good, and do not need Jesus as much as others? (Continue on your own to apply the other verses.)

NOTE: This is a sample of the process of observation, interpretation, and application. Undoubtedly as you study Luke 19:1-10, you will observe, interpret and apply things not mentioned here, as will others in the class. You should follow a procedure similar to this frequently in your private devotions.

V. SUMMARY: "The Best Investment of my Whole Lifetime"—Richard Woike. Richard Woike has spent 30 years in the insurance business, the last 18 as President of the Manhattan Casualty Company. He is now head of his own investment firm, with offices in New York and Beverly Hills, California. He is active in the work of the Christian Business Men's Committee, International, of which he has been chairman, and demonstrates his enthusiasm for the Bible by teaching three classes every week.

"While I was taking college freshman English the instructor said, 'Don't be a literary hummingbird. As you go through life, select some great work, like Shakespeare or the Bible, and become thoroughly familiar with it. Give more time to it than to the popular books of the day.'

"Eighteen years later I took this seriously and began reading my Bible on my 36th birthday. Before, I had read at it; now I set a pace which has taken me from Genesis to Revelation once a year for the past twenty years. The result? A growing conviction that: this is no ordinary book, but what it claims to be, the Word of God; it does not take a profound mind, only one seeking to know God better ;it does require more than one reading; it is not full of errors and contradictions; most of the arguments about its meaning are based on incomplete knowledge of what the whole Bible says on the question under debate; regular study will be rewarded intellectually and spiritually as one makes the Bible the focal point of his life.

"I have discovered that my businessman's mind is inclined to wander from almost any reading material unless I have a ballpoint pen in my hand to annotate what I am reading. So I 'edit' a new Bible every year by underlining verses or passages and a key to the meaning. One other thing: because I believe that the Holy Spirit is the best Teacher of the Bible, I always invite Him, as I open the Book, to show me something that I can understand.

"As an investment man, I consider the time I have spent with my Bible to be the best investment of my life."

LESSON PLAN

THE CHURCH

LESSON SIX   STEP ONE

OBJECTIVE: To demonstrate to the student the importance of the church
and to encourage him to be active in it.

I.   OPEN WITH PRAYER.

II. MEMORY VERSE: Colossians 1:18.

III. MOTIVATION: Ask the class, "Why do you think Jesus Christ
founded the local church?" Have them list as many
reasons as possible.

IV. BIBLE STUDY: Go over each question in the lesson with the class,
supplementing from the Lesson Amplification ma-
terial if necessary.

V.   PARALLEL PASSAGES:

A. Christ the Head of the church—Ephesians 5:23; Colossians 1:18.

B. The universal church—I Corinthians 16:1; Galatians 1:2; I Thessalonians 2:14.

C. The local church—Acts 5:11; 11:26; I Corinthians 11:18; 14:19,
28,34; Romans 16:4.

D. Marks of a church—II John 9; Matthew 18:19; 28:19; Acts 2:42;
I Corinthians 5:1-5 (discipline); 11:18; 14:19, 28,5.

VI. SUMMARY: Use quote by Theodore Roosevelt in the Lesson Amplification material.

VII. CLOSE IN PRAYER.

136

THE CHURCH

LESSON SIX   STEP ONE

INTRODUCTION:

Why did Jesus Christ found the local church? Through the years the church has been widely criticized and often subject to failure. Many have suggested it is an outmoded institution which Christianity could well do without. When the church is not true to Christ and not fulfilling its mission this is undoubtedly true; but when the church does the task He assigned to it, it is absolutely essential, not only to the growth and progress of Christianity, but to the spiritual welfare of the believer as well. Some reasons why Jesus Christ founded the local church:

1. For the Christian movement to succeed, some form of organization was necessary. If Jesus had left only a loose association of followers, Christianity might well have died out within a few years. Such powerful movements as Communism depend on organized local groups for their success.

2. The church provides a place of fellowship and mutual encouragement for Christians.

3. The church provides a place of instruction—here the doctrines contained in the word of God are explained to us.

4. The church provides a place of worship—here we can join together in worship of the risen Lord.

5. The church provides a place of service—here we can put our talents at His disposal so that we may help others.

I.   BIBLE STUDY:

A. Question 1 — The early Christians (1) studied the Bible, had fellowship with each other, celebrated the communion service and prayed together; (2) witnessed fearlessly; (3) preached Christ in every place possible.

Concerning this early church, which we read about in the Book of Acts and the New Testament Epistles, J. B. Phillips says:

"The great difference between present-day Christianity and that of which we read in these letters is that to us it is primarily a performance, to them it was a real experience. We are apt to reduce the Christian religion to a code, or at best a rule of heart and

137

life. To these men it is quite plainly the invasion of their lives by a new quality of life altogether. They do not hesitate to describe this as Christ 'living in them.' . . .

"Many Christians today talk about the 'difficulties of our times' as though we should have to wait for better ones before the Christian religion can take root. It is heartening to remember that this faith took root and flourished amazingly in conditions that would have killed anything less vital in a matter of weeks. These early Christians were on fire with the conviction that they had become, through Christ, literally sons of God; they were pioneers of a new humanity, founders of a new Kingdom. They still speak to us across the centuries. Perhaps if we believed what they believed, we might achieve what they achieved."

B. Question 2 — Note that the Bible *commands* Christians regularly to assemble for worship and fellowship. "The Christian life is not just our own private affair. If we have been born again into God's family, not only has He become our Father but every other Christian believer in the world . . . has become our brother or sister in Christ . . . Every Christian's place is in a local church . . . sharing in its worship, its fellowship, and its witness"—JOHN R. STOTT.

C. Question 3 — Matthew Henry says about the church as the body of Christ:

"Each (Christian) is a member of the body . . . each stands related to the body as part of it, and all have a common relation to one another, dependence upon one another, and should have mutual care and concern . . . Mutual indifference, and much more contempt, and hatred, and envy, and strife, are very unnatural in Christians. It is like the members of the same body being destitute of all concern for one another, or quarrelling with each other."

D. Question 5 — Ask the class, "What is the significance and importance of baptism to every believer?" As we review the pages of history, we note that every church has maintained the practice of this doctrine. It has taken on various meanings and modes, but the church has recognized that it was one of the specific things the Lord spelled out for His disciples to do. "Go . . ., teaching all nations, baptizing them. . . ." (Matthew 28:19). Baptism was an initiatory rite practiced by the Jews in the time of Jesus to signify that an individual was identifying himself with Judaism as a convert, or with a particular movement within Judaism, such as that led by John the Baptist. The early church took over this rite so that Christians could make a public proclamation of their faith and announce to the world that they had identified themselves with Christ and His cause. *The meaning of baptism. To some, baptism*

138

is a means of grace, and to others, such as the Baptists, it is a symbolic act. To the former, baptism is in varying degrees a special vehicle of grace, a sacrament which truly conveys grace to the participant. To the latter, there is nothing in baptismal service that is not equally present in an ordinary church service"—LINDSELL AND WOODBRIDGE. But to all churches, baptism is essential to an obedient walk with the Lord.

E. Question 6 — Ask the class members to share their understanding of the meaning of the communion service. Point out again that this specifically was given to the disciples to be incorporated into their remembrance of Him. It has taken on various meanings in churches, even as has baptism; but it is important to note again that the participation in the act is essential to the obedient walk of the believer and that every church observes the practice in some form. To some Christians the Lord's Supper conveys grace and provides spiritual food for the believer; to others it is purely symbolic and serves only as a reminder of the broken body and shed blood of the Lord Jesus. But all agree that it brings the believer face to face with the fact of our Lord's death and atoning sacrifice, and that it furnishes the Christian a sacred opportunity to examine his life before partaking of the meal.

"It was appointed to be done *in remembrance of Christ,* to keep fresh in our minds . . . His dying for us, as well as to remember an absent friend, even Christ interceding for us, in virtue of His death, at God's right hand. The best of friends, and the greatest acts of kindness are here to be remembered, with the exercise of suitable affections and graces. The motto of this ordinance, and the very meaning of it, is, 'When you see this, remember me' " — MATTHEW HENRY.

F. Question 7 — One of the basic purposes of the church is to preach the word of God. As a rule, we should not unite with a church which does not preach the word of God. "The preacher must present, not book reviews, not politics, not economics, not current topics of the day, not a philosophy of life denying the Bible and based upon unproven theories of science, but the Word. The preacher as a herald cannot choose his message. He is given a message to proclaim by his Sovereign. If he will not proclaim that, let him step down from his exalted position" — KENNETH WUEST.

G. Question 9 — Five basic points which a Church should believe, among other things, are listed here:

1. The Virgin Birth of Christ—Note:

    a. The miraculous birth of our Lord relates to the authority of the word of God. "If one denies the Bible's teaching on this subject he has rejected the authority of the Book. In such circumstances to speak of the Bible as an adequate and accurate source of spiritual truth is illogical and irrational"— LINDSELL AND WOODBRIDGE.

b. The Virgin Birth raises the question of supernaturalism. "Practically every person who denies the doctrine rejects the supernatural as such. The heart of Christianity is its supernaturalness. A valid test of one's attitude toward the supernatural is his acceptance or rejection of the doctrine of the Virgin Birth"—IBID.

c. The negation of the Virgin Birth is destructive of the whole fabric of the Christian faith. "It leaves us with surmise rather than fact concerning Christ's birth and deprives us of knowledge as to the manner in which He entered the world. It seriously weakens, if it does not destroy, the doctrine of the incarnation (God manifest in the flesh) upon which our confidence rests and without which the Christian faith cannot survive"—IBID.

2. The deity of Jesus Christ—"Everyone should be conscious of the implications of denying the deity of Jesus Christ. Unfortunately some believe that His deity is of little importance and are naive enough to think that the Christian faith is coherent, sufficient, and satisfactory even if Jesus is not God. They would remove the structure of the faith but retain the outward facade. . . . If Jesus is not God, then:

a. "He bore false witness. He was a liar and thus a sinner Himself. . . .

b. "The Bible itself would be an unreliable witness, and it would purport to reveal a system of religion founded on error rather than on truth.

c. "Usually the denial of Christ's deity leads to a denial of the supernatural in general. This, of course, eliminates the Virgin Birth of Christ, His physical resurrection, and His miracles" —IBID.

3. His death—"Man separates himself from God by sin, and death is the natural result. . . . But it was not that way that Jesus became subject to death, since He had no personal sin. In this connection it should be borne in mind that death is not merely the natural consequence of sin, but above all the judicially imposed and inflicted punishment of sin. It is God withdrawing Himself with the blessings of life and happiness from man and

visiting man in wrath. It is from this . . . point of view that the death of Christ must be considered"—LOUIS BERKHOF. When Christ died, God punished Him for our sins. From Christ's death all the blessings of Christianity flow.

4. The resurrection of Christ—When we speak of the resurrection of Christ we mean the coming forth from the grave of body and spirit. This is a most significant belief. The fact of the resurrection is supported by evidence as dependable and conclusive as any act of ancient history. (You may wish to review the material presented concerning the resurrection in this Teacher's Manual by looking at Lesson Four of the Introduction to the Ten Basic Steps, The Uniqueness of Jesus.)

The importance of the resurrection is summarized concisely in the following manner:

"The resurrection of our Lord teaches three important lessons: (1) It showed that His work of atonement was completed and was stamped with the Divine approval; (2) It showed Him to be Lord of all and gave the one sufficient external proof of Christianity; (3) It furnished the ground and pledge of our own resurrection, and thus 'brought life and immortality to light' (2 Tim. 1:10). It must be remembered that the resurrection was the one sign upon which Jesus Himself staked His claims—'the sign of Jonah' (Luke 11:29); and that the resurrection is proof, not simply of God's power, but of Christ's own power: John 10:18—'I have power to lay it down, and I have power to take it again'; 2:19—'Destroy this temple, and in three days I will raise it up' . . . 21—'He spake of the temple of His body' " (Strong, A. H., *Systematic Theology*, p. 131).

5. His Second Coming—"The faith in a second coming of Christ has lost its hold upon many Christians in our day. But it still serves to stimulate and admonish the great body, and we can never dispense with its solemn and mighty influence. Christ comes, it is true, in . . . revivals . . . in Reformation movements and in political upheavals. But these are only precursors of another and literal and final return of Christ, to punish the wicked and to complete the salvation of his people. That day for which all other days are made will be a joyful day for those who have fought a good fight and kept the faith. Let us look for and hasten the coming of the day of God"—A. H. STRONG.

All these teachings are at the heart and core of the Christian faith and the Bible so we should naturally expect every church to believe them. However, we should seek to worship in those churches which affirm the basic and traditional doctrines of the Christian faith as enunciated in the New Testament.

How can I know if a church is true to Christ? Ask yourself these questions:

a. Do the sermons make clear as a rule, that we become a Christian by accepting Christ personally, or do they leave a vague impression that a Christian is just a good moral person?

b. Do the church members seem to be those who have had a true conversion experience, or those who are just coming to church for social reasons?

c. Is the Bible really taught, or does the minister spend most of his time preaching his own opinions, political issues, etc.? Remember, good oratory is no substitute for the clear preaching of God's word!

It is not our responsibility as Christians to condemn and criticize those who disagree with us. Wherever possible, seek to explain in a loving, and diplomatic way the basic Scriptural truths to the pastor and church members who do not already embrace the original teaching of the word of God, and, incidentally in most cases the original teachings of their own denomination. In the event the response is not favorable, you should prayerfully consider the wisdom of identifying yourself by becoming active in a church with which you are more compatible.

H. Question 10 — Note some of those whom God gives to His church to strengthen its ministry: (1) Evangelists—those who present the gospel to the lost. Billy Graham, foreign missionaries, and many laymen effective in winning others to Christ have been given this gift. We are all to witness, and in most cases we should see many come to Christ through our witnessing. But some will be so effective in this area that it seems evident God has given them a special gift. This may be true of you or some of your friends. (2) Pastors and teachers. The original Greek makes clear that these are one and the same. A better translation would be "pastor-teacher," the term "pastor" originally meant "a feeder of sheep." In a figurative sense it came to be applied to Christians who teach and help other Christians. Ministers are, of course, pastors. But many who never enter the ministry also have this gift and are expected to exercise it. "Spiritual gifts are unusual manifestations of God's grace under normal and abnormal forms. The exercise of a spiritual gift implies service in the church. This practical approach is never lost sight of in the New Testament. The New Testament spiritual gifts are often divided into miraculous and non-miraculous; but since some are synonymous with specific duties they should be classified according to their significance for preaching the Word on one hand, and exercising practical ministries on the other"—JAMES G. S. S. THOMSON.

You may notice on your campus that some students seem especially able to teach the Bible and help other Christians grow. They may never go to seminary or into the ministry, but God expects them to exercise this gift. Many gifts given to the church are not listed here—but undoubtedly God has gifted you in some special area. He expects you to develop it and use it for His glory. Some ways in which God can gift us that we can use for Him:

1. Superior intellect—you can use this to gain a deeper understanding of the Scriptures and teach others.

2. Athletic ability—this is a natural gift from God. Any prominence you get from it should be used to the fullest to reach those who might admire your prowess.

3. Outgoing personality and physical attractiveness—You should be much more effective in witnessing than some who are more shy and introverted. You should use this to reach as many for Christ as you can.

4. Leadership and administrative abilities—You should help to organize and oversee some of the Christian activities on your campus, and accept some of the responsibility of the staff workers.

5. Maybe, as you evaluate yourself, you seem very average. Do not be discouraged. You probably have hidden talents which God will develop as you follow His will. You must never forget that many very average people in the Bible accomplished great feats because they trusted in a very great God. Study Hebrews 11.

I. Question 11 — Love is the great proof we are His disciples. "The qualities which should characterize the love we are to manifest toward our fellow-men are beautifully set forth in I Corinthians 13. It is patient and without envy; it is not proud or self-elated; neither does it behave discourteously; it does not cherish evil, but keeps good account of the good; it rejoices not at the downfall of any enemy or competitor, but gladly hails his success; it is hopeful, trustful, and forbearing—for such there is no law, for they need none; they have fulfilled the law"—WILLIAM EVANS.

II. SUMMARY:

Writing for the Ladies' Home Journal, in an article called, "Shall We Do Away with the Church?" President Theodore Roosevelt once said: "In the pioneer days of the West, we found it an unfailing rule that after a community had existed for a certain length of time, either a church was built or else the community began to go downhill.

"I doubt whether the frank protest of nothing but amusement has really brought as much happiness as if it had been alloyed with and supplemented by some minimum meeting of obligation toward others. Therefore, on Sunday go to church. Yes—I know all the excuses: I know that one can worship the Creator and dedicate oneself to good living in a grove of trees or by a running brook or in one's own house just as well as in a church,but I also know that as a matter of cold fact, the average man does not worship or thus dedicate himself. If he stays away from church he does not spend his time in good works or in lofty meditation . . . He may not hear a good sermon at church, but unless he is very unfortunate he will hear a sermon by a good man.

"Besides, even if he does not hear a good sermon, the probabilities are that he will listen to and take part in reading some beautiful passage from the Bible, and if he is not familiar with the Bible, he has suffered a loss which he had better make all possible haste to correct. He will meet and nod to or speak to good, quiet neighbors. If he doesn't think about himself too much, he will benefit himself very much, especially as he begins to think chiefly of others."

SUMMARY LESSON PLAN

THE CHRISTIAN AND THE ABUNDANT LIFE

STEP TWO

OBJECTIVE: To demonstrate that the abundant life is possible for every Christian and to explain the steps which one must take to be assured of the abundant life.

I. OPEN WITH PRAYER: "Lord, we pray for a clear insight into Your plan and purpose for our lives. May we enter into that abundant life which You have promised and planned for us from eternity past."

II. MEMORY VERSE: John 10:10b.

Go around the circle of those present, having each person take a word from "I" to "abundantly" of John 10:10b, explaining what each word means.

III. MOTIVATION:

A. Write your definition of a person who is living an abundant Christian life.

B. Make a list of qualities you feel should be true in your life but are not true at present.

IV. BIBLE STUDY:

Care should be given to cover each of the following points during the time allowed for *one* Bible Study session.

A. What is the nature of a new life in Christ (Lesson 1, A New Creation)?

B. Evaluate your life in relation to the four types of soil (Lesson 2, questions 1-4).

C. What is the secret of the abundant life (Lesson 3)?

D. What is meant by the expression, "the abiding life" (Lesson 4, questions 1-2)?

E. What is the condition of cleansing and forgiveness (Lesson 5, The Results of Sin and Self Will, 1-4)?

F. What is the battle in which we are engaged (Lesson 6, questions 1-2)?

G. What should be our attitude toward circumstances in the Christian life (Lesson 7, questions 2-4)?

V. PARALLEL PASSAGES:

A. II Cor. 5:17—A New Creation.

B. Matt. 13:1-23—Parable of the Sower.

C. Romans 6:4-18—Abundant Life.

D. John 15:1-27—Abiding Life.

E. I John 1:9—Cleansed Life.

F. Eph. 6:10-18—Armor and Warfare.

G. Ex. 14:1-15—Mental Attitude.

VI. SUMMARY:

A careful, prayerful, sincere study of these great truths will, if claimed in faith, change your life so that you will never again be the same. These are the keys which unlock the door to a full and abundant Christian life. A key is no good unless it is used to unlock the resources needed. Search these scriptures diligently and make these great doctrines true in your everyday experience.

VII. CLOSE IN PRAYER: "God, make us willing to take the time to apply these great truths from Your word to our lives. May we enter the abundant life to give glory to You."

(Invite non-Christians to receive Christ, stressing especially His Lordship.)

LESSON PLAN

WHAT IS THE CHRISTIAN LIFE?

LESSON ONE   STEP TWO

OBJECTIVE: To explain to the new Christian the difference between his new life in Christ and his old life, and communicate also how his new life relates to God, to others, and to self.

I.   OPEN WITH PRAYER: "Lord, may we understand what it means to be a new creature in Christ, and may we respond to what we learn today."

II. MEMORY VERSE:

Review memory verse together. Devote five minutes to this, allowing each one in the group to recite audibly. Assign next week's memory verse. *Care should be given to continue to emphasize the importance of memorizing scripture.*

III. MOTIVATION:

Make a list of qualities you would expect in the life of a person who had been made a new creation. (Contrast with your life before you became a Christian or, if you are not a Christian, what would you expect to take place in your life when you accept Christ.)

IV. BIBLE STUDY:

Divide entire Bible study into four groups. Count off in fours as follows:

Group I—A New Creation.

Group II—A New Relationship.

Group III—A New Motivation.

Group IV—A New Relationship to Mankind.

Request each group to discuss and review each verse under its chosen topic. The small groups should then reconvene and summarize their conclusions to the entire group.

147

V.   PARALLEL PASSAGES:

   A. Old Testament provision of a new heart, Ezek. 36:26.

   B. New Testament contrasts between old and new life.

      1. Titus 3:3-4.

      2. Eph. 2:1-13.

      3. Gal. 5:19-23.

VI. SUMMARY:

   A. What is the Christian life?

      1. Begins with new birth (explain the Four Spiritual Laws).

      2. A personal daily relationship with Christ—Christ living in you.

   B. Have you been born spiritually? (Give an invitation.)

   C. What changes have you seen in your life?

   D. What changes do you wish to see in your life?

      1. In relation to your life with Christ?

      2. In relation to your life with others?

      3. In your own personal life?

VII. CLOSE IN PRAYER: Leader should invite non-Christians to pray *silently* a "salvation prayer" and Christians a "new life" prayer.

WHAT IS THE CHRISTIAN LIFE?

LESSON ONE   STEP TWO

INTRODUCTION:

The Christian life is Christ living in you. It actually is Christ living on earth again through your body. He can move, talk, pray and change people's lives through you.

In Step One, we considered the person of Jesus Christ, the Son of God, who, as the revelation of God to men and His sacrifice for our sins, came among men to make it possible for them to be reconciled to God. Let us now consider the Christian way of life; that is, the kind of life which belongs to those who have received Him into their hearts.

I.   A NEW CREATION:

A. What is the nature of a new life in Christ?

1. John 3:3-7. The first consideration in the Christian life is how to experience "Christ living in you." This involves the new birth. Life in the physical realm requires a physical birth.
   At birth there is a time and place, and you receive a name. It is the same in the Christian life. There is a time when you personally receive Jesus Christ, there is a place (which may be church, home, walking under the stars or where you are now) and you receive a name—Christian. There are many genuine Christians who cannot point to the time or place of their conversion who know with certainty that Jesus Christ lives within them.

2. The new birth can be compared to the caterpillar example. "Take for example a caterpillar crawling in the dust, an ugly hairy worm. One day this worm weaves about its body a cocoon. Out of this cocoon there emerges a butterfly. We do not understand fully what has taken place. We only know that where once a worm has crawled in the dust, now a butterfly soars in the heavens. So it is in the life of a Christian. Where once we lived on the lowest level according to our own selfish and thus sinful motives, we now dwell on the highest plane according to the way and will of God."

3. In John 1:13 we read, "It is not by blood (we cannot inherit it), nor by the will of the flesh (we cannot earn the right), nor by the will of man (we cannot be voted into it), but of God!"

B. How can we have Christ living His life through us?

1. "As many as received Him to them (only) God gives the power to become children of God." And so the Christian life can only be lived by first receiving Christ as your own Saviour.

If you have already done so, why not ask Him into your heart and thank Him for so graciously forgiving your sins and becoming your Lord and Saviour.

Look at Romans 10:9-10 (Amplified).

2. This new birth results in an entirely new kind of life. Basically it changes one's perspective, or point of view. One sees things now from God's point of view. It also gives him the power of spiritual life just as in the natural birth he is given the power of natural life. II Cor. 5:17, "If any man be in Christ he is a new creation; old things are passed away, behold all things are become new." If everything is different, and it is when we receive Christ, what are some of the changes?

II. A NEW RELATIONSHIP WITH GOD:

A. What are some of the results of our becoming a Christian?

1. We are newborn children (I Peter 2:2-3).

2. We desire the word.

3. We are members of the family of God (John 1:12). We are told that we have the right (Greek word for power here is "authority") to call ourselves members of His family. We are called "babes" and as such we must immediately receive nourishment. Therefore, as soon as we accept Christ or become by birth a new member of God's family, it is essential that we immediately begin studying the word of God and also begin having fellowship with other members of God's family—in church and in other Christian groups.

4. We are partakers of the divine nature (II Peter 1:4). God imparts His nature to us immediately at birth. The evidence of God's nature is more apparent in some than in others. *If we give Him our all, He can accomplish more quickly that which He wills for us.* This means a total yielding of our lives to God.

B. Who is it that gives us assurance of our relationship with God?

1. God reveals Himself in each life in such a way that each person knows or has the assurance of his salvation. The way He

reveals Himself may be completely different in each case. The important thing is that you *know*.

    2. He sent His Holy Spirit to dwell within us (Gal. 4:6; Romans 8:16).

    3. God gives us assurance through His word (I John 5:11-13).

C. Because of His interest in our lives, can we totally yield our lives to Him without fear?

    1. I Peter 5:7, "Casting the whole of your care—all your anxieties, all your worries, all your concerns, once and for all—on Him; for He cares for you affectionately, and cares about you watchfully" (Amplified Version).

    2. Romans 8:28: So many people console themselves with, "All things work together for good." Note the verse explains, "to those that love God, to them who are called according to His purpose." This is a relationship to be cherished. Spend many wonderful times in prayer with God. Get to know Him above all others.

    3. Write out Hebrews 13:5 (Amplified Version).

    4. Write out I Thess. 5:16-19 (Amplified Version).

III. A NEW MOTIVATION:

A. What is this new motivation?

    1. To live for Christ (II Cor. 5:14-15).

    2. To seek those things which are above (Col. 3:1-3).

    3. Matt. 6:19-34.

    4. Matt. 4:19; John 15:8.

B. From where does this motivation come?

Christ lives in you. He loves, acts, talks through you. Your entire life becomes different because you are no longer living your life but Christ is living it (Galatians 2:20)! His motives are yours. Study the Bible to find how He moved among men, how He had a heart for those around Him. As you "let Jesus live" through you, you will be amazed at your reason for doing things—"for the glory of God."

IV. A NEW RELATIONSHIP TO MANKIND:

A. What is different about our relationship to others?

1. I John 1:3-4: "That which we have seen and heard . . ."

2. Through the Christians, Christ comforts lonely hearts, instructs and teaches, seeks and saves the lost, and can again walk among men and tell them of His love and sacrifice for their sin. He chooses to do this through *you*. God loves the world, not just a little section where you are now. Your concern becomes the world. You want others to know the Lord as you do because Jesus Christ died for the world. Your relationship now to man is world-wide and your responsibility is to let Jesus Christ live in you to reconcile the world unto Him.

V. SUMMARY:

The Christian life begins with a new birth. It is a personal daily relationship with Christ. Have you been born spiritually? What changes have you seen in your life? What changes do you wish to see in your life in regard to Christ, in regard to others, in your personal life?

The Christian life is simply—Christ living in you! "LET JESUS LIVE TODAY."

Leader should read the following prayers slowly to allow those representing each group to pray a similar prayer quietly:

Salvation: "Lord Jesus, come into my life, forgive my sin and change my life. Give me a new life—Your life. I exchange my life for Your life, Lord Jesus.

New Life: "Thank You, Lord, for giving me a new life. May I be more conscious of Your presence in my life and may others see the change in my life and come to know You."

After a period of silence the leader should close with a brief appropriate prayer.

SUPPLEMENTARY READING

God's Best Secrets—Andrew Murray.

Victory in Christ—Charles G. Trumbull.

LESSON PLAN

AN APPRAISAL OF YOUR OWN SPIRITUAL LIFE

LESSON TWO   STEP TWO

OBJECTIVE: To see ourselves as God sees us and to apply the things
which we learn from this lesson to our personal lives.

I. OPEN WITH PRAYER: "Lord, make us willing to respond positively to what You show us today."

II. MEMORY VERSE:

Give and check memory verse with the person on your left.

III. MOTIVATION:

Have students take out a piece of paper and number A to H. Give
orally this True-False test.

A. All good soil produces the same amount of fruit.   F

B. Stony ground refers to an unreceptive heart.   F

C. Thorny ground includes the deceitfulness of riches.   T

D. Every Christian should be fruitful.   T

E. This parable refers to people not in college.   F

F. Patience comes through the trying of our faith.   T

G. God's word offers the solution to every "care" in college. T

H. My life would be different if I learned God's solutions
and applied them.   T

Read correct answers and let each person correct his own paper. Stress
the need to know these truths.

IV. BIBLE STUDY: Read the parable of the sower.

A. Answer questions 1 and 2 of Lesson Two.

B. What three things will keep you from being productive for God?

1. Unreceptive heart—wayside soil.

2. Affliction and persecution—stony soil.

3. Cares of the world, deceitfulness of riches, lusts—thorny soil.

153

C. Define affliction and persecution in the college Christian's life.

    1. Fact of persecution, I Thess. 3:3; I Pet. 2:21.

    2. Sources of persecution, I John 3:13; Rev. 2:10.

D. What are some cares of the world that you experience in college?

E. What does the Bible refer to as lust?

F. What is the deceitfulness of riches? (False sense of security.)

G. Answer questions 5 through 8 of Lesson Two.

V. PARALLEL PASSAGES:

    A. Receptive heart—Heb. 3:15—wayside soil.

    B. Hear to believe—Rom. 10:17—wayside soil.

    C. Ridicule from world—John 15:18-21—stony soil.

    D. Persecution from Satan—Rev. 2:10—stony soil.

    E. Strife from within—Rom. 7:15-25—stony soil.

    F. Salvation—I Cor. 10:13; Rom. 8:28; Prov. 29:25—stony soil.

    G. Cares—I Pet. 5:7—solution to thorny soil.

    H. Material things—Matt. 6:19-21—solution to thorny soil.

    I. Lust—I John 2:15-17; I Cor. 6:18—solution to thorny soil.

VI. SUMMARY:

Only good soil brings forth fruit: some thirty-fold, some sixty, some one hundred. This is referred to in John 15 as fruit, more fruit, much fruit. THE CHOICE LIES IN YOUR HANDS (read choices).

VII. CLOSE IN PRAYER: "Father, give us a true sense of values. May we say, as did Joshua, 'As for me I will serve the Lord.' Also with Paul, 'Lord, what wilt Thou have me to do?'"

AN APPRAISAL OF YOUR OWN SPIRITUAL LIFE

LESSON TWO   STEP ONE

INTRODUCTION:

This lesson is a very personal one in that God and you are the only ones that know your heart. As we study this lesson let it be as if you alone were with Christ that day He gave this parable. Ask Him to show you on which ground you stand and be willing to take action on that which He reveals to you.

Choose and read one of the references of the parable of the sower: Matt. 13:1-23; Mark 4:3-20; Luke 8:4-15.

I. TYPES OF SOIL:

A. What is meant by seed sown in "wayside soil?"

Wayside soil: a life on which the word of God has fallen but where Satan by creating a hard heart or a lack of receptiveness has snatched away the seed.

B. Description of seed sown in stony (rocky) soil.

Those who, when they have heard the word, immediately receive it with gladness and follow Christ for a time, but when difficulty or persecution arises are not rooted enough to stand.

1. Ridicule from the world, John 15:18-21.

2. Persecution from Satan, Rev. 2:10.

3. Strife from within, Romans 7:15-25.

C. Seed sown on thorny soil.

"And the cares of this world, and the deceitfulness of riches, and the lusts of other things entering in, choke the Word, and it becometh unfruitful," Mark 4:19.

1. Cares: any burden, problem, or decision that is carried by self instead of casting it on the Lord.
Example: grades, boyfriend or girlfriend, athletics, finances, future, etc.

2. Deceitfulness of riches: allowing things to give you a false sense of security—believing that this is what brings security and happiness.

Example: tell of rich, successful men who end their lives in suicide.

3. Lusts: great, driving desires. Apply to college life: clothes, cars, girls, grades, etc.

D. Good ground:

"And these are they which are sown on good ground; such as hear the word, and receive it, and bring forth fruit, some thirtyfold, some sixty, and some an hundred," Mark 4:20.

II. SOLUTION IN MAKING SOIL PRODUCTIVE:

A. Wayside Soil.

1. Must have a receptive heart when we hear the word of God. Heb. 3:15, "While it is said, Today if ye will hear His voice, harden not your hearts, as in the provocation."

2. Must hear the word to have faith in it or to believe it. Romans 10:17, "So then faith cometh by hearing, and hearing by the word of God."

B. Stony Ground.

1. We are promised that persecution will come. I Thess. 3:3, "That no man should be moved by these afflictions: for yourselves know that we are appointed thereunto." I Peter 2:21, "For even hereunto were ye called, because Christ also suffered for us, leaving us an example, that ye should follow his steps."

2. God has not promised us anything too great to bear, I Cor. 10:13.

3. "All things work together for good to them that love God, to them who are the called according to His purpose," Rom. 8:28.

4. "The fear of man bringeth a snare: but whoso putteth his trust in the Lord shall be safe," Proverbs 29:25.

C. Thorny Ground.

1. Cares: "Casting the whole of your care—all your anxieties, all your worries, all your concerns, once and for all—on Him; for He cares for you affectionately,and cares about you watchfully," I Peter 5:7 (Amplified). Also see Psalm 37:1-7.

2. Deceitfulness of riches: "Lay not up for yourselves treasures

upon earth, where moth and rust doth corrupt, and where thieves break through and steal. But lay up for yourselves treasures in heaven, where neither moth nor rust doth corrupt, and where thieves do not break through nor steal. For where your treasure is, there will your heart be also,"Matt. 6:19-21.

3. Lusts: "Love not the world, neither the things that are in the world. If any man love the world the love of the Father is not in him. For all that is in the world, the lust of the flesh, and the lust of the eyes, and the pride of life, is not of the Father, but is of the world. And the world passeth away, and the lust thereof; but he that doeth the will of God abideth forever,"I John 2:15-17. I Cor. 6:18, "Flee fornication. Every sin that a man doeth is without the body; but he that committeth fornication sinneth against his own body."

4. Determine to be a single-minded man. James 1:8, "A double-minded man is unstable in all his ways." James 4:8, "Draw night to God, and He will draw night to you. Cleanse your hands, ye sinners; and purify your hearts, ye double minded."

D. Good Ground.

1. To live the victorious life is to live on "good ground" and to ABIDE in Christ. John 15:5, "I am the vine, ye are the branches. He that abideth in me, and I in him, the same bringeth forth much fruit: for without me ye can do nothing." (Scofield Note: "To abide in Christ is, on the one hand, to have no known sin unjudged and unconfessed, no interest into which He is not brought, no life which he cannot share. On the other hand the abiding one takes all burdens to Him, and draws all wisdom, life and strength from Him. It is not unceasing consciousness of these things and of Him, but that nothing is allowed in the life which separates from Him.)

2. As you will notice, this includes the solution to the problems of the other types of ground. Example: sin confessed—lust; no life which He cannot share—social relationships; takes all burdens to Him; draws all wisdom, strength and life from Him.

III. RESULT OF DWELLING IN GOOD SOIL:

A. Fruit of the Spirit.

Gal. 5:22-23, "But the fruit of the (Holy) Spirit, (the work which His presence within accomplishes) is love, joy (gladness), peace, patience (an even temper, forbearance), kindness, goodness (benevolence), faithfulness; (meekness, humility) gentleness, self-control (self-restraint, continence). Against such things there is no law (that can bring a charge)" (Amplified).

B. Fruitful.

Faith, virtue, knowledge, self-control, patience, godliness, brotherly love, divine love.

C. Fruit.

New Christians.

IV. SUMMARY:

Only good soil brings forth fruit: some thirty-fold, some sixty, some one hundred. This is referred to in John 15 as fruit, more fruit, much fruit. THE CHOICE LIES IN YOUR HANDS.

On the one hand	*On the other hand*
1. Neglect the Word	1. Hear the Word
2. Fear of man	2. Trust the Lord
3. Satan's snares	3. God's victory
4. Flesh pleased	4. Spirit fed
5. Burdened	5. Carefree
6. Materialistic	6. Spiritual
7. Worldly	7. Heavenly
8. Fruitless	8. Fruitful

V. PRAYER: "Father, give us a true sense of values. May we say, as did Joshua, 'As for ME I will serve the Lord'."

LESSON PLAN

ABUNDANT LIVING

LESSON THREE   STEP TWO

OBJECTIVE: To show that the abundant life is possible in practical, everyday life and to give steps to be taken which will result in
the abundant life.

I.   OPEN WITH PRAYER: "Lord, help us to see that the abundant
life is a life of faith in what Jesus Christ
has accomplished and can accomplish in
our lives."

II. MEMORY VERSE: John 10:10b.

Go around circle having each person take a word from the verse
beginning with "I" to "abundantly," explaining what each word means.

III. MOTIVATION:

A. Turn to Rom. 7:14-24 and read aloud stressing the personal pro-
nouns (I, me, my, etc.).

B. Now turn to Rom. 8:1-17 and read aloud stressing God, Spirit,
Son, Christ, etc.

C. Ask, "What do you think makes the difference in the life in Rom.
7 (defeat) and Rom. 8 (victory)?"

D. Ask, "How many of you are living in Rom. 8?"

E. Perhaps you are like the poor rancher who for years lived on land
which was rich in oil—but he didn't know it. Today you can know
how to draw upon your riches in Christ.

IV. BIBLE STUDY:

A. Go over "Directory of Terms" in Step Two, Lesson Three.

B. Do questions 1-4 in section on Rom. 6:1-16.

C. Now, how can we be sure God will take our lives and use them
as instruments of righteousness? Do questions 1-6 in section on
Psalms 37:1-7, 34.

V. PARALLEL PASSAGES:

A. Know—Col. 3:1-4.

B. Reckon—Col. 2:6.

C. Yield—Rom. 12:1-2.

D. Obey—Phil. 2:13.

E. Fret not—I Pet. 5:7.

F. Trust—Rom. 8:28, 32; II Cor. 1:8-10.

G. Delight—Psa. 16:11.

H. Commit—Prov. 16:3.

I. Rest—Matt. 11:28.

J. Wait—Isa. 30:18.

VI. SUMMARY:

Certain facts must be learned to live the abundant life. This should make us desire to read the Bible to find out how to solve our problems and answer our questions. Learn these facts and you will be one to find victory in the abundant life by applying them to your experience.

VII. CLOSE IN PRAYER: "Father, we rest in the fact of what You have done for us. Now we enter *by faith* into the abundant life which You have for us. We are trusting Your faithfulness alone, not ours."

160

ABUNDANT LIVING

LESSON THREE   **STEP TWO**

INTRODUCTION:

Jesus Christ has planned for each one who has trusted Him as Saviour to live an abundant, victorious life. Many Christians are defeated today, and do not know the means of appropriating the abundant life. This lesson seeks to show that the answer is Jesus Christ, Himself, living the life through each Christian. He has provided the means to victory and it is ours to claim in our daily walk with Him. In the last lesson (2) we looked at our own lives in contrast to what good soil produces and became aware of the great need which only He can supply.

I. THE DOCTRINE UNDERLYING THE ABUNDANT LIFE (Romans 6):

A. Directory of terms.

1. Know—to be fully assured of the facts (head-knowledge).

2. Reckon—count upon it in spite of feelings (will).

3. Yield—give up, to surrender, submit (physical members).

4. Obey—"your wish is my command" (emotion) Rom. 6:16—obey from the heart.

B. Do you know what happened to you when you became a Christian?

1. At the moment you became a Christian, God not only forgave all your sins, but also gave you all you need to live a victorious Christian life. *God does not need to do something new so you may live a victorious Christian life. He has already done all that needs to be done through the death and resurrection of Christ. You need only to take hold of this provision by faith, just as you took hold of forgiveness of sins by faith.* Rom. 6:3 says all who have received Jesus Christ were "baptized into His death." This does not refer primarily to water baptism. The word means primarily to dip, immerse or sink. Here it stresses that we were placed into Christ. We thus became part of Him, indissolubly joined to Him. Example: in John 15:1-6 Jesus pictures this union with Him as being like the union of a vine and its branches. Example: In I Corinthians 12 Paul pictures it as being like the union of a body with its members.

We have become, in the eyes of God, spiritually united to Jesus

161

Christ. Since this is true, what does it mean? It means that when Christ died, we took part in His death. In His death, He paid the penalty for sin and satisfied all of God's demands. Sin has no claim on Him whatsover. Since we were in Him, this now becomes true of us. He paid for our sins on the cross and sin now can make no demands on us. We are free from it just as Christ is free from it. "Our old self was crucified with Him . . . so that we should no longer be in bondage to sin" (Romans 6:6).

2. Since Christ paid for sin and rose from the dead to live in a resurrected life, this is true of all who are in Him. We have risen and can now live a resurrected life, a life of victory over sin. "For if we have become united with Him in the likeness of His death, we shall be also in the likeness of His resurrection" (Rom. 6:5). Thus all who are in Christ should live the life of Christ; that is, a life which overcomes sin. Christ has paid for your sins; you are free from them. You can live in victory over them through His power. Know these facts from God's Word!

C. What must you do in light of these facts?

1. *Reckon yourself to be dead to sin.* Count upon the fact that you are dead to sin and its control. But you say, I do not *feel* dead to sin. Sin seems as strong as ever in me. Paul does not say *feel,* he says *reckon.* Believe that you are dead to sin, count upon it in spite of feelings because *you actually are!* If you never count on it you are still dead to sin. Example: You are just like a man who has a bank account of thousands of dollars and never uses it. The money is really his even if he never uses it.

Victory is not fighting down your wrong desires. It is not concealing your wrong feelings. That is the counterfeit. Victorious living, the life of freedom from the power of sin is a gift of God. "But thanks be unto God which giveth us the victory through our Lord Jesus Christ." Acknowledge God's gift of victory, of being dead to sin, by faith, as you did His gift of salvation. Thank Him.

2. *Reckon yourself to be alive to Jesus Christ.* A dead man is no good to anyone. Count upon the fact that you are now alive to Jesus Christ.

Example: When our Lord was in Nazareth He could do "not many mighty works there because of"—their inactivity? No, *"because of their unbelief."*

Christ's power is not futile without our effort, but is made futile by our effort. To attempt to share by our effort in what only grace can do is to defeat grace. Acknowledge the fact that you are alive to Christ and then do not fool yourself into thinking you must help Him accomplish His will in your life in this life of victory. Believe God for the life of victory, of being alive to Him moment by moment.

D. To whom should you yield yourself as a Christian?

1. The obvious answer is to yield yourself to God. But have you ever considered why He asks for your "members," that is, your physical body? In Rom. 12:1-2 we find the same exhortation from Paul. *The Lord Jesus needs a body prepared for Him now, just as He did while He was on earth.* You and I are the only bodies He can possess. Gal. 2:20 becomes true in your life, "I am crucified with Christ, nevertheless I live, yet not I, but CHRIST . . ." By Christ taking your body and living through you, victory is not a problem because Christ conquered sin. As you yield your members of righteousness unto God, Christ will live through you and your life will be an abundant life.

2. The only thing that keeps the Lord from operating in your life at 100% potential is you. The Lord does not want you to try to live the Christian life. He wants to live the Christian life through and for you.

Example: When you pray, "Lord, help me," you are saying, "Lord, I can do most of this by myself, I only need you to boost me over the hump." Whatever percentage of you there is, by that much the Lord is deficient.

Example: If there is 30% of you, that limits the Lord by 30%.

E. What determines a man's allegiance?

1. Whomever you choose to obey, his servant you are. Here we need a proper perspective on life. Do not forfeit the lasting for the immediate pleasure which passes so quickly. Sit down and count the cost! The Bible says, "As a man soweth, that shall he also reap."

2. There are two powers in the world: God and Satan. *Many times we fool ourselves into thinking we are our own rulers when actually we are controlled by Satan.* Satan blinds our eyes to the truth, as he has been doing since the creation, and we are not smart enough to recognize him.

3. We are to obey God from the heart. You may say, "But my heart is deceitful." Yes, but when you yield yourself unto God, He says He will "give you a new heart which will cause you to walk in my statutes" (Ezek. 36:26). Obeying God will become the natural thing, the most blessed experience. This is the abundant life, the life for which you were created; victory over sin! If you do these things you will find that "sin shall not have dominion over you" (Rom. 6:14).

II. THE PRACTICE OF ABUNDANT LIVING (Psalm 37):

A. What is God's remedy for worry?

1. *Fret not!* God wants us to trust Him in all things and be "anxious for nothing." Every time we worry we are showing the Lord that we do not really believe that "all things do work together for good to them that love Him and are called according to His purpose." The saying goes, "why pray when you can worry." This is very true in many lives but it is not pleasing to God.

2. "In everything give thanks, for this is the will of God in Christ Jesus." Try thanking the Lord instead of worrying. Your whole attitude will be changed.

B. What is to be our attitude toward the Lord?

1. *Trust!* What does it mean to trust? The Amplified New Testament defines it as, "confidence in His power, wisdom, and goodness." If you have confidence in God you know that His way is best and that He is in control of your life, so why not trust?

2. *In the Lord!* It is one thing to trust someone who is not trustworthy and quite another thing to trust a trustworthy God who has never, no never, no never ever failed or let one of His children down. We can trust because of the One in whom we trust (Heb. 13:5).

C. What must we do to receive the desires of our hearts?

1. *Delight yourself in the Lord!* Most Christians think if they just serve God they'll get all they want. But this verse and all the rest of the scripture has first things first. First, delight in the Lord, then He will give you the desires of your heart.

2. Remember you cannot fool God. You may fool others, but "God looks upon the heart." He knows whether you are really "delighting" yourself in Him for Himself, or for what you can get from Him.

3. This goes back to "obeying from the heart." God makes it possible when you yield yourself to Him to delight yourself in Him—making His every wish your command.

D. What should we do with our future, before we make any plans?

1. *Commit our way to Him!* Jesus Christ came to do the Father's will. When we let Jesus Christ live in and through us, He does His will in and through us. God is glorified in us. This is the greatest privilege, to let God Himself show us His plan for our lives and then see Christ fulfill it in and through us.

2. There is no frustration as to our future because God, who knows the beginning from the end, knows what is the very best for us (Isa. 55:8-9).

E. What are we admonished to do in light of our circumstances?

1. *Rest in the Lord!* Many times in our lives we come to the point where we do not know what God's will is in a certain matter. What do we do then? *Rest in Him.* Take advantage of the time of indecision for being *with Him.* Learn of His ways. Memorize His promises on guidance. Do not waste this precious time when you could be learning so much from Him. Leave the decision or situation in His hands. He will work it out and will always tell you the answer in time to do what He wants you to do (Heb. 2:3).

2. *Wait patiently for Him!* "Be anxious for nothing, but in everything by prayer and supplication, with thanksgiving let your requests be made known unto God" (Phil. 4:6). *Lack of patience is lack of trust and God will often not let you know until you trust His judgment of time as well as will.*

III. SUMMARY:

How precious these truths are which we have considered. God does not call us to a life of victory and abundance and then leave us to find our own victory. *He has provided every means in His Son Jesus Christ. All that we need is in Him.* We have considered the means of appropriating all which we need in our everyday lives and find that all is in Him. KNOW what He has done; RECKON upon His victory; YIELD yourself to Him that He might live through you; OBEY from your hearts as He has given you a new heart which will keep His statutes. FRET NOT because He is in control; TRUST Him because He is trustworthy; DELIGHT yourself in Him, and He will give you the desires of your heart; COMMIT your way to Him as He knows the best plan possible for your life; REST and WAIT for Him, enjoying His presence as He reveals and brings to pass His will in your life.

IV. CLOSE IN PRAYER:
"Father, we rest in the fact of what You have done for us in and through the Lord Jesus Christ. Now we enter *by faith* into the abundant life which You have provided for us in Him. We are trusting in Him and in His faithfulness alone, not ours."

SUPPLEMENTARY READING

Victory in Christ—Charles G. Trumbull

Christ, Our Life—Major Thomas

Victorious Living—Ethel Wilcox

THE ABIDING LIFE

LESSON FOUR   STEP TWO

OBJECTIVE: To understand the principles of abiding life and how we can abide in Christ.

I.   OPEN WITH PRAYER: "Dear Lord, how we long to be conscious of Your presence with us constantly! Teach us today the true meaning of abiding in Christ and the results of such a life."

II. MEMORY VERSE: John 15:7, 16. Share verses with person on your left.

III. MOTIVATION:

A. Have you ever wondered why some Christians are not happy? Perhaps you have wondered about your own life, why are there times when the Lord seems so far away?

B. There are many keys in scripture which unlock great experiences. Today we shall discuss the key which unlocks real joy, joy which remains and which is full.

IV. BIBLE STUDY:

A. Read Scofield's definition of abiding: "To abide in Christ is, on the one hand, to have no known sin unjudged and unconfessed, no interest into which He is not brought, no life which He cannot share. On the other hand, the abiding one takes all burdens to Him, and draws all wisdom, life and strength from Him."

B. Assign each person one question from the lesson.

C. As they give the answer have them also give one result of abiding in Christ (fruit, answered prayer, Father glorified, disciples, love, joy, friends, persecution, Holy Spirit's presence).

D. Have them underline the word "abide" in its various forms in their Bible (John 15).

V. PARALLEL PASSAGES:

A. Fruit—Matt. 13:23.

B. Strength—Psa. 71:16.

C. Life—Phil. 1:21.

D. Wisdom—James 1:5.

E. Answered prayer—Rom. 8:26-27; John 14:13.

F. Faith—Heb. 11:6.

G. Fellowship—I John 1:9; James 4:8.

H. Joy—I Pet. 1:8.

VI. SUMMARY:

It takes time to grow into Jesus the Vine; do not expect to abide in Him unless you will give Him that time. You need time day by day with Jesus—to put yourself into living contact with the living Jesus. The wholehearted surrender to abide in Him alone brings the joy unspeakable and full of glory.

VII. CLOSE IN PRAYER: "Oh Father, let each one of us who has begun to taste the sweetness of this life yield ourselves wholly to be a witness to the grace and power of our Lord to keep us united with Himself, and seek to win others to follow Him wholly."

THE ABIDING LIFE

LESSON FOUR   STEP TWO

INTRODUCTION:

The abiding life is one of the most significant phases of the Christian life. To have real abiding joy we must learn to abide in Christ constantly. Many people never find the secret to a joyous life; consequently they feel the Lord has let them down. The Christian who is not enjoying his Christian experience should be taught the truth of God's word, "These things have I spoken unto you that My *joy* might remain in you, and that your *joy* might be full." The abiding life brings lasting joy. Abiding in Christ also makes our lives fruitful; our prayers are answered. We are obedient to Him because He lives in and through us.

In our last lesson we considered the facts concerned with the abundant life, the things we need to know for a life of victory. Now we will consider how to continue in the victorious, abundant life—abiding in Him.

I.   WHAT IS MEANT BY THE EXPRESSION, "THE ABIDING LIFE?"

   A. Defining Scofield's definition of "Abiding in Christ."

      1. "No known sin unjudged or unconfessed"—to have all your sin forgiven by accepting the Lord Jesus Christ as your personal Saviour. No one can abide in Christ until he has been forgiven his sin and received the righteousness of God. Then as a believer he must confess his sin and claim the forgiveness of God through the blood of Christ. Do you know of any sin unconfessed (unforgiven) by Christ? Confess it now if you desire to enter into the abiding life of Christ.

      2. "No interest into which He is not brought"—includes every activity in which you participate. Are there any activities in your life which would prevent Christ from living His life through you? He is the sinless Saviour and limits Himself to doing only the will of God. Can He live His life in every activity of yours? If not, confess this to Him now and allow Him to have absolute sovereign control of your life. You will never abide in Christ as long as there is an activity or interest in your life which hinders Jesus Christ from living His life through you.

      3. "No life which He cannot share"—includes any relationship

which Christ Himself does not have. In other words, joining yourself to someone who is not abiding in Christ is making Christ be joined to one with whom He cannot have fellowship. "Can two walk together unless they be agreed " (Amos 3:3)? You are united to Christ. If you are joined to someone who is not in fellowship with the Saviour, He cannot live His life through you because you have cut off the source of power by sin (disobedience). He has told us not to be united with unrighteousness (II Cor. 6:14-18). In order for you to have fellowship with the Lord, *every* relationship you have must be shared by Him. Is this true in your life? If not, you will never "abide in Christ" until you "come out from among them and be ye separate." (We must follow the example of our Saviour who is in the world but not *of* the world. Be a witness to the non-Christian world but avoid entangling alliances.)

4. "The abiding one takes all burdens to Him"—he does not carry even his burdens for himself. Jesus Christ lives completely in and through him, taking all responsibility on Himself. Next time you find yourself carrying your own burdens, just remind yourself that you are not abiding in Christ. You see, He wants to live His life through you and He cannot as long as you are doing anything—even carrying your burdens. Give them to Him, now.

5. "Draws all wisdom, life, and strength from Him"—receiving all the power to live the Christian life from Him. Have you let Him be wise through you? Have you let Him teach you from His word? If you are gaining your wisdom from anyone else but Him, you are not abiding in Christ. Your life comes from God; your life is His. Let Him live! Your whole life will be different as you yield every moment to Him to live through you. The times when you live your own life, you are not abiding in Him. Let Jesus live now! And now, a precious lesson to learn—that even your strength comes from Him. The times when you feel you cannot go on, He says, "Let me be your strength." Will you let Him? "My strength is made perfect in weakness" (II Cor. 12:9).

B. What is the parallel of the "Vine and the Branches" to the Christian Life?

1. Jesus Christ is the vine; we, as Christians, the branches.

2. When we abide in the vine, we bear fruit. A branch never worries about fruit bearing. The important thing is that the branch is in the vine. The only thing that can keep this branch from bearing fruit is an obstruction that keeps the sap from flowing through the branch.

169

3. The branch has to be pruned that it may bring forth more fruit. Sin obstructs the flow of life through us from the Lord Jesus. God has to prune our lives so as to keep them free from obstruction.

4. The branch does nothing of its own will, but only what the vine does through it. We as Christians cannot produce in our own strength, but only as we let the life of the vine accomplish His purpose through us.

II. WHAT ARE THE RESULTS OF ABIDING IN CHRIST?

A. Answered prayer.

1. We must abide in Christ to have our prayers answered, as this is how we know the Father's will. Also, we must be in the place of answered prayer—abiding in Christ—to receive the answers (John 15:7).

2. His words must abide in us so that we might know what is in accordance with His will when we pray. He cannot answer any prayer which is contrary to His word.

B. Glorify God.

1. God's word states that He is glorified by our bearing much fruit, which can only be accomplished by our abiding in Him.

2. Andrew Murray says, "The most heavily laden branches bow the lowest."

C. Become His disciples.

1. By our bearing much fruit we prove ourselves to be disciples of Jesus Christ (John 15:8). Every time Jesus Christ said, "follow Me," it was in connection with the souls of men. We fool ourselves when we call ourselves disciples of Jesus Christ when there is no fruit in our lives.

2. Jesus Christ's command to Peter was, "Follow Me, and I will make you to become fishers of men" (Matt. 4:19).

D. Continue in His love.

1. "As the Father hath loved Me"—What a love! It is an eternal love. It is with this infinite love that He invites you to abide in Him. "I have loved you with an everlasting love." It is a perfect love. It gives all, and holds nothing back. When it was needed, He sacrificed His throne and crown for you. He did not count

Heaven a thing to be grasped at, but left all to come and die for you—what love! It is an unchangeable love. "Jesus Christ is the same yesterday, today, and forever" (Heb. 13:8).

2. "Continue ye in My love"—It is faith in His love which will enable us to abide in His love. Let His love permeate your being. It is by abiding in His love that we learn to trust Him in all our circumstances. Meditate upon His love and care for you as an individual.

E. Joy is full.

1. A life of exquisite and overflowing happiness results from abiding in Christ. As Christ gets more complete possession of a soul, that soul enters into the joy of its Lord.

2. Abiding in Christ brings joy because the presence of Jesus, distinctly manifested, cannot but give joy. Why are not most Christians joyful? Because they are not abiding. Those who yield themselves unreservedly to abide in Christ have a bright and blessed life; their faith comes true—the joy of the Lord is theirs.

F. Fruitful lives.

1. The great blessing of offering to others that which will bless and transform their lives becomes the portion of the abiding one. We need to have only one care: to abide closely, fully, wholly. God will give the fruit.

   Example: branches do not struggle to bear fruit. They just let the life of the vine flow through them and fruit is inevitable. Many Christians worry and struggle to bear fruit. *But the responsibility of the branch is to ABIDE in the Vine.*

2. As you are more closely united to Him, the passion for souls which urged Him to Calvary begins to breathe within you, and you are ready to follow His footsteps, to forsake the heaven of your own happiness, and devote your life to win the souls Christ has taught you to love, and for whom He died.

3. Two lessons to learn: If we are abiding in Christ, let us work (in His power), and if we are working, let us abide in Him.

G. Persecution.

1. Right along with all the blessings received from abiding in Christ is another blessing in disguise, persecution. *Outward pressures only crush us closer to the heart of God if we are abiding in Him.*

2. "They which live godly in Christ Jesus shall suffer persecution" (II Tim. 3:12). This is a promise and we should thank the Lord for being able to suffer with Him. Don't look for trouble, but if it comes accept it as from the Father's hand. Rest in the promise of Romans 8:28 and practice I Thess. 5:18.

III. SUMMARY:

It takes time to grow into Jesus the Vine. Do not expect to abide in Him unless you give Him that time. You need day by day with Jesus—to put yourself into living contact with the living Jesus. The wholehearted surrender to abide in Him alone brings the "joy unspeakable and full of glory." Learn to abide in Him by being with Him. Fill your heart with His word, and pray at every spare moment acknowledging His presence with and in you. Confide in Him, live, and dwell in Him. Rely only upon Him in all circumstances of your life. Learn the secret of the abiding life, then share it with others that all Christians may know the joy of the Christian life and not live a frustrated, defeated existence.

And now, little children, ABIDE IN CHRIST,
that you may not be ashamed at His coming. (cf. I John 2:28)

IV. CLOSE IN PRAYER:

Give opportunity for those who have never trusted Christ to pray, placing their faith in Him to come into their lives and forgive their sin, and live through them from this moment on.

For Christians:

"Oh, let each of us who has begun to taste the sweetness of this life yield ourselves wholly to be a witness to the grace and power of our Lord to keep us united with Himself, and seek to win others to follow Him wholly."

LESSON PLAN

THE CLEANSED LIFE

LESSON FIVE   STEP TWO

OBJECTIVE: To teach the reality of moment by moment cleansing from sin (forgiveness) through immediate confession.

I.   OPEN WITH PRAYER: "Lord, teach us how to abide moment by moment in Your presence, we pray."

II. MEMORY VERSE: I John 1:9. Have each person take one word of the verse and explain. (Example, if, we, confess, etc.)

III. MOTIVATION:

   A. Some of the benefits of fellowship with God are pardon, purpose, peace, joy, power, fruitfulness, etc.

   B. Some of the penalties of sin in the life are separation from God, frustration, insecurity, no power, no joy, no peace, no fruit.

   C. The value of constant cleansing rests in fellowship with Christ and Christians, according to I John 1:5-10.

IV. BIBLE STUDY:

   A. Do the first seven questions, having student define key word in answer to question.
      Example: 1. Unstable.

              2. Result.

              3. Impure heart.

              4. Condition (confess).

              5. Acknowledged.

              6. Forsaketh.

   B. Do the first seven questions, assigning each to different individuals. Have all write out their own answer to question 2, under LIVING IN FELLOWSHIP.

V. PARALLEL PASSAGES:

A. James 1:14-15—Form in which sin begins.

B. I Cor. 10:13—No excuse for succumbing.

C. Psa. 24:3-4—Must be cleansed to glorify God.

D. Isa. 53:5—Price paid for forgiveness of sin.

E. Gal. 6:7-8—Future result of sin in life now.

F. Psa. 32:1-5—Example of David in sin.

VI. SUMMARY:

Confession of sin means agreeing with God concerning your sin, recognizing His opinion of the sin. Confession suggests a willingness to repent, to turn from going your way to going God's way. You name the sin to God, and you want it dealt with now. As you continue to claim I John 1:9, you are going to do one of two things. Either you will stop that sin, or you will stop praying.

VII. CLOSE IN PRAYER: "Lord, teach us, because of the price You paid on Calvary that we can have forgiveness moment by moment and abide in You."

THE CLEANSED LIFE

LESSON FIVE   STEP TWO

INTRODUCTION:

The Christian life on earth is a victorious life, but we are not perfect. When we became Christians, God united us with Christ, made us new creatures, gave us His Holy Spirit, but He also left us with the same sin nature we had before we accepted Christ. When Christ comes again we will receive a new body and at last lose our sin nature, but until then it will always be with us. I John 1:8 says, "If we say that we have no sin, we deceive ourselves, and the truth is not in us." Why has God not taken it away? II Cor. 4:7 tells us, "We have this treasure in earthen vessels, that the excellency of the power may be of God, and not of us." God has left us with these "earthen vessels" for a short while that we might live and walk by faith and demonstrate His power. It would be nothing for Him to use strong, well-equipped vessels to do great tasks. But to use weak, sinful vessels like us to accomplish great works is more to His glory, and the "excellency of the power is of Him and not of us." We often yearn for spiritual power and do not have it because of impure motives, double motives or unconfessed sin. God does not fill a dirty vessel with His power. We will consider how to keep our lives cleansed and filled with His power.

In our last lesson we covered another aspect of the victorious life. In this lesson we consider the importance of the cleansed life; how to receive forgiveness when we allow our old sin nature to rule in our lives and thus experience spiritual defeat.

I. LIVING "OUT OF FELLOWSHIP" WITH GOD:

    A. What type of man is unstable in all his ways?

        1. Instability is a result of being double-minded. A person who is trying to serve two gods, who sits on the fence, and who compromises to fit each situation in which he finds himself, is always unstable.

        2. In I Kings 18:21, Elijah said, "How long halt ye between two opinions? If the Lord be God, follow Him, but if Baal, then follow him." *Don't be double-minded!*

B. What is the result of evil in one's life?

    1. The result is separation from fellowship with God.

    2. Even the smallest sin denies us the joy of fellowship with our Lord.

    Example: Suppose you were dating a fellow or a girl on this campus. You know how it goes—a little thing comes between you—not a big thing, just a very small thing. You know what happens: that small thing builds a big wall between you and you can't get through to each other. There is no fellowship, no communication.

C. How does the Lord respond to an impure heart?

    1. The Lord does not answer our prayers when we have sin in our lives. "If I regard iniquity in my heart, the Lord will not hear me" (Psalm 66:18).

    2. God desires our fellowship and longs for us to come back to Him that we might walk together as before we allowed sin to come into our lives. The more sin we allow in our lives, the more miserable we are. God feels all of this with us and longs for us to come immediately for cleansing.

D. What is the condition for cleansing and forgiveness?

    1. In I John 1:9 we read, "If we confess our sins, He is faithful and just to forgive us our sins, and to cleanse us from all unrighteousness."

    2. We are immediately to confess sin to God. Confession in the Greek suggests the idea of "say together with." We are to say together with God, agree with God about our sin. We are to detest it and resolve that by His strength we will never do it again. This is the provision God has made for us to maintain our fellowship.

    Example: A man who had been a wonderful Christian for many years was telling another man that he had never known an hour of defeat in fifty years of his Christian life. "What!" said the other man in astonishment, "You have never known any defeat in your Christian life?" "No, I didn't put it that way," said the first man. "I've known moments of defeat, but never an hour. I always get back into fellowship immediately by confessing my sin and claiming a promise from God's word, I John 1:9."

    3. Psalm 32:5 is an example of David's confession of sin. It is impossible to hide our sin from God. He is aware of all that we

do. Some ask, "Then why do we have to confess to Him, if He already knows." (That is, in God's mercy, His provision for forgiveness is due to the fact that we could never make up for the sins we commit.) It takes faith in His provision to believe that He cleanses us completely apart from anything we can do. God is glorified by our acknowledging His forgiveness.

4. We in our own strength cannot "forsake" our sins. We must accept the victory over temptation from Christ, the Victorious One. The faith which lets Christ bring us into and sustain us in victory is just remembering that Christ is faithful, that it is His responsibility and duty to accomplish this miracle in our lives as we are faithful to confess to and abide in Him. He is always true to His responsibility toward us.

II. LIVING "IN FELLOWSHIP" WITH GOD:

A. How fellowship is lost.

1. Fellowship is lost through sins of commission—that is, doing things we should not do, a word, thought, motive or action which is not pleasing to God. Maybe it is a sex problem—petting, necking or even worse. Perhaps it is pride in our lives. The saying goes, "If I list them, I will probably miss yours," but it is still sin.

2. Fellowship is lost through sins of omission—that is, not doing the things we should be doing. Most Christians live out of fellowship with God their whole lives because they refuse to obey the commands of God.

Example: The Great Commission—Matthew 28:19.

Grudge not—James 5:9.

Love one another—I John 4:7.

Follow me—Matt. 4:19.

Abide in Me—John 15.

Wait for Promise of Father—Acts 1:4, 8, and many others.

B. How are we restored to fellowship with God?

By confessing our sin (I John 1:9).

C. What is the result of being in fellowship with God?

1. Purpose, peace, power and joy are the result of being in fellowship with God. Inner stability and all the qualities of Christ become ours because we are in Him.

2. God works in us both to will and to do His pleasure. Almighty God Himself lives, moves and has His Being in and through us.

3. All power in heaven and in earth is ours; therefore, I "can do all things through Christ which strengtheneth me." We have a life that has power because it is cleansed and filled with the Holy Spirit of God.

4. Jesus manifests Himself to those who are obedient to His commands (John 14:21).

III. SUMMARY:

God uses only those vessels which are cleansed and filled. The smallest sin will break fellowship with God and thus render us impotent and unfruitful for Christ. Immediately confess your sins to Him. Set your affection on things above. It is not enough to empty your life of former practices which you feel are not pleasing to God; you must let Him fill your life with His presence and let Him fill your life with friends and deeds which are pleasing to Him. Saturate yourself with Him if you desire to be a faithful Christian.

IV. CLOSE IN PRAYER: "Lord, teach us, because of the price You paid on Calvary, that we can have forgiveness moment by moment and abide in You. May our lives show forth the victory of the Lord Jesus in our every act."

Perhaps you have never appropriated the cleansing power of the blood of Jesus Christ. Perhaps you have never asked Him to forgive your sin, to come into your life and live in and through you. Wouldn't you like to invite Him to come into your life now? On the authority of Rev. 3:20, He promises to come into your life. Isa. 1:18 says, "Though your sins be as scarlet they shall be as white as snow; though they be red like crimson, they shall be as wool." Won't you accept His forgiveness for your sin now? (Allow for a brief silence.) Did you ask Christ to come into your heart and cleanse you of your sin? If you were sincere, you may be sure that He came in and you have been forgiven. Now, thank Him for what He has done for you—come and tell me what you have done that I may rejoice with you and help you in your Christian growth.

SUPPLEMENTARY READING

Full Surrender—J. Edwin Orr

Victory In Christ—Charles G. Trumbull

Record: *"Rebound"*—Bob Thieme

THE CHRISTIAN ARMOR AND WARFARE

LESSON SIX   STEP TWO

OBJECTIVE: To inform students of the constant spiritual battle in every Christian's experience. To explain that the battle is the Lord's, and to motivate usage of armor provided.

I.   OPEN WITH PRAYER: "Lord, open our eyes to the real issues of life and help us to understand how we can be more than conquerors through Christ."

II. MEMORY VERSE: Eph. 6:10-11. Quote verses to person on your left.

III. MOTIVATION:

A. Have students read Eph. 6:10-18.

B. Close Bibles and Steps.

C. Write down all the pieces of warfare they can remember.

D. Describe soldier with just a few pieces of armor. Ask, "Would he be well armed for battle?"

E. What else does a soldier need for battle?

IV. BIBLE STUDY:

A. Assign to each student present one question relative to the Christian spiritual warfare.

B. Allow time for each to look up his passage and find the answer.

C. Allow each student opportunity to answer his assigned question.

V.   PARALLEL PASSAGES:

A. Enemy.

1. Devil—Eph. 6:11.

2. World—I John 2:15-17; James 4:4.

3. Flesh—Gal. 5:17.

B. Warfare.

1. Truth—John 14:6; 8:32, 34, 36.

2. Righteousness—II Cor. 5:21; Rom. 3:22.

3. Gospel of Peace—I Cor. 15:1, 3-4; Phil. 4:7.

4. Faith—Gal. 2:20; II Tim. 2:13.

5. Salvation—Acts 15:11.

6. Word of God—John 1:14; Heb. 4:12.

7. Prayer—Rom. 8:26.

C. Victory.

1. In Christ—II Cor. 2:14.

2. In God—II Chron. 20:15.

VI. SUMMARY:

Great men and women of the past have died on the battlefield for the Lord Jesus Christ. Today, we are not even willing to live for Him. Many leave home, family, loved ones for our country. Few will leave all and follow Him. "No man that warreth, entangleth himself with the affairs of this life that he may please Him who hath chosen him to be a soldier" (2 Tim. 2:2). Perhaps, you've never become a soldier for Jesus Christ. (Give the Four Spiritual Laws.)

VII. CLOSE IN PRAYER: "Oh, God, may we realize we are on the battlefield for You. May we as a group of students be disciplined in our stewardship of the armor You have given us, that we may one day have the victor's crown to lay at the feet of our risen Lord."

THE CHRISTIAN ARMOR AND WARFARE

LESSON SIX   STEP TWO

INTRODUCTION:

The Bible teaches very clearly that the Christian life is not only a walk, but also a warfare. Many Christians do not realize this. They think that living the Christian life means escaping all trials, difficulties, temptations, and they expect to glide through their years on earth with scarcely a problem. As a matter of fact, we are strangers and pilgrims on this earth (I Pet. 2:11), living in a world ruled by Satan, and we must continually face opposition and difficulty. The Christian life should be a victorious one, but it is not always an easy one. We must continually be strengthened "in the Lord and in the power of His might" (Eph. 6:10). We cannot expect to win the battle unless we allow Christ to fight the battle for us. We have all that it takes to be a good soldier, Jesus Christ. The secret of victory is to be dead to self and alive to Him.

I. WE ARE ON THE BATTLEFIELD!

A. Why must all the armor be worn?

1. We must put on the whole armor of God to stand against the wiles of the devil. Ephesians 6:12 teaches that "we wrestle not against flesh and blood, but against principalities, against powers, against the rulers of the darkness of this world, against spiritual wickedness in high places." God's provision for victory against the devil is to take the whole armor of God.

2. Also we need it to withstand in the evil day. There are so many philosophies, false doctrines, etc., that would mislead us. Our only defense is to put on the whole armor of God. Each piece, as we study them later in the lesson, must be in place before we can expect the Lord Jesus to fight for us.

B. Who are the enemies in this warfare?

1. The *world* consists of the total of non-Christian humanity. It is ruled by Satan. It will ridicule us and try to get us to live by its standards.

2. Also we face opposition from our own *flesh,* our old sin nature. God has left us with a sin nature, which is always at enmity (Rom. 8:7) with God's Holy Spirit. Paul said that in his flesh dwelt *no* good thing (Rom. 7:18). Our flesh, or sin nature, will always be tempting us, always be asserting itself, always be trying to entice us away from God. We can never trust it, not even for a moment.

3. *Satan,* or the *Devil,* is our third enemy. We fight the strongest power in the universe next to God. Satan is very alive and very active, but he is nevertheless a defeated foe. John 12:31 tells us he was defeated at the cross. He continually tries to frighten the Christian. The Bible describes him as a roaring lion, going about seeking whom he may devour.

C. How are we to respond to these enemies?

1. In relation to the world the Bible says, "Set your mind on things above, not on things of the earth" (Col. 3:1). The Christian must not be conformed to this world (Romans 12:2), and he is not to love the world (I John 2:15). The world is passing away. All its pleasures and allurements, all its glitter and attraction are but for a moment. The Christian is living with eternal values in mind, not just temporary ones. Therefore, he should set his mind on Christ and His eternal rewards in heaven, and not on the allurements of the world which will soon pass away. This is the only intelligent approach to life. Why live for that which you won't be able to enjoy for more than a few years? Why waste all your time and energy on that which is fleeting, passing, temporal, hollow?

2. We have victory over our flesh also. When we realize that God judged it on the cross, and that it no longer has control over us, we can overcome it. Romans 6:11 says we must reckon ourselves, that is, count upon the fact, that we are dead to sin. The flesh will always make demands. We should ignore them, and ignore it. *We are not called on to fight the flesh, but count it dead by faith.* Rest in the victory God gave at the cross.

3. How can we conquer Satan? We conquer him by being strong *in the Lord.* We have no strength ourselves to match his, no cunning, no wisdom by which we can outwit him. He will defeat us every time. But when we trust in God and not ourselves, when we rely on God's strength and not our own, we have victory. No Christian need ever fear the devil. Whenever he attacks, resist him in God's strength and he will flee (James 4:7). When we pray, we should claim God's victory over him at the cross, and he will be driven out. The Christian, in the

name of Jesus Christ, has the right and privilege of trampling the devil, with all his power, underfoot. Christ defeated Satan at the cross—victory has already been announced with the resurrection of Jesus Christ from the dead. The need is to act upon these facts, and by faith claim victory over the desire in the name of Christ.

D. Name the protective pieces of armor God provided for you to wear.

1. *Loins girt with truth*—Jesus said, "I am the way, the *truth*, and the life" (John 14:6). "And you shall know the *truth* and the *truth* shall make you *free*" (John 8:32). "If the *Son* therefore shall make you *free,* you shall be *free* indeed" (John 8:36).

Example: Soldiers used a 6-8 inch belt to gather up their flowing garments and as a foundation upon which to hang their swords and other weapons. The belt facilitated movement for the soldier in battle. Truth (Jesus Christ) is the Christian's belt that facilitates movement in the Christian's warfare. Knowing the truth frees us from sin and allows us to obey the call of our new Captain, Jesus Christ, in this great battle in which we are engaged.

2. *Breastplate of Righteousness*—"For he hath made Him to be sin for us, who knew no sin; that we might be made the righteousness of God in Him" (II Cor. 5:21). "The righteousness of God which is by faith of Jesus Christ unto all and upon all them that believe" (Rom. 3:22). Jesus frees us from the penalty of our sin. We can fight the good fight of faith because He is our righteousness.

3. *Feet shod with the Gospel of Peace*—" I declare unto you, the Gospel . . . how that Christ died for our sins according to the Scriptures, and that He was buried, and that He rose again the third day" (I Cor. 15:1, 3-4). "The *peace* of God shall keep your hearts and minds through Christ Jesus" (Phil. 4:7). "Being justified by faith, we have peace with God through our Lord Jesus Christ" (Rom. 5:1). We were at war with God and now are reconciled to Him and are at peace. We are free from condemnation. This is the same message we should take with us wherever we go. Every step you take should bear the news—the Gospel of Peace.

4. *Shield of Faith*—"I live by the faith of the Son of God (Gal. 2:20). "If we believe not, yet He abideth faithful" (II Tim. 2:13). We take the faith of Jesus Christ which is free from doubt. He is always faithful. We fight in His strength, knowing "The battle is the Lord's" (II Chron. 20:15).

5. *Helmet of Salvation*—"We believe that through the grace of the Lord Jesus Christ we shall be saved" (Acts 15:11). Jesus Christ Himself becomes our salvation. Being assured of our salvation gives us the confidence we need to fight the battle. "If we make our calling and election (salvation) sure, we shall never fall" (II Pet. 1:10). Jesus Christ frees us from death.

E. What is our offensive weapon?

1. *Sword of the Spirit*—This is the weapon that the Holy Spirit uses to convict the hearts of men and women. We can expect no conviction of sin and need for the Saviour apart from the word of God. The Spirit holds the prerogative of using the sword. He does not say to us, "See how *good* you are."

2. *Which is the word of God*—not our brilliant oratory, our persuasiveness, etc., but the word of God. Learn it from cover to cover. Learn the answer to every problem you face by searching its pages. This is your only offense. Use it always!

F. How is God's word used as a weapon against temptation?

1. First of all it fills the vacuum left by the lack of thoughts which possessed our minds before we became Christians. Too much spare time is bad for us. We daydream and let our minds wander to subjects not pleasing to the Lord. We should fill our minds with the word of God.

2. Memorizing God's word facilitates our usage when we do not have a Testament or Bible with us. Often we need the scriptures or promises immediately. Memorize the key verses in the lessons we have covered and will cover. This will bring the solutions to the problems of life to your mind when needed.

G. In what way can you use the sword of God's word?

1. Doctrine—or teaching of spiritual things. This is the Christian's source of teaching. The victorious one knows the word of God and applies it to his everyday experience.

2. Reproof—To reprove is to rebuke one for wrong words or actions. We should always use the word of God when showing one something in his life is displeasing to the Lord. It should not just be our opinion.

3. Correction—Through the word of God we can correct the error of doctrine when taught by others. If we give our own opinion, theirs is as good as ours. Always use the word of God to correct error.

184

4. Instruction in Righteousness—The Bible is the *Holy* Bible. It alone has the perfect standard of righteousness. "God's word will keep you from sin, or sin will keep you from God's word."

H. What must the successful warrior always do?

    1. To succeed in our Christian warfare we must always be in prayer. That does not mean we must always be on our knees, but always in prayer. The battle is fought by the Lord Jesus Christ, but we allow Him to fight through us by yielding ourselves to Him in prayer.

    2. Then we must watch—this denotes a "keep on keeping on." Be alert, be watching for the enemy and the opportunities for offensive attack. Be aware of the battle, and be constant in your prayer to the One Who fights for you.

I. Who is fighting the battle?

    1. Jesus Christ, the captain of our salvation, is fighting our battle and He has already won the victory. We fight from victory, not toward victory.

    2. When you take over and fight in your own strength, this is not enough to win the battle. If you lose, you must know that you have taken over the battle. God ordained that you "stand still and see the salvation of the *Lord*" (II Chron. 20:17).

J. Is there any protection for the back?

    1. No—our command is to stand and to withstand, not run. God does not expect us to be namby-pamby soldiers, but strong in His might.

    2. Remember, our "weapons are not carnal, but mighty through God to the pulling down of strongholds."

II. WE ARE MORE THAN CONQUERORS!

A. Why can we have confidence?

    1. Our confidence comes from having Christ live our lives. Not from any merit or ability on our part do we win in this battle, but through the strength of the Lord.

    2. The Lord conquered Satan at the cross, so the conflict need not frighten or worry us. God has given us all we need to win, and to be "more than conquerors." We need only march forward, as

soldiers of Christ, claiming victory by His strength and His power. "This is the victory that overcometh the world, even our faith" (I John 5:4).

B. What should our attitude be toward adversity and temptation?

1. "God is for us" and that is enough for any battle. His strength is enough to give us confidence. God is omnipotent.

2. "Who can be against us" with any degree of victory except that given him from our God? No one. God is in charge and we can rest in His will and know that "All things work together for good to them that love God, and are called according to His purpose" (Rom. 8:28).

III. SUMMARY:

What a thrill! To be in the army of the Living God is indeed a great thrill and privilege. Great men and women of the past have died on the battlefield for the Lord Jesus Christ. Today we find few who are willing to live for Him. "No man that warreth entangleth himself with the affairs of this life, that he may please Him who hath chosen Him to be a soldier." Let us go forth to battle, clad with the whole armor of God, more than conquerors, because He has already won the victory. Do you believe Him for the victory in the battles of your life, in college, right now? Do you believe that He has the answer, He has the power to overcome any habit or problem in *your* life? Trust Him now for the victory. "Now thanks be unto God, which *giveth* us the victory through our Lord Jesus Christ." Thank Him.

IV. CLOSE IN PRAYER: "Oh, God, may we realize we are on the battlefield for You. May we as a group of students be disciplined in our stewardship of the armor You have given us, that we may one day possess the victor's crown to lay at the feet of our wonderful Lord."

Perhaps you've never become a soldier for Jesus Christ. (Give the Four Spiritual Laws.) Would you like to invite Him to be the Lord and Captain of your life now? (Allow a few moments for silent prayer.)

SUPPLEMENTARY READING

Bone Of His Bone—Huegel

Fox's Book Of Martyrs

ATTITUDE

LESSON SEVEN   STEP TWO

OBJECTIVE: To show the difference between the divine and human viewpoint and to motivate students to live by the divine viewpoint.

I.   OPEN WITH PRAYER: "Lord, we thank You that You have made
it possible for us to look at our circum-
stances through Your eyes. Enable us by
Thy grace to always possess the divine
point of view concerning all the issues of
our lives."

II.   MEMORY VERSE: II Cor. 1:3-4. Share verse with person on your
left.

III. MOTIVATION:

A. Present demonstration of divine and human point of view to several
different kinds of problems.

B. Use two members of the group.

C. Situation: Each is to receive news of a tragedy which would closely affect him. One should display the divine viewpoint and the
other the human.

(Example: Breaking up with a girlfriend.)

D. Ask the group, "What makes the difference in the attitude?"
(Answer: One trusts God no matter what, the other relies upon his
own resources and refuses to trust God.)

IV.   BIBLE STUDY:

A. Read Ex. 14:1-14 aloud, with group following in their Bibles.

B. Tell them to listen carefully as you will ask them questions.

C. Ask questions 1 a-d in step.

D. Does Rom. 8:28 refer to everyone?

E. Read James 1:2-4 asking, "What is the result of testing?" (Righteousness, patience, and maturity.)

F. What is the advantage in "giving thanks in all things?"

G. Do question 7.

V. PARALLEL PASSAGES:

A. David as an example—I Sam. 17:31-58.

B. Job as an example—Job 1:1-22; 13:15; 42:12a.

VI. SUMMARY:

This is one of the great lessons we must learn in the Christian life—to give thanks in all things. Our attitude can change the course of our life. We need to stay in such close fellowship with the Lord that we will have His mind in all circumstances.

VII. CLOSE IN PRAYER: "Lord, teach us Your viewpoint concerning all things in our lives. May we look at them as You do. Help us to have a positive witness every moment because we trust You. May we show the world the steadfastness and faith of a real believer."

ATTITUDE

LESSON SEVEN   STEP TWO

INTRODUCTION:

Victory or defeat occurs in the mind before it occurs any place else.
God has called on us to win the battle of maintaining a correct mental attitude before anything else. If we think right all else will be right. "As a
man thinketh in his heart so is he" (Prov. 23:7). Why are so many Christians defeated here? Why do so many give in to discouragement, despair,
self-pity when they face difficulty? We will consider the divine viewpoint
and how we can face life from God's point of view. In our last lesson we
considered our armor or the warfare. We learned that our battle is against
principalities and powers, the rulers of darkness. We must have the proper
attitude in the battle to win.

I.   AN EXAMPLE OF GOD'S PEOPLE IN THE BATTLE:

    A. How did the Israelites react to apparent danger?

        1. "They were sore afraid." The Bible tells us "perfect love cast-
           eth out all fear" (I John 4:18). If the Israelites had loved God
           "with all their heart" they would have trusted and not been
           seized with fear.

        2. Fear then brought forth torment—they began to gripe. They
           griped to Moses, to the Lord. They were discontented with the
           fact that they were not "back in bondage in Egypt." How true
           this is to human nature. We remember the good of situations of
           the past, but not the bad.

    B. How did Moses react to the situation?

        1. He trusted God! Moses was in the same situation that the others
           were in, but he trusted while they doubted. "Unbelief prevents
           the enjoyment of God's promises although they will be fulfilled."

        2. He gave the glory to God! Moses told the people to watch what
           God would do. He was Moses' only hope. Did God let him down?
           Never!

    C. How did God bless through this experience?

        1. The people were allowed to see God in action! It is so thrilling
           to be present when God does a mighty work.

189

2. God taught His people another lesson in faith. They could believe Him; He was always faithful. He had not forgotten His people.

D. How does God work through difficulties?

1. God must teach us to trust Him. When everything is going well, we do not often credit God, but our own ingenuity. God has to bring us to the place where we recognize that we cannot do anything in our own wisdom and strength—then He moves in and works. He does this to teach us to trust Him in all things (Psalm 37:5; I Peter 5:7).

2. The more difficult the situation, the more God is glorified by providing a solution. Learn to trust God in the little things of life and He will increase your faith to trust Him in great things for His glory.

II. TAKING THE PROPER ATTITUDE:

A. What does the Bible guarantee when we are tempted or tested (I Cor. 10:13)?

1. That our test or temptation is common to all. Often we think we are enduring something no one else has endured. Yet there are real comfort and lessons to be learned from others that have been through the same trial.

2. We will not be tempted above what we are able to withstand. This is a fact written by God. We can never rightfully think that we cannot endure the temptation. If we could not endure, God would not have allowed us to be tempted in this way.

3. There will always be a way to escape. The Christian should immediately seek God's word for the answer to the problem. When we do not seek the answer, we fall deeper into the temptation.

4. We will be able to bear it. Always remember that, "I can do all things through Christ who strengthens me" (Phil. 4:13). All power in heaven and earth is yours. You have all the resources you will ever need in Jesus Christ.

B. Does Romans 8:28 refer to everyone?

1. It is qualified to include those "who love God." Love for God brings trust. Therefore you know that whatever comes is from the Father's hand.

2. The second qualification is "those who are called according to His purpose." God's purpose is fulfilled in those who are yield-

190

ed to His purpose. Until we come to the point in our lives where we can accept His will, we will not see His perfect will being accomplished.

C. What is the result of testing?

1. The Christian life often includes suffering, heartbreak and tragedy. Why do these things come? Phil. 1:29 says, "It is given you in the behalf of Christ not only to believe in Him, but also to suffer for His sake." Suffering and tragedy come ultimately from God *to accomplish His divine purpose.* All sunshine and no rain creates a desert. *To mold our Christian character,* God must not only give us times of blessing and encouragement, but also allow times of trouble and difficulty. To most of us these are to be escaped at all costs, but God does not always intend for us to escape.

2. In times of trial we *learn to trust God and draw close to Him.* We learn of the comfort He can give; we learn of the provision He can make; and we learn how weak and self-centered we really are. We learn to see God's power in a new way.

3. Many, many Christians have never achieved real usefulness for God until He has sent a difficult trial their way.

4. Suffering often comes *to expose a rebellious attitude.* The world can see no meaning in suffering, no purpose for it; but for the Christian it is the hand of a loving God, who is tenderly disciplining His children, sending a blessing in disguise. Learn to accept God's victory in suffering and difficulties.

5. One can base his life upon his physical experiences or upon his spiritual relationship with God. If physical life is the most meaningful to us, when pressures come, there will not be the stability and reserve which an active spiritual life affords and which is necessary for victory over circumstances.

D. What is the advantage in "giving thanks in all things?"

1. First of all, by giving thanks in all things we acknowledge God's authority in our lives. We show our trust in His faithfulness. As Moses, we see the glory of God manifested, and enjoy it because we look for His "out," not our own.

2. We think more clearly when we think from God's point of view. Thanking Him reminds us that He is in control of the situation. We don't have to fall apart trying to manufacture an answer.

3. The person looking for the good is always quicker to find it.

THE CHRISTIAN AND THE HOLY SPIRIT

STEP THREE

OBJECTIVE: How to present the Ministry of the Holy Spirit.

I.   OPEN WITH PRAYER.

II. MEMORY VERSE:
Briefly review the memory verses.

III. MOTIVATION:

Every day can be an exciting adventure for the Christian who knows the reality of being filled with the Holy Spirit and living constantly, moment by moment, under His gracious control.

Almost every sincere Christian who does not understand the ministry of the Holy Spirit is dissatisfied and often discouraged with his impotent and fruitless life. In Ephesians 5:18, God commands every Christian to be filled with the Holy Spirit. Not to be filled and controlled by the Holy Spirit is an act of disobedience. Would you like to know how you can be filled with the Holy Spirit right now? (When the response is positive, proceed with the following.)

First of all, I would like to explain that you should not seek nor expect an ecstatic feeling, though according to the promise of John 14:21, Jesus said that He would manifest Himself to those who keep His commandments. Rather, the basis for this wonderful new relationship with God is faith in the fact of God's word. There are four basic truths involved in understanding how to be filled and controlled by the Holy Spirit (see Bible Study).

IV. BIBLE STUDY:

A. God has provided for us a full and abundant Christian life (I John 1:3-10).

   1. Our joy can be full.

   2. Our fellowship consistent.

   3. Our sins forgiven immediately.

B. It is possible for a Christian not to experience the full and fruitful life (Romans 7:15-24).

   1. Up and down experience.

   2. Actually doing things you are trying to avoid doing.

3. Having no power to do things you know that God wants you to do—i.e., pray, witness, love others, etc.

4. Carrying the burden of unconfessed sin (Romans 7:24).

C. Jesus told us the Holy Spirit is the only answer to a vital Christian life (John 7:37-39; John 16:7, 12-14; Acts 1:4-8).

1. He is the source of the overflowing life (John 7:37-39).

2. He has come to glorify Christ (John 16:14). Consequently, being filled with the Spirit is being filled with Christ.

3. Christ's last command told us to receive the power of the Spirit before we dare go forth to witness (Acts 1:8)!

D. We are filled with the Holy Spirit by faith (Ephesians 5:18; I John 5:14-15).

1. The Bible commands us to be filled constantly and continually moment by moment. Do not expect a dramatic once-and-for-all-time ecstatic experience. Feelings are a by-product of faith. To disobey a command of God is sin. Therefore, it is sin not to be filled with the Spirit (Ephesians 5:18)!

2. God can only fill a cleansed vessel. Sin in our lives keeps us from being filled. We must confess sin in the Christian life the moment it occurs (I John 1:9)!

3. We must present ourselves to God in a decisive dedication of our lives, our wills, our bodies and our total personalities (Romans 12:1-2).

4. Once sin is confessed, and the control of our lives is surrendered to Him, we are cleansed. We then simply thank God for filling us and BELIEVE Him, on the basis of His Word, that we are filled (I John 5:14-15).

"Without FAITH it is impossible to please God" (Hebrews 11:6).
"That which is not of FAITH is sin" (Romans 14:23).
"The just shall live by FAITH" (Romans 1:17).

V. SUMMARY:

In love, simply invite the Christian with whom you are speaking to pray with you, to confess any known sins (such as pride, unbelief, unwillingness to be used of God, etc.), to present himself to God willing to do His will and to thank God for filling him with the Holy Spirit.

Then go on to explain how to walk in the Spirit. Again, by faith!

A. Confessing sin immediately (I John 1:9).

B. Believing God moment by moment that you *are* filled.

C. Expecting Him to use you. (Anything not of faith is sin.)

Or, you might put it this way, "CONFESS, RECEIVE, BELIEVE."

VII. CLOSE IN PRAYER.

LESSON PLAN

WHO IS THE HOLY SPIRIT AND
WHY DID HE COME?

LESSON ONE   STEP THREE

OBJECTIVE: To gain an understanding of the ministry of the Holy
Spirit and learn how to appropriate His power for holy
living and Christian service.

I.   OPEN WITH PRAYER.

II. MEMORY VERSE: John 16:13-14 (Ask each class member to recite
the memory verse to another).

III. MOTIVATION:

Hold up a candle. "The Spirit of man is the candle of the Lord" (Proverbs 20:27). Until the Holy Spirit of God lights the candle of man's
spiritual life he cannot see and know God. Man is spiritually dead
(unlighted candle), but when the Holy Spirit takes up residence at
the time of spiritual birth (John 3:3,6) he becomes spiritually alive.
(Light candle.)

IV. BIBLE STUDY: Who is the Holy Spirit and why did He come?

A. The identity of the Holy Spirit.

1. The Holy Spirit's Personality.

a. What are the characteristics of personality?

b. Would you consider God a person (a personality)?

c. What do the scriptures teach about the Holy Spirit's personality (questions 1-3, Lesson 1)?

2. The Holy Spirit is the Spirit of God. Eph. 3:16 "His Spirit . . ."

What is the particular ministry of the Holy Spirit mentioned in
Paul's prayer for the Ephesians in Eph. 3:16-19? Note also in
what manner the other persons of the Trinity are mentioned.

a. V. 16 ". . . by His *Spirit* in the inner man."

b. V. 17 ". . . Christ may dwell in your hearts by faith."

c. V. 19 ". . . Filled with all the fulness of God."

B. The Ministry of the Holy Spirit: questions 5-7 of Lesson 1 point out to us the progressive ministry of the Holy Spirit.

1. John 16:13-14—The Spirit seeks to glorify Christ the Saviour.

   a. To call attention to Him for He is "the Way" (John 14:6).

   b. "The Son of man is come to seek and save that which was lost" (Luke 19:10).

2. I Cor. 3:16—The Spirit lives in us. We are the house (temple) of the Holy Spirit. Upon what experience do we base this? What scripture? (John 3:3,6; Revelation 3:20; John 1:12; etc.).

3. In the light of these facts what will be the result of the Holy Spirit controlling our lives? Discuss questions 6 and 7 of Lesson 1.

V. PARALLEL PASSAGES: See the Lesson Amplification.

VI. SUMMARY:

People often give the impression that God is an impersonal force which they exploit for a life of well-being. This is wrong! God is a person, and through His Spirit He wants to control and use us for His glory and our own good. We do not use God—God uses us. Through His Spirit in us He wants to call attention to Jesus Christ, the Saviour, "the Way."

VII. CLOSE IN PRAYER: "Dear Father, I want to allow the Holy Spirit to control my life each moment of every day in order that I may always know and do Your perfect will."

LESSON AMPLIFICATION

WHO IS THE HOLY SPIRIT AND WHY DID HE COME?

LESSON ONE   STEP THREE

INTRODUCTION:

The majority of Christians know very little about the Holy Spirit. All of us have heard sermons on God the Father, and many on God the Son, but a sermon on God the Holy Spirit is rare. The Holy Spirit is equal in every way with God the Father and God the Son. He vitally affects our lives as Christians. In fact, His presence or absence in a person's life makes the difference between life and death spiritually. We are born spiritually through the ministry of the Holy Spirit according to John 3:1-8.

I.   THE IDENTITY OF THE HOLY SPIRIT.

The Holy Spirit is known as the third member of the Trinity.

A. He was believed to be equal with God the Father and God the Son by the early Church and succeeding generations of the Church.

1. Nicene Creed (1600 years old) 325 A.D. "I believe in the Holy Ghost, the Lord and Giver of life, Which proceedeth from the Father and the Son, and with the Father and the Son together is worshipped and glorified."

2. Athanasian Creed (1300 years old). "Such as the Father is, such is the Son, and such is the Holy Ghost."

B. Hymn writers of all ages attribute Him with deity.

"Holy Ghost with light *divine,*
Shine upon this heart of mine.

Holy Ghost with power divine,
Cleanse this guilty heart of mine."

Written 100 years ago. Who could cleanse a guilty heart except God?

C. Webster's Dictionary defines the Holy Spirit as the third Person of the Trinity.

II. THE MINISTRY OF THE HOLY SPIRIT:

A. What was the work of the Holy Spirit in the Old Testament?

1. Job 26:13; Psa. 104:30; Gen. 1:2-3 (creation).

2. II Pet. 1:21; II Tim. 3:16 (revelation).

197

3. I Sam. 16:13; II Chron. 15:1-2; Judges 14:5-7; Judges 15:9-14 (power for service).

B. What was the work of the Holy Spirit in Jesus' ministry?

1. Matt. 1:18-20; Luke 1:30-35 (incarnation).

2. Jn. 1:32 (baptism).

3. Matt. 12:28 (miracles).

4. Jn. 3:5-6 (message of new birth).

5. I Pet. 3:18; Rom. 8:11 (resurrection).

The life of the Lord Jesus and the ministry of the disciples depended on the Holy Spirit. How much more should we depend on the Holy Spirit!

C. Special Question:

Compare Rom. 8:16, 26 in the King James and the Amplified translations. What mistranslation concerning the Holy Spirit do you find in the King James? (Holy Spirit should be translated "He" and not "it" because He is a person.)

At the Last Supper when the disciples were gathered in the upper room with Jesus, they were very sorrowful when Jesus said He would have to die. For three years they had been his closest companions. They had seen Him heal the sick, the deaf and the blind. They had watched Him as He fed five thousand with only five small loaves and two fishes. They had listened to His words and concluded with others, "Never man spake like this man spake." They even saw Him raise the dead. With such conclusive evidence that Jesus was the Messiah—the promised Messiah, the promised Redeemer—they "forsook all and followed Him." Imagine their dismay and grief when they realized that their beloved Master would have to die. But Jesus spoke words of comfort to them as He said, "Nevertheless I tell you the truth; it is expedient for you that I go away: for if I go not away, the Comforter will not come unto you; but if I depart, I will send Him unto you" (John 16:7).

In other words, Jesus said it was necessary for Him to go away, to die that they might benefit. But Jesus said He would send someone else to replace Him—the Comforter. Notice He did not say He would send His comfort, but the Comforter, a person. In John 14:16, Jesus said He would send "another Comforter" who would abide with them forever. This Comforter was to be just like Jesus!

There are two words for 'another' in the Greek:

"allos" —another, but similar (another of the same kind).

"heteros"—another as distinguished from (qualitative difference).

Jesus said He would send another (allos) just like Himself.

LESSON PLAN

HOW IS THE HOLY SPIRIT RELATED TO
EVERY CHRISTIAN?

LESSON TWO   STEP THREE

OBJECTIVE: To show that spiritual life (Christianity) is the Holy Spirit in us and that successful Christian living is based upon His control of the life.

I.   OPEN WITH PRAYER.

II.   MEMORY VERSE: Ephesians 5:18 (class members review with one another).

III. MOTIVATION:

In your estimation how are God the Father, God the Son and God the Holy Spirit individually related to you, the Christian? Write out answers and discuss briefly?

God the Father—The source of life, source of all that is holy and good, etc.

God the Son—God manifest in the flesh, our Savior, provides the way of salvation.

God the Holy Spirit—Regenerates, gives us the new life, seeks to control us, etc.

IV.   BIBLE STUDY:

A. The Holy Spirit initiates the new life and then wants to fill (control) the believer. Apply each of the following verses to the work of the Holy Spirit:

1. Proverbs 20:27—"Spirit of man is the candle of the Lord."

2. I Thessalonians 5:23—"Spirit, soul and body"—In order of importance.

3. John 3:5—Spiritual birth necessary.

4. Titus 3:5—Provided by the Holy Spirit, "Renewing of the Holy Spirit."

199

5. I Corinthians 2:14—A new perspective, a new understanding (also 2:13).

6. Galatians 5:16-17—The Holy Spirit seeks to control us.

7. Discuss the answers to question 1, Lesson 2. If the Holy Spirit is in us, is it important that we should yield to His control?

B. The results of the filling (controlling) of the Holy Spirit in the lives of the apostles.

1. See Lesson 2, question 2. (Discuss.)

2. According to Acts 4:31 how did they speak the word of God? (With boldness.)

3. Paul certainly was "Spirit-filled" and his message was powerful. Note his testimony in I Corinthians 2:4-5. How did he speak? What does he contrast this with? (*Demonstration of the Spirit and of power* vs. man's wisdom.)

4. Discuss how one can have this boldness and power.

V.   PARALLEL PASSAGES: See the Lesson Amplification.

VI.   SUMMARY:

It is evident that the Holy Spirit plays a major role in the life of the Christian. God carries out His purpose in the life of the Christian through the control of the Holy Spirit. To be a successful Christian one must yield to His control.

VII.   CLOSE IN PRAYER: "Dear God, teach me to live in the reality of my relationship with the Holy Spirit. May my life be a channel for His power to the end that the Lord Jesus Christ shall always be glorified."

HOW IS THE HOLY SPIRIT RELATED TO EVERY CHRISTIAN?

LESSON TWO   **STEP THREE**

INTRODUCTION: The Triune God and the Christian.

Have you ever heard the story of the three men who all claimed ownership of the same house? The first man was the builder of the house. He planned the whole thing and then put it up for sale. The second man was the buyer who paid the price to buy the house. He owns the house, but there is a third man who now lives in the house. So it is with us. God the Father made us; God the Son redeemed us with His precious blood at Calvary; and God the Holy Spirit has come to live within us. "Know ye not that ye are the temple of God, and that the Spirit of God dwelleth in you" (I Cor. 3:16)? In Christ we are indwelt by the Godhead: Father, Son and Holy Spirit (Col. 2:10).

It is almost inconceivable that God Himself lives in us when we receive Christ, but He does!

I.   THE WORK OF THE HOLY SPIRIT:

   A. *Regenerates.* John 3:5. "Generation is impartation of physical life; regeneration is impartation of spiritual (divine) life."

      1. Men are spiritually dead until regenerated. Romans 6:23, "The wages of sin *is* death " (Eph. 2:1).

      2. There is only one thing a dead man needs, and that is life (John 14:6; John 5:24; John 11:25).

   B. *Indwells.* I Cor. 3:16; 6:19; John 14:16-17.

      1. Is there a contradiction when we say that Jesus comes into our hearts, and we also say the Holy Spirit lives in us? (John 14:17-20; John 15:5; John 17:18-23, 26; Romans 8:9; Ephesians 3:17; Phil. 1:19-21.) *The Holy Spirit is the Spirit of Christ.*

      2. Every believer, no matter how weak and imperfect, has the indwelling Holy Spirit. The best references on the indwelling Holy Spirit (I Cor. 3:16; 6:19) were written to weak, carnal Christians at Corinth.

C. *Assures* us of our salvation. Rom. 8:16.

"Jesus Christ wanted to take religion out of the external and make it internal and put it on the same level as life itself, so that a man knows he knows God the same as he knows he is himself and not someone else. He knows God the same as he knows he is alive and not dead. Only the Holy Spirit can do that. The Holy Spirit came to carry the evidence of Christianity from the Bible and books of apologetics into the human heart, and that is exactly what He does. You can take the gospel of Jesus Christ to the heathen in Borneo, or Africa, people who could never conceive the first premise of your logical arguments, so that it would be totally impossible for them to decide on logical grounds whether Christianity was of God or not. Preach Christ to them and they will believe and be transformed and put away their wickedness and change from evil to righteousness and get happy about it all, learn to read and write and study their Bibles and become leaders and pillars in their church, transformed and made over. How? By the instant witness of the Holy Spirit to their hearts."

—A. W. Tozer, *How to be Filled with the Holy Spirit,* p. 13.

D. *Seals* the believer. Ephesians 1:13 (Cf. II Timothy 2:19) denotes:

1. Ownership.

2. Assurance.

"When Jesus comes again, like a great magnet there will be a response in the hearts of His people. What will that response be? The indwelling Holy Spirit will respond to the shout of the coming Bridegroom (Christ), and will present to Christ His own without spot or wrinkle. It is vital to know one is sealed by the Holy Spirit —that He indwells the heart and life. He is here to prepare for the glorious moment when faith will give way to sight—for the meeting with the Bridegroom face to face. Yes, the Holy Spirit is the Seal" (I Thess. 4:16-18).

—Harold Wildish, *Did Ye Receive the Holy Ghost?* p. 31.

E. The Holy Spirit is the *earnest* of our inheritance. Eph. 1:14.

1. If businessmen make a transaction, they want some guarantee. Suppose, for example, you were buying a $10,000 house. You would have to make a down-payment before business could be contracted. This down-payment or guarantee that the rest would be paid is called the "earnest." The Holy Spirit is our guarantee that the Lord will do all for us that He has promised.

2. Just like the engagement ring is the token or promise of the life to come in the marriage relationship, so the Holy Spirit is the promise to the believer of the life to come with the Lord.

F. The Holy Spirit *baptizes* us (the baptism of the believer by the Holy Spirit—Acts 1:4-5; I Corinthians 12:13). This is an act of the Holy Spirit in which He, at the moment of the individual's acceptance of Christ in faith, takes the person and places him into the body of Christ (note Romans 6:3).

II. RESULTS OF THE FILLING OF THE HOLY SPIRIT IN THE LIVES OF THE APOSTLES: Discuss questions 2 and 4 in Lesson Two.

III. SUMMARY: The Holy Spirit fills every yielded Christian for service, Acts 1:8.

A. Dr. R. A. Torrey, "There is not one single passage in the Bible, either in the Old Testament or the New Testament, where the filling with the Holy Spirit is spoken of, where it is not concerned with testimony for service."

B. Read the book of Acts and you will observe how the apostles were repeatedly filled.

LESSON PLAN

WHY ARE SO FEW CHRISTIANS FILLED
WITH THE HOLY SPIRIT?

LESSON THREE   STEP THREE

OBJECTIVE: To gain an understanding of the problems that would keep
the Christian from experiencing the "filling of the Spirit."

I.   OPEN WITH PRAYER.

II. MEMORY VERSES: I John 2:15-17 (each check with another).

III. MOTIVATION:

Ask each member of the group to write out four or five things which
he feels would keep an individual from experiencing the control of
the Holy Spirit (Spirit-filled life). Discuss together.

IV. BIBLE STUDY:

A. The battlefield within the heart.

   1. Galatians 5:16-17 points out to us that there is a battlefield
   within the heart:

   CHRISTIAN

   Physical Life   versus   Spiritual Life

   2. What are the descriptions given for the flesh (Galatians 5:19-
   21)?

   3. What are the descriptions given for the fruits of the Spirit
   (Galatians 5:22-24)?

   4. Is the issue "our doing" of these things or "our surrender" to
   the controlling principle which produces either the works of
   the flesh or the fruits of the Spirit?

B. Why the battle is often lost. See discussion of pride, fear of man,
   unconfessed sin, etc. in Lesson Amplification.

C. How to win the battle.

204

1. How does Paul describe the individual who seeks the control of God's Spirit in his life (Colossians 3:10)? Evidently he begins to reflect as "an image" some of the characteristics of God.

2. In Ephesians 5:8 we are told to "walk as children of light."

3. How is this to be accomplished (Ephesians 5:17-18)?

4. Discuss Galatians 5:25—What does Paul mean when he speaks of "living" in the Spirit as opposed to "walking" in the Spirit?

V.   PARALLEL PASSAGES: See the Lesson Amplification.

VI.   CLOSE IN PRAYER: "Dear God, help me to recognize sin and self-will. May I never let them become the controlling force of my life. May I continually yield to the control of the Holy Spirit."

WHY ARE SO FEW CHRISTIANS FILLED WITH THE HOLY SPIRIT?

LESSON THREE   STEP THREE

INTRODUCTION:

What are the reasons why many Christians are not filled with the Holy Spirit?

Lack of knowledge of the word of God is a key reason.

Illustration: "Suppose a young Christian who loved the Lord Jesus Christ and wanted to serve Him was very eager to get married. This Christian boy was in the Armed Forces in France. He became very fond of two French girls—he just didn't know which one he liked better—he liked them both. He really wanted to get married, but he didn't know which girl to ask. As a man who believed in God, he walked into a big church in France and sat down in one of the pews. He asked God to guide him, and then looking up at the stained glass windows, he seemed to see two words that guided him: "Ave Maria." Strangely enough the name of one of the French girls was Maria. He thought, "Have Maria, have Maria! I'll ask her to be my wife." But, sad to say, that girl was not a Christian. If that boy had been reading God's word diligently, and if he had read and digested that phrase in II Cor. 6:14 which says, "Be ye not unequally yoked together with unbelievers," he would never have looked to a stained glass window for guidance. If the word of God was dwelling in him richly, the Spirit of God would have shown him clearly that he could not ask an unsaved girl to be his wife. The Spirit-filled life is tremendously practical."

—Wildish, p. 57.

I. THE BATTLEFIELD WITHIN THE HEART: Discuss question 2 in Lesson Three in regard to Galatians 5:16-17.

II. WHY THE BATTLE IS OFTEN LOST:

A. Pride—Prov. 16:18.

1. Pride was the sin of Satan (Isa. 14:12-14).

2. Pride was the first sin of man as Adam and Eve wanted to be something they were not (Gen. 3:5).

3. The self-centered, egocentric Christian cannot have fellowship with God . . . "for God resisteth the proud and giveth grace to the humble" (I Pet. 5:5).

B. Fear of man—Prov. 29:25.

   1. One of the greatest tragedies of our day is that you can't tell a Christian from a non-Christian (generally speaking). We are "not to be conformed to this world, but transformed" (Rom. 12:1-2).

   2. All around us are hungry hearts who would respond if some Christian would be brave enough to fly his colors and let people know where he stands.

   3. Dr. Henrietta Mears said that a Christian should be like a lifeguard at the beach. Everyone knows who he is, but pays him scant attention. But when someone swims too far and begins to drown, he remembers the lifeguard and calls for him to help. If we will let it be known what we stand for, someone is bound to come for help when he gets in trouble and really needs help.

   4. No great leader for Christ fears man.

   Martin Luther, the great Protestant reformer, stood fearlessly before the Holy Roman Emperor and the Diet of Worms as an Archbishop questioned him about his writings. Luther replied, "The books are all mine, and I have written more."

   "Do you defend them all, or do you reject a part?" asked the Archbishop. Luther replied aloud, "This touches God and his Word. This affects the salvation of souls. Of this Christ said, 'He who denies me before men, him will I deny before my Father.'"

   Luther was given a day to think it over and asked the next day to recant his statements. Luther replied, "Unless I am convicted by Scripture and plain reason—I do not accept the authority of popes and councils, for they have contradicted each other—my conscience is captive to the word of God. I cannot and I will not recant anything, for to go against conscience is neither right nor safe. Here I stand, I cannot do otherwise. God help me."

   —Bainton, *Here I Stand, A Life of Martin Luther,* p. 144.

C. Unconfessed sin—Ps. 66:18.

   1. God will not fill an unclean or unyielded vessel.

   2. He wants you to confess all known sin, and in some cases make restitution—Ex. 22:3, 5-6, 12.

3. Review I Jn. 1:9.

4. Read "My Heart Christ's Home" by Dr. Robert Munger.

D. Worldly-mindedness—I Jn. 2:15-17.

    1. Love for material things and desire to conform to a secular society is the spiritual disease of many Christians.

    2. Every Christian should make careful and frequent evaluation of how he invests his time, talent and treasures in order to accomplish the most for Christ.

    3. "Only one life, 'twill soon be past,
       Only what's done for Christ will last."

E. Lack of trust in God.

    1. Basic reason why Christians are not filled with the Spirit is that they will not surrender their will to God's will.

    2. Some people are afraid that if they surrender to God's will He will take something away from them or make them unhappy. Nothing could be farther from the truth. A person who chooses to do God's will, will:

        a. Find the inner longings of his own heart gratified (selfward)—Ps. 23:5; Ps. 16:11; Ps. 63:5; Jn. 4:13-14; Jn. 7:37-38.

        b. Glorify God (Godward)—Jn. 15:8; Matt. 5:16; I Cor. 6:20; Eph. 1:6.

        c. Bring salvation and blessing to others (manward)—Acts 4:13, 9:15; I Cor. 4:9; II Cor. 4:10-11; Gal. 1:16, 6:10; Phil. 1:20; Luke 24:47-48; etc.

III.   HOW TO WIN THE BATTLE: See the Lesson Plan, Romans 12:1-2 and Ephesians 5:18.

A. SUMMARY: The unhappiest people in the world are not the unbelievers, but Christians who resist the will of God for their lives!

Illustrations:

    1. A professor in a Christian college once told his class, "I have lived most of my life on God's second best." God had called him to be a missionary in his younger years. He had turned away from this call through marriage. He practically gave up all Christian work and began a selfish business life as a cashier in a bank, with the primary purpose of setting up a nice home and making money. The Spirit of God kept dealing with him, but there was no yielding. A number of years passed. Then one

day there was a telephone call to the bank. Their small child had fallen from her high chair and was dead. It took that bitter experience to bring that Christian to a place of surrender. After he spent a night alone with God on his knees, in tears and agony, he surrendered to God. But it was too late to go to Africa. His disobedience in earlier years forever closed that door, though he knew God had once called him there.

2. A similar story was told by a man who resisted the call to the ministry in Sweden. He stubbornly resisted God's will even through the death of his wife and daughter. He went into business and prospered, only to be robbed by his own son. In his older years as he languished with cancer, he said, "I know that I am saved, but O, the loss, as I soon will be ushered into His presence only to give an account of a whole life of disobedience."

3. Frieda Schneider, invalid and bedridden for most of her life, said in her striking book, "A, B, C's for Christian Living," "It is better to yield now than to wait until God puts you on a stretcher as the chiropractor does with his unruly patients. This stretcher method often constitutes an avalanche of crucial circumstances which crush earthly hopes. Therefore, this admonition—prostrate yourself before Christ and invite His nail-scarred hands to adjust your life and correct your spirit . . . Rest your case in His hands. He died for you, now live for Him.

> "Were the whole realm of nature mine,
> That were a present far too small:
> Love so amazing, so divine,
> Demands my soul, my life, my all!"

4. The Christian who refuses to do the will of God must be prepared to pay the price of disobedience. Be assured, "As we sow, so shall we reap."

B. Explain that God is a loving Father, in whom we can trust without reservation, as a son trusts an earthly father who has proven his love.

C. Lack of faith. "That which is not of faith is sin" (Romans 14:23). "Without faith it is impossible to please God" (Hebrews 11:6). Most Christians grieve the Holy Spirit because of their unbelief.

HOW CAN A CHRISTIAN BE FILLED WITH THE HOLY SPIRIT?

LESSON FOUR   **STEP THREE**

OBJECTIVE: To discuss how one is filled with the Holy Spirit and counsel and pray with those who desire to be filled with the Holy Spirit.

I.   OPEN WITH PRAYER.

II.   MEMORY VERSE: Romans 12:1-2 (each check with another).

III.   MOTIVATION:

New Christian to counselor: "Don't you think one's conversion experience and sinful background determine the success in personal witnessing, in Christian work and in Christian growth? I do not have the power 'X' has because he has such a tremendous background." What would you say if you were the counselor? (If this is not true, what does make for success?)

IV.   BIBLE STUDY:

A. Practice Interview:

1. What does Jesus say in Matt. 5:6? The Holy Spirit indwells every believer from the moment he receives Christ. However, He does not continue to control the life in the sense of filling unless we want Him to do so.

2. In Ephesians 4:30-32 what sins of commission are spoken of as grieving the Holy Spirit? *(Ans.* Bitterness, wrath, clamor, etc.) Do you feel that these have been in your life?

3. In I Thess. 5:19, quenching the Spirit is spoken of. What does it mean to quench a fire? This is a sin of omission, omitting obedience to the Holy Spirit's leading.

4. In the light of Ephesians 5:18, do you feel that God wants you to have power in your life as 'X' does? When one is drunk with wine, what controls his life—the lowest nature or God's Spirit? Do you feel that God is trustworthy? Will you let Him control your life?

5. In I John 5:14-15 what is there to indicate that God would allow you to be filled with the Holy Spirit if you simply prayed, confessing any grieving or quenching you have done, and gave Him permission to take over?

6. Would you like to so pray now?

7. Why don't we exhibit our trust in God by going out right now to witness to some friends?

B. A short explanation of Filling—John 7:37-39.

1. Read John 7:37-39. In verses 37-38 pick out the verbs. *(Ans.* thirst, come, drink, believe.)

2. When one thirsts one must come to Christ, drink, and believe. Some come to Christ because they thirst, but they do not believe (trust, rely on, have faith in).

3. According to John 7:38-39 what can one expect will be the result in coming to Christ, drinking and believing? *(Ans.* An outflow of "rivers of living water.")

V. PARALLEL PASSAGES: See the Lesson Amplification.

VI. SUMMARY:

The Spirit-filled life is the norm of the Christian life. It is for every Christian. With a Spirit-filled life the Christian will experience the joy and reality of his Christian life; he will have power to witness. The simple prerequisites are confession, cleansing, complete yielding to His will by faith.

VII. CLOSE IN PRAYER: "Dear Father, thank You for helping us to understand and appropriate the fullness of Your power and love by faith."

HOW CAN A CHRISTIAN BE FILLED WITH THE HOLY SPIRIT?

LESSON FOUR   STEP THREE

Admonition to Be Filled.

Ephesians 5:18 admonishes us to "be filled with the Spirit" continually. The Spirit-filled life is the only life that God can use. To try to live the Christian life or do service for God apart from His Spirit is like trying to operate a car without gas. It doesn't work!

The Holy Spirit's Indwelling.

The very moment you trusted Christ as your Saviour, that moment the Holy Spirit, the third Person of the Trinity, came to live in your life. In other words, *God Himself* came to live *in* you! "What? know ye not that your body is the temple of the Holy Spirit which is in you, which ye have of God, and ye are not your own? For ye are bought with a price: therefore glorify God in your body, and in your spirit, which are God's" (I Cor. 6:19-20).

What the Indwelling Spirit Does for Us.

The Holy Spirit living in us is what makes us conscious of God's presence and gives us the assurance that we are children of God. "The Spirit himself bears witness with our spirit, that we are the children of God" (Rom. 8:16).

The Holy Spirit was responsible for our new birth. We are "born of the Spirit" (Jn. 3:5-6). The Holy Spirit guides our lives. "For as many as are led by the Spirit of God, they are the sons of God" (Rom. 8:14). Our hope of the resurrection lies in the power of the Holy Spirit. "But if the Spirit of Him that raised up Jesus from the dead dwells in you, He that raised up Christ from the dead shall also quicken your mortal bodies by his Spirit that dwelleth in you" (Rom. 8:11).

Since the Holy Spirit inspired the writing of the Bible, we cannot understand its true meaning apart from His control.

We pray with His assistance according to Romans 8:26 and witness in His power according to Acts 1:8.

Negative and Positive Aspects to the Filling of the Holy Spirit.

There are two negative and two positive aspects to being filled with the Spirit. First the negative: "Grieve not the Holy Spirit of God, whereby ye are sealed unto the day of redemption" (Eph. 4:30). To grieve the Spirit of God means to commit some sin or break one of God's laws. Then we are also told, "Quench not the Spirit" (I Thess. 5:19). When we "quench the Spirit," we do not openly break one of God's laws, but we refuse to do something God wants us to do. For example, the still, small voice of God may tell us to speak to a friend about Christ. If we refuse, we have quenched the Spirit.

If we have grieved or quenched the Spirit in our lives, then we must confess that sin to Him before He will fill us with His power. That is the first positive aspect to being filled with the Spirit. "If we confess our sins, He is faithful and just to forgive us our sins, and to cleanse us from all unrighteousness" (I Jn. 1:9).

In Ephesians 5:18 God commands every Christian to be filled with the Holy Spirit. In I John 5:14-15 God promises that if we pray according to His will He hears and answers our prayer. On the authority of God's word we may receive the fullness of the Holy Spirit right now.

The final step is to BELIEVE that God has filled you with His Spirit and you now have the power to witness and live for Him. "Without faith it is impossible to please Him" (Heb. 11:6).

Col. 2:6 says, "As ye have therefore received Christ Jesus the Lord, so walk ye in Him," . . . How did you receive Christ? By works or by faith? By faith, of course! So you must continue your Christian life by faith. Every time sin breaks your fellowship with God, confess that sin to Him, and then believe that God has filled you with His Spirit. Thank Him for filling you with His Spirit.

What About Surrender?

Of course it is absolutely necessary that your will be surrendered to God to have this power flowing through your life. Is there anything you would not do for God? Is there any place you would not go? If so, you are not fully surrendered to Him, and you are not filled with His Spirit. When you can say to God in sincerity, "I'll go where You want me to go, Lord; I'll do what you want me to do — no matter what it costs me," you are ready to be filled with His Spirit. The next step is to appropriate His fullness by faith.

Continue to Be Filled.

Don't forget that we are commanded to "be filled with the Spirit continually." It is not a once-and-for-all experience, as salvation is. There is nothing strange or odd about the Spirit-filled life. It's the way that God intended the Christian life to be lived. It is the act of allowing the Lord Jesus Christ to express Himself through my life. When I am filled with the Spirit, I am filled with Christ; and the fruit of the Spirit (love, joy, peace, long-suffering, etc.) is manifest in my life. It is impossible to live the Christian life without being Spirit-filled. Also, the Holy Spirit gives me power to witness (Acts 1:8). The same Holy Spirit that led Philip to the Ethiopian eunuch, will begin to lead me to hearts that are prepared to receive His word. Witnessing will no longer be a chore, but a joy.

Finally, remember that the Holy Spirit is not an influence or a substance, but a Person. It is not how much we have of the Holy Spirit that counts, but how much He has of us. There is one baptism, but many fillings of the Spirit.

> Spirit of the living God,
> Take control of me;
> Spirit of the living God,
> Take control of me;
> Spirit of the living God,
> Take control of me;
> Melt me! Mold me! Fill me! Use me!
>
> —Daniel Everson.

We are commanded not to be drunk with wine, but to be filled with the Spirit (Eph. 5:18).

"Strong drink is known to make men talkative—mean, stingy men become generous—timid men become bold—mournful, sad men become filled with joy for a little time until the intoxication wears off. Do not be drunk with wine wherein is excess, but be filled with the Spirit. Have you let the Spirit of God fill your spirit and radiate out through your soul and body, displaying Christ?"

> —Wildish, p.55.

The Spirit-filled life is not just for Christian leaders, but for all Christians. (See Additional Material in Step Three.)

Example: Samuel Morris, an African prince who was educated in a mission school and there converted to Christ, set out to America with no funds. His chief purpose was to learn about the Holy Spirit, who he had heard could "teach him all things." He miraculously found his way to America. In New York, he asked a bum on the street if he knew where he could find a certain man that the missionaries had told him about. The bum knew the man because he was head of a gospel mission. Sammy exemplified the Spirit-filled life. He was guided by the Spirit and his down-to-earth prayers were not only answered, but touched many hearts. He was a tremendous influence on fellow-students at Taylor University. The story of his life has been made into a movie called "Angel in Ebony" and has a challenging message for both Christians and non-Christians.

214

LESSON PLAN

HOW CAN A CHRISTIAN KNOW WHEN HE IS FILLED AND WHAT ARE THE RESULTS OF BEING FILLED WITH THE SPIRIT?

LESSON FIVE   STEP THREE

OBJECTIVE: To give the Christian assurance of his Spirit-filled relationship and encourage him to continue to walk in the Spirit
by faith.

I.   OPEN WITH PRAYER.

II. MEMORY VERSE: Galatians 5:22-23 (each check with another).

III. MOTIVATION:

Illustration: A bride and groom do not feel very married five minutes
after the ceremony. It is all so new and uncertain to them. They have
not really begun to experience the marriage relationship although the
legal transaction of binding them together has taken place. Ask them
a year later if they feel married and you'll get a much different
answer than at the time of the ceremony.

Likewise, don't be discouraged if you have not had a supercharged
change immediately after yielding to the filling of the Spirit. The
changes will come. Expect them and prepare for them.

Illustration: One day Mr. Fact, Mr. Faith and Mr. Feeling were walking along a wall. Mr. Fact was first, Mr. Faith second and Mr. Feeling was tagging along behind. Whenever Mr. Feeling took his eyes
off Mr. Fact and Mr. Faith he fell off the wall. But as long as he
kept his eyes on Mr. Fact and Mr. Faith he stayed on the wall. Feeling may be a result of the filling of the Holy Spirit, but let Feeling
tag along behind and not take his eyes off Fact and Faith.

IV. BIBLE STUDY:

A. Have them discuss what they think the results of the filling of
the Holy Spirit should be. If possible ask them to back this up
with scripture (see questions, Lesson 5).

B. Look up and discuss the following:

   1. John 4:34—The same motive for living that Jesus had.

   2. John 7:37-39—You will have an exuberant, abundant life flowing over into the lives of others.

   3. Acts 1:8—You will have power for witnessing.

C. Discuss fact, faith and feeling.

   1. What is the fact?

   2. Why is faith so important?

   3. Why should we make feeling subordinate to fact and faith? (Feeling fluctuates when fact does not change—faith anchors.)

V. PARALLEL PASSAGES: See the Lesson Amplification.

VI. SUMMARY:

The Christian is filled with the Holy Spirit by *faith*. He continues to be filled and controlled by *faith*. Evidence of a Spirit-controlled life will be a more fruitful witness for Christ. Matt. 4:19; John 15:8; the fruit of the Spirit, Gal. 5:22-23.

VII. CLOSE IN PRAYER.

HOW CAN A CHRISTIAN KNOW WHEN HE IS FILLED AND WHAT ARE THE RESULTS OF BEING FILLED WITH THE SPIRIT?

LESSON FIVE   STEP THREE

1. CHECK LIST OF THE FRUIT OF THE SPIRIT:

    A. Do you realize your utter dependence on Jesus Christ hour by hour, moment by moment?

    B. Are you looking to Him in all things?

    C. Are you slow to speak, to act, to plan, until you have been in touch with Him?

    D. Are you letting Christ live His life through you, instead of trying to live your life for Him (Gal. 2:20)?

    E. Do you realize that He is Love?

    F. Have you given up self-love and made it a supreme purpose of your life to love others? To let Christ love through you?

    G. Are you experiencing boldness in your witness for Christ?

    H. Are you producing fruit according to Mt. 4:19 and John 15:8?

    I. Are you convicted by every harsh word?

    J. Do you resent every selfish thought?

    K. Do you refuse to do selfish acts because they violate your new purpose?

    L. Do you understand that this love means practical, constant, life-long ministry and service for others, even as He served when on earth?

    M. Are you keeping both commandments continuously (faith, love)?

N. Are your quiet hours given to communion?

O. Are your busy hours given to ministering in love, however humble and commonplace the task may seem?

P. Are you so busy looking to Him and loving others that you are beginning to understand "It is no longer I that live, but Christ that liveth in me?"

II. RECOGNIZE THE ENEMY OF THE SPIRIT-FILLED LIFE:

A. Satan has bitterly opposed the doctrine of the Spirit-filled life.

1. He has confused it, opposed it and surrounded it with false notions and fears.

2. He does this to keep believers from winning others to Christ and thus taking them from his control.

B. Be on guard against Satan's temptations.

C. Expect persecution from the world. Jn. 15:18, 20; Matt. 5:11-12.

D. Realize that "greater is He that is in you, than he that is in the world" (I Jn. 4:4).

III. WHAT TO DO ABOUT POSSIBLE DIFFICULTIES:

A. Check impulses to see if they are of the flesh or the Spirit.

B. Allow the Holy Spirit to develop within you a new attitude of having "no confidence in the flesh."

C. Out of our failures to abide and our sinfulness shall come a deep sense of the need to abide, and more and more we shall lean on Christ.

IV. If there is time, have the class members each take one of these chapters on abiding and list the suggestions which will help one to abide in Christ:

John 14, 15, 16; Matt. 6; Col. 3; Eph. 5; Rom. 6, 8, 12, 14; I Cor. 13:1; Heb. 11; Gal. 5; Ps. 37:1-7; Ps. 23; Ps. 34. Keep these in a notebook for future reference. Add other chapters as you study.

HOW CAN A CHRISTIAN CONTINUE TO BE FILLED WITH THE HOLY SPIRIT?

LESSON SIX   STEP THREE

OBJECTIVE: To help each Christian reach a point of understanding which will result in the continual filling (control) of the Holy Spirit in his daily life.

I. OPEN WITH PRAYER.

II. MEMORY VERSES: John 14:21 or John 15:10.

III. MOTIVATION:

An experiment in role play: This is an excellent means to help individuals in the group identify their problems. Have three individuals play the roles (briefly) of:

1. A Christian just returning from a meeting with a friend in which he has successfully witnessed to him. (What does witnessing indicate to the Christian? Ans. One who is Spirit-controlled will witness.)

2. A Christian who has just been defeated by sin, but has used I John 1:9 and rebounded. How long does a Christian have to remain defeated?

3. A Christian who has been defeated and has not taken care of his sin problem and lacks faith to claim I John 1:9 and the refilling of the Holy Spirit (I John 5:14-15).

Discuss the roles played and why they reacted as they did.

IV. BIBLE STUDY: (Follow the basic outline in lesson 6).

A. Basically what are the steps one would take to be Spirit-filled? Discuss.

1. *Cleansing* from sin and self-life by I John 1:9.

2. *Claiming* God's will and purpose (the filling of the Holy Spirit, Ephesians 5:17-18; Rom. 12:1-2; and Acts 1:8) in prayer (I John 5:14-15).

3. *Believing God's promise* and acting in *faith* (Hebrews 11:6 and James 1:6).

B. How do you translate "continuing to be filled" into daily language? How does one live this way each day? (See Lesson Amplification for additional help.)

1. What part does cleansing play in our daily life?

2. What part do faith, trust, belief play in daily life (Heb. 6:12; 11:16)?

   a. In obedience and abiding—I John 3:24?

   b. In the adversities of life—Romans 5:3-5; I Thess. 5:18; Romans 8:28?
How do we display faith in adversity? (Praise and thanks to God.)

   c. In witnessing?

3. How should we present ourselves to God each day? (Rom. 12:1-2; Luke 9:23 and Rom. 6:11, 13).

V. PARALLEL PASSAGES: See the Lesson Amplification and Bible Study above.

VI. SUMMARY:

To have a continuous day by day Spirit-filled life is God's norm for the Christian and results from cleansing, and uncompromising faith which believes God and claims His promises to be truth *each day*, moment by moment.

VII. CLOSE IN PRAYER: Thank God for what He is going to do in each life that is yielded to Him.

HOW CAN A CHRISTIAN CONTINUE TO BE FILLED WITH THE HOLY SPIRIT?

LESSON SIX   **STEP THREE**

INTRODUCTION:

We have become so used to depending on feelings instead of facts in the Christian walk that we tend to doubt God's word and inwardly question whether He will do what His word says He will. Many of you have come to realize that you have been living a powerless Christian life and you honestly asked the Holy Spirit to fill you. Now, a few days later, you may be doubting the validity of this filling because there has been no big emotional reaction or drastic change.

Remember this, what God says is fact and whether your response be calm assurance, excited enthusiasm, or no definite emotional reaction at all, you can be positive that the Spirit has filled you if you've met the qualifications we discussed in Lesson Four, surrendered your will to Christ, asked in faith and expected Him to fill you.

I.   HOW TO BE FILLED WITH THE HOLY SPIRIT (Review):

II.   HOW TO WALK IN THE SPIRIT:

     A. *Results of the Spirit-filled life* (other than Gal. 5:22-23).

         1. You will have the same motive for living that Jesus had—John 4:34.

         2. You will have an exuberant, abundant life flowing over into the lives of others—John 7:37-39.

         3. You will have power for witnessing and aggressive spiritual warfare—Acts 1:8; Phil. 4:13; John 14:12.

         4. You will live a life of constant prayer and intercession.

            a. Because you have the inmost self of Christ in you.

            b. Only the Holy Spirit can teach you to pray—Rom. 8:26-7.

         5. You will have the character of Christ, the fruit of the Spirit. (It is not my trying to live like Christ, but letting Him live His life in me—Gal. 2:20.)

         6. Greater understanding of Scripture—I Cor. 2:9-13; John 14:26.

B. *Abiding.*

Abiding is not only communion but ministry *expressed in* love—I John 3:23.

1. God, who is love, can manifest Himself only to those who are willing to love others. John 3:16; I John 3:16; 3:1; 4:8, 4:19; John 13:1; John 15:9.

2. That child of God will have the fullest manifestation of the Spirit who adopts as the deliberate purpose and principle of his life, THE LOVE OF CHRIST INSTEAD OF THE LOVE OF SELF.

    a. He ceases to grasp all, and begins to give all.

    b. He ceases to seek all, and begins to surrender all.

    c. He ceases accenting "take care of number one," and begins to accent "let every man take care of the things of others."

    d. He no longer seeks the high place, but the lowly one.

    e. He seeks to minister, instead of being ministered to.

    f. He no longer seeks, but shuns the praise of men.

    g. He no longer seeks to save his life, but to lose it for others.

    h. He no longer seeks to lay up, enjoy and be at ease, but suffer, and spend and be spent for Christ Himself.

    i. He seeks to love as God loves, regardless of his treatment by others. "He is kind to the unthankful and the evil." If some grievous wrong, insult or unkindness goads you from your attitude of love, justify it not, but hasten to confess, and find forgiveness from Him who prayed for those who murdered Him, as well as for those who loved Him.

    —James McConkey, *Three-fold Secret of the Holy Spirit,* p. 86.

III. SUMMARY:

Read and meditate on the words of the hymn *"Trust and Obey."* Make personal application.

LESSON PLAN

THE CHRISTIAN AND THE HOLY SPIRIT

LESSON SEVEN   STEP THREE

OBJECTIVE: To give a panoramic view of the Spirit-filled life which would lead the group into the reality of this truth.

I.   OPEN WITH PRAYER.

II. MEMORY VERSE: Eph. 1:13-14.

III. MOTIVATION: Quiz—if any element of the question is false it is all false.

   A. When we accept Christ, God spiritually comes into our lives to produce good works. True or False? (True.)

   B. The Spirit of God is an impersonal force. True or False? (False.)

   C. If a man allows God's Spirit to control him he will find he will get to heaven, but will have to live a very restricted, pious life. True or False? (False.)

   D. Once a man has accepted Christ there is nothing he can do that will make him lose the Holy Spirit's control or filling. True or False? (False.)

   E. A person who is Spirit-filled is usually not very rational and therefore would not appeal to others unless they are Christians and understand. True or False? (False.)

IV. BIBLE STUDY: Read Ephesians 3:16-20 and 5:14-18.

   A. Who is the Holy Spirit? Read John 14:16-20 and John 16:7-15. What have you found out about the Holy Spirit?

      1. "Another comforter"—another person like Christ, vs. 16.

      2. "He will abide with you forever," vs. 16.

      3. "Spirit of truth," vs. 17.

223

4. Dwelleth in you (Christian), vs. 17.

5. Through the Holy Spirit Christ lives in us, vs. 20.

B. Why do we need His control—His filling of our lives?

1. There are two forces which can control us: the material or the Spiritual. We will gravitate to one or the other. Which will you be servant to?

2. List the things the Spirt will do in our lives in Ephesians 3:16-20 and 5:14-18.

   a. Strengthened with might, vs. 16.

   b. Power, vs. 20.

   c. Love, vs. 17.

   d. Fullness of God, vs. 19 (becomes reality).

   e. Using time (buying it), 5:16 (purposeful living).

   f. Give light, vs. 14.

   g. What does a little wine do? Compare this with the filling of the Spirit, vs. 18 (freedom from self and inhibitions).

3. What is the prerequisite for these things in our life? Eph. 5:18; Eph. 3:16 —By whom?

C. How can He fill us with the Holy Spirit?

1. Eph. 5:14—Sin puts the Christian to sleep and makes him for all practical purposes as if dead in spiritual life. Recognize it— Confess it—Be clean—I John 1:9.

2. According to Ephesians 5:17-18 what is the will of the Lord?

3. According to I John 5:14-15 if we ask anything according to His will what did He say would happen?

4. You must believe God—Faith—Heb. 11:6.

D. Let's bow for prayer, confess sin, ask God to fill us and believe Him that He will do that which is already His will.

E. Let this attitude of yieldedness be a practice of your daily life— Romans 12:1-2.

V. SUMMARY:

The Spirit of God seeks to control us. As we received Christ by faith for salvation, now we must receive the filling control of the Holy

Spirit by faith (Colossians 2:6). This is a necessity for all Christians, if they are to live in this material world effectively and abundantly as Christians.

VI. CLOSE IN PRAYER.

SUPPLEMENTARY READING

Augsburger, Myron, *Quench Not the Spirit,* Herald Press.

McConkey, James H., *Three-fold Secret of the Holy Spirit,* Back to the Bible, Box 233, Lincoln, Nebraska, 25¢.

Murray, Andrew, *Full Power of Pentecost.*

Murray, Andrew, *God's Best Secrets.*

Orr, J. Edwin, *Full Surrender,* Marshall, Morgan & Scott.

Pache, Rene, *The Person and Work of the Holy Spirit.*

Rees, Tom, *The Spirit of Life,* Moody, $2.50.

Taylor, Howard, *Hudson Taylor's Spiritual Secret,* Moody, 89¢.

Thieme, Rev. R. B., Jr., *What is Spirituality?* Berachah Church, 2815 Sage Road, Houston, Texas.

Torrey, R. A., *The Holy Spirit, Who He Is and What He Does,* Revell, $2.50.

Tozer, A. W., *How to Be Filled with the Holy Spirit,* Christian Publications, 25¢.

Unger, Merrill, *The Baptizing Work of the Holy Spirit,* Scripture Press.

Wilcox, Ethel, *Victorious Living,* Gospel Light Press.

THE CHRISTIAN AND PRAYER

STEP FOUR

OBJECTIVE: To challenge students to a regular and effective prayer life.

I. OPEN WITH PRAYER.

II. MEMORY VERSE:

Briefly review the verses which the students should have committed to memory.

III. MOTIVATION:

Hand out sheets of paper and ask the students to write down as many reasons as they can think of as to why we should pray. After three or four minutes, have each one read his list. The leader may then add any of his own and conclude the discussion by pointing out the importance of prayer.

IV. BIBLE STUDY:

A. Ask the key questions listed below, which are taken from the Step. For Lesson Amplification, refer to the Teacher's Manual as it discusses these various questions. If the student fails to answer correctly, direct him to the Scripture or quotation given in the Step. After the student has answered, the leader may conduct a brief discussion as he sees fit, or add any other material he wishes from the Manual.

B. Discussion:

1. What is a devotional time and why is it necessary (pp. 6-7)?

2. What kind of example did Christ set in relation to the quiet time (p. 7, Mark 1:35)?

3. What kind of things do you include in your quiet time? (This is a good opportunity for the group to share different methods which are helpful.) Definite suggestions from the leader should conclude the discussion.

4. What is the chief purpose of prayer (John 14:13—see essay in Lesson Two)?

5. How are God the Father, God the Son and God the Holy Spirit involved in our prayers? (Lesson Three—prayer is directed to God the Father, through Christ, in the power of the Spirit.)

6. What are at least four procedures which should be involved in prayer and what does each mean (pp. 14-16)?

7. What is the difference between intercession and petition in prayer? (Intercession is for others; petitions are requests in general, pp. 16-17.)

8. What are some things which make us powerful in prayer (p. 18)?

9. Name some promises God has made concerning prayer (Lesson Seven).

10. About how much time do you think you should spend in prayer regularly, in light of its importance? (Close this with discussion. Leader should point out that time varies for different individuals, but most of us spend all too little time in prayer.)

V. PARALLEL PASSAGES:

A. Quiet Time—Psalm 5:3; 55:17; Matt. 6:5-15; Acts 6:4.

B. Purpose of Prayer—Prov. 15:8; Psalm 42:1-2; John 4:23-24.

C. Privilege of Prayer—Matt. 6:9; John 16:24; Acts 12:5; Romans 8:26.

D. Procedure in Prayer—Psalm 15:1-3; 107:1; I Sam. 12:23; Matt. 7:7-8; Eph. 3:14-21; I John 1:9.

E. Power in Prayer—II Chron. 7:14-15; Matt. 21:22; Phil. 4:6-7; James 5:17-18.

F. Promises of Prayer—Jer. 33:3; Psalm 37:1-9; Luke 11:11-13.

VI. SUMMARY:

The world little knows what is accomplished through prayer. It is one of the most important things anyone can do. Through prayer, often prayer alone, men and women can be brought to Christ, Christians can be strengthened, holiness infused into their lives, circumstances altered, tragedies averted, perplexing problems solved, governments and kingdoms overturned, forces of evil defeated and Satan rendered helpless. When we have such a great privilege, are we not foolish to spend so little time and effort in prayer? When we arrive in heaven, one great question we will have burning in our hearts is, "Why did I not pray more?"

VII. CLOSE IN PRAYER:

Ask one of the group to close in prayer.

DEVOTIONAL BIBLE STUDY AND PRAYER

LESSON ONE   STEP FOUR

OBJECTIVE: To explain the meaning of devotional time and its importance as a daily practice.

I.   OPEN WITH PRAYER.

II. MEMORY VERSE: Isaiah 40:31.

III. MOTIVATION:

Discuss the following questions in relation to the memory verse:

A.   What does it mean, in the memory verse, when it says, "Wait on
the Lord?" Ans.—"Wait on the Lord" means to look to and expect
help from Him. This, of course, is an attitude we have all the time,
but it is something we especially do in our daily devotional time.
Daily waiting on the Lord means a daily time alone with Him in
prayer and meditation.

B.   What is the result of daily "waiting on the Lord?" Ans.—It gives
us strength we would not otherwise have to live the Christian life.
Note the context of Isaiah 40:31. Verse thirty has just told us
that even the young and strong shall faint and collapse under
strain, but those who wait upon God shall "renew" their strength;
daily they can obtain strength for the tasks at hand by spending
time with God.

C.   What does it mean, when it speaks of mounting up "with wings as
eagles," running without being weary and walking without fainting? Ans.— This gives us a picture of the strength we gain from
daily waiting on God. We are able to begin what God has for us
with zeal and enthusiasm, as an eagle, with great power, is suddenly able to rise in flight. We are able to continue at what God wants
us to do over a long period, as one who walks a great distance without fainting.

IV. BIBLE STUDY:

Use a panel discussion method, and assign each member *in advance of the class* one of the following topics to discuss for two minutes. At the end of each discussion add helpful comments of your own.

A. Definition and necessity of devotional time.

B. Having a definite time.

C. Setting a definite place.

D. Making the devotional time unhurried.

E. Goal and content of a quiet time.

Subjects may be condensed or expanded according to the number in the class.

V.   PARALLEL PASSAGES:

    A.   Matt. 7:7-11; Mark 11:22-26; John 15:7; I John 5:14-15—God promises to answer prayer.

    B. Gen. 18:23-32; Ezra 9:5-15; Dan. 9:3-19; John 17—examples of prayer.

VI. SUMMARY:

Read Psalm 145 and spend several minutes in prayer letting each one who wishes pray briefly.

VII. CLOSE IN PRAYER.

DEVOTIONAL BIBLE STUDY AND PRAYER

LESSON ONE   STEP FOUR

INTRODUCTION: The aim of this lesson is to explain the meaning of the devotional time, and its importance as a daily practice. Many young Christians know almost nothing about an effective devotional time, and many older Christians are very lax in their practice of it. This is one of the foundation stones of an effective Christian life. It can make or break your effectiveness as a Christian.

I.   HELPFUL SUGGESTIONS TOWARD A DEFINITE DEVOTIONAL TIME:

A. Set a definite time.

The important thing to note here is that we should regularly meet with God. It should not be haphazard or intermittent if we are to have sound spiritual health. Haphazard sleeping and eating habits cannot produce sound physical health. Christians are not under the Law. If we fail to have our devotional time one day, or if we do not have it at a certain exact time every day, this does not mean we are failing in our spiritual lives. But if we go for days at a time without a devotional time, or if it is not an important and meaningful part of our lives, something is wrong in our relationship with God. Note that David, in Psalm 5:3, had the habit of spending time with God regularly in the morning. This is a good example to follow. In Mark 1:35, Christ did two things. He arose early in the morning and went to a solitary place where he would not be distracted. He had just finished an extremely busy day. He was worn out. But not too worn out to get up to pray. Why? Because He recognized that the effectiveness of His ministry depended on time alone with God. *A man or woman too busy for time with God is too busy*. Why shut out the most important thing in life? Martin Luther, when once asked what his plans were for the following day, answered, "Work, work, from early morning until late at night. In fact, I have so much to do that

I shall have to spend the first three hours in prayer." If the Son of God, with all of His power, needed to pray, how shall you and I with all our weakness get by without praying?

B. Decide on a definite place.

In Mark 1:35 Christ selected a place where He could be alone and without distraction. This is essential in the devotional time. We must be able to turn all of our time and attention to God. If possible, select a place of beauty—a church, or some place surrounded by the beauties of nature. Sometimes, if this is impossible, by singing a hymn to yourself or playing one on a record, you can transform your devotional time to a time of real worship. This is a time when you can draw aside from the busy hours to rest and come close to God. You should enjoy it as much as any time in the day.

C. The goal of devotional time.

Two things are important in the devotional time: (a) **First and foremost,** God should get something out of it. It should be God-centered, ascribing praise and worship to Him. It should be a time when we show our love for Him. (b) We ourselves should get strength and help from it. From reading the Bible we should learn more about God. From praying we should find our burdens lifted and gain strength for the activities of the day.

"The object of the devotional time should not be to prepare addresses for your Bible study group, your Sunday school class, or anything of the kind, but to nourish and upbuild your own soul . . . In the devotional time, the consciousness of the soul must be, '*I need Thee, Oh, I need Thee.*' "

II. CONTENT OF THE DEVOTIONAL TIME:

A. Objective.

The content of the devotional time will include many things. It should include a simple, practical and effective method of Bible study. "Your object in the devotional time is not so much to gather information as to gain inspiration, and so you should discover what is the application of what you read to your present circumstances and need. Turn the truth into terms of life, and use the word of God to light and feed the fire of devotion."

Remember, you cannot lead anyone higher than you yourself have gone. You cannot enrich anyone beyond your own actual experience of God, hence, the absolute necessity of the Bible in the devotional time.

232

B. Prayer.

The devotional time should also include prayer. "Men who have moved the world for God have been men of sustained prayer habits." Your prayer should not be all supplication—it should include adoration and confession as well. Prayer is one of the most important disciplines of the Christian life. In John 4:23 it says the Father *seeks* those who worship Him in prayer. Why relegate it to second or third place in your life?

III. SUMMARY:

In conclusion, once again, we need to see the strategic importance of the devotional time in the life of the Christian:

"There is no true, deep conversion, no true, deep holiness, no clothing with the Holy Spirit and with power, no abiding peace or joy, without being daily alone with God. There is no path to holiness but in being much and long alone with God.

"What an inestimable privilege is the institution of daily secret prayer to begin every morning. Let it be the one thing our hearts are set on, seeking, and finding, and meeting God. Take time—O my soul, take time, to be alone with God. The time will come when you will be amazed at the thought that one could suggest that five minutes was enough"—Andrew Murray, *God's Best Secrets.*

"Harken unto the voice of my cry, my King and my God, for unto Thee I pray" (Psalm 5:2).

PURPOSE OF PRAYER

LESSON TWO   STEP FOUR

OBJECTIVE: To teach us the basis for making our prayer scripturally sound and meaningful.

I.   OPEN WITH PRAYER.

II. CHECK MEMORY VERSE: I John 5:14-15 (Review verses phrase by phrase to facilitate learning).

III. MOTIVATION:

Write a short paragraph of approximately fifty words based on the information in the lesson about one of the following topics:

A. Reasons why you pray according to your personal experience.

B. Man's relationship to God and why it is important before he can pray (based on John 3:5-8).

C. The qualifications for effective prayer (based on John 15:7-11).

D. Some purposes of prayer (based on Matthew 7:7; Matthew 26:41; Luke 18:1).

IV. BIBLE STUDY:

Have each one read his paragraph and discuss each. Conclude by doing question 4 together.

V.   SUMMARY:

A. Two definite conclusions are understood from this lesson:

1. Receiving Christ as Saviour puts one on praying ground and is a "must" according to John 3:3.

2. One must realize the law of the "abiding life" to be effective in prayer. Note the description of abiding on p. 26 of Step Three.

B. The Christian's fellowship with the Father is two-fold:

1. God speaks to us in His holy word. The Bible is the Father's message to His dear children.

2. We have the privilege of addressing Him in prayer. Prayer ought to be the Christian's native breath, his constant delight, his refuge in the moment of distress, his recourse in time of struggle, his solace in the hour of need.

C. Start a definite prayer list. (Leader give 4 or 5 specific requests for group to begin to pray for. Expect answers and acknowledge when answers are received.)

VI. CLOSE IN PRAYER.

Each person pray silently that God will reveal unconfessed sin so it may be confessed and not hinder the future effectiveness of his prayer. Prayer session should be closed by a brief prayer by leader.

PURPOSE OF PRAYER

LESSON TWO   STEP FOUR

I.   REASONS WHY YOU PRAY:

A. To Glorify God.

There are many reasons for prayer, but above all, the purpose of prayer is to glorify God. Jesus said in John 14:13, "Whatsoever ye shall ask in my name, *that will I do, that the Father may be glorified in the Son.*" In Acts 4:29-31, the early Christians were undergoing persecution. Did they pray that all persecution and difficulty would be removed from their lives? Did they pray all would be easy for them? They did not. They prayed that God would give them boldness to speak the Word, despite difficulty. Prayer is not an "escape hatch" to get us out of trouble. It is not merely something to make life easy for us. It is a means of glorifying God, whatever the cost may be to us. Prayer that moves God is prayer that ". . . seeks first the kingdom of God and His righteousness . . ." In Acts 4:31, God answered the prayer of the apostles by filling them with the Spirit so that they could speak the Word.

B. Other reasons.

Other reasons for prayer which we might list are: communion with God, adoration of God, confession to God, thanksgiving to God, supplication to God. But all of these are united by the common purpose of glorifying God. If they are done merely for personal pleasure, and not to glorify God, they are, for the most part, in vain.

II.   MAN'S RELATIONSHIP TO GOD IN PRAYER:

It is important to realize, as we pray, that prayer is a spiritual activity, an activity which must be motivated and carried out by the Holy Spirit. John 3:5-8 and John 4:23-24 emphasize this. John 4:24 tells us that "God is a Spirit . . ." This is the form God takes. The person who is not a Christian is a "natural man" (I Cor. 2:14). He ". . . receiveth not the things of the Spirit of God, for they are foolishness unto him, neither can he know them, because they are spiritually discerned." This is why so much of prayer is an empty experience for the man who is not a Christian. This is also the reason that prayer can be a dead and dull experience for the Christian who does not pray by the power of the Holy Spirit. "True prayer is prayer in the Spirit; that is, the prayer the Spirit inspires and directs. When we come into God's presence, we should recognize . . . our ignorance of what we should pray for and how we should pray for it, and in the consciousness of our utter inability to pray right, we should look up to the Holy Spirit, casting ourselves utterly upon Him to direct our prayer, to lead out our desires and to guide our utterance of them."

—R. A. Torrey, *How to Pray.*

III. THE QUALIFICATIONS FOR EFFECTIVE PRAYER:

Question 3 emphasizes the qualifications for effective prayer. These conditions are wrapped up in the two phrases taken from John 15:7 —"If ye abide in me" and "My words abide in you." Abiding in Christ means total dependence on Christ. There are at least three ways to cross the Pacific Ocean. You can swim the ocean, which would be total dependence on your own strength. In this case you would go a few miles at the most, and drown. You can paddle in a canoe, which would be partial dependence on your own strength, and you might get several miles farther, but the first strong wind would overturn you. Finally you could travel on a great ocean liner, which would be the total committing of yourself to another to do what you could not do. This would guarantee you a safe trip, even through storms and gales. So, abiding in Christ means total dependence on the strength and power and ability of another. We do not trust ourselves even in part. Lack of abiding, laboring in our own strength, being out of fellowship with God, makes our prayer lives empty and vain. Christ's words also must abide in us. His words must rest in our hearts and control our lives. In the military a soldier who refuses to obey instructions can be court-martialed. An employee who refuses to obey instructions is fired. A student who does not obey instructions in his courses often lowers his grade. The Christian who, whether from ignorance or unwillingness, does not obey God's instructions in the Bible, will see his whole life suffer—especially his prayer life. Right living means right praying. And to obey God's word we must know it, which means we must read it often.

IV. THE DEEPEST LONGINGS OF THE HUMAN HEART ARE SATISFIED THROUGH PRAYER:

Question 4 emphasizes that prayer satisfies the longings of our hearts. Psalm 63 describes the longing of a heart for God. One reason for prayerlessness is lack of desire to seek God. Do we seek God for Himself alone—apart from all He can give us? In Exodus 33:1-17 is the story of how Moses pled for the presence of God after Israel's sin with the golden calf. In verse 15 Moses said, "If thy presence go not with me, carry us not up hence." God had said He would send an angel, but this was not enough for Moses. Moses wanted the best . . . God's presence with him. "In the grief of that sad day, how glad God must have been to find one man who at all costs wanted the best . . . God never forgot it. The time came when Moses failed God; nevertheless at the end of his life they both went together up the slopes of Nebo's lonely mountain, communing as they walked, and there God gave His beloved friend sleep, and with His own hands laid him away to rest until the great resurrection day. God did not consider angelic ministration good enough that day for the man who in his life time would have nothing less than God Himself . . . In our zeal for the better are we missing the best? The word of our Lord to us is still 'He that loveth Me shall be loved of My Father, and I will love him, and will manifest Myself unto him.' Up there 'His servants shall serve Him, and they shall see His face,' but it is also blessedly true that He will manifest Himself on earth to those who love and serve Him here."

PRIVILEGE OF PRAYER

LESSON THREE   STEP FOUR

OBJECTIVE: To show the divine operation of the Father, Son and Holy Spirit in their functions regarding our prayers.

I.   OPEN WITH PRAYER.

II. CHECK MEMORY VERSE: Phil. 4:6-7.

III. MOTIVATION:

Take a pencil and paper and list these four names: Jesus, God, Holy Spirit and You. Now assign one or two of the Scripture passages listed to each person in the Bible study and have him or her relate the Scripture verse to the proper name:

Hebrews 4:14-16 *Jesus*   I Timothy 2:5 *Jesus*   Isaiah 59:2 *God*
Ephesians 6:18 *HS*   Matthew 6:9 *w*   Romans 8:26 *H S*
John 14:6 *Jesus*   I John 3:22-23 *w*   Jude 20 *H S*

Summarize by pointing out how these Scripture verses show that the Father, the Son and the Holy Spirit are all involved in prayer.

IV. BIBLE STUDY:

Ask each one present to answer a question; then encourage discussion using the information in the Lesson Amplification.

V.   PARALLEL PASSAGES:

A. How many mediators are there between God and man?

1. I Timothy 2:5.

2. Romans 5:15.

3. I Corinthians 8:6.

B. How should we pray?

1. Pray without display—Matthew 6:5.

2. Pray in faith, believing—James 1:6.

239

3. Pray fervently—James 5:16.

4. Pray in line with God's will—I John 5:14-15.

5. Pray unceasingly—I Thess. 5:17.

VI. SUMMARY:

The fact that all three persons of the Godhead are involved in our prayers shows how vitally important prayer is to God. Of all the privileges we have in life, a personal audience with our Father through His Son in the power of the Spirit is one of the greatest. Suppose that for every day you spent at least twenty minutes in prayer, someone would give you at least a thousand dollars. Would you be more diligent and faithful in your prayer life than you are now? Is it possible that you and I would be willing to do for money what we would not be willing to do for God just because He is God and has given us access to Himself? Prayer is not just a dull duty imposed on us by God; it is not a ritual which we are to fulfill legalistically; it is the privilege of being able to pray to our Father in heaven. You should not have to force yourself to pray; you should feel the need of prayer and want to pray.

VII. CLOSE IN PRAYER.

PRIVILEGE OF PRAYER

LESSON THREE   STEP FOUR

I.   UNTO WHOM DO WE PRAY?

On question 1, it is important to note the matchless privilege of praying unto God. The realization of this gives power to our prayers.

"But some will say, 'Is not all prayer unto God?' No. Very much so-called prayer, both public and private, is not unto God. In order that a prayer should be really unto God, there must be a definite and conscious approach to God when we pray; we must have a definite and vivid realization that God is bending over us and listening as we pray. In much of our prayer there is little thought of God. Our mind is not taken up with the thought of the mighty and loving Father of Whom we are seeking. Often-times it is the case that we are occupied neither with the need nor with the One to Whom we are praying but our mind is wandering here and there throughout the world . . . But when we really come into God's presence, really meet Him face to face in the place of prayer, really seek the things that we desire *from Him,* then there is power."

—R. A. Torrey, *How to Pray.*

II.   THROUGH WHOM DO WE PRAY?

We pray unto God, but as question 2 points out, we pray only through His Son Jesus Christ. Jesus said, "I am the way, the truth and the life; no man cometh unto the Father, but by Me" (John 14:6).

A college student at an eastern university was once invited by a friend to go with him to Washington, D.C. The college student had no idea that anything out of the ordinary would happen, but when they arrived in Washington, his friend took him to the White House. Here they spent the day with the President and his wife, as their guests. It turned out that the friend had known the President for years, and through him the college student was able to spend a day that he would never forget. This would have been impossible on his own initiative, but when an acquaintance of the President opened the way for him, he received a priceless privilege—one he would never forget. The way to God is opened for us, but many of us think very lightly of it. We would not be too busy to see the President, but we have no time for an audience with the King of Kings, the Ruler of the universe.

III. IN WHOM DO WE PRAY?

Question 3 points out that we are to pray *in the Spirit*. This has already been discussed in earlier lessons, but we should note again that unless our prayer is in the Spirit it can never be effective before God. Only the filling of the Holy Spirit can produce vital, believing prayer. No matter how we may work up our emotions, no matter what our feelings, no matter how great our desperation—unless God the Holy Spirit is behind our praying, it is fleshly, self-centered, powerless prayer. To pray in the Spirit, it is important to realize what our relationship to the Spirit is.

"The Holy Spirit will not come to us, nor work within us only at certain times when we think we need His aid. The Spirit comes to be our life companion. He wants us wholly in His possession at all times; otherwise He cannot do His work in us . . . When once this truth is grasped, we shall realize that it is possible to live always praying in the Spirit! By faith we may have the assurance that the Spirit will keep us in a prayerful attitude and make us realize God's presence, so that our prayer will be the continual exercise of fellowship with God and His great love."

Thus we see, as a result of this lesson, the great privilege of prayer, and how God the Father, God the Son and God the Holy Spirit all participate in it.

We cannot afford to neglect this priceless privilege. No wonder prayer accomplishes so much; no wonder it does what nothing else can do.

C. H. Spurgeon said years ago: "You have no place in which to pour your troubles except into the ear of God. If you tell them to your friends, you but put your troubles out for a moment, and they will return again. Roll your burden onto the Lord, through prayer, and you have rolled it into a great deep out of which it will never by any possibility rise. Cast your trouble where you cast your sins; you have cast your sins into the depths of the sea, *there* cast your troubles also. Never keep a trouble half an hour before you tell it to God in prayer. As soon as the trouble comes, quick, the first thing, tell it to your Father in prayer." Read I Peter 5:7 in the Amplified New Testament. Continual prayer means continual freedom from burdens and anxieties. It is the only way to be a happy Christian.

IV. SUMMARY:

That God *desires* our fellowship is, perhaps, one of the most amaz-

242

ing facts conveyed to us through the Scriptures. This fact is so staggering in its conception that it is extremely difficult for us to grasp and consider its significance.

That God should allow His creatures to have fellowship with Himself is wonderful enough; but that He can *desire* it, that it gives Him satisfaction and joy and pleasure, is almost too much for understanding.

"The Father seeketh such to worship Him . . ." Let this reflection fasten itself upon us, and it will inspire us with a passionate desire to seek His face morning by morning. The usual conception—that we read our Bibles and say our prayers for our own benefit and satisfaction—will fade into insignificance. Let this simple thought of His desire for our fellowship obsess us morning by morning and day by day.

It will carry us through times of deadness and darkness, give us patience to continue and persevere, when we remember that He is waiting to be gracious to us, waiting till He sees that we wait upon Him.

PROCEDURE IN PRAYER

LESSONS FOUR AND FIVE   STEP FOUR

OBJECTIVE: Lessons four and five will be considered as one unit. We are considering a simple guide that you may use in your daily prayer time. This order can be easily remembered by the first letter of each word: ACTS.

I.   OPEN WITH PRAYER.

II. CHECK MEMORY VERSE: I Corinthians 14:40.

III. MOTIVATION:

Ask for student's definition of terms: adoration, confession, thanksgiving, supplication (see the Lesson Amplification).

IV. BIBLE STUDY: Cover only the verses noted here.

We may categorize the section into two phases: giving to God (adoration, confession, thanksgiving) and receiving from God (supplication).

A. Giving to God:

   1. Adoration or praise—gives honor to God because:

      a. Jeremiah 32:17—NOTHING is too hard for God.

      b. Romans 8:28—of His omnipotent, sovereign rule in all of life. (See the Lesson Amplification.)

   2. Confession—presents a clean vessel to God (see the Lesson Amplification).

      a. Psalm 51:6, 16-17.

      b. I John 1:9.

   3. Thanksgiving—indicates appreciation to God as the supplier of all our needs.

      a. Thanks should be offered.

         (1) Continually—Hebrews 13:15.

         (2) For every single thing—Ephesians 5:18-20.

         (3) Because it is God's will—I Thess. 5:18.

b. The Scripture teaches us thanksgiving is to be offered continually and for all things—even for what seems adverse. Why can adversities really be blessings in disguise? Discuss.

B. Receiving from God—Supplication:

1. Intercession

   a. Colossians 1:3,9—Paul prays for Christians.

   b. I Timothy 2:1-4—prayer for non-Christians.

2. Petition:

   a. What are some things that hinder our prayers? Discuss.

      (1) Doubt—James 1:6-8.

      (2) Pride—Psalm 66:18.

      (3) Wrong motives—James 4:3.

   b. What are some things we should realize to have successful prayer?

      (1) God's willingness to give—Romans 8:32.

      (2) Faith—I John 5:14-15.

      (3) Right living means right praying—Psalm 84:11-12.

   c. Have students give personal experiences of prayers that went unanswered and why.

V. PARALLEL PASSAGES:

A. Adoration—Habakkuk 3:17-19; Psalm 113.

B. Confession—Psalm 32; Ezra 9:5-15.

C. Thanksgiving—Psalm 107:1-2; Luke 17:11-19.

D. Supplication—Philippians 4:6-7; Ephesians 6:18-20.

VI. SUMMARY:

A. Use poem in the Lesson Amplification.

B. Once again we are faced with the importance of prayer. We can carefully use these methods and procedures, but they in themselves will not make great prayer warriors. To learn these things effectively, we must pray.

"Though a man shall have all knowledge about prayer, and though he understands all mysteries about prayer, unless he prays, he will never learn to pray."

VII. CLOSE IN PRAYER.

LESSON AMPLIFICATION

PROCEDURE IN PRAYER

LESSONS FOUR AND FIVE   STEP FOUR

I.   ADORATION: Act of paying honor to a Divine Being; to regard with
     fervent devotion and affection.

Comment on Romans 8:28.

One authority notes on this verse: "This working of all things for good
is done quite naturally to 'them that love God' because such souls
are persuaded that He who gave His own Son for them cannot but
mean them well in all His procedure. Life cannot but have purpose and
meaning when it is His purpose."

Another authority notes: "It is only the loyal soul who believes that
God engineers them. Although we say we do, we treat the things that
happen as if they were engineered by men." We must learn to worship God in the trying circumstances.

II. CONFESSION: To make confession of one's faults, especially to con-
     fess one's sins. (The Greek word means "say the
     same thing with." We "say the same thing with"
     or agree with God about our sins.)

Comment on I John 1:9.

In confession of sin, note these principles: (1) We do not need to feel
"spiritual" to confess our sins. If we need to confess them, it is a sign
we are not spiritual anyway at the moment. Confession need not depend on moods or feelings. The time to confess is immediately after
realizing we have sinned. (2) Confession should be real and honest,
but beware of torturous self-examination or unhealthy extremes of in-
trospection. Lord Wariston, a devout young man of the seventeenth
century, describes himself in his diary as being God's "poor, naughty,
wretched, useless, passionate, humorous, vain, proud, silly, imprudent
. . . barrow man . . . the unworthiest, filthiest, passionatest, deceit-
fulest, crookedest, backslidingest, rebellionest . . . of all thy servants."
Whatever truth there was in this, this cataloging of sins seems tainted
with a bit of pride in the thoroughness of his self-condemnation. (3)
Confession should be willing to accept God's forgiveness and then
change behavior appropriately. I John 1:9 says we are cleansed from
all unrighteousness. When some confess their sins they still retain

their guilt feelings and self-pity because they do not want to accept the fact God cleanses from all unrighteousness. Someone has well said, "The great men of the Old Testament, like David and Moses, were not perfect men. But they were men who, when they sinned, had the ability to confess, be restored to fellowship, and go on once more with God."

III. THANKSGIVING: Act of rendering thanks, especially to God. A prayer expressing gratitude.

Note especially here that we are to thank God not only for good times, but also for adversities. Ephesians 5:20 says, "Giving thanks *for* all things." Here it is made a sign of the filling of the Holy Spirit. I Thessalonians 5:18 says to give thanks *in* all things because this is God's will for us. To fail to do this is to sin against God, just the same as violating the Ten Commandments is sin against God. In Job 1:21 it is recorded that after Job had lost his money and his family, he worshipped God and said, "Blessed be the name of the Lord." If you were to lose your whole family and every cent you have in the next twenty-four hours, would this be your attitude? If we are filled with God's Holy Spirit and recognize that He controls all things, it can be. "Oh that men would praise the Lord for His goodness and for His wonderful works to the children of men" (Psalm 107:8).

IV. SUPPLICATION: To implore God. A humble petition, entreaty.

Supplication is of two types: intercession, which is for others, and petitions, which are requests in general. Christians often do not realize the importance of intercession. Paul continually prayed for his converts, as the first chapters of almost all his epistles show. He also asked them to pray for him (Romans 15:30-31, etc.). Paul, probably the greatest Christian of them all, felt it necessary to request prayer for his work. How shall we succeed if others do not pray for us, and we for them. Early in your Christian life, you should try to form prayer partnerships with your friends. This will bring you closer together and will profoundly affect your life. Discuss with the group and try to motivate them to form prayer partnerships whether with one another, or with others. Every Christian should have other Christians praying for him regularly.

"God rules the world and His Church through the prayers of His people. 'That God should have made the extension of His Kingdom to such a large extent dependent on the faithfulness of His people in prayer is a stupendous mystery and yet an absolute certainty.' God calls for intercessors: in His grace He has made His work dependent on them; He waits for them"—Andrew Murray, *God's Best Secrets*.

THE PLACE OF PRAYER

There is a place where thou canst touch the eyes
    Of blinded men to instant, perfect sight;

There is a place where thou canst say, "Arise"
    To dying captives, bound in chains of night;

There is a place where thou canst reach the store
    Of hoarded gold and free it for the Lord;

There is a place—upon some distant shore—
    Where thou canst send the worker and the Word.

Where is that secret place—dost thou ask, "Where?"
    O soul, it is the secret place of prayer!

—Alfred Lord Tennyson

POWER IN PRAYER

LESSON SIX   STEP FOUR

I.   OPEN WITH PRAYER.

II.   MEMORY VERSE: Check any or all memory verses up through this lesson.

III. MOTIVATION:

The teacher should narrate the story of Acts 12 briefly to show the power of prayer. Notice: (1) There was a serious problem here out of which there was no conceivable escape. Peter was an important leader in the early church and his death might have meant catastrophe for the early church at this time. James had already been killed, and it looked as if Peter would be also. So we are often faced with great problems, which, if they continue, might result in tragedy, and out of which there seems no human escape. (2) The church resorted to its only weapon at such a time—and really best weapon. The church had no army with which to free Peter; it had no means of wisdom or craft to get him out of jail; it was shut up to God alone. Yet "one man with God is a majority." So we should not despair when prayer is the only way out, for prayer is more effective than anything else we can use. We should be spending more time in prayer about our problems and less time worrying or fretting and trying to devise means of escape. (3) The result of the church's prayer was that Peter was set free, and Herod, the one who put him in jail, was removed by a judgment of God (Acts 12:20-25).

"Prayer is the great problem-solver. Yet even the church found it hard to believe prayer would work (Acts 12:15). 'Power belongeth unto God,' but all that belongs to God we can have for the asking. God holds out His hands and says, 'Ask and it shall be given you . . .' The powerlessness and poverty of the average Christian finds its explanation in the words of the Apostle James, 'Ye have not because ye ask not' "—R. A. Torrey.

IV. BIBLE STUDY:

Assign each one a question to answer.

V. PARALLEL PASSAGES:

Note Genesis 32:24-29—Jacob wrestled with God and prevailed. After much prayer he came away with a NEW NAME (prince of God), and a NEW BLESSING AND COURAGE to face his brother, Esau. Gen. 32:26, "I will not let go except Thou bless me," should be our motto in prayer. Note also I Kings 18:36-37.

VI. SUMMARY:

If we are to have powerful prayer, we must learn how to pray in groups as well as individually. What are some suggestions as to how we can improve group praying? (See the Lesson Amplification.)

VII. CLOSE IN PRAYER.

LESSON AMPLIFICATION

POWER IN PRAYER

LESSON SIX   STEP FOUR

I. WHAT MAKES A MAN POWERFUL IN PRAYER?

A. *Hebrews* 11:1,6—Faith.

B. *Romans* 12:1-2—Yieldedness.

C. *I Corinthians* 15:58—Steadfastness and abounding in God's work.

D. *James* 5:16—Righteousness.

E. *Ephesians* 5:18—The filling of the Spirit.

F. *John* 15:7—Abiding in Christ and letting His word control us.

G. *Ephesians* 5:20 and *I Thess.* 5:18—Thanksgiving in all things.

H. *I John* 5:14-15—Praying according to God's will as revealed in His word.

These verses will help us solve many of our problems concerning unanswered prayer. Answered prayer is not just automatic. It is the experience of those who only truly want to live for God and put Him in first place. If your prayers are powerless before God, perhaps the difficulty is not just in your prayers, but in your life. Perhaps you are not surrendered on some issues. Perhaps you are not doing anything for God. Perhaps some sin is hindering you. "One unconfessed act of disobedience on our part will shut the ear of God against any petitions." R. A. Torrey tells the story of a woman who came to him and said she did not believe in the Bible any more. When he asked her why, she replied, "Because I have tried its promises and found them untrue." "The Bible says," she continued, " ' Whatsoever ye ask believing, ye shall receive.' Well I fully expected to get things from God in prayer, but I did not receive them, so the promise failed." Dr. Torrey then turned her to I John 3:22—"Whatsoever we ask, we receive of Him, because we keep His commandments, and do those things that are pleasing in His sight." Then he said, "Were you keeping His commandments and doing those things pleasing in His sight?" She confessed she was not. Her trouble was not the Bible's promises; it was her own disobedience.

II. THE CONDITIONS FOR ANSWERED PRAYER:

A. *I John* 5:14-15—Asking according to God's will.

B. *Matthew* 18:19—Praying in agreement with another. (Though prayer can be answered individually, this increases our power in prayer.)

C. *John* 15:7—Abiding in Christ and His word in us.

D. Some questions to discuss in regard to answered prayer:

1. Would God really be doing the best thing for us if He answered prayers which were not His will? A baby playing in the kitchen might see a shining steel knife and want it. Yet his mother, knowing the danger of giving it to him, keeps it from his grasp. Many times things we want with all our hearts, and things which will ultimately bring misery and spiritual weakness to our lives, are outside of God's will.

2. What is the value of several praying for something as opposed to just one? There are times, of course, when God answers the prayer of just one individual. But when several share the burden of a prayer, the Scripture teaches that there are greater results. Paul requested others to pray for him (Eph. 6:18-19). Just as an ember by itself will soon die out, but when surrounded by other embers will burn for some time, so with the Christian, there is strength in unity. When many pray, many have a chance to witness God's power instead of one. When many pray, a closer fellowship both with God and one another results. Seek a prayer partner and share your prayer burdens. Christians in the same living group should meet together for prayer. There is *power* in united prayer.

3. Why is it necessary to abide in Christ, and His word in us, that prayer may be answered? We noted above that we must pray *in the will of God*. But the important question is, how do I know the will of God when I pray? The answer is first of all, through God's word. This lays down the general principles of Christian living. Many times we pray outside the will of God because we do not know the word of God.

   "My words must abide in you." But we can also know even further than this. If we abide in Christ, putting all our dependence on Him, He will guide our prayers by the Holy Spirit. We cannot pray for everything. God knows what He is going to do, and will guide our prayers. John 16:13, "He will guide you into all truth." But this experience becomes true in our lives as we walk close to God and spend much time in prayer with Him. Ask God to guide your prayers. Guided praying is the most effective praying.

III. PREVAILING PRAYER:

Many Christians pray for something which it is God's will to give

them, but they never obtain it only because *they give up too soon!*
They want to see results immediately. "The fruit of the Spirit is patience." God waited many years before He sent Christ. He may wait
many more years before He sends Him the second time. He waited
patiently for years while some of us lived without knowing or wanting
to know Him. Even today He bears patiently with all kinds of weaknesses and rebellious attitudes. So, if He requires us to wait days,
weeks, even years before prayers are answered, we should have no
complaints. Through waiting patiently our faith grows and our characters are refined. Note the example of George Mueller on page 20 of
Step Four. "God may cause us to wait, but He will never be too late."
The farmer works all through spring and summer, month after month,
but he does not see a harvest right away. Yet when the harvest does
come his waiting has made it worthwhile.

IV. SUMMARY: Some practical suggestions for group praying:

A. Make your prayers sentence prayers.

B. Wait in silence until the Spirit impresses you to pray about something specific.

C. Avoid praying in a circle. Such practice tends to hinder the Spirit's
free working in the group.

D. Feel free to pray more than once about different individuals and
circumstances.

E. Be thankful for the silences between prayers. Let God speak to
your heart at that time.

F. Be specific—avoid the over-use of general words like "bless" and
"help." Ask God not just to bless in a general way, but to bless
in specific ways.

G. Make praise and thanksgiving an important part of your time of
prayer.

LESSON PLAN

PROMISES OF PRAYER

LESSON SEVEN   STEP FOUR

OBJECTIVE: To show that God answers prayers to meet our needs in every area of life.

I.   OPEN WITH PRAYER.

II. MEMORY VERSE: Jeremiah 33:3.

III. MOTIVATION:

In Detroit, Michigan, an old couple was taken to the hospital suffering from malnutrition and starvation. After they went to the hospital, police began to search through their rubbish-cluttered home, and they discovered $40,000 stored away. The husband said he was not even aware that he possessed over a thousand dollars. This is exactly the plight of most Christians in relation to prayer. "Ye have not because ye ask not" (James 4:2). "He that spared not His own Son, but delivered Him up for us all, how shall He not with Him also freely give us all things?" God does not expect us to live like spiritual misers, suffering malnutrition in our Christian life, when He has vast treasures of blessings ready to give us only on the condition that we come in believing prayer. Let all of us ask ourselves if we are really appropriating His blessings. If not, the trouble is not with God but with us. In this lesson let us seek to discover how we can appropriate what God has for us.

IV. BIBLE STUDY:

A. Have one person look up the condition and another recite the promise for each of the following verses in the Step:

1. Jeremiah 33:3.

2. Matt. 21:22.

3. I John 5:14-15.

4. John 14:14.

5. Phil. 4:19.

254

6. Psa. 84:11.

7. Prov. 3:5-6.

8. Eph. 1:3.

9. Isaiah 41:10.

B. Have one person read one verse and comment on it for each verse listed under part two of Lesson Seven. The leader should add to the discussion from the Lesson Amplification.

V. PARALLEL PASSAGES: See above.

VI. SUMMARY:

A. Through this Bible Study we see again how important prayer is. It is like the pipe which carries water from the great city reservoir into our homes. Though it is but a channel, if the pipe is broken all of the water is held back and nothing comes through. Prayer is our channel to God.

B. Read the quote of E. M. Bounds on page 23 of the Step.

VII. CLOSE IN PRAYER.

PROMISES OF PRAYER

This lesson should drive home to the heart of every believer how willing God is to answer prayer. "If a son shall ask bread of any of you that is a father, will he give him a stone? Or if he ask a fish, will he for a fish give him a serpent? Or if he shall ask an egg, will he offer him a scorpion? If ye then, being evil, know how to give good gifts unto your children: how much more shall your heavenly Father give the Holy Spirit to them that ask Him" (Luke 11:11-13)? Jesus here draws from human analogy. No parent would refuse his child an honest request. No parent would deliberately hurt his child. If sinful humans are this way, what about our heavenly Father who is perfect? Shall He not outgive any human father? The difficulty, however, is that men take advantage of this. They think the best things to have are material things, things of the world, things that will make life easy and pleasant for them. Jesus said, "How much more shall your heavenly Father give the Holy Spirit." While He makes material provisions for His children, His greatest and most lasting gifts are gifts connected with the Spirit of God and spiritual things. "Desire earnestly the best gifts." In taking hold of God's willingness to give, let us not only believe He will give, but let us ask for the best He has—spiritual blessings.

I.   WHAT GOD HAS PROMISED CONCERNING PRAYER:

A. Ask expectantly.

Jer. 33:3—If we but call on God, He will answer and show us "great and mighty" things. At the time God made this promise to Jeremiah, he was being held captive by the unbelieving rulers of Israel. Israel had strayed far from God. They were a nation given to idolatry, and the horrible judgment by Babylonian captivity was about to descend on them. In the midst of this dark, discouraging picture, God says, "Call unto Me and I will answer thee, and show thee great and mighty things." God showed Jeremiah (in the rest of chapter thirty-three) that a day was coming when He would utterly transform and change this idolatrous nation, and "it shall be to me a name of joy, a praise and an honor before all the nations of the earth" (v. 9). What a marvelous revelation for such an hour! What an encouragement to the heart of God's prophet! So in praying we need to realize God has "great and mighty" things to show us as individuals about our relationship to Him and what He can do for and through us. We need only call upon Him to receive these things. We are so governed by earthly circumstances we lose the heavenly vision. We need to take our eyes off the discouragement of self and circumstance and call upon God. Perhaps you are going through a difficult and discouraging time right now. Perhaps on your campus or in your life there seems nothing but mediocrity. Call on God to show and to do "great and mighty" things. In his darkest hour Jeremiah had a great revelation from God. In your dark hours God can do this for you—IF you call on Him.

B. Ask believing.

Matthew 21:22—God promises that whatsoever we ask *believing*, we shall receive. "Without faith it is impossible to please Him" (Hebrews 11:6). This is a stumbling block for most of us because we are always tempted by Satan to doubt God's love and willingness to make provision for us. The first sin entered the human race because Eve began to doubt God's word (Gen. 3:1-6). We cannot believe God for just anything, however, for sometimes it is not His will to do just the things we ask. We must therefore ask God to lead us to ask for the right things, and when He does this, along with it He will give us the faith to believe. But we should be far more willing to believe God than most of us are. Why be content to trust Him for the little things only? Why not ask God to "move mountains?" Why not ask Him to work in a special way in your life or the life of a friend to glorify Himself. William Carey, the great missionary said, "Expect great things from God, attempt great things for God." Pray in accordance with the promise of God. Claim the promises by faith. Dr. Henrietta Mears, after a long and fruitful ministry frequently stated, "If I had my life to live over again I would just believe God."

C. Ask according to God's will.

I John 5:14-15—The condition of prayer here is that we ask *according to His will,* and then we receive the petitions, or answers to prayer, we desire of Him. The railroad train cannot travel in just any direction it would like. It must always follow the track. So God is restricted to the path of His will in answering prayer. God is all-knowing and all-loving. He knows every possibility and contingency. He sees into the future. He knows what others will do. Therefore His answers will correspond only to His will, which is "good, and acceptable, and perfect" (Rom. 12:2). The problem is not that God refuses to answer prayer, or is ungenerous; the problem is that we do not ask according to His will. How can we know His will? (1) By studying the word of God. (2) By really thinking carefully whether our prayer is for the glory of God and according to His will, or just something to gratify selfish desires. "Ye ask and receive not because ye ask amiss, that ye may consume it upon your lusts" (Jas. 4:3). (3) By asking the Holy Spirit to lead us. "For as many as are led by the Spirit of God, they are the sons of God" (Romans 8:12).

D. Ask in Jesus' name.

John 14:14—If we ask in the name of Christ, He will do it. What does it mean to ask in the name of Christ? It means far more than saying "in Jesus' name" glibly at the end of a prayer. To ask in the name of Christ means to ask on the basis of the authority Christ has given to us. We are to ask in His authority for His glory, so that "the Father may be glorified in the Son" (v. 13). Outside of many public schools in the United States, small boys wearing white bands are given authority by the school and the state to halt traffic so school children may cross the street. Just a small boy, yet because he has the authority of another greater than himself, dozens of motorists on their way to work will bring their cars to a screeching halt at the sign of his uplifted hand. No matter how weak and unbelieving we may think we are, we come to God on the basis of the authority from His Son. If we recognize this, and if we ask things which will glorify the Son, not just ourselves, God says He will do it.

II. WHAT GOD HAS PROMISED CONCERNING PROVISION FOR OUR NEEDS:

A. Material needs.

Philippians 4:19—God will supply all your needs according to His riches in glory. Notice God says He will supply your *needs*, not necessarily your desires. Notice also it is according to His riches in glory. If you had a benefactor who had a 50 million dollar fortune, would you worry about where tomorrow's meals were coming from? God's fortune is far greater than a paltry 50 million, and we need have no worry about His willingness to supply. Psalm 84:11—God withholds no *good* thing from those who walk *uprightly*. Notice God gives only *good* things. Sometimes the things that are good for us in the long run may not make us happy for the moment. Sometimes it is good for us to go through privations, and we need to consider these as gifts from God too. We must also walk *uprightly* to have God's blessing on our lives. Men who have prayer answered are men who live uprightly.

B. Guidance.

We continually need guidance as we walk the path of the Christian life. God does not promise to show us the whole future at once, but He does promise to guide us day by day. But this comes only as we "trust in the Lord." Before making any important decision we should always pray for guidance; and in even the little things of life, there should be an attitude of surrender and trust. Why rely on your wisdom when you can have God's?

C. Spiritual needs.

These are the greatest needs of life. These are also things which God alone can satisfy. We need happiness and satisfaction in our hearts. We need victory over sin. We need courage to overcome Satan and face trial. These are spiritual needs. The Bible promises that God will supply these generously and in abundance—more so than any other kind of blessing He gives. God does not allow every person on earth to be a material millionaire. Some are living in elegant mansions and some live in one-room shanties. But God made all Christians universally spiritual millionaires. "He has blessed us with every spiritual blessing in Christ." This is sufficient for every need. And, it has been done already in Christ, so all we need do is possess the possessions He has given us.

III. SUMMARY:

As a teacher of this lesson you may make this lesson more meaningful to yourself and thereby to your class by following the subsequent exercises:

1. List items which hinder answered prayer, those sins implied by the promises. Are you guilty? Have you confessed and forsaken them?

2. Notice what area you may have failed to submit to the Lord in prayer, an area in which you have felt competent to govern details.

3. Think about the statement, "God helps him who helps himself." Is there a false conviction underlying this statement? What is it that allows God to help you?

SUMMARY LESSON PLAN

THE CHRISTIAN AND HIS BIBLE

STEP FIVE

OBJECTIVE: To impress the student with the greatness of the Bible; to show that the unity of the Bible lies in one theme; to give Christians confidence in the authority and inspiration of the Old Testament; to discover what the Bible claims for itself, and to awaken a desire for the word of God as daily food, essential for life.

I.   OPEN WITH PRAYER.

II. MEMORY VERSE: II Timothy 3:16-17.

Weave the entire lesson around these verses.

III. MOTIVATION:

Use Lesson One's Motivation.

IV. BIBLE STUDY:

A. The historical and scientific accuracy of the Bible is a demonstration of its inspiration. Use the material on Creation (Genesis 1) from Lesson Three for further study section.

B. Christ is the theme of the Bible. Use the ten Old Testament prophecies fulfilled in Christ, Lesson 2, (pp. 8-9). Fill in these questions in the Step if the students have not done this previously.

C. The Bible is our food and power. Use the first half of Lesson 5, (p. 18). Tell what the Word is or what it does, or both.

The Motivation illustration of Lesson 6 provides a useful conclusion.

V.   PARALLEL PASSAGES:

A. Matt. 5:17-18.

B. Luke 4:16-21.

C. John 5:38-40.

D. John 7:16-17.

VI. SUMMARY:

Two solid reasons have been given for our belief that the Bible is what it claims to be—the very word of God. First, its instruction contains a small amount of science and a great deal of history which is of such a nature that a supernatural origin is the only logical explanation. Secondly, its instruction is powerfully helpful; it gives us spiritual life and health here on earth and in the life to come. Review II Timothy 3:16-17.

VII. CLOSE IN PRAYER.

THE CHRISTIAN AND HIS BIBLE

STEP FIVE

SUPPLEMENTARY READING

Bruce, F. F., *The New Testament Documents: Are They Reliable?* Eerdmans, $1.25, pb.

Culbertson, William, "Faith's Sure Foundation," American Tract Society, 3¢.

Free, Josph P., *Archaeology and Bible History,* Van Kampen, $4.00.

Gaebelein, Frank E., "Is the Bible Inspired?" American Tract Society, 2¢, pb.

Grounds, Vernon, *The Reason for Our Hope,* Moody, 39¢, pb.

Lindsell and Woodbridge, *Handbook of Christian Truth,* Part I, Revell, $3.50.

Lott, Ernest E., ed., *The Miracle Book,* Moody, 39¢, pb.

Martin, James, *Did Jesus Rise from the Dead?* Association, $1.25.

Moody, D. L., *Pleasure and Profit in Bible Study,* Moody, 39¢, pb.

Olson, Nathanael, "How to Read Your Bible More Effectively," American Tract Society, 1¢.

Orr, William, "Ten Reasons Why," Van Kampen, 25¢, pb.

Packer, J. I., *Fundamentalism and the Word of God,* Eerdmans, $1.25, pb.

Ramm, Bernard, *Protestant Christian Evidences,* Moody, $3.50.

Short, A. Rendle, *Modern Discovery and the Bible,* Eerdmans, $2.00.

Smith, Wilbur M., *Profitable Bible Study,* Wilde, $2.00.

Stoner, Peter, *Science Speaks,* Moody, 39¢, pb.

Stott, John F. W., *Basic Christianity,* Eerdmans, $1.25, pb.

Torrey, R. A., *Difficulties in the Bible,* Moody, 39¢, pb.

Vos, Howard F., *An Introduction to Bible Archaeology,* Moody, 39¢, pb.

Young, E. J., *Thy Word Is Truth,* Eerdmans, $3.50.

Note: If the lessons of Step Five are being taught separately, the leader should purchase and read the invaluable paperback by Grounds.

LESSON PLAN

THE BOOK OF BOOKS

LESSON ONE   STEP FIVE

OBJECTIVE: To whet the appetite by introducing the Bible and the lessons to follow (in this Step); to impress the student with the greatness of the Bible.

I.   OPEN WITH PRAYER.

II. MEMORY VERSE:

II Timothy 3:16-17 is used as part of the Motivation; discuss it and memorize it.

III. MOTIVATION:

II Timothy 3:16-17 makes two claims for the Bible. What are they? If you were a Moslem or a humanist or any other type of non-Christian and you wanted seriously to investigate Christianity, how would you evaluate these two claims? What would be your criteria for the first claim? . . . and for the second?

IV. BIBLE STUDY:

Follow outline given in the Lesson Amplification.

V.   PARALLEL PASSAGES:

None.

VI. SUMMARY:

Two arguments for inspiration of the Bible have here been touched upon: (a) the amazing composition of the Bible; its unity and progression, despite centuries of differences among authors; (b) the moral uplift and drive of the Bible; its helpful influence, and its saving power.

VII. CLOSE IN PRAYER.

THE BOOK OF BOOKS

LESSON ONE   STEP FIVE

INTRODUCTION:

Note to OBJECTIVE: This is an introductory lesson; study the objective carefully and limit yourself to it. Even if a student is agnostic, the facts regarding the Bible's content and influence should draw his interest and open his mind to want to know more.

Therefore keep off the subject of inspiration; if it comes up, table the topic until Lesson Two (and especially 3-5). Your object here is to lay a good foundation for teaching the high view of the Bible as God's word.

Note on MOTIVATION: How would you evaluate these claims? The leader should study ahead, for you will find help in working out some answers in the four foundations of faith in Lesson Two, as well as in the points of Lesson Three. (In other words, let the others talk; then fill in where they have not.) The object of the Motivation is to preview some of the discussions which are to come. As they mention points, tell them when (in what lesson) their inquiry will be studied.

I.   THE AMAZING COMPOSITION OF THE BIBLE:

We shall begin our evaluation of the Bible with a look at its composition and human authorship.

A. Read the paragraph on pp. 4-5 in the Step.

B. Turn to the Table of Contents in your Bible and we shall survey the composition of the whole Book. *Note:* There are two objectives in this survey: (1) the practical value of being familiar with Bible books (many students feel lost when asked to look up verses; so inform them of the fact that the Table of Contents is put there to be used—this will save time and embarrassment); (2) to grasp better the weight of the argument regarding the Amazing Composition. Return to the paragraphs in the Step and discuss them now.

Note: Consult the historical chart in Step Nine. The Historical Books cover the period from Moses to Ezra on the chart. Poetry: dates sometimes unknown; David and Solomon were the major authors. Prophets: from Elijah to Ezra on chart.

265

1. The Old Testament is divided into five parts. The first of these is the *Pentateuch* which consists of the first five Historical Books. It was written by Moses and is also called the books of the Law. *Genesis* contains the creation of the universe and man. It shows how man was created to have fellowship with God, but because of his own stubborn self-will, he chose to go his own independent way and that fellowship was broken. It gives the first promise of the coming Redeemer (3:15), and shows the establishment of the Jewish nation through which He was to come. *Exodus* is the story of Israel leaving the bondage of Egypt and the beginning of their journey to the promised land. While on their journey, God gives the Law by which His nation is to live. *Leviticus* contains the more detailed instructions of the Law. *Numbers* and *Deuteronomy* tell of Israel's wandering in the wilderness and coming to the promised land.

2. The next section contains twelve more *Historical Books.* They tell of the establishment of the Kingdom of Israel in their own land, of Israel's repeated turning from God to sin, and finally, God's punishment—their being taken into exile by Assyria and Babylonia. The last three books tell of the exile and post-exile periods. Paul tells us in the New Testament that these narrations of Hebrew history were given to be examples to us.

3. The five books of *Poetry* make up the next section. The book of *Psalms* is probably the best known. It is the Hebrew hymn book, but each Psalm applies to us in some way.

4. Another section of five books follows, called the *Major Prophets.* They were written during the days shortly before Israel was taken into captivity and during the exile period. They contain prophecies concerning the coming Messiah, warnings of impending disaster if Israel did not turn from her wicked ways, as well as prophecies concerning world events. Some of these are still to be fulfilled.

5. The last division of the Old Testament is the *12 Minor Prophets.* They are called this not because they are less important, but because their writings are shorter. Their prophecies mainly concern Israel and the coming Messiah.

6. The divisions of the New Testament are mentioned in the first paragraph of this lesson in Step Five. The four *Gospels* tell of Christ's life and ministry. *Acts* is a history of the early church describing the ministry of Peter and Paul. There are two groups of epistles, the *Pauline* and the *General Epistles.* The epistles, or letters, written by Paul are thirteen in number and are named for the church or individual to whom they were sent. Next comes the book of *Hebrews.* We do not know the author,

but its very content puts it on the same level as other Scripture. There are seven *General Epistles,* which are named not for the recipients but for the authors. *Revelation* describes the ultimate triumph of Christ in His Second Coming.

II. IT IS THE BOOK FOR IMPORTANT MEN:

A. Do not fail to read pages 44-51 and 82-90 of *The Reason for Our Hope,* for more on this point. Anyone teaching this Step should buy or borrow a copy of the 39¢ paperback.

B. Some additional quotations:

Robert Millikan, past-president of California Institute of Technology and Nobel Prize winner: "I consider an intimate knowledge of the Bible an indispensable quality of a well-educated man."

William Lyon Phelps of Yale: "I thoroughly believe in a university education; (yet) I believe a knowledge of the Bible without a college course is more valuable than a college course without the Bible."

Goethe: "Let mental culture go on advancing, let the natural sciences progress in ever greater extent and depth, let the human mind widen itself as much as it desires; beyond the elevation and moral culture of Christianity, as it shines forth in the Gospels, it will not go."

Horace Greeley: "It is impossible to enslave mentally or socially a Bible-reading people. The principles of the Bible are the groundwork of human freedom."

Mark Twain: "The things that bother me in the Bible are not the things which I do not understand, but the things I *do* understand!"

III. THE BIBLE IS OFTEN CALLED VARIOUS NAMES BY ITS WRITERS:

A. Look up "scriptures" in the dictionary, so that its meaning is clear.

B. Why do you think the Bible is called the Sword of the Spirit?

Explain how the Holy Spirit uses the word to teach and convict; and how we need to be familiar with it, so that we are able "to take" this sword and use it effectively. This brings the lesson back to the personal and practical, as in II Timothy 3:16-17, at the beginning.

LESSON PLAN

CHRIST IS THE CENTRAL PERSON OF THE BIBLE

LESSON TWO   STEP FIVE

OBJECTIVE: To show that the unity of the Bible lies in one theme; and
that this theme is the touchstone for determining whether
the Bible is the word of God.

I.   OPEN WITH PRAYER.

II.   MEMORY VERSE: I Corinthians 15:3-4.

III. MOTIVATION:

Admiral Byrd illustration.

IV.   BIBLE STUDY:

A. What did Christ say about the Old Testament Scriptures?

B. Why do we rest in the authority of the Christ of the Bible?

C. How many of the ten prophecies listed on pp. 8-9 appear to you
   to have been fulfilled in Christ?

D. How much of the Old Testament is fulfilled in Christ?

E. What do the four Gospels tell us?

F. In the Epistles what were Christians directed to do?

G. The last book of the Bible has what purpose?

V.   PARALLEL PASSAGES:

John 5:45-47; Neh. 8:10; John 16:33; II Tim. 1:7; John 8:31-32;
1:1-5; Mark 13:31; Matt. 5:17-18; Luke 4:16-21; Matt. 5:17-
29; 28:18-20; Mark 10:42-45; Luke 7:36-50; 14:1-6; 15:1-2; John
1:1-18.

VI.   SUMMARY:

Why is Christ the central person of the Bible? Let each one think in
silence and then talk this over. Refer to the four foundations of our
faith in Christ.

VII. CLOSE IN PRAYER.

268

CHRIST IS THE CENTRAL PERSON OF THE BIBLE

LESSON TWO   **STEP FIVE**

INTRODUCTION:

During his first Antarctic expedition Admiral Byrd was flown to the Pole itself and spent the six-month-long night there alone. Snow after snow and blast after blast buried his small hut.

Each day he shoveled his way to the surface for exercise. There was enough light to see only a dozen yards or so as he walked the few steps he dared to take. One day he turned to go back, but was shocked to discover that he could not see his stove pipe. Veteran that he was, he controlled any tendency to panic, refusing to move because he knew his danger. To wander about would probably place him farther from the hut.

He drove a stake into the snow, and using it as his center, he walked a large circle around it. Not finding the hut, he extended his radius and walked another circle, always with one eye on the stake, the other searching through the blackness. The third time he tried this, the circle was so large that he almost lost his stake. He returned and resolved to make one more attempt, with a still larger circle.

The range of visibility was strained to its limit as he walked holding on to his point of reference. Yet he knew that if he lost that point of reference, the ice and snow would quickly claim another victim. It was enough. He walked right into the hut's tunnel. Some people get lost reading the Bible. This lesson holds the secret for understanding the Bible. The Bible has a point of reference, around which one must move. Learn to keep your eyes on Christ, and you will find that as your spiritual eyesight improves and allows you to penetrate the gloom and darkness of this world, you will be able to extend your radius of faith further and further, exploring more and more of the exciting and adventurous life in Christ.

Have you ever heard this one?

> "You Christians provide the best examples of reasoning in a circle. You quote the Bible as God's word and therefore the final authority, yet when you are challenged as to why one should consider the Bible to be so authoritative, you can only say, 'It claims to be God's word.' What kind of logic is that? 'It is God's word because God's word says it is God's word.' So does the Koran!"

This is a vital question for any clear-thinking Christian, as well as for the sincere investigator of Christianity. And it is important that we grant to the critic the correctness of his logic, and then proceed to explain to him that there are solid facts behind our Christian convictions—facts which elevate the Bible far above all other books—facts which logically point to just one conclusion: the Bible is the word of God. These facts are focused partially on the Bible itself but more on the Bible's central message: God-in-Christ.

I. WHAT CHRIST SAID ABOUT THE OLD TESTAMENT IN RELATION TO HIMSELF:

A. What did Christ say about the Old Testament Scriptures?

1. The men addressed by Jesus did accept Scripture, but what judgment did He make on their profession? John 5:38, 42, 45-47.

2. The key question therefore is: what will you do with Jesus Christ? Go over question 2, a-d, dealing with Luke 24 given in Step Five.

3. Certainly these first Christians were not reasoning in a circle; they had very objective data to work with, namely, Christ Himself—all that He was, and all that He taught. They came to a place of unconditionally accepting Jesus Christ's authority because in Him they were brought face to face with the God who fulfills *heart* and *mind, natural* and *supernatural*.

We live twenty centuries later. Yet the same confrontation is made today. Let us enlarge these four points with modern man in mind.

B. Why do we rest in the authority of the Christ of the Bible?

1. *Because in Him we meet the God who lays claim to our hearts with an unparalleled offer of love, joy and peace* . . . freeing us, on the one hand, from self-centered living with its guilt, anxiety and sensuality, its petty purposes, recurring friction and inevitable loneliness; and arming us, on the other hand, with power to become creative and redemptive servants—in God's image.

"The joy of the Lord shall be your strength"—the Old Testament. "I have spoken this to you that in me you may have peace; in the world you have tribulation, but be of good cheer, I have overcome the world"—Jesus, on the eve of His execution.

"God has not given us a spirit of timidity, but a spirit of power and love and self-control"—Paul, writing from a Roman prison.

A very vocal opponent of Christianity has reluctantly admitted: "There are certain things that our age needs. . . . The root of the matter is a thing so simple that I am almost ashamed to mention it for fear of the derisive smile with which wise cynics will greet my words. The thing I mean—please forgive me for mentioning it—is love, Christian love, or compassion. If you feel this, you have a motive for existence, a guide in action, a reason for courage, an imperative necessity for intellectual honesty"— Bertrand Russell, *Impact of Science.*

2. *Because in Him we meet the God who calls for intellectual allegiance to the highest philosophy,* to a logical world-view which is "a light for our feet and a lamp for our path" and is "the power of God unto salvation" because it converts evil into good and suffering into blessing. The realism and discipline of Jesus Christ forces us to confront the drabness, the rawness and the grandness of life (including ourselves and God) in such a radical way that we are transformed in the process; we discover meaning, beauty, virile purpose, dynamic energy, for our lives and for all mankind (John 8:31-32).

3. *Because in Him we meet face to face the same God who is only viewed dimly in nature;* the God whose word and Spirit are found to lie in and through, beneath and above the facts of life whether known through common experience or through our physical, social and historical sciences.

The divine activity is rooted in nature as well as ancient history, and it is expressed today in living persons and events. All our sciences therefore touch upon it, some more and some less. And—when stripped of philosophical presuppositions and allowed to be purely scientific instruments—all of them do supplement the Christian revelation, and confirm it; far from contradicting it, they find their ultimate significance in it—John 1:1-5, 10-14, 18; Acts 17:24-29.

4. *Because in Him we meet the God who answers our desire for a voice direct from Him to us.*

Through fulfilled prophecy and miracles, providential guidance and answered prayer, but pre-eminently in the person of Christ Himself and our experience of His Holy Spirit within us, God personally validates the message of Scripture so that our faith rests confidently in it as His true word and nothing less—Acts 1:1-5.

5. *We may conclude, therefore, that true Christian thinking does not reason in a circle at all. It begins with objective data.* In the mission and message of Jesus we find the deepest harmony of the demands of our own hearts and minds and the facts of life with a sure word straight from God.

None of these four points is complete in itself. Nevertheless each one is very convincing, even without the support of the others. Where else can you go to find a religion or philosophy offering that which equals even one of these? Many a man is so thrilled when he discovers Christ fulfilling *just one or two* of these that that he is converted before investigating the others. However, when added together, the case for Christianity is just that much weightier. "Heaven and earth will pass away," said Jesus, "but my words will never pass away."

The case for the Bible rests fundamentally on the case of Christ, for Christ identified the Bible indissolubly with Himself.

II. OLD TESTAMENT PROPHECY CONCERNING CHRIST FULFILLED IN THE NEW TESTAMENT:

A. How many of the ten prophecies listed on pp. 8-9 appear to you to have been fulfilled in Christ?

1. If limited in time, assign one question to each person for an answer.

2. This lesson introduces the student to one of the many remarkable features of Christianity's foundation, namely, the phenomenon of fulfilled prophecy. Suppose that there were only 50 predictions in the Old Testament (instead of approximately 300) concerning the first advent of Christ, giving details of the coming Messiah which meet in the person and work of Jesus. The probability of chance fulfillment, as calculated by mathematicians, is less than one in 1,125,000,000,000,000 (1125×10^{12}).

B. How much of the Old Testament is fulfilled in Christ?

1. It is important to realize that—impressive as they are—the specific predictions are only half the weight of the evidence of Lesson Two. For the references to the Old Testament on pages 6-7 are equally as important as those on page 9, even though they are much more general.

2. Have three students each read one of the following: Matthew 5:17-18; Luke 4:16-21; John 5:38-40.

3. It is not merely in the isolated predictions which are fulfilled with precision, but it is also in the entirety of the Old Testament that one finds a looking forward to something yet to come, something beyond itself; and if that something is not a delusion, it is to be found in the New Testament and in Christ. For Jesus' life and work give a fullness of meaning *to the whole Old Testament* that it could not otherwise have. This total fulfillment provides us with firm ground for the belief that the Old

Testament not only *did* lead to Christ, but *was intended* by the God whose partial revelation it records to lead to Christ.

4. According to Romans 15:8-12 what did Christ confirm by His ministry?

5. According to Acts 3:18 how many of the Old Testament prophets wrote of Christ?

III. CHRIST, THE CENTRAL PERSON OF THE NEW TESTAMENT:

A. What do the four Gospels tell us?

1. Each of the Gospels presents different aspects of Jesus' life and ministry:

a. Matthew, written to the Jews, presents Jesus as the "Messiah" (the "Christ," the "Anointed"); the Law-giver who is far greater than Moses and the Ruler who is far greater than King David; the Son of God who is Authority and Power; Matthew 5:17-18, 21-22, 27-29; 28:18-20.

b. Mark wrote with the Romans in mind—men of action who built roads and conquered nations. In Mark's gospel you will find the words "immediately" and "straightway" used over and over again as the writer pictures Jesus with divine power and compassion, constantly serving rather than being served; the Son of God who is the Servant; Mark 10:42-45.

c. Luke, the only Gentile writer in the New Testament, wrote perhaps for a Greek nobleman with the Greek ideals of the development of fine manhood—"perfect mind," "perfect body," etc. He presents Jesus as the perfect Man, the Son of God who is the Son of Man; Luke 4:16-21; 7:36-50; 14:1-6; 15:1-2.

d. John, writing years after the other three, provides a deeper perspective than they. From the very first there was an intensity of divine glory in Jesus which human thick-headedness appreciates only partially. After years of contemplation, John saw this more clearly and presents Christ to the world as God incarnate—God become man; the Son of God who is God Himself; John 1:1-18.

2. Does the fourth Gospel purport to record all that Jesus did (John 20:30)?

3. How did the disciples of Jesus know of what they wrote (I John 1:3)?

4. Why are the historical facts and teachings of Jesus Christ written (John 20:31)?

5. What did Christ command us to do (John 15:16)?

6. What are we to teach (Matthew 28:19-20)?

B. In the Epistles what were Christians directed to do?

1. Colossians 2:6. After the student has answered this question ask: "How had the Christians received Christ?" (Answer: by faith.) "This is the manner in which they were to continue to live and walk in Him. They were to have a child-like faith in Christ and a complete obedience to Him."

2. How (2:7)?

3. Of what were they to beware (2:8)? Is this warning still needed today?

C. The last book of the Bible has what purpose (Rev. 1:1)?

1. What is its authority (Rev. 1:2)?

2. What is its promise (Rev. 1:3)?

3. Who gave such knowledge to its writer, John?

4. How?

5. What is its warning (Revelation 22:18-19)?

FOR FURTHER STUDY:

For another array of impressive predictions, see *The Reason for Our Hope,* page 52. Note that these prophecies on a specific subject are being fulfilled in our own times as well as earlier. *Protestant Christian Evidences,* p. 81ff., has still another type of historical fulfillment of definite prophecies. These are the three main lines of Old Testament prediction: the Jewish nation (as in *The Reason for Our Hope),* the Gentile nation *(Protestant Christian Evidences),* and Christ (Step Four). However, it is not recommended that you use any of this additional material, since it is much farther from the main theme of Lesson Two.

LESSON PLAN

AUTHORITY OF THE OLD TESTAMENT

LESSON THREE   STEP FIVE

OBJECTIVE: To give Christians confidence in the authority of the Old
Testament so that any sense of shame or doubt regarding
the trustworthiness of the Book of Books may give way to
the joy and freedom of assured understanding.

I.   OPEN WITH PRAYER.

II.   MEMORY VERSE: II Peter 1:20-21. (Cover this in the motivation
discussion.)

III. MOTIVATION: Refer to the five questions included in the Introduction.

IV.   BIBLE STUDY:

A. Did the writers have a genuine confidence in their own product?

B. Does inspiration mean that the writers lost their individuality and
became stenographers or dictaphones in their relation to their own
writings?

C. Summarize the evidence for the divine origin of the Old Testament.

D. Is Scripture trustworthy in both fact and doctrine according to
Jesus?

E. Does Christ's teaching prove anything?

F. Is the Old Testament scientifically and historically accurate?

V.   PARALLEL PASSAGES:

A. Isaiah 6:1-8.

B. Amos 7:14-15.

C. Hebrews 11:32-38.

D. Jeremiah 23:16-17.

E. Isaiah 55:6-11; 40:6-8.

VI.   SUMMARY:

Repeat the evidence listed at summary of Section I C of the Lesson
Amplification, then use the verse and the question at the conclusion
of the lesson, page 13 in Step Five.

VII. CLOSE IN PRAYER.

AUTHORITY OF THE OLD TESTAMENT

LESSON THREE   STEP FIVE

INTRODUCTION:

Here are five questions for you to work on, preferably working out your own answers *before* you have studied through the material of this lesson and those to follow. Then add your answers as you study.

- a. What is meant by the inspiration of the Bible?

- b. What part does God play and what part does man play in writing the Bible?

- c. If the Bible were not God's inspired word, what difference would it make to you personally?

- d. What are the main arguments in favor of the Bible's being the word of God?

- e. What do we do with difficulties and apparent errors in the Bible?

(The ideal would be to have the members of your group come to the session with their answers to these questions written out.)

Take time to discuss the first of the questions. Consult II Peter 1:21 and II Timothy 3:16 and Hebrews 1:1. Then proceed to introduce question 1 of the lesson.

I.   TESTIMONY OF ITS WRITERS:

A. Did the writers have a genuine confidence in their own product? In daily life we trust people for three reasons: because they claim our confidence, because their claims are supported by the testimony of others, and because we can test them for ourselves by our own experience. For instance, every time you take medicine you are trusting a pharmacist. You trust him because he claims to be a competent dispenser; because that claim has been verified by recognized medical authorities and a host of customers; and, perhaps, because you have had other prescriptions made up by him before. Of course, it is not necessary to have all three elements present in any one act of trust. (a) We may, for example, have confidence in a man who has no confidence in himself; or, (b) we may trust him on the basis of our own experience without the confirming evidence of the experience of others; (c) and there is always a first time of trusting when we have no experience of our own to rely upon.

But for complete certainty of the reliability of a person *all three* elements should be present.

Therefore, in evaluating the case for inspiration, it is important that we ask:

1. What kind of conviction regarding themselves did the Bible writers themselves have?

2. What is the testimony of other experts (in religion and science)?

Let's take the first question first: Did the writers have a genuine confidence in their own product? II Samuel 23:2; Jeremiah 1:9; Ezekiel 3:4.

B. Does inspiration mean that the writers lost their individuality and became stenographers or dictaphones in their relation to their own writings?

1. Critics of the Bible's claim to be divinely inspired often interpret this as meaning that the Book was mechanically dictated by God, that it has no more of the human personality in it than a girl imparts to the letters she types from the dictation of her business employer. This is miles from the truth. Every author has his own literary style. Each displays his intellectual and emotional characteristics in varying ways and to varying degrees. Paul's letters, for instance, are so loaded with his own personality that a famed scholar has rightfully asserted that no man of antiquity is better known to us than he. In his letters to Christians whom he had not yet met we are introduced to the Apostle's tremendous analytical mind and the depth of his experience with Christ, with sin, with life; and in the letters to his own converts we feel the personal warmth of his great heart. Plainly, there is in the Bible a human element which is itself magnetic.

Intellectual difficulties which some people feel toward the Bible are discarded once they realize that "inspiration" does not mean that God used writers as though they were dictaphones. Dr. B. B. Warfield, the greatest writer on this subject, has said:

"These books were not produced suddenly, by some miraculous act—handed down complete out of heaven, as the phrase goes; but, like all other products of time, are the ultimate effect of many processes cooperating through long periods. There is to be considered, for instance, . . . the preparation of the men to write these books, a preparation physical, intellectual, spiritual, which must have had its beginning in their remote ancestors, and the effect of which was to bring the right men to the right places at the right times, with the right endowments, impulses, acquirements, to write just the books which were designed for them . . .

"If God wished to give His people a series of letters like Paul's He prepared a Paul to write them, and the Paul He brought to the task was a Paul who spontaneously would write just such letters . . .

"As light passes through the colored glass of a cathedral window, it is light from heaven we are told. So, any word of God which is passed through the mind and soul of a man must come out discolored by the personality through which it is given, and just to that degree ceases to be the pure word of God. But what if that personality has itself been formed by God into precisely the personality it is, for the express purpose of communicating to the word given through it just the coloring which it gives it? What if the colors of the stained-glass window have been designed by the Architect for the express purpose of giving to the Light precisely the tone and quality it received from them?"

2. The selection of Scripture in this section may be misunderstood in that it gives the impression that these writers were without character—just nameless nonentities, machines of God. Actually, the exceptional character and veracity of these men provides one of the strongest evidences for their divine inspiration. Note also paragraphs like the following:

Isaiah 6:1-8, noting the prophet's consciousness of his own inadequacy to deliver God's message, his unworthiness.

Amos 7:14-15, spoken as the prophet's answer to royal orders to "shut up or get out" (like Peter's word in Acts 4:19-20).

Hebrews 11:32-38 might be added also.

Men do not ordinarily maintain their messages when extreme suffering and isolation is their payment. They, rather, trim their talk to suit the listener's applause. Jeremiah 23:16-17 has a good description of the false prophet who—*because he lacks God's inspiration*—cannot resist the "organization-man complex" toward conformity.

3. The prophets themselves lay down high standards as characteristic of the word of God:

a. Above and beyond, outside of the self-centered and sensual interests of sinful men; and powerful, therefore—infallibly effective and invincible—Isaiah 55:6-9, 10-11.

b. Eternal, lasting, universally true—Isaiah 40:6-8.

The writers of the Old Testament were fully convinced that their messages met these standards; and they would be the first to discard them *if* they did not. Such was the quality of their objectivity and devotion to God's truth.

C. Summarize the evidence for the divine origin of the Old Testament. On chalkboard or on paper, list these point by point so that all can see them. The leader should list the numbers and the lessons (i.e., the underlined material), leaving the rest of each line to be filled in by the others.

The evidence for the divine origin of the Old Testament may be summarized as follows (i.e., the evidence discussed in these *Steps;* this is by no means the totality of the evidence):

1. *Lesson One*: The amazing composition of the Bible; its unity and progression despite centuries of differences among authors.

2. *Lesson One*: The moral uplift and drive of the Bible, its beneficial influence, its saving power. (Lesson Two; Further Study also.)

3. *Lesson Two*: The fulfilled prophecy of the Bible, especially its specific and general fulfillment in Christ. (The Further Study section gives two other major areas where extensive prophecies have been and are being fulfilled.)

4. *Lesson Three-A. Testimony of Its Writers:* The confidence of these men in the fact that their messages originated with God, not themselves, i.e., their claim to divine inspiration.

5. *Lesson Three-A. Testimony of Its Writers:* The character and veracity of the writers; their lives backed up their claims. In particular, they received from divine revelation an objectivity toward the evils of their times which was displayed with the compassion of social surgeons—without bitterness or cynicism (though the people resented and resisted them).

6. *Lesson Three-C. Testimony of the Apostles* (to be covered shortly, so leader must fill in this answer): The remarkable harmony of science and history with the Old Testament.

7. *Lesson Three-B. Testimony of Christ* (Since this is next, make this the transition point): The Old Testament can and should be independently evaluated regarding its claims. Nevertheless, it is inseparably linked to Christ, as Lesson Two demonstrated. The final evaluation therefore rests upon the testimony of Christ, which follows.

II. TESTIMONY OF CHRIST:

A. Is Scripture trustworthy in both fact and doctrine according to Jesus?

1. Move steadily through these questions, without devoting a lot of time to any one of them. The main point comes at the conclusion, and the questions are laying the groundwork for it. So, if time prohibits covering all of them, assign a different question to each person to answer; or, if necessary, take only 2-6 and 9-10.

2. Refer to *For Further Study* section when necessary for questions 2 and 5 of the Step.

B. Does Christ's testimony prove anything?

1. Do you believe Christ's claim to be divine is true or false? Can a divine person lie or err?

2. "We have to choose whether to bow to the authority claimed by the Son of God, or whether on our own authority to discount and contravene a part of His teaching; whether to rest content with Christianity according to Christ, or whether to go hankering after a Christianity according to the spirit of our age; whether to behave as Christ's disciples, or as His tutors" (Packer, p. 170).

Let this point drive home to your mind. Do not fail to grasp its significance. (If a student will not bow to the authority of Christ, then it is time to return to the four points of Lesson Two's argument. Material of Lessons Three through Five, of course, provides part of the evidence which supports those points.)

III. TESTIMONY OF THE APOSTLES:

A. Questions 1, 3, 4, 5 and 6 point to fine passages on the claim to inspiration. Be familiar with these so that you can go over as many as your discussion group may require. For the most part, these verses have already been used under "Motivation," and no discussion should be required.

B. Questions 5 and 8 of the previous section, plus 2, 7, 8 and 9 of this section, refer to passages which deal with specific facts of the Old Testament: Creation (5), Jonah and the Fish (8), Noah and the Flood (2), Abraham, father of the Hebrews (7), Rahab, the harlot of Jericho (7), Job (7), Elijah (7), Cain (8), and Adam's fall into sin (9).

Is the Old Testament scientifically and historically accurate?

This provides us with an invitation to examine the factual accuracy of the Bible, an invitation which any Bible believer should relish, because there is such a wealth of corroborative evidence available today. See For Further Study section for a purely random treatment of these first five events mentioned above.

The simple fact is, that the extent of the scientific evidence is so great today that it is possible to lay down a challenge to anyone. Make a random selection of *any* Biblical events. You will come up with the same degree of factual confirmation of the Bible.

Unfortunately, popular opinion is always 20 to 40 years behind the experts.

And still more unfortunate, even catastrophic, is the fact that the educated of our country, including those on our university faculties, are rarely educated *in the Biblical field*. Hence they are unable to rise above the popular ignorance. Many pose as critics who are ignorant of the facts.

IV. FOR FURTHER STUDY:

A. Additional Material for Testimony of Christ.

"Christ's claim to be divine is either true or false. If it is true His Person guarantees the truth of all the rest of His teaching (for a divine person cannot lie or err; therefore, His view of the Old Testament is true). If His claim is false, there is no compelling reason for us to believe anything else that He said. If we accept Christ's claims, therefore, we commit ourselves to believe all that He taught—on His authority. If we refuse to believe some part of what He taught, we are in effect denying Him to be the divine Messiah—on our own authority. The question, 'What think ye of the Old Testament?' resolves the question, 'What think ye of Christ?' " (Packer, p. 59.)

B. Additional material for question two, page 11 of Step Five.

False neo-orthodox view of inspiration: There are those today who do not teach that the Bible *is* the word of God, but that it merely *contains* the word of God. They say that if a particular passage of Scripture speaks to you, it is the word of God for you.

There is some truth in this, for it is an essential part of a true view of Scripture. But it is only one part, and when it is enlarged to become the total doctrine it is very dangerous. For there are three parts: *revelation* is God's disclosure of truth to the prophet or apostle; *inspiration* is God's moving of the prophet or apostle to declare to men the truth disclosed to him; *illumination* is God's opening of the minds of the recipients so that they understand the truth. Neo-orthodoxy substitutes illumination for inspiration.

Inspiration is "a supernatural, providential influence of God's Holy Spirit upon the human authors of the Bible so that they recorded exactly what He wished" (Warfield). It is our guarantee that we have the truth which God revealed thousands of years ago, our guarantee that the Bible is free from error, though written by sinful men like ourselves.

If the Bible only *contains* the word of God, then which part is His word? Our criterion can only be our subjective response, a very fluctuating measuring instrument indeed. As we read, the first things that we discard are the passages dealing with the actual inspiration of the Bible: these cannot be from God. Next we glean out other parts that are difficult or questionable. What is left we remain uncertain about, for we cannot claim understanding outside of our knowledge and experience . . . and consequently we see a Biblical fact reversed; we are making God in our image.

We cannot be sure which promises, if any, are God's and therefore cannot with any kind of assurance claim any for our lives. In this uncertain stand we find ourselves adrift from an absolute standard and assurance, forced to a reliance upon our sinful natures' partial response to God. We are as a wave tossed to and fro by any wind of doctrine and our changeableness. We can rely on nothing except ourselves and we enter once again into spiritual defeat . . . until by God's grace we are given the faith to believe that Christ is God and that He guarantees the Scripture's reliability to us.

C. Additional material for question five, p. 11 of Step Five.

"The more poetic, imaginative and symbolic the form in which the truth is presented, and the further the truth is presented, and the further the truth transcends our present experience and comprehension (as when Scripture tells us of life before the Fall, or in heaven), the harder it is . . . to determine the limits of the symbolism with any finality. (But) Genesis 2 and 21 or Rev. 3 and 22 are not typical of the Bible as a whole. In most passages the use of the ordinary rules of exegesis enable us to determine accurately enough the limits of the intended assertions. . . .

"The idea that the doctrine of the inerrancy of the word of God commits its adherents to a literalistic type of exegesis is wholly groundless. There is nothing inconsistent in recognizing that real events may be recorded in a highly symbolic manner, and Evangelicals do in fact recognize this. . . . The use of symbolic modes of representation in the story of Adam and Eve is explicitly acknowledged" (Packer, pp. 98-99).

That Christ believed the story of man's creation and subsequent fall was a *real event* is taught in Matthew 19:4. This is clear; and the answer to No. 5 is therefore easy. That Christ believed this real event *was recorded in a highly symbolic manner* is neither affirmed nor denied in Matthew, for the first century was not concerned with such questions.

D. Additional material for the factual accuracy of the Old Testament.

Ever heard this one?

"The Bible is the source book of Christianity. Now that it has been proven to be a hodge-podge of old wives' tales, Christianity deserves to dissolve into the mists of mythology and take its place in the museums alongside other pre-scientific cults. All that we need is some of its good ethics."

We shall examine this criticism, first through five specific events in the Bible and then through some more general references by reputable scholars.

1. Creation.

The following ten events will be found in Genesis 1 as having been accomplished in the order given:

a. "In the beginning God created the heaven and the earth."

b. "And the earth was without form and void; and the darkness was upon the face of the deep."

c. "And God said, Let there be light . . . And God called the light Day, and the darkness He called Night."

d. "And God said, Let there be a firmament (literally, an expanse) in the midst of the waters, and let it divide the waters (above) from the waters (below)."

e. "And God said, Let the waters under the heaven (that is, of the universal ocean) be gathered together in one place, and let the dry land appear . . ."

f. "And God said, Let the earth bring forth grass, the herb yielding seed, and the fruit tree yielding fruit . . ."

g. "And God said, Let there be lights in the firmament of the heaven to divide the day from the night; and let them be for signs, and for seasons, and for days, and years . . ."

h. "And God said, Let the waters bring forth abundantly the moving creature that hath life, and fowl that may fly above the earth in the open firmament of heaven." And God created great whales, and every living creature that moveth, which the waters brought forth abundantly, after their kind, and every winged fowl after his kind . . .

i. "And God said, Let the earth bring forth the living creature after his kind, cattle, and creeping thing, and beast of the earth after his kind: and it was so."

j. "And God said, Let us make man in our image, after our likeness . . ."

(1) Let us compare the scriptural data with that of modern science: (Unmarked quotations are from A. Rendle Short.)

Thanks to the theories of both atomic physics and astrophysics, there is a good deal of agreement today that matter did have a beginning, that it is not eternal.

Sir James Jeans: "Everything points with overwhelming force to a definite event, or series of events, of creation some time or other, not infinitely remote. The universe cannot have originated by chance out of its present ingredients, and neither can it always have been the same as now."

Lincoln Barnett, in summarizing *Albert Einstein's* thought (and with Einstein's endorsement):

"The universe is thus progressing toward an ultimate 'heat-death,' or as it is technically defined, a condition of 'maximum entropy' . . . when . . . all the processes of nature will cease . . .

"If the universe is running down and nature's processes are proceeding in just one direction, the inescapable inference is that everything had a *beginning*: somehow and sometime the cosmic processes were started, the stellar fires ignited, and the whole vast pageant of the universe brought into being. Most of the clues, moreover, that have been discovered at the inner and outer frontiers of scientific cognition suggest a definite time of Creation" (*The Universe and Dr. Einstein*, pp. 102, 105-6; 2nd ed., 1957).

"In the evolution of scientific thought, one fact has become impressively clear: there is no mystery of the physical world which does not point to a mystery beyond itself. . . . Standing midway between macrocosm and microcosm, man finds barriers on every side and can perhaps but marvel, as St. Paul did nineteen hundred years ago, that 'the world was created by the word of God so that what is seen was made out of things which do not appear (pp. 117-18)."

(2) "The Earth, after solidifying, would emit great quantities of water vapor and carbon dioxide, so that it would be covered with a universal ocean and swathed in dense masses of clouds.

(3) "By degrees the clouds would diminish sufficiently to transmit light from the sun, and as the Earth rotated on its axis, there would be an alternation of day and night, though the sun was not yet visible. Only infrared rays would get through. (It is probable that Jupiter is at this stage now.)

(4) "At first the ocean and cloud would be continuous; later (with the cooling of the Earth) an atmosphere would separate them.

(5) "Further earth-contraction due to cooling of the Earth and atmosphere would separate them.

(6) "When, at last, blue rays from the sun would penetrate, the time would arrive when life could first appear, and there are convincing reasons for believing that vegetable life appeared before animal. Oxygen, both in the atmosphere or dissolved in water, is necessary for animal life, and it is normally only derived from the action of chlorophyll in plants. Fossil plants are known from the Devonian rocks . . . were highly developed and specialized, and included large trees. . . . Others were relatively simple. . . . It is noteworthy that the Coal Measure ferns were seedbearing.

(7) "After the first plants appeared, a further clearing away of the dense clouds was probably taking place, and the sun, moon and stars would become visible to the Earth's surface. (Genesis does not say that God here *created* the sun; that happened in verse one; rather, it says that He made it 'to rule the day,' etc.)

(8) "(In the Genesis account) The beginnings of animal life (are) in water, not on land. This accords with the geological record. No notice is taken of trilobites or shellfish; here, again, as with plants, the Scripture narrative only deals with the obvious. Fish appeared first in the Ordovician, and became abundant in the Silurian. The great amphibians would aptly be described as sea monsters. . . . Numerous insects flourished in Carboniferous times. . . .

(9) "Reptiles first appeared in Permian times, and mammals (later). The mammals of the Mesozoic period, how-

ever, were few in number, and very small, no larger than a squirrel. Doubtless, therefore, birds were flying over the Earth before the 'cattle and creeping thing, and beast of the field' (which in the Bible usually means the great carnivores) made their first appearance.

(10) "Fossil man appeared on the Earth much later than the animals, certainly during the Ice Age, perhaps during Pliocene times."

There is therefore an amazing harmony between the Scripture's account of Creation and the discoveries of modern science. We are familiar with the creation-narratives of ancient Egypt, Babylon and numerous other cultures; they are but fantasies. *By contrast the simplicity, beauty, and accuracy of the Genesis story stands out in solitary grandeur.* Neither guesswork nor intuition is sufficient to explain how Moses so accurately stated these facts in their accurate order. Only one explanation does justice to reason: divine inspiration.

A West Coast scientist has attempted to compute the mathematical probability of Moses' ever achieving such by guess. He compares Moses' chances with yours if you were in a lottery which had small tickets piled a couple of miles high covering the entire continental United States. Put on your blindfold, says this scientist, and start searching for the *one* marked ticket. Dig as deep as you wish, travel over the pile as far as you wish (from Canada to Mexico, from the Atlantic to the Pacific). Take as long as you wish—so long as eventually you come up with just one ticket and (eyes still blinded) you say with all the confidence of Moses, "This is it!"

2. Jonah in the Fish.

For information regarding the plausibility of this story, the Library Research Service of Encyclopedia Britannica was consulted.

Their reply stated, first, that from the standpoint of the biologist as well as the professional whaler, there is no question whatsoever that the sperm whale is physiologically capable of swallowing the largest of men: mouth, throat and stomach handle much larger food without the least inconvenience.

Further, the Research Service goes on to cite two instances of men in modern times being swallowed alive and living to tell the story. One of these cases was subjected to careful scientific investigation by a British and two French scientists. A whaler disappeared after his small boat was upset by a harpooned whale; two days later he was found in the dissected whale's stomach. Except for a two-week period of shock and a permanent bleaching of his skin from the gastric juices, the man lived a normal life thereafter.

3. The Flood.

"A great sensation was caused in March, 1929, when Sir Leonard Woolley announced that during his excavations at Ur of the Chaldees he had found a layer, eight feet thick, of water-laid clay, evidently deposited by a deluge of stupendous proportions. To use his own words:

" 'Eight feet of sediment imply a very great depth of water, and the flood which deposited it must have been of a magnitude unparalleled in local history. That it was so is further proved by the fact the claybank marks a definite break in the continuity of the local culture; a whole civilization which existed before it is lacking above it and seems to have been submerged by the waters. . . . There could be no doubt it was the flood of Sumerian history and legend, the flood on which is based the study of Noah.'

"A few days later, Professor Langdon announced that he had made exactly the same discovery at Kish, hundreds of miles away: 'We were loth to believe that we had obtained confirmation of the Deluge of Genesis, but there is no doubt about it now.' "

Short (pp. 133-35) gives this material in great detail, plus other corroborative evidence.

4. Abraham.

His magnificent home-city in Babylonia has been excavated; the culture of the time has become well-known to modern scholars. One of the greatest of these, Jack Finegan, has said, "These stories fit in very well with what is now becoming known through archaeological research of ancient life, laws and customs in upper Mesopotamia."

The reversal in scholarly circles of opinion and attitudes toward the historicity of the Old Testament is well illustrated by the account of Abraham's raid upon the Babylonian armies in Genesis 14. Fifty years ago it was charged (1) that the names of the Mesopotamian kings were fictitious—they have now been identified satisfactorily, though not conclusively; (2) that Palestine at that early date could not have been under Eastern control—we now know that Hammurabi's code of laws and even his postal system were in operation throughout Palestine and Syria;

(3) that the cities named in 14:5-6 were fictitious—Halley cites our foreemost archaeologists on this: "Albright, who once considered the cities here named to have been legendary because they were so far east of the known trade routes, in 1929 discovered a line of great mound-ruins of cities that flourished about 2000 B.C., indicating that it was a well settled region in Abraham's time . . ."; (4) that Abraham's band could never defeat the united armies of four powerful kings—Hamilton cites Kyle and then concludes: "We thus see that it was entirely possible for such a night attack . . . small though it was, to accomplish its purpose by surprising the unsuspecting imperial rear guard, and making off with plunder and prisoners. Modern wars are full of just such exploits." Most significantly, Hamilton comments, "Bear in mind the fact that all the evidence on the subject that has come to light has supported the narrative and not one bit of evidence tending to discredit the story has been discovered." *This is the commentary which modern science is writing in bold letters over the historical material of the entire Old Testament.* (See Grounds for Abraham and the story of Lot's wife, p. 63.)

5. Rahab and the Fall of Jericho.

See Grounds for the incontestable discoveries of the archaeologist, Garstang, regarding the collapse of the city's mammoth wall which allowed the attacking Israelites to destroy the city.

Short continues the account (in *Why Believe?*), "Garstang has shown (also) that on three historical occasions the waters of Jordan have been cut off exactly as described by Joshua."

6. General.

Historical accuracy is established on three foundations: geography (and topography), ethnology, and chronology. In all three areas modern science has been building a stronger and stronger case for the Bible during the past hundred years of extensive research in the Near East.

We are discovering piece by piece (1) that the peoples, places and events of Scripture are to be found in the same locale and under the precise geographical circumstances as those described in the Bible; (2) that whenever statements are made in the Bible concerning kinship, origin, or customs of peoples, these statements can be depended upon to be in accordance with the finds of archaeology; (3) that when we compare events in the Old Testament with the records on the tombs and monuments of Egypt, or the records of Babylonia, Assyria and elsewhere, we find that the different parts of the chronology fit extremely well, in spite of the unscientific chronological systems which the ancients used.

See Grounds, p. 65, for the intellectual conversion from radical criticism to orthodoxy of one of the greatest Near Eastern archaeologists of the previous generation (when so many scholars were being forced by their own discoveries to reverse their criticisms of the Bible).

"If we consider the Exodus . . . the general setting is such that the emergence at that time of the children of Israel into a more unified people devoted to the worship of the Lord is thoroughly credible. If we follow them in the conquest of the Promised Land, we find through actual archaeological excavation in Palestine that many Canaanite cities suffered destruction at just about the time the Israelites are supposed to have come. Also, at about this time, we find the Israelites mentioned on an Egyptian monument as a people actually in Palestine.

"When we advance to the time of Solomon, we are able to point to an excavated city which was probably one of his chariot cities, and to a seaport city at the head of the Gulf of Aqaba where the same king conducted extensive manufacturing and commercial activities. In the case of yet later kings, we find their actual names appearing on contemporary Assyrian and Babylonian monuments"—Prof. Jack Finegan.

"The progress during the present century of research in science, and in Sumerian, Assyrian, Egyptian and Babylonian archaeology, and in classical geography and history, has produced scarcely one discovery to support the critics, and a spate of discovery to confound them. Books have poured from the presses in incessant stream showing that the fault-finding of the critics of the Bible has been based on insufficient information"—A. Rendle Short.

LESSON PLAN

AUTHORITY OF THE NEW TESTAMENT

LESSON FOUR   STEP FIVE

OBJECTIVE: To discover for ourselves the absolute reliability of the New
Testament.

I.   OPEN WITH PRAYER.

II.   MEMORY VERSE: Matthew 24:35.

The fact that we, in the twentieth century, still have access to the
word of God, is living proof that God's word does not pass away.
Throughout the centuries attempts to destroy the Bible have been
to no avail, for God Himself will not permit it.

III. MOTIVATION:

Some people, who have not examined all the evidence, attempt to discredit the authority of the Scripture. If I were one who doubted, could
you give me valid reasons for your belief in the authority of the New
Testament? As we study this lesson, jot down the evidences you find
for the authority of the New Testament.

IV.   BIBLE STUDY:

A. What authority was given the apostles by Christ?

B. What does the resurrection of Christ prove?

   1. How trustworthy are our documentary sources which report that
      Jesus rose from the dead?

      a. Was the claim actually made?

      b. Did the study develop like the legends that have grown up
         around history's great heroes?

      c. Do the reports bear the marks of authentic eyewitness ac-
         counts? What are the judgments of experts on legal evidence?

   2. Is the reporting of Jesus' resurrection substantiated by other
      historical data?

   3. Is the resurrection substantiated by logic and rationality?

   4. Can the resurrection of Christ be pragmatically verified by mod-
      ern man?

5. What is the pivotal point in Paul's faith in Christ's authority? What does the resurrection prove?

C. Were the apostles conscious that they wrote under Christ's authority rather than their own?

D. Is the New Testament we have today reliable?

1. What is your greatest assurance that the Bible is God's word?

V. PARALLEL PASSAGES:

A. John 20:26-31.

B. Acts 2:22-32.

C. Acts 3:13-15.

D. Luke 1:1-14.

E. Acts 4:13-22.

F. Acts 7:54, 8:3.

G. II Corinthians 11:24-29.

H. Deuteronomy 21:22-23.

VI. SUMMARY:

Five valid reasons for our belief in the authority of the New Testament as God's word have been discussed. List these, using the notes which the students have jotted down during the study.

A. Christ's authentication, not only of the Old Testament, but also of the New Testament (Section I).

B. Christ's resurrection, proving that His authority was truly divine, and endowing the apostles with unique authority because they were the eyewitnesses of this foundation to salvation (Section II).

C. The character, integrity and historical accuracy of the New Testament writers, combined with their claim to be under Christ's authority (Sections II and III).

D. The endurance and preservation of God's word (Matthew 24:35 and Section IV).

E. The witness of the Holy Spirit directly to the Christian, authenticating the New Testament (Sections II-D, IV-B).

VII. CLOSE IN PRAYER.

AUTHORITY OF THE NEW TESTAMENT

LESSON FOUR   STEP FIVE

I. WHAT AUTHORITY WAS GIVEN THE APOSTLES BY
    CHRIST?

    A. No 1: what four things did Christ say the Holy Spirit would
       do for the apostles? Allow students to answer.

    B. "B" of No. 1: did Christ authenticate their teaching beforehand?

    C. No. 2: what authority did Christ give the apostles?

    D. No. 4: What did Christ say which indicates that He planned for
       His teachings and His gospel to be reduced to writing later?

    E. No. 3: On what basis did Christ select the apostles to tell of His
       gospel? (Whom had Paul seen according to I Corinthians 15:7-9
       and Acts 26:1-20?)

    F. No. 5: What authority did Christ give Paul?

II. WHAT DOES THE RESURRECTION OF CHRIST PROVE?

    New Testament authority rests upon Christ's authority. And this
    authority of Christ, founded upon His unique life and teachings, was
    first studied in Step One. Then in Lesson Two of this Step, our
    foundation for faith in His authority was broken down into four
    points. One aspect of this foundation is so crucial that it should be
    investigated carefully.

    A. How trustworthy are our documentary sources which report that
       Jesus rose from the dead?

       1. The claim was made (that Jesus had risen). Few men can deny
          that this is historical fact because the claim was not only made
          orally but in writing. And we have in our possession today
          copies of the written reports, which are authentic (accurate)
          copies of the originals (with only inconsequential deviations).
          This is scientifically established, so that no scholar anywhere
          will argue the point. (See the Section in student's manual—Is
          the New Testament Reliable?)

       2. The various New Testament writings have been fairly precisely
          dated; and it is established that they were all written in the
          first century. They are, in fact, exceptionally early, so early

292

that the suggestion that myths and legends arose around the figure of Jesus is ruled out: there was not a long enough time lapse between Jesus and the writings. Legends require several generations to develop and spread, but the New Testament writings come from the first generation, that is, while the actual eye-witnesses still lived.

For the latest written witness, read John 20:26-31 and I John 1:1-3, dated about 90-95 A.D. (And we have a portion of a manuscript of John's Gospel which the experts have dated at 125 A.D., only 30 years after the original writing!)

For the earliest written reports, read I Thessalonians 1:10 and Galatians 1:1 (dated 50 A.D., just 20 years after the event); and note especially I Corinthians 15:3-9 with its statement that, *25 years after the event,* there were *a few hundred* eye-witnesses still alive to tell the story.

A few of the earliest oral reports of the resurrection have been preserved in writing in the speeches of Acts, dating from the week after the risen Christ was last seen (e.g., Acts 2:22-32; 3:13-15). It is noteworthy that the resurrection was *the central point* of these first Christian sermons. Down through the years we can trace the development of Christian doctrine around this central point, but the point itself did not develop; *it was the same in the earliest as in the latest teachings.*

There is therefore *no historical evidence whatsoever* that a legend gradually developed.

3. Do the reports bear the marks of authentic eye-witness accounts?

   a. Each account of Jesus' resurrection appearances contains much material that the others do not have, even some minor points which appear on the surface to conflict in detail; yet they are all unanimous regarding the central issues. These three features led one of Britain's greatest legal minds (Lord Lyndhurst) to assert: "I know pretty well what evidence is; and, I tell you, such evidence as that for the Resurrection has never broken down yet."

   "Reports taken from each of several eye-witnesses of any exciting event—a street accident, say, or a riot or a battle—will invariably contain differences. But if the witnesses are honest and sincere, their reports will show agreement on the main points. This is just what we find in the Gospels. . . . If the narratives had been exactly the same on every point, that would have been more disquieting, as giving grounds for suspicion that there had been deliberate intention to avoid any suggestion of disagreement" (James Martin, *Did Jesus Rise from the Dead?* pp. 35-36).

b. Several of the reports of the resurrection are recorded in Luke and Acts, whose author meets the requirements of a modern researcher. Luke, a non-Jew to begin with, displays the finest Greek literary style of any writer since the classical period; and his prologue (cf. Luke 1:1-4) reveals that his superb training led him to follow principles of careful research which are true to the best historical tradition. Because he gives events precise dating, detailed description, etc., Luke's writings can be, and have been, quite exhaustively checked for accuracy.

Sir William Ramsey, authority second to none on the archaeology of Asia Minor, began his research firmly convinced of the 19th century's theory that Luke's "history was written long after the events and was untrustworthy as a whole." The facts he unearthed through years of digging gradually compelled him to a complete reversal, so that he wrote, "I take the view that Luke's history is unsurpassed in regard to trustworthiness. . . . You may press the words of Luke in a degree beyond any other historian's and they stand the keenest scrutiny and the hardest treatment."

c. As for Paul, James Martin (pp. 74-75) *Did Jesus Rise from the Dead?* emphasizes four points:

(1) "Saul was a man of outstanding intelligence, by common consent one of history's intellectual giants, and was also a man of extensive education and academic attainment. Here was no unthinking, unquestioning, credulous mind that might be easily captured. . . . Such a man is not likely to have been won to a faith that rested upon a deception or a few hallucinations."

(2) "An exceptionally ardent Pharisee, Saul's whole training and background were such as to set him in opposition to the possibility of the Christians' being right. The mere suggestion that a crucified man could be Messiah was anathema to him."

"Occupying so prominent a role in the campaign against the Resurrection preaching, he would be acquainted with all the facts as known to the Jewish headquarters, and would be well briefed in all the 'natural' explanations and in all the means employed to refute the affirmation that Jesus was risen from the dead. Intellectually as well as emotionally, he was strongly predisposed against the Christian claim."

(3) "His conversion was no half-hearted affair. He did not merely begin to think that perhaps he was wrong;

he became utterly convinced that they were right. He did not merely stop persecuting; he began preaching . . . a man who was sure beyond any possibility of doubt."

(4) "His conversion was not only thoroughgoing, it was enduring. When Saul changed his position on the Damascus road, he changed it for life . . . even though it cost him dearly. It led him to much pain and trouble . . . but nothing could turn him from it."

The strength of Paul's witness, therefore, lies not only in the fact that he claims, along with the others, to have seen the risen Christ personally; but also in this, that he became fully convinced that *all* the aspects of the resurrection story were true. And, as Martin comments, "Such a man would accept the Christian case only if he were left with no alternative."

d. The reporting of Christ's resurrection brought persecution, suffering and death to the witnesses. They lost rather than gained by it. They, therefore, can be said to be witnesses without personal motive outside their passion for the truth. Study Acts 4:13-20; 7:54-8:3, or II Corinthians 11:24-29 before proceeding.

Regarding this, consider the opinion of a great legal mind— Simon Greenleaf, author of the *Treatise* which is still considered the greatest single authority on evidence in the literature of legal procedure. In his book, *An Examination of the Testimony of the Four Evangelists by the Rules of Evidence Administered in Courts of Justice,* he writes:

"Their Master had recently perished as a malefactor, by the sentence of a public tribunal. His religion sought to overthrow the religions of the whole world. The laws of every country were against the teachings of His disciples. The interests and passions of all the rulers and great men in the world were against them. . . . Propagating this new faith, even in the most inoffensive and peaceful manner, they could expect nothing but contempt, opposition, revilings, bitter persecutions, stripes, imprisonments, torments and cruel deaths. . . .They had every possible motive to review carefully the grounds of their faith and the evidences of the great facts and truths which they asserted; and these motives were pressed upon their attention with the most melancholy and terrific frequency. . . . If it were morally possible for them to have been deceived in this matter, every human motive operated to lead them to discover and avow their error. To have persisted in so gross a falsehood, after it was known to them, was not only to encounter all the evils which man could inflict, but to endure also the pangs of inward and conscious guilt; with no testimony of a good conscience . . . no happiness in this life or in the world to come."

B. Is the reporting of Jesus' resurrection substantiated by other historical data?

1. Established historical fact: the tomb was empty.

The testimony of the resurrection was made continuously in Jerusalem, only half a mile from the tomb outside the city walls. Both the Roman governor and the Jewish leaders had every reason to want to quell the turbulence which the new "sect" was creating by its testimony. Producing the body of Jesus from the tomb would have solved all their problems and squelched the Christians once and for all.

In the book, *Who Moved the Stone?* written by an English lawyer, there is an unusual first chapter entitled, "The Book That Could Not Be Written." In it the author explains that the original objective of his research was to present an unimpeachable case disproving the myth of Jesus' resurrection. He labored for years, only to discover that that was "the book that could not be written," not by an honest lawyer at any rate. For one solid historical fact had blockaded progress on his case —the empty tomb. Explaining this forced him to empty every hypothesis conceivable; his conclusions are in the present book . . . which turns out to be one of the finest defenses of the resurrection written in our times.

2. Established psychological fact: the disciples' lives were transformed.

"Perhaps the transformation of the disciples is the greatest evidence of all for the resurrection, because it is entirely artless. They do not invite us to look at themselves, as they invite us to look at the empty tomb, and the collapsed graveclothes and the Lord Whom they had seen. . . . The men who figure in the pages of the Gospels are new men and different in Acts. . . . Two examples stand out. The first is Simon Peter. . . . He has denied Christ three times. . . . When Jesus is dead, he joins the others in the upper room, behind barred doors 'for fear of the Jews' (John 20:19), and is utterly dejected. We turn over one or two pages in the Bible and we see him . . . preaching so boldly and so powerfully to a vast crowd that three thousand people accept Christ. We turn on to the next chapters in the Acts and we watch him defying the very Sanhedrin who had condemned Jesus to death."

"Or take James, who later assumed a position of leadership in the Jerusalem church. He is one of 'the brethren of the Lord' who throughout the Gospels are represented as not believing in Jesus (John 7:5). . . . What convinced him? (Cf. I Corinthians 15:7.) . . . It was the resurrection which transformed Peter's fear into courage, and James' doubt into faith" (John R. W. Stott, *Basic Christianity*, pp. 57-58).

3. Established sociological fact: the Christian Church was born.

Two solid facts are enough to mention here. First, people's lives continued to be changed; a dynamic of new, contagious life had been injected into the human race by the resurrection. The Roman author Pliny, in his famous letter to the Emperor Trajan, provides non-Christian testimony to the moral purity and power, and the rapid spread of the Church (written in 107 A.D.).

Secondly, the Church—Jewish though it was at first (including numerous priests) and therefore *strictly* monotheistic — was founded upon the belief in the deity of *the man Jesus*. The disciples had never come as far as this "preposterous" understanding of Him. The general populace and the leadership had crucified Him specifically because He had clarified this claim to deity when on trial in their presence. What can account for the conversion to this belief of both friend and (some) foe?—especially for the emergence of this belief *after He had died?* Can God die? Can God die what to the Jews was the most abhorrent of all deaths (cf. Deut. 21:22-23)?

"Throughout the whole book of Acts, it is made plain that to the first Christians the Cross was an object of shame and horror, which only the Resurrection had transformed. They worshipped Jesus, not because of the Cross, but in spite of it. It was only the interpretation of the Cross in the light of the Resurrection which produced, after a time, that changed attitude which is to be seen, for example, in Philippians and the Fourth Gospel, where the Cross itself is seen as the manifestation of the glory of God. Such a change could have been brought about only by an unmistakable certainty in the truth of the Resurrection. . . .

"The suggestion, even while He lived, that Jesus was divine would have filled nearly every Jew with repugnance; but the making of such a suggestion after the Crucifixion must have filled them with a horror so great that most of them would refuse to listen any further to what the Christians had to say. It is, therefore, of arresting import that so many who did condescend to listen were, in spite of their angry prejudice, convinced and converted. They, too, must have been very sure that Jesus had risen from the dead" (James Martin, *ibid,* p. 78).

C. Is Jesus' resurrection substantiated by logic and rational argument?

The failure of skeptics to refute the above facts or to provide alternative explanations for them is supporting evidence to their validity. Whenever Critic A has come up with a new theory to account for the facts, invariably the history of criticism reveals that within ten or twenty years Critic B emerges with a newer theory that rips to shreds the first "explanation." No critic has ever been able to offer an alternative theory with which even a minority of critics themselves have been satisfied. Fraud? Legend? Delusion?—each runs around the facts. Hallucinations come to individuals, but not to so many of them; and never to groups, especially a crowd of five hundred. Legends require time and isolation from the facts in order to develop. Fraud requires motivation, and careful conniving, plus freedom from close scrutiny.

D. Can the resurrection of Christ be pragmatically verified by modern man?

The claim is that Christ not only rose from the dead, but that He continues to live; so the claim is open to investigation and verification in this or any other year—by any man. For a man can know Christ and the power of His resurrection now. Note Paul's descriptions of the experience of the resurrected Christ in Galatians 2:20; Ephesians 1:15-20; Philippians 3:7-10.

The disciples in Acts 5:32 maintain that they are not the only witnesses to the resurrection, but *"so is the Holy Spirit."* The Apostles are dead, and their witness continues in their written records. The Spirit of Truth lives on—and continues to corroborate their witness by His own.

In Revelation 3:20 Christ is speaking; but note that it is the Risen Christ who speaks—and He speaks not to the original disciples but to a later generation of men. He speaks these words to the twentieth century also, to each among us . . . saying,

> "Behold, I stand at the door and knock; if any man hear my voice, and open the door, I will come in to him, and sup with him, and he with me."

E. What is the pivotal point in Paul's faith in Christ's authority, according to Acts 26:1-20 and Romans 1:4? What does the resurrection prove?

III. WERE THE APOSTLES CONSCIOUS THAT THEY WROTE UNDER CHRIST'S AUTHORITY RATHER THAN THEIR OWN?

A. Let us examine some of the statements of the New Testament writers which show that they wrote with authority. Have the students answer the following questions from Lesson Four, Step Five:

1a: From whom did Paul receive what he preached?

4a: What does John declare?

4b: John wrote Revelation by what authority?

7: On what writings is the foundation of the Church of Jesus Christ established?

IV. IS THE NEW TESTAMENT WE HAVE TODAY RELIABLE?

A. Comment on these paragraphs. The student can use these facts to answer attacks on the Bible.

B. Conclude with the lesson's final question: What is your greatest assurance that the Bible is God's word?

GLIMPSES OF BIBLE POWER

LESSON FIVE   STEP FIVE

OBJECTIVE: To find what the Bible claims for itself, and also how we can understand it personally.

I.   OPEN WITH PRAYER.

II. MEMORY VERSE:
     Hebrews 4:12.

III. MOTIVATION:
     The key to understanding the word of God is in this lesson. The next two studies are probably the most important in this Step, for here the Bible's practical power is learned.

     What would be your answer if challenged by another student: "I don't believe the Bible is the word of God. I can't go along with a lot of the miracles . . . and I can't understand so much of it. Do I have to believe the Bible 100%—from cover to cover—in order to become a Christian?"

IV. BIBLE STUDY:
     A. What does the word claim to be able to do?
     B. How is the word of God understood?

V.   PARALLEL PASSAGES:
     A. Isaiah 55:10-11—word shall not return void.
     B. Jeremiah 23:29—word like a fire and a hammer.
     C. Matthew 5:17-18—word all to be fulfilled.
     D. John 7:16-17—if any man will . . . he shall know the doctrine.
     E. II Timothy 3:16-17—all inspired.
     F. Romans 1:16—power unto salvation.
     G. John 1:39—Come and see.

VI. SUMMARY:
     You, a new Christian, have the same teacher that great Bible scholars have, the Holy Spirit. Every time you sit down to study the Bible, ask the Holy Spirit to show you the things He wants you to learn from His word, and to help you understand the difficult parts.

VII. CLOSE IN PRAYER.

300

GLIMPSES OF BIBLE POWER

LESSON FIVE   STEP FIVE

INTRODUCTION:

Someone says, "I don't believe the Bible is the word of God."

Answer: "If you had a sword and wanted to prove to a man that it was sharp, you would not talk about it, you would poke him with it. Use the Sword of the Spirit; it will prove itself. The doubter probably has never read the Bible himself, and is just repeating what he has heard from someone else.

"You cannot know for sure that a lamp will go on until you have flicked the switch and tried it. So, too, you cannot know whether the Bible is God's word until you have tried it in your own life. Christ is the central issue of salvation. Questions of science and history can wait; but the question of one's relationship with God cannot wait."

In giving such an answer, there is no need for one to hide the fact that he does believe the Bible is true and trustworthy. This we believe without apology, knowing that the facts clearly lead to such a conclusion.

But such an answer places the emphasis where Scripture itself places it. *The demonstration of the inerrancy and infallibility of God's word lies in its effectiveness, its power.* (If God's word does not accomplish what it says it will, we may conclude that it is not inspired.) Study Isaiah 55:10-11 carefully; then the memory verse, Hebrews 4:12. These are key verses (cf. Jer. 23:29; Matt. 5:17-18).

A Chinese man, after hearing the Bible for the first time, said to the missionary, "I know this is God's word because it tells me all that I am."

I.   WHAT DOES THE WORD CLAIM TO BE ABLE TO DO?

   A. Campus Crusade has a short and clear creed. Each year the staff reaffirms their faith as expressed in it. The fourth article is as follows:

   "We personally accept the Bible as God's infallible word, uniquely inspired, the Spirit's supreme and final authority for man in all matters of faith and conduct, His sustenance for every believer."

   We believe that this states the central issue in a nutshell—it is toward faith and conduct, toward spiritual sustenance, that the

Lord's word is unerringly aimed. Let us place our concentration where He places His. Then, and not till then, will our doctrine be characterized by the Prophets' and Jesus' and the Apostles' *confidence in the power* of the word itself to do its own work and to carry its own conviction. Read John 7:16-17.

B. Fill in the blanks in the lesson for the following: John 17:17; 8:31-32; I Peter 1:23; 2:2; Ephesians 6:17; Romans 10:17; John 15:3. (See Further Study section for a note on John 8:31-32.)

C. The insistent directing of the inquiring student to Christ Himself is not meant to deny that there is a rightful place for extensive historical research and for hard-headed scientific examination of the Bible; but it is a warning that undue emphasis in these areas *misses the point.*

D. To the non-Christian we lay down the challenge: *begin where the Bible applies to you and can therefore be tested by you.* "Come and see" was Andrew's answer to his brother in John 1:39.

When Jesus said, "Come unto me all ye that labor and are heavy laden, and I will give you rest," what did that mean to a Galilean villager? First of all, it meant simply, "Listen to me today . . . and tomorrow *come* again and listen some more." As the man listened, he would soon learn more deeply the meaning of "come to me"—but he would never learn more without just plain *listening.* When Jesus says in our day, "Come to me, all ye that labor (at school) and are heavy laden (with term papers, problem-sets, etc.) and I will give you rest," what can that mean to a collegian? First of all, it demands the same elemental response that it did in 30 A.D.; except that today we read His words instead of hearing them. "Listen to me today by reading my word, and tomorrow *come* again and listen some more." As you read and listen, you will learn more deeply the meaning of "come unto me" . . . "and you will find rest for your souls."

In the experiential and scientific way (and in this way *only*) a man comes to know truly that the Bible is uniquely inspired, the infallible expression of God's plan for our lives.

Through the written word, God speaks His living word to us day by day, hour by hour. And soon we learn what Jesus both practiced and taught in His wilderness temptations: "Man shall not live by bread alone, but by every word that proceeds from the mouth of God" (Matthew 4:4,RSV).

II. HOW IS THE WORD OF GOD UNDERSTOOD?

A. What should we first know (II Peter 1:20-21)?

What kind of interpretation *is* valid?

B. Does this mean that the true interpretation must be that of "The Church" or of God's Spirit (I Cor. 2:14)? (See Further Study section for the fallacy in the often-heard argument that "The Church must be our interpreter of Scripture.")

The "natural man" is the "old man" before God took hold of the life in rebirth; it is the "carnal man" with all that is fallen and sinful, proud and sensual in man. Galatians 5:16-24 describes the contrast between the natural man and the spiritual.

One of the most famous Confessions (or Creeds) of Church History has this to say: *"The supreme judge,* by which all controversies of religion are to be determined, and all decrees of councils, opinions of ancient writers, doctrines of men, and private spirits, are to be examined, and in whose sentence we are to rest, *can be no other but the Holy Spirit speaking in the Scripture."*

C. What must occur in one's life in order to understand and know God and His plan for our lives (John 3:3)?

A young woman once picked up a certain book to read but soon laid it down, finding it too dull and difficult to read. Shortly afterward she met a young man to whom she became quite attached. During the course of their courtship she learned that he was the author of this book. She began to read the book a second time, and this time she read it from cover to cover. Why the tremendous interest? Now she knew and loved the author. When we come to know and love Jesus Christ, His Book, the Bible, becomes alive and vital to us.

D. Are we dependent for our understanding upon scholars who are specialists in Bible and theology? (Must we obtain that kind of training ourselves before we can understand?) Who is our Teacher (I Corinthians 2:10-12)? Quoting the same Confession, *"Those things which are necessary* to be known, believed, and obeyed, for salvation, *are so clearly propounded* and opined in some place of scripture or other, *that not only the* learned but the unlearned, in a due use of the ordinary means, *may attain unto a sufficient understanding of them."*

E. Question 5: Does one who has experienced the new birth have this great Teacher according to Romans 8:9? Then what should be our response to "ministers" and "brilliant" professors who deny the deity of Christ, the inspiration of the Bible and other basic teachings in the printed word of the Holy Spirit?

III. FOR FURTHER STUDY:

A. Additional material on John 8:31-32.

"Do evangelical principles inhibit the freedom of reason? On the contrary, they establish it. Freedom is no merely negative conception; anarchy is not freedom, either on the moral or on the intellectual level. True freedom is something positive: to possess it is to fulfill one's human destiny.

"Man's mind becomes free only when its thoughts are brought into captivity to Christ and His word; till then, it is at the mercy of sinful prejudice and dishonest mental habits within, and of popular opinion, organized propaganda and unquestioned commonplaces without. Tossed about by every wind of intellectual fashion and carried to and fro by cross-currents of reactions, man without God is not free for truth; he is forever mastered by the things he takes for granted; the victim of a hopeless and everlasting relativism.

"Only as his thoughts are searched, challenged and corrected by God through His word, may man hope to rise to a way of looking at things which, instead of reflecting merely passing phases of human thought, reflects God's eternal truth. This is the only road to intellectual freedom, and its sole safeguard is the principle of absolute subjection to Scripture.

"If, as our critics say, Evangelicals at present are not entering into this heritage, that does not mean that it is not theirs to enter into. The truth is that, in principle, it is theirs and no one else's; for they alone treat the idea of Biblical authority seriously enough to secure and preserve this freedom. If anyone in the present debate lacks intellectual freedom, it is rather those whose minds are governed by the tyrannical modern axiom that what is newest must be truest; what is old must be out-of-date; and change is always progress; those who feel they must deny what Christ affirmed about Scripture rather than break with nineteenth-century ideas of what assumptions are 'scientific' and what are not. . . . By maintaining a fancied freedom (non-subjection to God's Word), they forfeit the possibility of real freedom; nor can they gain the second till they renounce the first" (Packer, pp. 143-144).

B. Additional Material for Science and Scripture.

"We must allow Scripture itself to define for us the scope and limits of its Biblical teaching. . . . The biblical authors wrote of God's sovereignty over His world, and of man's experiences within that world, using such modes of speech about the natural order and human experience as were current in their days, and *in a language that was common to themselves and their contemporaries.* This is saying no more than that they wrote to be understood. Their pic-

304

ture of the world and things in it is not put forward as normative for later science, any more than their use of Hebrew and Greek is put forward as a perfect model for composition in these languages. They do not claim to teach either science or grammar. (Attempts to make Scripture teach science, either explicitly or by implication, have occasioned much *fruitless* labor. . . .) Sometimes their grammar lapses; often the mental picture of the created order which their phraseology suggests to the twentieth-century mind differs from that of modern science; but these facts do not bear on the inerrancy of the divine Word which the writers' conceptual and linguistic resources were being used to convey. This distinction between the content and the form of the written Word of God needs more discussion than we can give it here, but it seems clear enough in broad outline. . . .

"The infallibility and inerrancy of Scripture are relative to the intended scope of the Word of God. Scripture provides instruction that is true and trustworthy, not on every conceivable subject, but simply on those subjects with which it claims to deal. We must allow Scripture itself to tell us what these are" (Packer, pp. 96-98).

C. Additional Material for "How the Word of God Is Understood," II Peter 1:20-21.

The Roman Catholic reads this verse as asserting that no individual can interpret Scripture. For does not Peter here forbid a private interpretation, they ask? So we look to The Church and we receive Her interpretation. But then we are in the same dilemma all over again: for as an individual, how can I read and understand the official interpretation? That would be private interpretation, wouldn't it? So back I go to The Church for an interpretation of the interpretation, *ad infinitum*.

In other words, sooner or later I *must* do my own thinking and interpreting. Relying on The Church cannot save me from this necessity.

The big question is: When I do my own thinking, will it be my own private interpretation—or will it be guided by the same Spirit who originally inspired the Scripture? Then and only then will it cease to be a human or private exposition.

LESSON PLAN

SOUL-FOOD IN PSALM 119

LESSON SIX   STEP FIVE

OBJECTIVE: To awaken desire for the word of God as daily food essential for life.

I.   OPEN WITH PRAYER.

II. MEMORY VERSE: Psalm 119:105.

God has promised to guide us by His word. "Lead Kindly Light Amidst the Encircling Gloom" is certainly an appropriate prayer for the age in which we live. Who does not long for a sure word, for clearly spoken directions? This is what God promises to those who will study His word.

III. MOTIVATION:

There are certain essentials to physical health and growth which find their parallels in the spiritual realm. Without food, air, rest and exercise we cannot live physically. So, too, without spiritual food, and air, and rest, and exercise, we shrivel up and die spiritually.

Just what are these spiritual equivalents of food, air, rest and exercise?

A. The Christian's FOOD: I Peter 2:2; Matt. 4:4. The Word.

B. The Christian's BREATHING: I Thess. 5:16-18; Phil. 4:6-7. Prayer.

C. The Christian's REST: John 14:21; 15:10. Abiding in Christ.

D. The Christian's EXERCISE: Acts 1:8. Witnessing.

It is with the first of these absolute necessities that we have been concerned in this Step, and now in this lesson. "Give us this day our daily bread" is a universal prayer of mankind. In answer to that prayer, the word of God replies, *"I am the food of the full-grown man; become a man, and you shall feed on Me."*

IV. BIBLE STUDY:

A. How to study the Bible.

306

1. Hearing and meditating.

2. Reading.

3. Studying.

4. Memorizing.

B. Discussion questions.

1. Are there any terms in question one that you do not understand?

2. Consider question five: See the Lesson Amplification.

3. Study question seven: Consider the difference between secular and spiritual wisdom as suggested in I Cor. 13:2; I Tim. 1:3-5; John 14:6.

4. Consider question twelve: Discuss the difference between the peace of God and peace with God. Col. 1:20-22; Rom. 5:1; Phil. 4:7; Gal. 5:22-23.

V. PARALLEL PASSAGES:

I Peter 1:22-23.

VI. SUMMARY:

Summarize "Private Bible Study Methods," Lesson Seven of Step Five.

VII. CLOSE IN PRAYER.

SOUL-FOOD IN PSALM 119

LESSON SIX   STEP FIVE

INTRODUCTION:

The relationship between the Church, a group of individual believers, and the Lord Jesus Christ has been compared to the marriage union. We are collectively Christ's bride, and as such we should lovingly place ourselves under His sovereignty. A wife should find consolation in her husband, not only during periods of adversity, but at all times. It is this vital love relationship that draws them together, keeps them together, and produces a home that makes a positive contribution to the community. If we are ever to expect a fruitful Christian life, we must realize that the key is a love union with Jesus Christ. (See Romans 7:4; Ephesians 5:22-23.)

HOW TO STUDY THE BIBLE:

Here is a visual method of demonstrating the way we "eat" the Bread of Life. Hold your Bible in your hand with a firm grip, noting that it takes all five fingers for the firmest grip. Then put the book down and count off on your fingers the following *ways of appropriating the Word*: (The larger and heavier the Bible, the more effective is this demonstration.)

(1) hearing (little finger); (2) reading (next finger); (3) studying (middle finger); (4) memorizing (index finger); (5) meditating (thumb).

I.   HEARING AND MEDITATING: We attend church services and we hear the word preached. Psychologists will tell you that most of what you retain from the worship service will be inspirational; you will actually *remember* only about 5% of what you heard, though that percentage might run as high as 15% depending on how much meditation (thumb) goes into the hearing. (Pick up your Bible and hold it with the thumb and little finger only.) Hearing is vitally important. Romans 10:17 tells us that "faith comes by hearing . . . . the word of God." But 5% or even 15% does not give you a very strong grip on the word of God, does it? Would it be difficult for you to take this Bible away from me when I'm holding it this way?

II. READING: Reading enables us to cover the broad sweep of the Scriptures, and this is absolutely essential. Nevertheless, it is true that you

308

will remember ordinarily only about 25% of what you read. (Now hold the Bible with the thumb, little finger and the next finger.) When we add personal reading of the Bible to hearing, we certainly begin to have a firm hold on God's word . . . but it's still a rather weak grip, wouldn't you say? Why use only three fingers? Why overlook the strongest fingers?

III. STUDYING: Studying contrasts to merely reading in that we use a pencil. We may make notes, outlines, word studies and file them away for future reference. Or, we may make notations in the margins of our study Bible concerning related passages, chapter outlines, and paragraph titles. Sometimes we may write a synonym above a difficult word. In this way we may retain up to 50% of what we study.

VI. MEMORIZING: Memorizing may seem like child's play—something that is done in the Junior Department in Sunday School. But think again. Have you ever heard of a doctor, a physicist, a lawyer or a stock broker who has not found it necessary to commit to memory many of the throught-tools of his profession? What good would a football or basketball player be if he refused to memorize the plays? We memorize the things that are absolutely essential, the things we dare not forget. For in memorizing we are not looking for 5% retention, or 25%, or 50%, but 100%.

(Hold the Bible with all fingers now.) When I add memorization to my methods of learning and understanding God's holy word, then I have the firmest grip possible. "Thy word have I hid in my heart, that I might not sin against Thee" (Psalm 119:11).

V. SUMMARY:

Before teaching Lesson Six, read over Lesson Seven (in the student's manual); and insert that material into the Lesson Six discussion.

LESSON PLAN

PRIVATE BIBLE STUDY METHODS

LESSON SEVEN   STEP FIVE

OBJECTIVE: To encourage the student to continue in the TEN BASIC
STEPS and learn the various methods of Bible study thereby.

I. OPEN WITH PRAYER.

II. MEMORY VERSE: Colossians 3:16-17. Spend time reviewing all the
verses of this Step.

III. MOTIVATION:

This is not a lesson to be used as a full study by groups. The material in brief outline should be incorporated in the discussions which are
centered on Lesson Six.

IV. BIBLE STUDY:

A. Explain how one should approach the Bible.

B. Methods of Bible study.

1. *Book Study*. The student has been reading a number of Bible
books as he progressed through the study of these TEN BASIC
STEPS TO CHRISTIAN MATURITY. This program of study
is designed to ground the young Christian in the basics of Bible
knowledge *and* in good habits of regular, systematic feeding upon the Bread of Life.

When the student has completed Step Ten, he should be more
than ready to launch out into profitable study of one Bible book
after another. However, it is recommended—with emphasis—
that this foundation of the TEN STEPS first be laid before
one moves to the more advanced work.

2. *Chapter Study*. This is the core of any good book study, and
the student is introduced to it in several of the STEPS. For
example, Step Two, Lessons 2 and 4.

3. *Topical Study*. The first eight STEPS are based on this method,
so it is familiar already; nothing more need be said.

4. *Biographical Study.* Step Nine, Lessons 4, 5, 6, 7 are designed to whet the appetite for the inspiration and education to be found in character studies. Once the taste has been created through the TEN STEPS, the young Christian will be eager to get going on his own!

V. SUMMARY:

Most of the material of Lesson Seven is for future reference, rather than immediate usefulness. When the TEN STEPS have been completed, the student will need to refer to these instructions in order to carry on fruitful personal Bible study without the use of study questions and other aids. Campus Crusade Leadership classes should make extensive use of this lesson.

VI. CLOSE IN PRAYER.

THE CHRISTIAN AND OBEDIENCE

STEP SIX

OBJECTIVE: To know the secret of a fruitful life in Christ which comes from definite obedience to the Word and action prompted by the Holy Spirit.

I. OPEN WITH PRAYER: "Father, we pray that You will search us and know our hearts; try us and know our thoughts and lead us into a practical understanding of how to obey You every day."

II. MEMORY VERSE:

Use each of the eight verses suggested in Step Five by having four students give two references each, and four other students name the verses which go with the references given. Ask for one volunteer to give an example as to how God has used one of the verses to help him in his life.

III. MOTIVATION:

Write the following four key words on a large sheet of paper or blackboard—TRUST . . . OBEDIENCE . . . FELLOWSHIP . . . UNION. Have three students relate the other three words to obedience and explain how they are connected. Then summarize with the following example of our relationship to Christ.

TRUST . . . We walk *before* the Lord as children.

OBEDIENCE . . . We walk *after* the Lord as servants.

FELLOWSHIP . . . We walk *with* the Lord as friends.

UNION . . . We walk *in* the Lord as members of the body.

IV. BIBLE STUDY:

Since obedience is the supreme test of our love for Christ, we should know some practical hints as to exactly what obedience means. First of all, what obedience is NOT:

A. Obedience is not telling God what we can or will do for Him. Example: Many Christians spend a lifetime refusing to surrender to

313

the will of God for fear He will send them to Africa—only to find that when they do finally surrender willingly, God never intended them to be in Africa; and as a result of an unwilling heart, they have missed His best for their lives right here at home. Remember, though, it is His will for some to go to Africa.

B. Obedience is not asceticism, or the giving up of all fun and personal possessions in order to appear humble and simple.

C. Obedience is not the outward conformity to a list of external rules of do's and don'ts.

Obedience is, rather, that attitude of heart which willingly conforms to the instruction of the Spirit of God as set forth in the word of God. Obedience involves, not mere knowledge, but the practical application of what is learned to one's every day Christian experience. True obedience is only initiated and continued by the fullness of the Holy Spirit who alone can live a Christ-honored life through the believer.

D. Human factors in obedience.

1. Heart.

a. Prov. 4:23, "Keep thy heart with all diligence; for out of it are the issues of life."

b. Prov. 14:30, "A sound heart is the life of the flesh . . ."

c. Romans 6:17, ". . . but ye have obeyed from the heart . . ."

d. Isa. 29:13; Matt. 15:8—Professing to believe in Christ does not please Him when our heart is far from Him.

2. Tongue.

James 3:2, ". . . if any man offend not in word, the same is a perfect man, and able also to bridle the whole body."

3. Thoughts.

a. Matt. 5:27-28—To lust in one's heart is equal to the outward act of sin.

b. II Cor. 10:5—Every thought should be brought into obedience.

4. Body and its members.

a. I Cor. 3:16-17—Body is the temple of God.

b. Romans 6:12-13—Don't yield to unrighteousness.

5. Flesh, eyes, heart (proud spirit).

a. I John 2:15-17—Love not the world.

b. Prov. 16:18, "Pride goeth before destruction, and an haughty spirit before a fall."

6. Mind.

Phil. 2:5—Christ's mind is to be in you.

E. How to please the Lord in practical, possible obedience.

1. Present yourself to Christ to be used to His glory and to give out His message.

a. Romans 12:1-2, ". . . present your bodies, a living sacrifice, holy, acceptable to God . . ."

b. Joshua 1:9, "Have not I commanded thee? Be strong and of a good courage; be not afraid, neither be thou dismayed; for the Lord thy God is with thee whithersoever thou goest!"

c. II Cor. 5:19-20—With reconciliation comes an automatic ambassadorship to bear the name of Christ.

(1) Question for discussion:

Is it more difficult to live for Christ, or to die for Him? Would one be willing to die for Him if he refuses to live for Him?

(2) Question:

What are some general responsibilities of any ambassador representing the U.S.?

(3) A Reminder:

a) An ambassador does not support himself.

b) An ambassador does not offer his own message.

c) An ambassador does not choose himself.

d) An ambassador cannot compromise his stand.

2. Present a cleansed vessel to be used.

a. Gal. 5:16, "Walk in the Spirit and ye shall not fulfill the lust of the flesh."

b. Eph. 5:18, "Be not drunk with wine, wherein is excess; but be filled with the Spirit."

F. Obedience in being an example to others.

1. I Tim. 4:12, "Let no man despise thy youth, but be thou an example of the believers in word, in conversation, in love, in spirit, in faith, and in purity."

2. Concerning questionable or doubtful things, use the following 4 laws as a basis for judgment and guidance.

   a. The law of liberty—James 2:12; Romans 8:2. Every Christian has certain rights based on a working knowledge of the word of God.

   b. The law of life—Romans 14:21; I Cor. 8:1-2. A Christian may have certain rights, but may refrain from doing a certain thing for the sake of his testimony and to keep down false issues (giving others an occasion to criticize him).

   c. The law of expediency—I Cor. 10:23-24; 6:12. In the case of unbelievers, a Christian may consider doing a thing, but decide to refrain to keep another from the possibility of stumbling.

   d. The law of supreme sacrifice—I Cor. 9. The life of Paul is our example. There are certain normal, legitimate phases of life which, ordinarily, are ordained of God for a maximum number of human beings; but in the case of some, God chooses to use their lives in a special way, and directs them to refrain from even wonderful, blessed ways of life. E.g., Paul had the right before God to marry, to rear a family and live a Christ-centered life in that way. But, to fulfill his particular calling, God chose Paul to be single and completely free from home and family responsibilities.

3. We are to live a separated life.

   a. Separated from what is contrary to the will of God (implies desires, motives, acts—the world system). II Cor. 6:7-8.

   b. Separated unto Christ—Rom. 6:11; 12:1-2.

V. PARALLEL PASSAGES:

Review the result of obedience and disobedience in the lives of Saul (I Sam. 15) and Paul (Acts 9). See the Lesson Amplification on Lesson 1.

VI. SUMMARY:

There is no substitute for obedience. God calls us individually. He does not call me and expect me to send someone else to take my place. There are no substitutions in the will of God. We are to respond to the highest privilege ever offered to man—to represent the King of Kings and Lord of Lords until He comes again—and in His own word He has said, "Behold I come quickly!"

VII. CLOSE WITH PRAYER OF THANKSGIVING TO GOD FOR PROVIDING OBEDIENCE—WE LIVE IN HIS PROVISION!

LESSON PLAN

OBEDIENCE AND THE PRIVILEGE OF GOD'S WILL

LESSON ONE   **STEP SIX**

OBJECTIVE: That the student might desire to know and do God's will regardless of how it may affect his present dreams and plans.

I.   OPEN WITH PRAYER: "Lord, make me willing to discover and do Thy will, regardless of the cost."

II. MEMORY VERSE: John 14:21.

Review memory verse and have one student suggest how it applies to his life.

III. MOTIVATION: (See the Lesson Amplification.)

IV. BIBLE STUDY:

The principal topic of the Scripture reading of this lesson centers around the conversion of Saul, but the deeper implications involve the result of his conversion and the man whom God chose to bring the "good news" of salvation to Saul. Use the two Scriptural examples set forth in the Lesson Amplification to illustrate the wonderful result of true obedience.

A. Saul: his disobedience and its result.

B. Paul's call: his obedience and its result.

C. One man's obedience: how it greatly affects another.

V.   SUMMARY:

If we were as willing to do God's will as we are to know it, we *would* know it, even as Jesus says in John 7:17—"If any man desires to do His will (God's pleasure), he WILL know . . ."

VI. CLOSE IN PRAYER.

OBEDIENCE AND THE PRIVILEGE OF GOD'S WILL

LESSON ONE   **STEP SIX**

INTRODUCTION:

The importance of obedience cannot be overemphasized. As we are admonished to discipline our children to save them from spiritual bankruptcy (Prov. 23:13-14), so are we taught to bring up our spiritual children (II Tim. 2:2). As a disobedient child grows up to be a problem child, so will the disobedient Christian grow into a problem to himself, to others and especially to the Lord if he does not learn the lesson of obedience in his early Christian experience.

Henry Drummond once stated, "There is a great instrument for finding God's will; this instrument can penetrate where others cannot go. It has a name which every child may understand, even as the stupendous instrument itself with all its mighty powers is sometimes moved in infant hands when others have tried in vain. The name of that instrument is OBEDIENCE." Perfect obedience would be perfect happiness if we had perfect confidence in the power we are obeying.

Present the following two Scriptural examples to illustrate:

I.   SAUL: HIS DISOBEDIENCE AND ITS RESULT, I Sam. 15:

    A. Saul, who was King of Israel, had been commanded by God to utterly destroy Amalek, his company, and his possessions (vs. 1-3).

    B. Incomplete obedience.

        1. Saul spared Agag, King of the Amalekites, and the best of the cattle for a sacrifice (v. 9).

        2. Saul then reported, "I have performed the commandment of the Lord (v. 13).

    C. Result.

        1. God was displeased and dissolved Saul's kingship (vs. 11, 23).

        2. Saul called his action 100% obedience. Samuel called it rebellion, stubbornness and rejecting the word of the Lord (v. 20, 23).

318

D. Key verse: "BEHOLD, TO OBEY IS BETTER THAN SACRI-FICE" (v. 22b).

II. PAUL'S CALL: HIS OBEDIENCE AND ITS RESULTS, Acts 9:

A. Background of Paul . . . Phil. 3:4-6.

1. Circumcised (covenant status).

2. Stock of Israel (pride of family).

3. Pharisee (pride of religion).

4. Zealous persecutor of the church (pride of conviction).

B. Transformation of his life—Acts 9.

1. Call by God (v. 6).

2. Chosen vessel to be God's witness (v. 15).

3. Restored to sight (v. 8, 17).

4. Filled with the Spirit (v. 17).

5. Baptized (v. 18).

6. Preached Christ (v. 20).

C. Paul's life is an example that one's calling should always precede his preaching!

1. In his earlier ministry he prayed, "That I might finish my course with joy, and the ministry, which I have received of the Lord Jesus, to testify the gospel of the grace of God" (Acts 20:24). At the end of his ministry he stated, "I have fought a good fight, I have finished my course, I have kept the faith" (II Timothy 4:7-8).

2. Paul did obey. His faithfulness in the trials of his early Christian life laid the foundation for greater trials and more faith to follow; thus a lifetime testimony to the saving and keeping grace of God.

3. Exhortation to believers today: "Brethren, give diligence to make your calling and election sure; for if ye do these things, ye shall never fall" (II Peter 1:10).

III. ONE MAN'S OBEDIENCE: HOW IT GREATLY AFFECTS THE LIFE OF ANOTHER:

A. Ananias, a disciple of Damascus, was commanded of God to go find Paul and restore his sight. Ananias immediately responded with the human viewpoint, "But, Lord . . . ." A second time the

Lord said, "Go . . . ." Much of our Christian way of life today has resulted from the simple obedience of Ananias, because God has used Paul to reveal the most abundant life ever possible to mankind. Never underestimate the value of complete obedience, however insignificant it may seem at the time. Again, "To obey is better than sacrifice!"

B. Parallel Passages.

1. Obedience to God—John 14:21; 15:10, 14.

2. Obedience to man—Hebrews 13:17; I Peter 5:5-6.

3. Obedience to higher authority—Romans 13:1-7.

4. Disobedience leads to slothfulness—Proverbs 18:9; 19:15.

IV. SUMMARY:

In 1948 these words were recorded by a young missionary who was later martyred in the jungles of Ecuador: "As your life is in His hands, so are the days of your life. But don't let the sands of time get into the eye of your vision to reach those who sit in darkness. They simply must hear. Wives, houses, practices, education, must learn to be disciplined by this rule:

Let the dead attend to the affairs of the already dead; GO THOU and attend the affairs of the dying."

LESSON PLAN

OBEDIENCE AND PERSONAL PURITY

LESSON TWO   STEP SIX

OBJECTIVE: To motivate and inspire the desire for purity in the students' thoughts and actions.

I.   OPEN WITH PRAYER: "Lord, examine our thoughts and see if there be any wicked ways in us."

II. MEMORY VERSE: I Corinthians 6:18.

Take five minutes to review the verse together. Ask one person to recite it; then ask one person to explain the verse.

III. MOTIVATION: (See the Lesson Amplification.)

IV. BIBLE STUDY:

Assign certain members of the group to look up and read aloud the references for the following questions. Then ask other members of the group to answer the corresponding questions, as found in the Lesson Amplification.

A. Matthew 5:27-28.
B. Romans 13:14.
C. I John 1:9.
D. Romans 14:21.

V.   PARALLEL PASSAGES:

A. Compromising with impurity and its results in the spiritual ministry.
   1. David's sins—II Samuel 11:1-4.
   2. Solomon's sin—I Kings 11:1-4.
   3. Samson's sin—Judges 14:1-4.

B. Purity and its results.
   1. Rebecca—Genesis 24:14-18.
   2. Joseph—Genesis 39:7-20; 41:38-44.

VI. SUMMARY:

Since impure actions are the results of impure thinking, it is especially important that we occupy our minds with Christ.

VII. CLOSE IN PRAYER.

OBEDIENCE AND PERSONAL PURITY

LESSON TWO   STEP SIX

INTRODUCTION:

An old Quaker lady who apparently never lost her temper under the most trying circumstances was approached one day by a young girl who said, "Why, if some of the things happened to me that I have seen happen to you, I would just boil over! Why is it that you never do?" The old lady answered quietly, "Perhaps I don't boil over, my dear, but thee doesn't know what boiling is going on inside!" This woman met the outward requirement but did not know the inward reality.

I.   WHAT DOES CHRIST SAY OF IMPURE THOUGHTS (Matthew 5:27-28)?

Jesus speaks here of two things, an *outward requirement* and an *inward reality*.

1. Which is the outward requirement (See v. 27)?

2. Which is the inward reality (See v. 28)?

3. Why is meeting the outward requirement without the inward reality unacceptable to God (See below)?

4. How can one attain the inward reality (See I Cor. 2:16)?

The Sermon on the Mount, in which these verses are found, is the classic condemnation of external religion. The religion of Jesus' time, as is ever the case, was largely a matter of obedience to external laws and rules. Mark 7:1-14 illustrates this. In our own time many believe that they are justified before God if they are outwardly moral, cultured, polite, considerate and refined. Likewise many philosophers and social reformers feel that the basic solution to our problems is an external one, merely the improvement of our environment through legislation and welfare programs. Against all such thinking Jesus stands. He shows that the real problem is internal: "There is nothing from without a man, that entering into him can defile him; but the things which come out of him, those are they that defile the man" (Mark 7:15). Many Christians are diligent in reading their Bibles, in praying, in church attendance, even in witnessing for Christ, but their works are unacceptable to God because they do not reflect the right condition in the heart. Are you one of them?

A policeman was shot to death by a gunman in California, and a Michigan business executive shot his best friend in a hunting accident. In the case of the policeman, search was made for the killer and he was prosecuted. In the case of the business executive, there was no prosecution; for it was apparently not his fault. He even received sympathy. Both men had done the same thing—they had shot and killed another human being with a gun. But their motives were entirely different.

"As a man thinketh in his heart, so *is* he" (Proverbs 23:7). Evil thoughts will eventually result in evil actions. The source of personality is within the thought processes.

How, then, can one attain the inward reality which Jesus here required? Since the problem is internal, the solution must be likewise. In I Cor. 2:16 it says the Christian has the mind of Christ. If Christ dwells in my heart, so does His thinking process. I can have pure thoughts, but not by trying to think pure things. I can have them by letting Christ think through me. Turn over your mind to Him that He might think through it.

II. HOW CAN A CHRISTIAN AVOID IMPURE THOUGHTS (Romans 13:14)?

A further suggestion about overcoming impure thoughts is in Romans 13:14. We are told to "put on" Christ. This means that as we live each day we are to do it claiming the strength, power and protection Christ provides. The victory over impure thinking does not come from us, but from Christ.

"Purity is too deep down for us to get naturally. The only exhibition of purity is the purity in the heart of our Lord, and that is the purity He implants in us."

The religious philosophies of the world are similar to the case of a drowning man, trying to swim ashore. People call to him, "swim harder, swim harder." This is of no help. To tell us we *should* be good and think purely is pointless. But to *enable* us to be pure is the victory of Christianity.

There is also a negative in this verse. We are to give no occasion to the flesh, so that it can fulfill its desires. Any choice you face in life will find two voices beckoning, each in opposite directions: the flesh, representing Satan; the Spirit, representing Christ. We are to give no occasion to the flesh, i.e., provide it with no opportunity. We often fail because we put ourselves in positions where we will be tempted. To look at or read material which promotes sinful thoughts and then expect God to protect us is equivalent to leaping from a building and asking God to keep us from falling!

III. HOW IS FELLOWSHIP RESTORED BETWEEN YOURSELF AND THE LORD (I John 1:9)?

The most difficult aspect of keeping our hearts right before God by confessing our sins is admitting that what we have done is sin. The human personality is so constructed that it would always prefer to rationalize or justify wrong rather than admit it.

Questions for discussion:

1. To whom does the "we" refer in I John 1:9? (Answer—believers.)

2. What is the responsibility of believers according to the verse? (Answer—confess our sins.)

The Greek meaning of the word *confess* is "to agree with" God concerning the sin. This implies being specific. Is there anything wrong with praying, "Lord, forgive me for all of my sins?" (Answer—yes, it is too general.)

When should we confess sin? The *moment* we fail God we must confess it. The *moment* we are unkind or unfaithful to a friend we must ask forgiveness of them and confess the sin to God.

As Christians, we often forget that our relationship to God depends upon our being cleansed, moment by moment, and not a haphazard attitude of "anything goes if I am sincere, or if I am trying."

A. God's promise is *unconditional* forgiveness.

    1. Our forgiveness is not based on how guilty we feel or if we promise never to do it again. But it is based on the unconditional promise of God's faithfulness. He only is faithful and just. He only can forgive.

    2. Example of Thomas—John 20:24-28. Confession also means restoration, not blame. The Lord did not blame Thomas for doubting, but appeared to him in love and proved to him the fact of the resurrection.

    3. When God forgives sin, He also removes and forgets it.

        a. Psalm 103:12.

        b. Isaiah 43:25.

B. Unconditional forgiveness provides complete cleansing.

    1. Question: Since we can only confess the sin we know, what happens to the unknown sin in our life? Is it possible to commit sin without knowing it?

    (Answer: I John 1:9b—He promises to cleanse us from "all unrighteousness." This includes all the "unknown sin" in our life.)

    2. When God forgives sin, on what is His forgiveness based? (Answer: Eph. 1:7; Col. 1:14—the blood of Christ.)

THE *SACRED FIRE*

Jesus, Thine all-victorious love, shed in my soul abroad
    Then shall my feet no longer rove, rooted and fixed in God.

Oh, that in me that sacred fire might now begin to glow
  Burn up the dross of base desire and make the mountains flow.

Thou, Who at Pentecost didst fall, Do Thou my sins consume
  Come, Holy Ghost, for Thee I call, Spirit of burning come!

Refining fire, go through my heart, illuminate my soul
  Scatter Thy life through every part and sanctify the whole.

My steadfast soul from falling free shall then no longer move
  While Christ is all the world to me, And all my heart is love.

Charles Wesley

IV. MAY A CHRISTIAN ENGAGE IN QUESTIONABLE PRACTICES (Romans 14:21)?

A. What is a "questionable practice?"

B. What determines whether I should engage in a "questionable practice" or not?

The Bible classifies the things we do into three general areas—things that are *wrong* (murder, immorality, drunkenness, etc.), things that are *right* (marriage, eating, etc.), and things that are *dependent on our own personality, the circumstance and the potential effect upon others,* as to whether they are right or wrong. It is like contrasting black, white and gray.

A "questionable practice" is something that falls into the third class.

We may engage in many activities with no personal harm, if we are strong Christians. But those who follow our example may fall. If such happens, God holds us responsible.

Such things are not usually sin in themselves, but our participation in them is to be governed by a "law of love," a consideration for others. If our participation will weaken, or somehow lead astray another Christian or even a non-Christian, the law of love says we should refrain. A trapeze artist may smoothly perform many acrobatic feats in the air. But an inexperienced and uncoordinated grade-school child would kill himself doing the same things.

Fortunately, the Bible is not a book of petty rules and regulations, but of broad principles which span time and culture. The Bible will not tell a girl how long her sleeves should be, or how high the neck on her dress. It will not tell a young man when he should and should not kiss his date. But it gives general principles which by the wisdom of the Holy Spirit we are to apply to our own situations. We are to avoid two extremes—license and legalism. It is never safe to lay down specific rules in these areas as to what one can and cannot do. Rather each must decide for himself on the basis of the fact that our bodies are temples of God, and of I Cor. 10:31—"do *all* to the glory of God."

LESSON PLAN

OBEDIENCE AND THE PRIVILEGE OF SECURITY

LESSON THREE   STEP SIX

OBJECTIVE: To show the student that physical, material and spiritual
security depend on Christ and our obedience to Him.

I.   OPEN WITH PRAYER: "Lord show me that You take care of all
my needs, wants and desires, and make me want only You."

II. MEMORY VERSE: Matthew 6:33.

Review verse individually for a few minutes. Ask someone to quote
the verse, and explain what "all these things" means.

III. MOTIVATION:

Read the story of the "Nine Successful Financiers" in the Lesson
Amplification.

IV. BIBLE STUDY:

Discuss the parable of the rich fool in Luke 12:13-21. Discuss the
questions in the lesson and use the Lesson Amplification.

A. The men who came to Christ.

B. Christ Himself.

C. The rich fool.

V.   PARALLEL PASSAGES:

A. Achan—security through possessions. Joshua 7.

1. Disobedience—took of the spoils of battle.

2. Reason—coveted them for self.

3. Result—Israelites killed in battle, Achan and family stoned.

327

OBEDIENCE AND THE PRIVILEGE OF SECURITY

LESSON THREE   STEP SIX

INTRODUCTION: "Nine Successful Financiers."

"In 1923 a very important meeting was held at the Edgewater Beach Hotel in Chicago. In attendance were nine of the world's most successful financiers. Those present were: the president of the largest independent steel company, the president of the largest utility company, the president of the largest gas company, the greatest wheat speculator, the president of the New York Stock Exchange, a member of the President's Cabinet, the greatest stock broker, the head of the world's greatest monopoly, the president of the Bank of International Settlements.

"Certainly we must admit that here was gathered a group of the world's most successful men; at least, men who had found the secret of making money. Twenty-five years later let's see where these men were:

> The president of the largest independent steel company, Charles Schwab, died bankrupt and lived on borrowed money for five years before his death. The president of the largest utility company, Samuel Insull, died a fugitive from justice and penniless in a foreign land. The president of the largest gas company, Howard Hopson, went insane. The greatest wheat speculator, Arthur Cotton, died abroad, insolvent. The president of the New York Stock Exchange, Richard Whitney, was released from Sing Sing Penitentiary. The member of the President's Cabinet, Albert Fall, was pardoned from prison so he could die at home. The greatest "bear" on Wall Street, Jesse Livermore, died a suicide. The head of the greatest monopoly, Ivan Krueger, died a suicide. The president of the Bank of International Settlements, Leon Fraser, died a suicide. All of these men learned well the art of making a living, but not one learned how to live."

From Billy Rose, *Pitching Horse Shoes*, 1948. The meeting at the Edgewater Beach Hotel was a youth congress.

In the parable of the rich fool, Luke 12:13-21, note the characters in both the parable and its setting. Ask the class to identify and describe each.

I.   THE MAN WHO CAME TO CHRIST: His interest in Jesus was only material, that Christ might use his influence to provide him with money. Is it possible to come to Christ for only material motives?

      Books are often written by well-meaning Christians almost giving the impression that if we come to Christ we are guaranteed an improvement in our material condition. A recent advertisement told of a book which had discovered the secret of making money and guaranteed this to its readers.

The secret, it said, was taken from the teaching of Jesus. But the blessings of Christianity are not material, though these sometimes incidentally result. They are spiritual and eternal. Don't make Christ just a divine bill-payer!

II. THERE IS CHRIST HIMSELF: The One who spoke of detachment from material things was Himself detached. Jesus, the ruler of the universe, often had no place to sleep and owned no property but His cloak. Can Christ live through me and have me still be materialistic? Ask the class how wealthy Christ was.

III. THE RICH FOOL: He was concerned about a material problem. This was his life. This was what he desired above all else. No doubt in his mind was the thought after *after* he had expended his fortune he could straighten out his life with God. God says "this night" your soul shall be required. The real problem in his life was spiritual, and all his efforts in the material direction were useless. Ask the class in what ways we can be overly concerned about material things, to the neglect of the spiritual. Notice this in the areas of studies, clothes, expenses on our social life, expenses on cars, etc. Note I John 2:15-16. What is the difference between *using* the things of the world and *loving* them? Use the illustration of the man who gave the woman an expensive ring. She then came to love the ring more than the one who gave it. When we love *things* more than God, we are guilty of one of the worst kinds of sins.

A. Discuss what true security is.
    1. Is it to be found in money?
    2. Is it to be found in the security of family relationships?
    3. Is it to be found in the possession of clothing and goods?
    4. Is it to be found in God?

B. Explain your answer.

IV. THE LIFE OF C. T. STUDD:
C. T. Studd was a wealthy young Cambridge student famous for his skill as a cricket player. He studied the Scripture, especially the story of the rich young man to whom Jesus said, "One thing thou lackest: go thy way, sell whatsoever thou hast, and give to the poor, and thou shalt have treasure in heaven: and come, take up the cross, and follow me" (Mark 10:21).

C. T. Studd felt impressed to do exactly what the rich young man had failed to do. There was no question of feeling or emotion, nor was there any kind of special supernatural guidance. It was simple obedience to the black and white statements of God's word. He gave away his inheritance, which was by our standards approximately $200,000. He proved what all prove who put God to the test, that He never fails those who trust Him. Neither he nor his wife nor their children ever lacked the necessities of life. He was a great man of God and went as a missionary to China, India and Africa; and through his ministry thousands of people were won to Christ.

Here is what he said: "Seeing that some 40 years ago at God's command I left mother, brethren, friends, fortune and all that is usually thought to make life worth living, and have so continued ever since, I have been called fool and fanatic again and again, yet lived to prove that the worldly counselors were the fools. 'Cursed is he that trusteth in man' does not make a very good pillow for a dying man, but there is much comfort in the other one, 'Blessed is he that trusteth in the Lord.' "

In a letter to a friend he said, "The Committee I work under is a conveniently small Committee, a very wealthy Committee, a wonderfully generous Committee, and is always sitting in session—the Committee of the Father, the Son and the Holy Ghost. We have a multi-millionaire to back us up, far and away the wealthiest person in the world. I had an interview with Him. He gave me a cheque-book free and urged me to draw upon Him. He assured me His Firm clothes the grass of the field, preserves the sparrows, counts the hairs of the children's heads. He said the Head of the Firm promised to supply all our need."

The life of C. T. Studd was a testimony to the world that when a believer is obedient to the commands of Jesus Christ every NEED in life will be supplied.

God's word says this: "Ask and it shall be given you; seek and ye shall find; knock, and it shall be opened unto you; For every one that asketh receiveth; and he that seeketh findeth; and to him that knocketh it shall be opened. Or what man is there of you, whom if his son ask bread, will he give him a stone? Or if he ask a fish, will he give him a serpent?

"If ye then, being evil, know how to give good gifts unto your children, how much more shall your Father which is in heaven give good things to them that ask him?" (Matthew 7:7-11).

"What shall we then say to these things? If God be for us, who can be against us? He that spared not His own Son, but delivered him up for us all, how shall He not with Him also freely give us all things?" (Romans 8:31-32).

Can you trust a God like that—a God who loved you enough to die for you?

Security lies only in being obedient to God's word: "Love not the world, neither the things that are in the world. If any man love the world, the love of the Father is not in him. For all that is in the world, the lust of the flesh, and the lust of the eyes, and the pride of life, is not of the Father, but is of the world. And the world passeth away, and the lust thereof; but he that doeth the will of God abideth for ever" (I John 2:15-17). False security lies in the world and the "things" of the world, but true security lies in doing the will of God.

LESSON PLAN

OBEDIENCE AND THE FEAR OF WHAT
MEN WILL THINK

LESSON FOUR   STEP SIX

OBJECTIVE: To show the student how to overcome the fear of what men
will think of him.

I.   OPEN WITH PRAYER: "Lord, teach us to be more concerned about
what You think of us rather than what
others think of us. Help us never to be
ashamed of You."

II. MEMORY VERSE: Luke 9:26.

Review individually for a few minutes. Ask someone to quote the verse
and to tell what it means to be ashamed of Christ and His words—
possibly give an example.

III. MOTIVATION:

Jerome Hines, Metropolitan Opera star, before singing at the Presi-
dential Prayer Breakfast, which was attended by the President of the
United States, the Cabinet, the House, the Senate, and the Supreme
Court, stated clearly his faith in Jesus Christ. He minced no words.
His stand was strong and dynamic. Other Christians, when presented
with golden opportunities, become afraid and never say a word for
their Lord. Why the difference? Let's study this lesson and see if
we can discover why—using examples from the life of Peter.

IV. BIBLE STUDY:

A. The example of Peter—Matt. 26:57-75; Acts 2:13-14.

B. What transformed Peter?

C. The example of Esther—Esther 4:11-16.

V.   PARALLEL PASSAGES:

A. We are to please God, not men. Gal. 1:10; Acts 5:29.

B. Biblical examples of the fear of man.

1. Abraham—Genesis 12:11-19. He said that Sarah was his sister rather than his wife.

2. Aaron—Exodus 32:22-24. He yielded to the Israelites who were demanding an idol.

3. The Israelites—I Samuel 17:24. They were afraid of men when they faced the Philistines.

4. Pilate—John 19:12-16. He yielded to the demands of the people.

VI. SUMMARY:

This lesson might be the answer to the problem of many professing Christians, who have no power or authority in their lives. They want to be men of God, but they are defeated by the overwhelming sense of the fear of man. This is especially true on the college campuses where great social pressures are brought to bear on each individual. The only way to overcome the fear of man is to yield to God, become obedient to Him and be faithful to the command, "Be ye filled with the Spirit" (Eph. 5:18). If you want power and authority and if you want to be a man or woman of God, then let the Holy Spirit have full and complete control of your life.

VII. CLOSE IN PRAYER.

LESSON AMPLIFICATION

OBEDIENCE AND THE FEAR OF WHAT
MEN WILL THINK

LESSON FOUR   STEP SIX

I. THE EXAMPLE OF PETER:

A. His strong faith (Matthew 16:13-16). He promised Christ that he would never be ashamed of Him (Matthew 26:33).

B. His denial—Matthew 26:69-75. And it was in front of a young girl.

C. His transformation.

1. Some days later, he stood before thousands of people and boldly preached Jesus Christ (Acts 2:14-41).

2. Again he preached Christ, before all the leaders in Jerusalem who had been responsible for the death of Christ (Acts 4:8-20). Everyone marveled at his boldness.

3. Again he preached Christ before the religious leaders, claiming that he must obey God rather than men (Acts 5:29-42).

II. WHAT TRANSFORMED PETER?

The Resurrection and Pentecost.

A. Because of the resurrection he understood the Messiahship of Jesus Christ. Previous to the resurrection he had too much of a human concept of Jesus. After the resurrection he understood that Christ is the Messiah who must suffer for our sins and be raised again for our justification, and that was the message he preached!

B. Because of Pentecost he had living within him the power to tell others the good news of the Gospel. It was a power which rested not in self, but in the Holy Spirit who dwelt within him.

C. Christ had predicted that it would be so.

1. *Resurrection*—Matthew 16:21; Matthew 26:31-42.

2. *Pentecost*—John 14:16-17; John 16:13-14.

III. THE EXAMPLE OF ESTHER:

A. Situation: King Ahasuerus had ordered queen Vashti to appear before a great feast. When she refused his command he dissolved Vashti's queenship and sought a fair young virgin to take her place (Esther 1).

B. Choice of Esther.

1. Preparation.

a. Groomed by God—Esther 2:7.

b. Costly planning—Esther 2:12.

c. Favor gained—Esther 2:15.

d. Loved and crowned—Esther 2:17.

2. Principle: First chosen by God, then the King (Psalm 75:6-7).

C. Esther's great trial—Esther 4:8.

1. Haman, the head of the King's princes, conspired to destroy all Jews (Esther 3:6).

2. Mordecai, who reared Esther, commanded her to go to the King in behalf of her people, the Jews. Under the law of the land, however, to go into the King without his request meant certain death unless the King held out his golden sceptre to indicate his approval of the visitor (Esther 4:8-11).

D. Esther's attitude of ultimate trust—"so will I go in unto the king, which is not according to the law, and if I perish, I perish" (Esther 4:16).

1. We have little conception of what Esther's faithfulness meant in spite of certain death. The fate of the whole Jewish race was at stake, and yet she fulfilled her duty as Christ commanded in Mark 8:35, ". . . whosoever shall lose his life for my sake and the gospel's, the same shall save it."

2. God never requires perfect understanding of the circumstances from His children; rather perfect obedience. He promises personal responsibility for the result when we carry out His commandments. Esther feared God more than she feared people and because of this attitude God showed Himself strong in her behalf (II Chron. 16:9).

E. Conclusion—a faithful stand and a faithful God—Esther 5:12.

1. Esther approached the King in her royal apparel. Principle of our life—we approach the Father in the perfect imputed righteousness of the Son.

2. The King held out the sceptre to her. Implications:

   (a) Her life was spared.

   (b) Her people were delivered.

   (c) Her Lord was glorified.

IV. SUMMARY: Questions for discussion:

A. Is it possible for the Lord to demand more of us than we are able to produce (I Cor. 10:13)?

B. What is our source of strength during times of trial (II Cor. 12:9-10; Romans 8:37)?

C. Is production in the Christian life ever dependent on human talents and abilities? On what is it dependent (John 15:5; Philippians 3:3b)?

LESSON PLAN

OBEDIENCE AND THE TONGUE AND
INSINCERE OBEDIENCE

LESSONS FIVE AND SIX   STEP SIX

OBJECTIVE: To show that true obedience affects the inward attitude and
the outward act.

I. OPEN WITH PRAYER: Have two or three students open with short
    prayers.

II. MOTIVATION AND MEMORY VERSE:

Ask the group to discuss the relationship between the two memory
verses, James 3:2 and Colossians 3:23. Leader should also check the
Lesson Amplification.

III. BIBLE STUDY:

A. Study on the *Tongue*—James 3.

    1. Have students read James 3:1-13 and find reasons why the
       tongue needs controlling. Examples:

        a. V. 2—The tongue is like a bridle and if we can control the
           tongue, we can control the body. Question: How does James
           illustrate this in verses 3 and 4?

        b. V. 5—The tongue does much damage with little effort. Ques-
           tion: How much does it take to start a fire?

        c. V. 6—An unruly tongue can wreck one's whole Christian life.
           Question: What is the origin of evil speech?

        d. V. 9—We need to prevent an inconsistent example of blessing
           God and cursing men with the same tongue. Question: How
           does James illustrate this in vs. 11-12?

    2. Summarize with James 1:26, "If any man among you seem to be
       religious, and bridleth not his tongue, but deceiveth his own
       heart, this man's religion is vain."

B. Importance of a Christian testimony before the world.

1. Have students read the account of Ananias and Sapphira in Acts 5:1-11.

2. Assign one student to each part of question 1, page 16.

3. Leader should review the Lesson Amplification.

C. Have group show the relationship between Acts 5 and James 3.

IV. PARALLEL PASSAGES:

A. Warnings concerning the use of the tongue for evil.

1. Psalm 12:3—against mischief, deceit and lying.

2. Psalm 52:2-4—against flattery and pride.

3. Matthew 15:8—against lip service without life testimony.

B. The use of the tongue for the glory of God.

1. Proverbs 14:25—soul-winning.

2. Proverbs 15:4—a tree of life.

3. Col. 3:16—praise.

4. Romans 10:9—confessing Christ.

C. The tongue and the heart in obedience.

1. Luke 6:45—"Of the abundance of the heart, his mouth speaketh."

2. Proverbs 23:7—"As a man thinketh in his heart, so is he."

3. Eph. 6:5-6—True servants obey from the heart.

V. SUMMARY:

The tongue does not function by itself as an independent member of your body, but is completely controlled by the mind. It responds to thought impulses. "Out of the abundance of the heart the mouth speaketh" (Matthew 12:34). Since our tongue is controlled by our mind, our mind must be renewed (Romans 12:2). Renewal is conformity, not to the world, but to Christ by the Holy Spirit working on the inside .

VI. CLOSE WITH PRAYER OF THANKSGIVING.

OBEDIENCE AND THE TONGUE AND
INSINCERE OBEDIENCE

LESSONS FIVE AND SIX   STEP SIX

INTRODUCTION:

These verses reflect two aspects of obedience, the outward result in the control of the tongue, and the inward sincere attitude of the heart. Both aspects must be stressed in the Christian life. We need instruction and exhortation concerning the outward manifestation so that we can know what God expects of us and whether or not we are approaching His standard. We need to look at the heart attitude which is the inward source of the outward obedience.

Compare the illustration of an apple tree. We do not produce an apple tree by taking a bushel of apples and pinning them on an oak tree. So, mere exhortations to outward obedience neglect the heart of the problem. On the other hand, if an apple tree is planted and grows properly, the natural result is large red apples. For one to claim he has the right attitude and true faith in God and have nothing to show for it is senseless. "But wilt thou know, O vain man, that faith without works is dead" (James 2:20).

I.   THE TONGUE:

Why should we control the tongue? Why does the Scripture devote most of a chapter here, plus numerous passages in other books, and why does Christ Himself have so much to say about the tongue? Why is this so important?

A. Because if we can control the tongue, we can control the whole body. Jesus said, "For out of the abundance of the heart his mouth speaketh" (Luke 6:45). The tongue is not something independent; it merely reflects the condition of the heart. A book may advocate atheism and undercut the faith of many Christians. No one blames the printing press for the book. The fault lies with the author. The press is but an instrument. The tongue is the instrument of the heart. Therefore, if we can control it, it indicates a heart which is totally submitted to Christ!

B. Because the tongue can do so much damage with so little effort. All sin is sin. But some sins do more damage than others. Many times we have sins in our lives for which God will still hold us

338

accountable, but which do not do so much damage and are not so public. Note the difference between harboring a secret grudge and spreading lies openly. Careers of people in public life have been virtually destroyed by "gossip campaigns" and secret rumors.

C. Because an unruly tongue may wreck the whole Christian life. Our speech is so public that failure in this area can ruin an otherwise good example. Few people would even want a new car if it were painted an obnoxious color, unless they could repaint it. Your thoughts are not written for others to see, but your words are public to all. A new suit with a large stain on it which we could not get out would destroy the value of the suit. A few drops of ink in clear drinking water would also destroy its value. So an evil tongue can mar and even wreck a Christian testimony.

D. Because controlling the tongue keeps us from inconsistency and hypocrisy. Verses 9-12 point out how inconsistent a life our tongue may reveal. Many Christians know all the "language," can pray eloquently, and speak as if they were very holy. But in almost the same breath their gossiping tonges reveal their hypocrisy. Remember, your speech is just like a large neon sign telling everyone what you *really* are.

II. THE IMPORTANCE OF A CHRISTIAN TESTIMONY BEFORE THE WORLD:

After finishing the Bible study on James, read Acts 5:1-11 and relate the two. Both passages speak of an outward obedience, but the passage in Acts speaks of an insincere heart. Ananias and Sapphira gave money to God, but not to please Him, only to please men. An obedience not backed by the right heart attitude is not only unacceptable, but will sooner or later reveal itself in sin. Suppose these two had been given the job of handling the fund of the church. No doubt they would have been dishonest in this area also. Note these things further about the sin of Ananias and Sapphira, and bring them out to the group, perhaps using some of your own illustrations:

A. This sin of Ananias and Sapphira was within the fellowship of the church. The church is rarely harmed or hindered by opposition from without; it is perpetually harmed or hindered by perils from within. Consider the damage wrought by Judas and Saul. Hypocrisy is a sin which can do irreparable damage.

B. The sin of Ananias and Sapphira was not in refusing to contribute to the church; it was not in the amount they gave and the fact they held back part of the price. There was no rule that they should give, or give a certain amount. Their sin was that of pretending they had done more than they had—in other words, hypocrisy.

The one thing that made Christ angry, the one thing against which He uttered His severest words, was the sin of hypocrisy. What severe things He said to the men who pretended to be religious; what scorching, blasting words fell from His lips against such! He had no attitude toward the hypocrite but that of denunciation.

III. SUMMARY:

Have the class give some present-day examples of types of hypocrisy, and contribute some of these to the discussion:

A. Hypocrisy toward God. We tell God we are surrendered to Him when we are not, instead of honestly expressing our feelings, no matter how sinful they may be, and obtaining His forgiveness. We presume we love Him and His will. He who said "I am the truth" never made any peace with a lie! Be *honest* in prayer.
If you do not want to do God's will on any issue, far better to tell Him so and ask for His help, rather than hide it because dedicated Christians are supposed to have no such feelings.

B. Hypocrisy toward other believers. We try to put on a show of being dedicated, sincere Christians, experiencing victory in most of our life when in reality we are defeated and in desperate trouble. Do not broadcast your defeats before others, nor wallow in self-pity, but be unafraid to seek help from mature Christians when help is needed.

C. Hypocrisy toward non-Christians. We profess to them that we are Christians; we read our Bibles; we attend church. But we cheat on exams, become just as frustrated, worried or exasperated as they are when the pressure comes. Or, even worse, our lives show drastic moral inconsistencies—we sin in the areas of sex or drunkenness, etc. Our lives will never be perfect. But we must ask Christ to enable us to live godly lives if we are to impress the non-Christian world for Christ.

SUMMARY LESSON PLAN

THE CHRISTIAN AND WITNESSING

STEP SEVEN

OBJECTIVE: to encourage Christians to be effective witnesses for Jesus Christ.

I. OPEN WITH PRAYER: "Lord, teach us how to be an effective instrument in bringing others to Christ."

II. MEMORY VERSES: Review all the verses in the lesson.

II Corinthians 5:14-15   I Peter 3:15
John 4:35   Acts 4:31
Matthew 4:19   John 15:26-27

III. MOTIVATION:

J. B. Phillips, in his introduction to *The Young Church in Action*, said this: "In the pages of this unpretentious book, written by the author of the third Gospel, the fresh air of Heaven is plainly blowing. Many problems comparable to modern complexities never arise here because the men and women concerned were of one heart and mind in the Spirit. Many another issue is never allowed to arise because these early Christians were led by the Spirit to the main task of bringing people to God through Christ and were not permitted to enjoy fascinating sidetracks."

What "fascinating sidetracks" do you think we are enjoying? Why is it that we have deviated from the purpose of bringing others to Jesus Christ?

IV. BIBLE STUDY:

A. Motivation for witnessing.

1. To be obedient to Jesus Christ who gave the Great Commission.

2. The fact that people are lost and in need of a Saviour.

3. People are hungry for the Gospel.

B. Methods of witnessing.

1. Public Meeting.

(a) Characteristics of these meetings.

(b) Examples of these meetings.

2. Private encounters.

341

   (a) Characteristics of these encounters.

   (b) Examples of these encounters.

  C. Modern Witnessing.

   1. Every Christian is to be a witness.

   2. Every Christian is to produce some fruit.

   3. Practical suggestions.

V. PARALLEL PASSAGES: (See Bible Study in the Lesson Amplification.)

VI. SUMMARY:

The Value of One Soul—

> "I believe that if an angel were to wing his way from earth up to Heaven, and were to say that there was one poor, ragged boy, without father or mother, with no one to care for him and teach him the way of life; and if God were to ask who among them were willing to come down to this earth and live here for fifty years and lead that one to Jesus Christ, every angel in Heaven would volunteer to go. Even Gabriel, who stands in the presence of the Almighty, would say, 'Let me leave my high and lofty position, and let me have the luxury of leading one soul to Jesus Christ.' There is no greater honor than to be the instrument in God's hands of leading one person out of the kingdom of Satan into the glorious light of Heaven"—D. L. Moody.

Christ considered the human soul to be of such transcendent value that He gladly exchanged the shining courts of glory for a life of poverty, suffering, shame and death as an expression of His desire to "seek and save the lost." He was "not willing that any should perish, but that all should come to repentance" (II Pet. 3:9).

Christ had a concern for the individual and for the multitude. His concern was so real and so deep that at times the flood of manly tears could no longer be restrained, and rolled down His compassionate face. Jesus, the manliest of men, wept. Paul, the brave, besought men night and day with tears to be reconciled to God. When a young missionary who had been sent home by illness was asked why he was so eager to get back to his people, he said, "Because I cannot sleep for thinking about them."

What about your concern?

> "Lord Crucified, give me a love like Thine,
> Help me to win the dying souls of men,
> Lord, keep my heart in closest touch with Thine
> And give me love, pure Calvary love,
> To bring the lost to Thee."

VII. CLOSE IN PRAYER.

342

WHY WITNESS?

OBJECTIVE: To demonstrate the reason for a verbal witness and to remove the barriers which prevent it.

I.   OPEN WITH PRAYER: "Lord, remove any false barriers to our verbal witness that Christ may be glorified in us."

II. MEMORY VERSE: II Cor. 5:14-15 (Each class member recite to another).

III. MOTIVATION:

A young man rushed back from the Billy Graham meeting to the apartment he shared with a friend. They had lived together for several years since they both worked for the same company. "I must tell you something," he said to his friend. "Tonight I invited Christ to be my Saviour, and He has changed my life." His friend smiled and said, "Wonderful. I have been hoping you would do that. I have been living the Christian life before you all these years hoping that you would trust Christ as your Saviour." Much surprised the new Christian said, "You lived such a perfect life that I kept trying to do it without Christ, inasmuch as you seemed to be doing it without Christ. Tonight I invited Him to become my Lord and Saviour because I failed to live up to your standard. You should have told me why you lived the way you live. Why didn't you tell me how I could know Christ too?" This is a good illustration of the fact that we need to witness with our lips or our life can be misinterpreted, doing harm to the Gospel, and perhaps even keeping people from receiving Christ.

IV. BIBLE STUDY:

A. What is a witness?

B. Motivation for witnessing.

   1. What some men of God have said.

   2. The Biblical position.

3. Christ, our example.

4. Our responsibility.

C. Modern witnessing.

D. Methods of witnessing.

    1. Public encounter.

    2. Private encounter.

    3. Practical suggestions.

V.   PARALLEL PASSAGES:

A. Other reasons for witnessing:

    1. Christ's command . . . Mark 16:15; John 14:21.

    2. Our responsibility . . . Ezek. 3:18.

    3. Out of love . . . II Cor. 5:14-15; I Thess. 2:8.

    4. To glorify God . . . John 15:8.

    5. That our prayers may be answered . . . John 15:16.

B. Examples in Scripture:

    1. In Acts 20:17-38, how did Paul feel about those to whom he witnessed?

    2. Compare Acts 20:20-21 and Ezekiel 33:9.

VI.   SUMMARY: Challenge to witness . . .

"You and I do not want to witness! Is not that the case? Satan is interested in keeping us from being vital, and you can be sure that his fifth column agent within us—the old nature—is working with the enemy of our souls to defeat us here. You may even feel fatigued, sick, rushed, worried, but Christ feels wonderful. Give Him a chance. If your heart is cold, think of all Christ has done for you and what it would mean if one of your friends came to know Him, too."

VII. CLOSE IN PRAYER.

WHY WITNESS?

LESSON ONE   STEP SEVEN

I.   WHAT IS A WITNESS? Have students suggest answers and then
           give this definition:

A witness is any Christian who bears testimony to the death, burial
and resurrection of Jesus Christ by life and by lips.

   A. I Cor. 15:1-4. Paul preached this message, thus defining the gospel:
      "Moreover, brethren, I declare unto you the gospel . . . for I
      delivered unto you first of all that which I also received, how that,
      1) Christ died for our sins, 2) that He was buried, 3) that He
      rose again the third day according to the scriptures."

   B. A witness is one who first receives the Gospel himself, then pro-
      claims that truth to others. One can never teach or testify to a
      truth which he does not first personally believe and practice.

   C. Some people want a god, but they must know THE Gospel about
      THE God if their lives are to be transformed. Paul expressed the
      exact responsibility of believers in Rom. 10:14-15.

II. MOTIVATION FOR WITNESSING:

Question: What are several reasons for telling others about Christ?
           Have several answer before leader answers.

   A. What some men of God have said.

      1. *C. T. Studd,* missionary to China, Africa and India . . . "If
         Christ be God and died for me, then there is nothing too great
         that I can do for him."

      2. *Jim Elliot,* martyred in Ecuador trying to reach Aucas . . .
         "Lord, pour out my life as an oblation for the world. Blood is
         only of value as it flows before Thine altar."

      3. *V. Raymond Edman,* president of Wheaton College . . . "There
         can be no self-confidence, no cockiness of Spirit, no contempt
         for any path in which He might lead or for any cross that He
         might give."

345

B. The Biblical position on witnessing.

    1. To be obedient to Jesus Christ, who gave the Great Commission. It is a command (Matt. 28:19).

    2. The realization that people are lost and in need of a Saviour. "The untold millions who are dying untold" (Luke 19:10; John 14:6; Acts 4:12; I Timothy 2:5).

    3. People are hungry for God (Matt. 9:37-38; John 4:35-39).

    4. Psalms 126:6 . . . go with the message and you will bear fruit.

    5. Prov. 14:25 . . . "A true witness delivereth souls" (Rom. 7:6).

    6. Luke 19:10 . . . "For the Son of man is come to seek and to save the lost" (Heb. 13:8).

    7. Acts 1:8 . . . commission and responsibility: ye shall receive power; ye shall be witnesses unto me . . .

        a. early church witnessed: Acts 8:4; 11:19; 15:35.

        b. the Lord added the harvest: Acts 2:41, 47; 4:4; 11:18.

    8. Matt. 28:18-20 . . . great commission: Go . . preach . . make disciples.

C. Christ, our example.

    1. Dealt with individuals (Nicodemus, Jn. 3; Samaritan woman, Jn. 4).

    2. Dealt with groups (5,000, Jn. 6; taught in temple, Jn. 8; Pharisees, Jn. 8:13 ff.).

    3. Dealt with disciples (Jn. 13:1 ff.; Jn. 9:2 ff.).

D. Our responsibility is the same; talk with individuals, talk with groups and talk with family and close friends.

III. MODERN WITNESSING:

A. Every Christian is to be a witness (Matthew 28:19).

B. Every Christian should produce some fruit (Romans 7:4; John 15:6). The natural result of marriage is children. We are spiritually married to Christ that we might bring forth spiritual children.

Characteristics of fruit:

    1. Fruit is always a product of a tree. There can be no fruit without the life-giving principle in the tree.

346

2. There can be no fruit without dependence upon Jesus Christ, who is our life.

3. Not every tree produces fruit at the same rate. Every tree is different.

4. If you are not seeing fruit, don't get discouraged. It is not yet your season (Psalms 1:3). Just be faithful in witnessing.

5. Always remember! Some plant, some water, but God gives the increase (I Corinthians 3:5-8). No man has ever won another person to Christ; soul-winning is strictly the job of the Holy Spirit.

IV. METHODS OF WITNESSING:

A. Public meeting—these meetings were held in the synagogues, and in the homes of the Christians, and outside in the cities and countryside.

1. Characteristics of these meetings.

   a. A bold spokesman—no fear of man or of what people would think (Acts 4:13; 18:26; 5:28-29).

   b. They stressed the crucifixion, resurrection and Lordship of Christ (Acts 3:15; 4:10).

   c. There was a clear presentation of salvation in Christ—no compromise (Acts 4:12).

   d. They spoke from the Scriptures (Acts 3:18; 7:52).

   e. Their message brought conviction in the hearts of those who listened, and some believed, some asked questions, others mocked and persecuted (Acts 17:32-34; 5:40).

2. Examples of some of these meetings.

   a. Acts 5:29-42, Peter, when meeting before the high priest and the Sanhedrin (which included the Sadducees and the Pharisees).

   b. Acts 17:22-34, Paul, when speaking to the Greeks at Athens.

   c. Acts 26:1-32, Paul, on trial before King Agrippa at Rome.

B. Private encounter.

1. Characteristics of these encounters.

   a. Tactful, but bold (Acts 8:30).

  b. The crucifixion, resurrection and Lordship of Christ were stressed (Acts 10:39-40).

  c. The witness had a personal knowledge of the Scriptures (Acts 8:31-32).

  d. Salvation in Christ and a personal faith in Him were stressed (Acts 8:35).

  e. People were won by one another (Acts 8:37).

 2. Examples of these encounters.

  a. Acts 10:7-33, Peter witnessed to Cornelius.

  b. Acts 16:25-34, Paul and Silas witnessed to a Philippian jailor.

  c. Acts 24:24-25, Paul witnessed to Felix, the governor of Rome.

C. Practical suggestions.

 1. Pray every day for God to make opportunities for you to witness.

 2. Make Jesus Christ central in your witnessing experience.

 3. Be sure you have the "Four Spiritual Laws" memorized, as well as the verses that go with them, so you can clearly and effectively present the Gospel.

 4. Be in a constant attitude of prayer so as to determine when the Spirit is leading you to witness.

 5. Be sure that all sin is confessed, and that you are filled and controlled by the Holy Spirit.

 6. Carry a small pocket Bible or New Testament so you can show the salvation verses to the person to whom you are witnessing.

 7. Pray for the individual's salvation after presenting him the Gospel.

 8. Rest in God's sovereign purposes and be faithful and obedient in spite of opposition. "All who live godly in Christ Jesus shall suffer persecution" (II Timothy 3:12).

JESUS DEMONSTRATES HOW TO WITNESS

LESSON TWO   STEP SEVEN

OBJECTIVE: To discover new approaches and techniques of witnessing.

I.   OPEN WITH PRAYER: (Have one or two students open.)

II. MEMORY VERSE: Review John 4:35.

III. MOTIVATION:

Ask one of the group, "Suppose you wanted to share your Christian faith with a person you knew in your dorm or house. How would you begin?" After the student has answered, leader should make helpful comments, and elicit further suggestions from the group. Then turn to John 4 to discover the techniques Jesus used.

IV. BIBLE STUDY:

A. Methods of Jesus.

B. Response of the Samaritan woman.

C. Reasons why we don't witness.

V.   PARALLEL PASSAGES:

A. Witness to the person of Christ—He is the only one.

1. John 14:6, no other way.

2. Acts 4:12, no other name.

B. Note Jesus' methods of witnessing with other individuals in John's Gospel:

1. John 3:1-15, Nicodemus.

2. John 5:1-14, man by the pool.

3. John 8:1-11, woman taken in adultery.

4. John 9:1-41, the man born blind.

VI. SUMMARY:

(See the Lesson Amplification.)

VII. CLOSE IN PRAYER: "Father, use us to bring Christ into the lives of our friends that they might find the abundant life He offers."

349

JESUS DEMONSTRATES HOW TO WITNESS

LESSON TWO   STEP SEVEN

INTRODUCTION:

In Lesson One we considered the question, "Why Witness?" Many reasons were suggested. An additional reason is that we would never have received Christ if someone had not told us. It is because we are debtors to Christ and to the individual or individuals who told us that we in turn must witness. One reason that so few Christians never get off the ground, so to speak, in this very important area of witnessing is that they don't know how to witness. We have not been left to shift for ourselves, but our Lord has given explicit instructions as to the why and how and then has given us examples from His own personal life to follow. Nowhere in the life of our Saviour has this methodology been written so large as in the account of His discourse with the Samaritan woman in John's Gospel, the fourth chapter. This session together might well be entitled, "How to and How not to!"

I.   METHODS OF JESUS:

Jesus used some techniques in witnessing to the Samaritan woman that we can also use. What were they?

A. He began His conversation with her on a topic of natural and common interest to both of them. Jesus was sitting by the well at noontime when it was hot, and His being there would suggest to her that He, too, was thirsty. She had naturally come for water as she was carrying a water pot.

B. He talked about something which would hold her interest, viz., water.

C. Jesus used a subject that could easily be a springboard to spiritual discussion.

D. Jesus sent away the disciples, all twelve, to buy provisions. Two would have accomplished the feat easily. It is quite evident that Christ wanted to be alone with the woman.

E. Jesus was willing to talk to anyone who had a need, regardless of race, creed or social status. It was unheard of for a Jew to go to Samaria, let alone talk to a Samaritan woman.

F. The Saviour had a set purpose and was not sidetracked by questions. The woman tried several times to turn the conversation from Christ's obvious intent to bring her face to face with her sin and need. When we witness, the person will often try to get the issue from himself or herself to some unrelated or side issue. We must never permit this in our own witnessing. Always return to the person's need of Christ.

G. Jesus brought this woman to grips with His own claims about Himself and her need for what He could do for her.

H. Jesus was tactful, kind and considerate in His dealings with the woman.

I. Jesus answered her questions that were pertinent but always returned to her problem.

J. Jesus was a good listener and did not always try to get over His points. What a necessary characteristic in witnessing! Often one must listen and hear the other person out before he can give the Gospel message. The individual usually has misconceptions which he will often talk himself out of if we will listen.

II. RESPONSE OF THE SAMARITAN WOMAN:

A. Notice how her attitude changed as Christ's graciousness won her respect and admiration to Himself.

B. She knew very little, but she told the whole town what she had seen, heard and felt.

C. The town turned out to hear Christ because of her report and many believed when they heard Him. This is our job, to bring men and women to a hearing of the word of Christ as found in the Scriptures. They will not believe because of what we say but rather what God the Spirit says to them via the written word. It is as we become skillful in using the word that we become effective in leading men and women to a saving knowledge of Christ.

D. Christ demonstrates very concisely that the reason for the woman's conversion is that He drew from her a faith in who He was and the veracity of all that He was and said. It is obedience to what Christ says that brings us to fully and clearly understand and know Him.

E. How do you feel about the approach of Christ to the woman? Do you agree that He had a methodology which He followed?

III. REASONS WHY WE DO NOT WITNESS:

A. There are three "sound barriers" to witnessing. These are much like the sound barrier through which an airplane passes. There is much stress and nervousness.

1. The first "sound barrier" is just starting to mention to a person the name of Jesus Christ and the value of knowing Him. Once we get the conversation around from girls, guys, the fraternity or sorority, politics, etc., to spiritual things, we have broken the first barrier. It is hard to do and it never becomes easy. Never!

2. The second "sound barrier" is to ask the person if he would like to receive Christ. That nervous feeling returns once again. We must blast through this one also. Remember, many people, when they understand who Jesus Christ is and what He has done for them, *will* want Him in their lives.

3. The last barrier is the most difficult. It is to ask him to receive Christ *right now*. This is the most important step. Often we tell the person how and then just leave him high and dry. We have not really witnessed until we ask the person to trust Christ. Never take the first no as final. Ask him over and over in the interview to receive Christ. Appeal to him through several different ways. If he says no, ask him why not. His answer will help you when you witness to others. Often it is some slight misconception or misunderstanding which prevents his making the right decision in favor of Christ.

IV. SUMMARY:

The only real way to learn to witness and become effective at it is to *do* it. It is only by trying that one ever succeeds. Nothing succeeds like success and the word of God in Proverbs says, "he that winneth souls is wise." You will be amazed how many people will appreciate your concern for them and be genuinely pleased that you talked to them. Remember, he that aims at nothing will hit it every time. Aim the word of God at the minds and hearts of the unregenerate and it will hit the mark every time and will accomplish that which the Spirit of God intends.

SUPPLEMENTARY READING

God's Plan for Your Life   Campus Crusade Publication
The Van Dusen Letter   Campus Crusade Publication
The Questionnaire   Campus Crusade Publication

QUALIFICATIONS FOR WITNESSING

LESSON THREE   STEP SEVEN

OBJECTIVE: To take a personal inventory of spiritual qualifications for
witnessing.

I.   OPEN WITH PRAYER.

II. MEMORY VERSE: Matthew 4:19.

III. MOTIVATION: I am sure that you are a sincere Christian and that
it is your desire to become an effective witness for Jesus Christ. In
Acts, chapter 8, God gives certain qualifications which are necessary
in the lives of those who desire to become effective witnesses for Him.

IV. BIBLE STUDY:

A. Read Acts 8:25-40 with this title in mind: CHRIST WINS MEN
TO HIMSELF THROUGH ME IF I AM YIELDED.

B. Ask these discussion questions:

1. Why was the Ethiopian open to the Gospel?

2. What supernatural events indicate God delighted in using
Philip?

3. What indicates Philip witnessed everywhere he went? Would
this mean that God was thereby able to use him more?

C. Survey the qualifications of Philip.

D. Hindrances to our witnessing.

V.   PARALLEL PASSAGES:

A. Philip:

Acts 8:3-5. When persecution came, did Philip think that he should
stop witnessing because God had let him down?

B. Paul:

1. I Corinthians 9:19-27. Who did Paul think was a servant? What does he say about his body?

2. I Corinthians 9:27. The Amplified New Testament gives the sense of "disqualified" for the King James "castaway."

3. What does the Bible say about keeping the body under God's will?

   a. I Thessalonians 4:3-5.

   b. I Peter 2:15-16.

   c. I Thessalonians 5:18.

VI. SUMMARY: What assets have we found valuable in soul winning? What about the qualities of your life? Can you say that you are content with today's behavior and thoughts? Make tomorrow a new beginning in Christlike qualifications because you are letting Christ live out through you. Deal with sin as it appears by confessing it. Always remember, "Not by might, nor by power, but by My Spirit, saith the Lord of hosts" (Zechariah 4:6).

VII. CLOSE IN PRAYER.

QUALIFICATIONS FOR WITNESSING

LESSON THREE   STEP SEVEN

INTRODUCTION:

It has been said, "Dependability is the best ability." In Philip, God
had a dependable person. He could witness anywhere. He could be depended upon to fulfill the Great Commission. Philip was not only dependable, but he had other qualities which were an asset.

In the last analysis, it was Christ in Philip who did the work. The
flesh is not prayerful, tactful, compassionate or humble. How often have
you hungered for a fantastic, miraculous conversion from a life of past sin
to help you win others to Christ. It is not what you are or were, but what
He is through you that wins men. Our responsibility is to deny self and
daily take up the cross, an instrument of death, and let Him live through
us. We must allow Him, His Spirit, and His word to be central in our
lives.

You will notice that persecution did not stop Philip. It only opened
the door for a vital witness in Samaria. Philip's disappointments were God's
appointments. No "poor-little-me" attitudes. How about you?

The Ethiopian was ready because of the Holy Spirit's preparatory
work. However, God used a man, a ready, willing man, to win him. Philip
had earned the right to be used. God had an angel appear, while he was
praying, and commanded Philip to leave a revival and go to the desert.
He was humble and obedient. Would you be the same? Then, God's Spirit
brought him to Azotus after he had baptized the eunuch. Philip was God's
key man. God used him. God depended on him because he was dependable.
Are you?

I. QUALITIES NECESSARY FOR WITNESSING:

A. The purpose of this lesson is to deal with the question, "What
qualifications are necessary for witnessing?" First, read Acts 8:25-
40 with this title in mind: Christ wins men to himself through me
IF I am yielded.

B. Discussion Questions.

1. Why was the Ethiopian open to the gospel? The Ethiopian was
open to the gospel because he had been reading the word of
God in Isaiah 53. The word of God is the only effective means
of opening up the minds and hearts of people to the Gospel.

Philosophy, sociology, etc., though good studies in themselves, will not avail in meeting the needs of the heart of man. The reading of the Word had so prepared the Ethiopian for Philip that the man asked him about whom Isaiah was speaking.

2. What supernatural events indicate God delighted in using Philip? A supernatural event that is most evident is the miraculous way the Holy Spirit transported Philip from place to place in the account. It is interesting that when the Holy Spirit said arise and go, Philip arose and went. Are we as faithful?

3. What indicates Philip witnessed everywhere he went? Would this mean that God was thereby allowed to use him more? Verse 40 of Chap. 8 states that when Philip was taken by the Holy Spirit to Azotus and from there through all the cities of the plain, he preached in ALL the cities until he came home to Caesarea. A wise man has said that "dependability is the best ability." This is also true of availability. In Philip, God had a dependable and available man; thus God used him to a great degree.

II. QUALIFICATIONS IN PHILIP'S LIFE:

Let us survey briefly the qualifications that are referred to in Philip's life that contributed to his effectiveness for Christ. Some of them are: *knowledge* of the word of God, *boldness, compassion, humility, obeience, prayerfulness, tact* and *enthusiasm.* Too much stress cannot be laid on enthusiasm; possess it and gain an audience!

III. SOME HINDRANCES TO OUR WITNESSING:

A. Lack of preparation—personal dedication to Christ and understanding of how to witness and what to say are imperative.

B. Fear of man—we will be persecuted by unbelievers, as well as believers, but . . . "The fear of man bringeth a snare" (Prov. 29:25). Christ said of those who feared to confess His name . . . "For they loved the praise of men more than the praise of God."

1. "Don't count your critics; weigh them."

2. "To avoid criticism: say nothing, do nothing, be nothing."

3. Jesus Christ is King . . . not to reign, but to fight our battles. "The battle is the Lord's!"

C. Fair of failure—"they won't believe; they won't accept such simple truth." Certainly some will reject or neglect the gospel, but never believe the lie of Satan that people aren't interested. Christ said, "Lift up your eyes, and look on the fields; for they are

(present tense . . . 'now') white already to harvest." Matt. 9:37
. . . "Then saith he unto his disciples, the harvest truly is plenteous, but the labourers are few; Pray . . . that He will send forth labourers into his harvest."

D. Fear that new converts will not go on and grow in the Lord. Review the parable of the sower (Matt. 13:1-23). Every seed of the word of God will fall on one of these types of soil: wayside, thorny, rocky and good. Some will be disciples. Keep up the faithful search for disciples!

IV. SUMMARY:

In the last analysis, it was Christ in Philip who did the work. The flesh is not prayerful, tactful, compassionate or humble. How often have you just stopped and thanked God for the impossible . . . that your feelings and attitudes, under the control of the Spirit, were right with genuine love and compassion for that lost person. To believe God is to possess the answer for which we have prayed. Thank God that we have been made "more than conquerors through Him that loved us!"

V. SUPPLEMENT TO STUDY:

Philip was not the kind of person who was eccentric, rubbing his friends the wrong way. He was known for his wisdom and fullness of the Holy Spirit (Acts 6:1-5). You can see that he was willing to do menial tasks, too, for he was selected to take care of the widows. You will notice that Stephen was also one of those seven deacons. Both Stephen and Philip could be depended upon to do menial tasks as well as preach effectively. How about you? A soul winner is neither eccentric nor lazy.

Paul was another great soul winner. He spoke of himself as debtor to everyone because he had Christ (Romans 1:14). Paul's behavior would not usually bring offense. He treated all as creditors. The only offense was the offense of the cross.

Paul adds a new thought about keeping our body under if we are to be soul winners. Anger, argumentation, selfish living are not permitted. Interestingly enough, God's will is spoken of specifically four times in the New Testament—John 6:40; I Thessalonians 4:3-5; 5:18, and I Peter 2:15-16. God wills our resurrection with Christ, our purity, thankfulness in everything, and complete civil obedience, in that order. One deals with heaven and three deal with phases of our witness. Are you placing a corresponding emphasis upon yourself? What about speeding in an automobile or disobeying stop signs? What about being thankful for adversities? This adds up to taking up our cross daily (Lk. 9:23), denying self and letting Christ live through us.

LESSON PLAN

WITNESS AND THE WORD OF GOD

LESSON FOUR   STEP SEVEN

OBJECTIVE: To demonstrate and convince the student of the value of
memorizing and using Bible verses when witnessing.

I.   OPEN WITH PRAYER.

II. MEMORY VERSE: I Peter 3:15.

III. MOTIVATION:

Why is the Bible important to use in witnessing? Have the group
suggest reasons. The leader should note these reasons: (1) The Word
is living ("quick") and powerful (Heb. 4:12). (2) Christ used the
Word extensively (Mk. 12:35-37, etc.). (3) The Word tells of Christ
(Jn. 5:39).

IV. BIBLE STUDY:

A. The place of Scripture in Peter's first sermon.

Peter's first sermon after Pentecost contained much of the word
of God and was preached in the power of the Holy Spirit. What
were the results? (No. 6.) The Spirit of God uses the word of
God to exalt the Son of God which makes people become children
of God. (See the Lesson Amplification.)

B. The value of Scripture memory.

1. What part did memorized Scripture have in the success of
Peter's message?

2. Do you think it was worthwhile for Peter to memorize these
passages?

C. Techniques in memorization.

1. What techniques do you use in memorizing material for your
school courses which would help you memorize Bible verses?

2. Are you memorizing Scripture verses? If not, why not?

V.   PARALLEL PASSAGES: The value of Scripture memory.

A. Give knowledge.

    1. To know Jesus Christ better (II Peter 1:2-3).

    2. To know His promises (II Peter 1:4).

B. Aids in Bible study.

    1. Gives a key to Scripture.

    2. Gives spiritual food for thought (I Peter 2:2-3; Hebrews 5:12-14).

    3. Enables you to reap the greatest returns for the time invested.

C. Gives sure doctrinal foundations.

D. Aids in meditation (Joshua 1:8; Psalms 1:1-3).

E. Gives guidance (Ps. 32:8).

    1. In worship (I Chronicles 29:11-13).

    2. In prayer (John 15:7; I John 5:14-15).

F. Builds faith (Romans 10:17).

G. Builds character (Luke 6:45).

H. Gives victory in the Spirit (Ps. 119:11).

VI. SUMMARY: Why memorize?

A. It is the best way to know the word of God—which is a means to the end of knowing Christ.

B. By having the promises and commands of the Word memorized we can apply them to any life situation at a moment's notice (Ps. 119:9, 11).

C. The word of God is necessary for new birth (I Peter 1:23). The best way to use it is to have it memorized (Ephesians 6:17 and Hebrews 4:12).

VII. CLOSE IN PRAYER.

LESSON AMPLIFICATION

WITNESS AND THE WORD OF GOD

LESSON FOUR   STEP SEVEN

INTRODUCTION:

One of the most important areas in which many Christians fail in living a life for Christ is the all-important area of memorizing and using effectively the word of God. The Psalmist states clearly that it is the word of God which keeps the Christian from sinning against God and it is the means by which the Christian cleans up his or her life (Psalm 119:9,11). The word of God is the most effectual weapon in dealing with persons about their need of Christ. Their questions are only truly answered in the word of God. Analogies and illustrations are helpful only to clarify what the Scriptures say. There is convincing power *only* in a presentation of what the word of God has to say. In answer to any question or argument I Peter 3:15 says we are to set aside our hearts for the Lord God and then be ready to give a Scriptural answer to any question which men can ask concerning the hope (which is actually a firm conviction) of a salvation, with reasonableness, humility and respect for them as individuals. For this and many other reasons, we should study the Scriptures diligently if we are to be effective witnesses for Christ. Let us examine the record in Acts 2 of Peter, who certainly was effective in presenting Christ in this instance, as 3,000 persons were to become believers in Christ.

I.   THE PLACE OF SCRIPTURE IN PETER'S FIRST SERMON:

Peter's first sermon after Pentecost contained much of the word of God and was preached in the power of the Holy Spirit. What were the results? (See question six in the lesson.) As we have already said, 3,000 people were converted to the new faith in Christ as their Messiah and Saviour. It was the word of God as found in the Old Testament which the Holy Spirit used to bring great conviction about their sins, and particularly the sin of crucifying Christ.

II. THE VALUE OF SCRIPTURE MEMORY:

A. What part did memory have in contributing to Peter's success? Peter had no notes to which he could refer. His address was impromptu and based upon Old Testament Scripture with which He had saturated his mind from an early age. No doubt the disciples actively engaged in the study of the Scriptures as they traveled with the Lord Jesus. Often He explained or expounded the Scriptures to the disciples as they journeyed about. The success of what Peter said was due entirely to the word of God administered to the hearts of the hearers by the Holy Spirit.

B. WAS IT WORTHWHILE FOR PETER TO MEMORIZE SCRIPTURE?

It proved to be worthwhile for Peter to memorize the Scriptures and use them, because God's blessing accompanied their use.

III. TECHNIQUES IN MEMORIZATION:

What techniques do you use in memorizing material for your school courses which would be helpful in memorizing Bible verses? Some helpful ways are:

A. Read the verses through several times.

B. Read the verses that come before and after in order that you might understand the trend of thought.

C. Read the verses again from comma to comma, colon or semi-colon. Look for the verbs first, as they convey the action of the verse. Note the thought of the words between the commas.

IV. SUMMARY: Are you memorizing Scripture verses? If not, why not? The disciples of Christ who have been most used and used successfully have been those who have memorized systematically the word of God and then obeyed it. In order to win men and women to Christ we must learn the Scriptures, and memorizing is a vital part in the process.

WITNESS AND PRAYER

LESSON FIVE   STEP SEVEN

OBJECTIVE: To demonstrate the vital part prayer plays in effective witnessing for Christ.

I.   OPEN WITH PRAYER.

II. MEMORY VERSE: Acts 4:31.

III. MOTIVATION: "Have you wondered why some are successful in their witness for Christ and others not successful; why God seems to use some Christians and not others? Can you think of some reasons why this may be?" Student mentions several things, one of which will probably be prayer. "In Lesson Five it is stated that prayer is really the place where people are won to Christ; service is just gathering in the fruit. If we really believe this, we should certainly spend more time praying before witnessing."

IV. BIBLE STUDY:

   A. What did these early Christians pray?

   B. What was the answer to their prayer?

   C. Basically who is it that opposes the Christian today? (Ans. Satan.)

   D. What is the best way to rout the enemy and win victory? (Ans. Prayer!)

   E. Why? (Ans. Eph. 6:10-12.) Have student look up the reference.

V.   PARALLEL PASSAGES: Unique Prayer Answers.

   A. Jehoshaphat, II Chronicles 20:1-30.

   B. Hezekiah, II Chronicles 32:1-23.

   C. Peter in prison, Acts 12:1-17.

   D. Paul and Silas in prison, Acts 16:25-40.

VI. SUMMARY: Have the students give some examples of persons who have come to know the Lord as a result of their prayer, or that of someone else. If they cannot give any instances then cite a few of your own experiences.

VII. CLOSE IN PRAYER.

WITNESS AND PRAYER

LESSON FIVE   STEP SEVEN

INTRODUCTION:

A Canadian missionary knelt to pray as his Chinese Communist interrogator commanded him to pray and demonstrate that God answers prayer. The missionary knelt and prayed that God would make it apparent that He answers prayer, even if it meant that their brash interrogator lose his vision. Immediately he was blinded, just as Elymas was (Acts 13:11). Seven clergymen were converted to Christ along with the Communist. The Communist died as a martyr at the hands of his comrades. Events such as these are little seen today. In the Bible they happen over and over again. God has not changed; we have changed. Our confidence in our own ability and our own self-sufficiency keeps us from asking God to deal with our problems in mighty power. Prayer changes things, even men's lives. The reason we are not seeing more people converted and Christians witnessing is prayerlessness.

George Mueller of Bristol, England, cared for hundreds of orphans, meeting their needs through daily miracles of answered prayer. He tells the story of one memorable morning when he had them bow their heads to thank God for the provision of breakfast. Unknown to the children nothing had been prepared for the cupboard was bare. Then it was that a large sack of breakfast meal was delivered by a wealthy man who felt strangely constrained to do so. Truly, living from hand to mouth does not seem very desirable, *unless* it is God's hand and your mouth.

I.   WHAT DID THE EARLY CHRISTIANS PRAY?

The early Christians in Acts 4 (vs. 29), prayed that they might have boldness in the face of persecution. They did not pray for themselves that they might be spared nor did they keep silent. They wanted power and boldness that they might not fail to proclaim Christ. When things got tough they prayed! They were to be found praying in every instance. They moved forward on their knees and how they moved! One Roman writer said of the early Christians, "These Christians are turning the Empire around." Acts 17:6 says they turned the world upside down. In reality it was right side up. They prayed for boldness because it is innate with every individual to preserve that which is most precious to him, his life. Their very lives were in

363

jeopardy, and the flesh faints when the body is in danger of harm or death. Boldness is a very scarce commodity today in Christian circles. "The fear of man bringeth a snare," says the Scriptures, and we are all afraid of what men will think of us and even do to us. Today in America we do not presently face physical harm for our witness to Christ, but the day may come when our very lives may be in danger. Now the attack of Satan comes in terms of fearing what men will think. In both instances we must pray for boldness and fearlessness. God, when we pray and in every instance of stress, has given us not the spirit of fear, but of love and power and of a sound mind (II Tim. 1:7). We need to pray for boldness!

II. THE ANSWER TO THEIR PRAYER:

The answer to their prayer was immediate and definite. It was in the affirmative. They prayed and God answered as He promised He would do. The place where they were was shaken; they were filled or controlled by the Holy Spirit and they spoke the gospel with boldness. None could stand against them, and they were victorious in Christ.

III. WHO OPPOSES THE CHRISTIAN TODAY?

Although many believe Satan is a ludicrous person in long, flannel underwear with horns and a pitchfork, or simply non-existent, Christ and the word of God state his existence and his work against God in very concrete terms. Satan cannot overcome and defeat a praying Christian. Jesus told Peter, "Watch and pray lest thou comest into temptation." Battles are being waged in the heavenlies between the hosts of Satan, and Christ and the angels. It is the prayers of the believers that avail to bring victory on earth and in the heavenlies. God has included us in the battles and victories of the ages, and nowhere can we have a more powerful part than in the field of prayer.

IV. THE BEST WAY TO ROUT THE OPPOSER:

A. Prayer.

B. The armor of God. (Cf. Ephesians 6:11-13.)

Put on the complete armor of God, that you may be able to stand against the deceitful tricks of Satan, the Devil, for we laboriously struggle not against flesh and blood, which appears tangible, but against governments, powers that energize this world system, and against spiritual corruptness high and low and all around us. Seeing this, put on the complete armor of God, that you may be able to bear up under the onslaught in the day of the evil one, Satan, and having done all that there is to do, so to stand steadfast, unmovable.

364

V. SUMMARY:

Prayer is the God-ordained way to bring the heavenly life of Christ into the lives of men and to make men alive that they might live the heavenly life here on earth and afterwards in heaven. We must pray for the lost! Praying for the lost will cause us to go to them and win them to Christ.

VI. CLOSE IN PRAYER:

Lord Jesus, cause us to see, as You see, the fields white unto harvest, and thrust us out to them with the message, the compassion and the boldness to tell and tell and tell. In Your name, Amen!

SUPPLEMENTARY READING

E. M. Bounds, *Power through Prayer*.

WITNESS AND THE HOLY SPIRIT

LESSON SIX   STEP SEVEN

OBJECTIVE: To demonstrate the vital necessity of the Holy Spirit to our
witness, and encourage utter dependence upon Him.

I.   OPEN WITH PRAYER.

II.   MEMORY VERSE: John 15:26-27.

III. MOTIVATION: Many attend Billy Graham's evangelistic crusades
in order to find out the techniques of crowd psychology that are used.
Non-Christians try to explain Billy Graham's phenomenal success by
natural means rather than spiritual. Why? Simply because they would
like to have the same dynamic without being under God's control. To
attempt to explain Billy Graham in these terms leaves such men
frankly baffled. As you read Acts 6 and 7, you will note that one cannot locate the techniques which Stephen used to influence people. This
is because Christ is being lived out through his life in the power of
the Holy Spirit. A dynamic personality appears, not oratorical effects.
Is this the answer to Billy Graham's success?

IV.   BIBLE STUDY:

Examine Acts 6 and 7 to discover the role of the Holy Spirit in
Stephen's life and ministry. You can have the best method, personality, testimony and arguments, but they will not do the job. The
Holy Spirit gives us the courage, the witness and the results. (See
the Lesson Amplification.)

V.   PARALLEL PASSAGES:

A. II Corthians 3:5-18.

1. Did Paul feel capable of winning men, even though he had the
finest seminary background in the world at that time?

2. What happened to Moses when he was in communion with God
and what bearing does this have on God's part in Christian
service (II Corinthians 3:7)?

3. Why did Paul have liberty to witness (II Cor. 3:17)? Does this explain why you may not have liberty?

B. I Corinthians 12:4-11.

1. Does God's Spirit make Christians differ in function?

2. What antidote is there for pride at having a more conspicuous gift (I Cor. 4:7; 12:12-31)?

3. Who is a truly superior Christian in God's estimation (I Cor. 13:1-3)?

4. Should every Christian be a witness (Mt. 4:19; II Cor. 5:14-15; II Tim. 4:5)?

VI. SUMMARY:

The same power that was evidenced in Stephen's life and ministry, in the life and witness of the early church and in Billy Graham's ministry today is also ours if we will but take it. How do we appropriate it? Ans: "Yield my life completely to Christ and appropriate the control or filling of the Holy Spirit."

Leader says, "Would you like to pray and ask the Holy Spirit to fill and control your life, and place Christ on the throne of your life? Would you like to do it right now as we conclude in prayer?"

VII. CLOSE IN PRAYER.

WITNESS AND THE HOLY SPIRIT

LESSON SIX   **STEP SEVEN**

In the previous lessons we have been examining various important aspects of witnessing for Christ. It is our purpose to demonstrate the vital necessity of the Holy Spirit to our witness and encourage utter dependence upon Him. No amount of persuasiveness or imagination or ability on our part will ever avail to move any person one whit closer to a saving knowledge of Jesus Christ apart from the work of the Holy Spirit in His convicting and regenerative power. Salvation, as the Psalmist says, is of the Lord, totally and completely. This is nowhere made more clear than in the life of the first Christian martyr, Stephen. He was an ordinary man, fearful, inadequate and powerless. However, controlled by the Holy Spirit, he became fearless, and moved multitudes with the sincerity and power of his life and witness for Christ. By an examination of his life, as revealed in Acts 6 and 7, we will discover that the reason for the effectual witness of this man, Stephen, was the person and work of the Holy Spirit who produced in him a mighty likeness to the Son of God himself. The Holy Spirit gave him the courage, the witness and the results.

I. QUALITIES OF LIFE WHICH INDICATE STEPHEN WAS CONTROLLED BY THE HOLY SPIRIT:

A. A two-fold purpose in life.

As a Spirit-filled man, what two purposes were Stephen's greatest concerns, as seen in his desire to witness and in his dying prayer? Stephen had as his two-fold purpose in life to present Christ as He is to men as they are so that sins might not be laid to their charge. Another way of stating this is that his fellow Jews might come to know Christ and have Him forgive their sins.

B. Full of faith.

The early testimony of the Scriptures concerning Stephen was that he was a man full of faith and filled with the Spirit. As a result we find all of the necessary qualities for a true and effectual witness for Christ present. He was absolutely fearless, he did not compromise his message regardless of circumstances, and he told men what was wrong with them. He spoke of the person of Christ, not pious platitudes. The presentation of the person of Christ always has a reaction on the part of the hearers. In this case, rejection and anger resulting in the death of Stephen is manifest. The other reaction is acceptance of Christ and the man bearing the message about him. In any case the work of the Holy Spirit is the same, conviction of sin in the heart of the sinner.

C. Fearless.

A Spirit-filled man is always selfless. Stephen did not fear what man could do to him nor was he defeated by self-consciousness. Probably no greater foe to witnessing is ever more evident or present than self-consciousness. Self prevents the Saviour from being known.

D. Selfless.

Many are concerned with what part or parts the Triune-God should play in their lives. It is not a case of what part should the Holy Spirit play in my life; but rather the Holy Spirit is my life, all of it. Stephen was full of the Holy Spirit. This statement reveals no place for self or self-manifestation. His experience of Christ was that Christ was all.

II. CLOSE IN PRAYER:

Father, we confess the sin of running our lives as we want, and ask the Holy Spirit to take complete control of our lives and place the Lord Jesus Christ on the throne of our lives right now. Thank you for doing this. In Jesus' name we ask it, Amen!

SUPPLEMENTARY READING

Step Three, *The Christian and the Holy Spirit:* Campus Crusade Publication.

THE CHRISTIAN AND STEWARDSHIP

STEP EIGHT

OBJECTIVE: To show God's ownership of everything and everyone, and to encourage joyfulness and submission to His authority.

I.   OPEN WITH PRAYER: "Father, we recognize that You are the sovereign God, worthy of all our praise."

II. MEMORY VERSES: Review all the verses to be memorized from Step Eight. (I Chron. 29-11; Psa. 139:23-24; Gal. 2:20; Phil. 2-13; Luke 16:13; II Cor. 5:10.)

III. MOTIVATION:

If the owner of the property you were managing had a serious character and a deep personal interest in your welfare, would you not gladly submit to his wishes? God's character traits are immeasurably marvelous. Why not submit to His control?

IV. BIBLE STUDY: (See the Lesson Amplification for the details.)

A. Attributes of the Master.

B. Accountability of His stewards.

1. To be yielded to His ownership.

2. To be faithful in His service.

V.   PARALLEL PASSAGES: (See the Lesson Amplification.)

VI. SUMMARY:

God is the sovereign owner of everything and everyone. His attributes are wonderful, beyond all comprehension. All He desires of His stewards is that they be yielded and faithful to Him. In consideration of who He is, will you allow Him to reign in *your* life?

VII. CLOSE IN PRAYER: A silent time of adoration and personal dedication.

THE CHRISTIAN AND STEWARDSHIP

SUMMARY LESSON   STEP EIGHT

I.   DISCUSS THE FOLLOWING ATTRIBUTES OF THE MASTER:

A. *Omnipotent*—All power and authority belong to Him. No individual, nation or combination of forces, terrestrial or celestial, can thwart His sovereign purposes.

Psa. 33:6-10—"By the word of the Lord were the heavens made; and all the host of them by the breath of his mouth. He gathereth the waters of the sea together as an heap: he layeth up the depth in storehouses. Let all the earth fear the Lord: let all the inhabitants of the world stand in awe of him. For he spake, and it was done; he commanded, and it stood fast. The Lord bringeth the counsel of the heathen to nought: he maketh the devices of the people of none effect."

Matt. 28:18—"And Jesus came and spake unto them, saying, All power is given unto me in heaven and in earth."

B. *Omnipresent*—He is present everywhere; not just a part of Him, but all of Him.

Jer. 23:24—"Can any hide himself in secret places that I shall not see him? saith the Lord, Do not I fill heaven and earth? saith the Lord." Matt. 28:20—". . . and, lo, I am with you alway, even unto the end of the world."

C. *Omniscient*—He knows the past, present and future. His knowledge not only comprehends all things, but also all possibilities. We suffer when we deny His knowledge and do not lean upon Him for guidance.

Isa. 46:9-10—"Remember the former things of old: for I am God, and there is none else; I am God, and there is none like me, declaring the end from the beginning, and from ancient times the things that are yet done, saying, My counsel shall stand, and I will do all my pleasure." Luke 5:22—"But when Jesus perceived their thoughts, . . ."

D. *Immutable*—He never changes, develops or grows.

> "Change and decay in all around I see;
> Oh, Thou who changest not, abide with me."

Num. 23:19—"God is not a man, that he should lie; neither the son of man, that he should repent: hath he said, and shall he not do it? or hath he spoken, and shall he not make it good?"

Heb. 13:8—"Jesus Christ the same yesterday, and today, and forever."

E. *Eternal*—There never was a time when He was not; there never will be a time when He will cease to be. He is the everlasting God.

Psa. 90:2, 4—"Before the mountains were brought forth, or ever thou hadst formed the earth and the world, even from everlasting to everlasting, thou art God. For a thousand years in thy sight are but as yesterday when it is past, and as a watch in the night."

Heb. 13:8—"Jesus Christ the same yesterday, and today, and forever."

F. *Holy*—He is separate from that which is morally evil or sinful.

Psa. 99:9—"Exalt the Lord our God, and worship at his holy hill; for the Lord our God is holy."

Isa. 6:3—". . . Holy, holy, holy, is the Lord of hosts: the whole earth is full of His glory."

At the contemplation of God's holiness one is prone, not to analyze, but to worship!

G. *Just*—He is impartial in all His dealing, equitable in all His works. Deut. 32:4—"He is the Rock, his work is perfect: for all his ways are judgment: a God of truth and without iniquity, just and right is He." Rev. 15:3—". . . Great and marvellous are thy works, Lord God Almighty; just and true are thy ways, thou King of saints."

H. *Love*—His holiness and justice caused Him to mete out the penalty of death for our sins. But His love caused Him to send His Son to bear the penalty for sin. At the cross God's holiness and love were beautifully revealed. There "mercy and truth are met together; righteousness and peace have kissed each other" (Psa. 85: 10).

I Jn. 4:10—"Herein is love, not that we loved God, but that he loved us, and sent his son to be the propitiation for our sins."

Eph. 3:19—" . . . the love of Christ, which passeth knowledge . . . "

II. ACCOUNTABILITY OF HIS STEWARDS:

A. To be yielded to His ownership.

Isa. 64:8—"But now, O Lord, thou art our father; we are the clay, and thou our potter; and we all are the work of thy hand."

Isa. 45:9—"Woe unto him that striveth with his Maker! . . . Shall the clay say to him that fashioneth it, What makest thou? . . ." (Also Rom. 9:20).

Job 12:10—"In whose hand is the soul of every living thing, and the breath of all mankind."

Phil. 2:10-11 and Prov. 21:1 are extra verses which can be used.

B. To be faithful in His service.

I Cor. 15:58—"Therefore, my beloved brethren, be ye stedfast, unmoveable, always abounding in the work of the Lord, forasmuch as ye know that your labour is not in vain in the Lord."

II Tim. 4:5—"For yourself, stand fast in all that you are doing, meeting whatever suffering this may involve. Go on steadily preaching the gospel and carry out to the full the commission that God gave you" (Phillips N. T.).

II Tim. 2:2-4; 2:15; 4:2; I Cor. 4:1-2 are verses which can also be used.

LESSON PLAN

THE OWNERSHIP OF GOD OUR FATHER AND
EXAMPLES OF PERFECT STEWARDSHIP

LESSONS ONE AND TWO   STEP EIGHT

OBJECTIVE: To show that God owns our lives and to encourage absolute
surrender through the example of the Lord Jesus Christ
and the Holy Spirit.

I.   OPEN WITH PRAYER: Lord, teach us to realize that You are the
supreme Owner of the universe. Impress on our hearts and minds the
perfect stewardship of Your Son and of the Holy Spirit.

II. MEMORY VERSES: I Chronicles 29:11 and John 8:28. Review
them individually and ask a couple of students to quote them.

III. MOTIVATION: What is a steward?

The steward is not the owner. He does not possess the estate he
manages. It is derived property, the ownership of which is vested in
another. The true owner has the right to demand an accounting from
the one to whom his possessions have been entrusted.

IV. BIBLE STUDY: Review these main principles:

A. God's creation of man (question 1—Lesson 1).

B. Man's sins and separation from God (questions 2 and 3—Lesson 1).

C. God's reconciliation (questions 4 and 5—Lesson 1).

D. The perfect stewardship of Jesus Christ.

E. The perfect stewardship of the Holy Spirit.

V.   PARALLEL PASSAGES:

A. Proofs of God's ownership.

1. He created us through His Son (Genesis 1:1; John 1:1-3; Colossians 1:16).

2. His Son purchased us with His blood (I Cor. 7:23; Mark 10:45).

375

3. He drew us to Himself and gave us to His Son (John 6:37, 44; Ephesians 1:22-23).

4. He convicted and converted us by His Spirit, giving us life (John 3:17; 16:7-11).

5. His Son found us (Luke 19:10).

B. Purpose of God's ownership.

1. Does God love you? How has He shown it (Romans 5:8)? How much does He love you (John 3:16)?

2. What kind of a character does God have (Psalm 86:5, 15)? Can you trust that kind of a God to run your life in the right way? Does He lie? Will He break His promise (Psalm 32:8)?

3. What are the blessings we lose by going our own way and failing to recognize His ownership (Isaiah 48:17-19)?

VI. SUMMARY:

God does own us—every bit of our time, talents and treasure. Scripture tells us that Christ died for us, that we should "not henceforth live unto ourselves, but unto Him who died for us and rose again" (II Cor. 5:15). To not acknowledge and act upon God's total ownership of everything we are, have or will be, is to rob ourselves of His blessing and make ourselves unfit for His service and use (II Tim. 2:19-21).

VII. CLOSE IN PRAYER: Silent prayer, confession and dedication.

THE OWNERSHIP OF GOD OUR FATHER AND EXAMPLES OF PERFECT STEWARDSHIP

LESSONS ONE AND TWO   STEP EIGHT

I. THE CREATION OF MAN:

Man was created in the "image" of God. What does this mean? Man is not *physically* in God's image, for "God is a Spirit" (John 4:24). Man is not *morally* in God's image, for man is sinful and God is holy (Rom. 3:23). Man is *constitutionally* in God's image. God has intellect, emotions, will—the elements of personality. Man was given intellect with which he might know God, emotions with which he might love God and a will with which he might serve God. Man was created not only *by* God but *for* God. Of His earthly creatures, man alone could have real fellowship with God. God and man *conversed*. The most intelligent animals lack any God-consciousness.

II. THE FALL OF MAN:

Man fell from God, not vice versa. What happened? Did Adam get drunk, commit gross immorality, become suddenly debauched? No. Earth's first couple decided that they could no longer depend on God to give them the best, but that they must strive themselves to gain what God could not give them. They wanted to remove their lives from divine control, and control themselves. The grass was greener on the other side of the fence. In other words, they made man the goal of existence, instead of God, and moved into independence from Him. "Godlessness" is nothing more than being independent of God. Man's mind now became blind toward God. He could no longer know Him. His emotions became perverted. He could still love, but he could not love God. Eph. 2:1 tells us that man became spiritually dead. Total chaos invaded humanity.

Some Illustrations:

The mind of man is now blinded to God (I Cor. 2:14). Some non-Christian scholars have suggested in all honesty that Jesus fed the 5,000 with five loaves and two fishes by hiding the bread in a cave and having His disciples secretly pass it out to them. Millions of intelligent people believe in such obvious foolishness. They say Jesus did not exist, or that God does not exist (it is our imagination); even that death does not exist, or that sin does not exist. Others teach that Adam is God, that Jesus got married to Mary and Martha and had children, that only 144,000 will be saved, etc. The modern cults of our day suggest the blindness of the human mind.

The emotions of man have fallen, too. The brutalities of Naziism and Communism, the love for sex which drenches our society, the pursuit of wealth above all things and the worship of idols through history are testimony to this. In ancient religions of New Testament times, some pagan temples had prostitutes serving as part of the religious worship, and this was considered devotion to God.

The will of man is now enslaved. Rom. 6:20—the non-Christian is the servant (lit. "bondslave") of sin. Man does not serve God because he cannot. Thus Adam in the garden (1) hid from God, (2) became afraid of God, (3) became ashamed before God. The sweet communion was now broken.

The Point of the Story. If Adam's act of independence has so ruined the human race, caused all the death, misery, suffering and sorrow that the world has ever known, and yet God in His grace, at the price of Christ's blood, has redeemed us and restored us, will we NOW REPEAT ADAM'S SIN ALL OVER AGAIN? This is what the Christian who refuses to submit to the Lordship of Christ does.

A common medical practice of the pre-scientific era was that of "bleeding." When one became seriously ill, it was thought that by draining out much of his blood the illness could be removed. Such a practice, we know, is unsound and dangerous. It does not help, but hurts. This probably caused the death of our nation's first President, George Washington. With all of our modern knowledge, remembering the fact that many have died from such a practice, what folly it would be for every hospital in the United States suddenly to re-institute it again. It is the same kind of stupidity for a Christian to marry a non-Christian, for your main goal in life to be money, a position, a sports-car, a fraternity, football or anything else besides God! Genesis, Chapter 3, should serve as an example of the folly of sin. "Who hath hardened himself against Him and hath prospered" (Job 9:4)?

III. RECONCILIATION:

The Example of Christ. Imagine it! A life without a single moment of sin. Even those who were closest to Him, His own disciples who would certainly have seen any flaws which would have been in His character, testify most strongly to His sinlessness. One writer describes this fact in this way: "The outstanding characteristic of Jesus in His earthly life was the one in which all of us acknowledge we fall so short, and yet which at the same time all men recognize as the most priceless characteristic any man can have, namely, *absolute goodness,* or to phrase it otherwise, perfect *purity,* genuine *holiness,* and, in the case of Jesus, nothing less than sinlessness. . . Fifteen million minutes of life on this earth, in the midst of a wicked and corrupt generation—every thought, every deed, every purpose, every word, privately and publicly, from the time He opened his baby eyes until He expired on the cross, were all approved of God. Never once did our

Lord have to confess any sin, for He had no sin. Here was One who, as Dr. Schaff said, never put Himself in the attitude of a sinner before God; never shed a tear of repentance; never regretted a single thought, word, or deed; never needed or asked divine pardon; was never concerned about the salvation of His own soul; and boldly faced all His present and future enemies in the absolute certainty of His spotless purity before God and man" (Smith, Wilbur M., *Have You Considered Him?* Chicago: Moody Press, n. d., pp. 8-10).

But was Christ sent merely to give us an example—merely to show us a model of life to which we could never attain? No!!! The Scripture says He came to save us from (not in) our sins (Matt. 1:21). He promised, "Blessed are they which do hunger and thirst after righteousness, for they shall (not might) be filled" (Matt. 5:6). He told His disciples that it was profitable for them for Him to leave because when He left, He would send the Holy Spirit to indwell them (John 16:7). The Holy Spirit is the Spirit of Christ, and, as Christ lived in absolute dependence on His Father (cf. John 5:19, 30; 6:57; 8:28), so we are to live in absolute dependence on Christ. "As ye have therefore received Christ Jesus the Lord, so walk ye in Him" (Col. 2:6), the Scripture commands. When we came to Christ, we came as those who had no strength, as sinners, and as those who had to depend on Jesus Christ absolutely. We surrendered ourselves to Him (Rom. 5:6-9). He did all the rest. So now, will you allow Him to fill you, possess you, control your entire being and body?

IV. THE PERFECT STEWARDSHIP OF JESUS CHRIST:

A. What did Jesus Christ come to do (John 6:38; Heb. 10:7)?

B. What was the most important aspect of His Father's will that He came to do (Luke 19:10; I Tim. 2:3-4)?

C. How well did He fulfill His Father's will (John 8:29, 46; II Cor. 5:21; I Pet. 2:22; I John 3:5)?

D. Was He a faithful steward merely because He was not tempted (Heb. 4:15)?

V. THE PERFECT STEWARDSHIP OF THE HOLY SPIRIT:

A. Who is the Holy Spirit (Rom. 8:9)?

B. In whose heart does the Holy Spirit live (Gal. 4:6)?

C. What has He come to do (Acts 1:8; Gal. 5:22-23)?

D. How must I cooperate (Acts 4:31; Eph. 5:18-20; Rom. 12:1-2)?

THE STEWARDSHIP OF OURSELVES

LESSON THREE   STEP EIGHT

OBJECTIVE: To motivate to faithful stewardship of one's body and soul.

I. OPEN WITH PRAYER: "Lord, teach us how to be pure in our thoughts as well as our actions."

II. MEMORY VERSE: Psa. 139:23-24.

III. MOTIVATION:

What is your standard of morality? Is it conscience? Is it the crowd? Is it circumstances? *Is it Christ?* How is it possible to consistently keep His standard?

IV. BIBLE STUDY: (See the Lesson Amplification for the details.)

A. Why should we be stewards of our bodies?

B. What is the Biblical view of sexual expression?

C. How does one deal with temptation in his or her sexual life?

D. Why should we be stewards of our minds and hearts? How can we be?

V. PARALLEL PASSAGES:

A. Sin in relation to sex:

1. Why is immorality in a Christian so shocking (I Cor. 6:15-16)?

2. As a Christian, a part of the Church, the bride of Christ, are you in any way guilty of spiritual immorality (James 4:4-8; Jer. 3:1, 13-14; Matt. 22:37)?

B. Sin in relation to the tongue (Prov. 6:17, 19; I Pet. 3:10).

C. Sin in relation to the heart and mind (Mark 7:21-23; Prov. 4:23, Phil. 4:6-7; Psa. 119:9, 11).

D. How to keep our bodies and souls for Christ:

   1. Dedicate them once and for all to God (Rom. 12:1-2).

   2. Do not yield your body's members to sin, but to God (Rom. 6:11-13).

   3. Walk by means of the Holy Spirit (Gal. 5:16-17).

VI. SUMMARY:

Our lives will either be used to further the cause of Christ or to hinder His purposes and further the ends of Satan, depending upon to whom we have yielded our bodies. Right now, surrender yourself to the King of Kings, saying, "All that I am, and all that I have are Thine" (I Kings 20:4).

VII. CLOSE IN PRAYER.

LESSON AMPLIFICATION

THE STEWARDSHIP OF OURSELVES

LESSON THREE   STEP EIGHT

I. WHY SHOULD WE BE STEWARDS OF OUR BODIES?

Rom. 12:1—"With eyes wide open to the mercies of God, I beg you,
my brothers, as an act of intelligent worship, to give Him your bodies,
as a living sacrifice, consecrated to Him and acceptable by Him"
(Phillips N. T.).

I Cor. 6:19-20—"Have you forgotten that your body is the temple of
the Holy Spirit, who lives in you, and is God's gift to you, and that
you are not the owner of your own body? You have been bought, and
at what a price! Therefore bring glory to God in your body" (Phillips
N. T.).

II. WHAT IS THE BIBLICAL VIEW OF SEXUAL EXPRESSION?

A. Sex is a gift of God, good and holy. It is to be expressed only within the marriage bond. Sex needs marriage and marriage needs sex.
   The two are interdependent in the design of God.

   Gen. 2:18-24—God said it was not good for man to be alone, so
   He instituted marriage.

   v. 18—"I will make him a help meet for him"—literally means: "I
        will make a helper who will in every way complement and
        supplement him."

   v. 18—"I will make."

   v. 21—"God caused."

   v. 23—"God took."

   v. 22—"God brought."

   As we can clearly see, it was all of God!

B. The Bible views the body as the vehicle for the expression of spiritual values. Thus, sex cannot be separated from the love which
   gives it true meaning.

   Eph. 5:22-25.
   Col. 3:18-19.
   I Pet. 3:8.

C. What about sex apart from marriage?

I Cor. 6:18—"Avoid sexual looseness like the plague! Every other sin that a man commits is done outside his own body, but this is an offense against his own body" (Phillips N. T.).

I Thess. 4:3-8—"God's plan is to make you holy, and that entails first of all a clean cut with sexual immorality. Every one of you should learn to control his body, keeping it pure and treating it with respect, and never regarding it as an instrument for self-gratification, as do pagans with no knowledge of God. You cannot break this rule without in some way cheating your fellow-men. And you must remember that God will punish all who do offend in this matter, and we have warned you how we have seen this work out in our experience of life. The calling of God is not to impurity but to the most thorough purity, and anyone who makes light of the matter is not making light of a man's ruling but of God's command. It is not for nothing that the Spirit God gives us is called the HOLY Spirit" (Phillips N. T.).

Col. 3:5—"Have nothing to do with sexual immorality, dirty-mindedness, uncontrolled passion, evil desire . . ." (Phillips N. T.).

Whatever the standard of the non-Christian, the standard for the Christian is clear: his body is a sacred trust from God; its functions are meant to be restricted to and preserved for the ends designed by God.

"Sexual experiences penetrate to the very depths of man's being. That is why sexual desire can lead to such sublime heights of joy, happiness, and fullness when used correctly; yet when used incorrectly it can drag a man down to unfathomable depths of sin, impurity and misery. When put to any other use than that for which it was created, sexual desires have a diabolical power to ruin and pollute lives. The abuse of sexual desire causes nature to take revenge by sowing destruction and havoc in the moral, psychological and physiological life of the abuser. What the author of Proverbs 6:32 wrote concerning adultery is equally true of all other sexual abuses: 'He that committeth adultery . . . is void of understanding: He doeth it who would destroy his own soul.'

Another warning from Scripture comes from the story of Tamar and Prince Amnon in the Old Testament. The prince in the court of David seduced a young girl and thought he had gotten away with it. But the Bible says bluntly: '. . . the hatred with which he hated her was greater than the love with which he had loved her . . .' " (Design for Christian Marriage, Small, Dwight Hervey, Fleming H. Revell Company, p. 174).

III. HOW DOES ONE DEAL WITH TEMPTATION IN HIS OR HER SEXUAL LIFE?

A. Negative aspects:

II Tim. 2:22—"Flee also youthful lusts . . ."

I Cor. 6:18a—"Flee fornication . . ."

Rom. 13:14b—". . . give no chances to the flesh to have its fling" (Phillips).

I Thess. 5:22—"Abstain from all appearance of evil."

B. Positive aspects: The Lordship of Christ.

Rom. 14:8-9—"For whether we live, we live unto the Lord; and whether we die, we die unto the Lord: whether we live therefore, or die, we are the Lord's. For to this end Christ both died, and rose, and revived, that He might be Lord both of the dead and living." Col. 3:23—"And whatsoever ye do, do it heartily, as to the Lord, and not unto men."

C. Illustration: David and Joseph contrasted.

David was considered "a man after God's own heart" (Acts 13:22), yet he failed under the attack of Satan. As we study the story of David's fall (II Sam. 11:1-5), we notice that David was vulnerable to this sin because he had committed others previously. First we see the sin of laziness. Instead of leading his men into battle, he sent them to fight while he stayed in Jerusalem. He stayed in bed until evening. Upon arising, he did not spend time with God in prayer and the study of the Scriptures, but went about his own business. These sins have broken his vital fellowship with God and he is helpless in the face of the attack of Satan. David, walking on the palace roof, sees a woman bathing. Note how the verbs denote David's descent into adultery. He *saw* (note, not just a glance) . . . she was beautiful to *look* upon . . . (steady gaze in view, see Strong's Concordance), *inquired, sent, look,* and *lay.* Then adultery led to betrayal, and murder, and open disgrace. There is more in the Bible about David's sin than there is about any victory he ever had.

How different is the story of Joseph! (See Genesis 39:7-12.) When tempted by Potiphar's wife, so vital and real was his fellowship with his Lord that his first thought was that this would be a sin against God (Gen. 39:9). This kept him from falling under the weight of *constant* temptation (Gen. 39:10). When faced with a direct assault by Satan, his fear of God had given the needed wisdom (see Prov. 1:7) to foresee the Biblical injunction to flee from immorality (I Cor. 6:18 . . . not to stay there, try to resist it, entertain it, and be overcome by it). His obedience did not result in immediate happiness for him, but rather prison. (Why are you obedient? Because you love Him or are you merely obedient so long as He blesses you?) Ultimately Joseph was given a place of honor and power and was used to save his people from death.

IV. WHY SHOULD WE BE STEWARDS OF OUR MINDS AND HEARTS ... OUR THOUGHT LIFE?

A. Because our actions proceed from our thoughts! That is what Jesus said:

Matt. 23:27-28—"Woe unto you, scribes and Pharisees, hypocrites! for ye are like unto whited sepulchres, which indeed appear beautiful outward, but are within full of dead men's bones, and of all uncleanness. Even so ye also outwardly appear righteous unto men, but within ye are full of hypocrisy and iniquity."

Matt. 15:18-19—"But those things which proceed out of the mouth come forth from the heart; and they defile the man. For out of the heart proceed evil thoughts, murders, adulteries, fornications, thefts, false witness, blasphemies."

Matt. 5:27-28—"Ye have heard that it was said by them of old time, Thou shalt not commit adultery: But I say unto you, That whosoever looketh on a woman to lust after her hath committed adultery with her already in his heart."

B. How can our thought life be pure?

By thinking on the things of God . . . occupation with Christ!
II Cor. 10:5—"Casting down imaginations, and every high thing that exalteth itself against the knowledge of God, and bringing into captivity every thought to the obedience of Christ."

Isa. 26:3—"Thou wilt keep him in perfect peace *whose mind is stayed on thee*: because he trusteth in thee."

Phil. 4:6-7—"Don't worry over anything whatever; tell God every detail of your needs in earnest and thankful prayer, and the peace of God, which transcends human understanding, will keep constant guard over your hearts and minds as they rest in Christ Jesus" (Phillips N. T.).

LESSON PLAN

THE STEWARDSHIP OF A BODY TO BE USED

LESSON FOUR   STEP EIGHT

OBJECTIVE: Leader should pray that the Holy Spirit will convict the
students of any lack of dedication of their bodies to the
Lord; this lesson should not "preach on externals," but
should present the *Biblical* view of a dedicated body.

I.   OPEN WITH PRAYER: "Lord, take our lives, our bodies and all
that we are and use them for Your glory."

II. MEMORY VERSE: Galatians 2:20—Have one student quote it; then
leader should explain the meaning of being crucified with Christ.

III. MOTIVATION:
                "Only one life
                  'Twill soon be passed
                Only what's done
                  For Christ will last."

IV. BIBLE STUDY:
     A. Relation of spirit and body.
     B. The body as a vessel.
     C. Stewardship of the body.
     D. Stewardship of time.
     E. Necessity of stewardship.

V.   PARALLEL PASSAGES: (See the Lesson Amplification.)

VI. SUMMARY:
     I Tim. 4:12 . . . *"Let no man despise thy youth. . . ."* We are to have
     a good time, plenty of recreation, some rest and relaxation. But, *"Be
     thou an example of the believers. . . ."* We can show the world who
     Christ is and what He is like; we are to live like regenerate believers,
     not unbelieving members of the world system. How are we examples?
     "In word, in conversation, in charity, in spirit, in faith, in purity." Do
     all to the glory of God!

VII. CLOSE WITH PRAYER OF GRATITUDE FOR THE WELL-
     BALANCED LIFE IN CHRIST.

LESSON AMPLIFICATION

THE STEWARDSHIP OF A BODY TO BE USED

LESSON FOUR   STEP EIGHT

If we could only get a really comprehensive grasp of the power and relentlessness of that dread monster, death, how our attitude would change toward it. The world's population is about 2,500,000,000. Suppose the average life of a man is about 45 years, then one-forty-fifth of the total is 55 millions who die every year, 150,685 every day, 6,278 every hour, 104 every minute and more than one every time the clock ticks a second. Think: A city with a population of over 100,000 passes into eternity every day. Let the full force of it come home to you. . . .

> "Time is earnest passing by;
> Death is earnest, drawing nigh:
> Comrade, wilt thou trifling be?
> Time and death appeal to thee."

(Laidlaw, R. A. *The Reason Why*. Chicago: Moody Press, n. d., p. 5.)

I. RELATION OF SPIRIT AND BODY:

A. Man is to be renewed in the spirit of his mind if he is to be converted to Christ. Conversion means to change one's mind, and to be converted to Christ one must change his mind about who Christ is and what He did on the cross to present us to God perfectly restored to righteousness. Rom. 8:8 says, "They that are in the flesh (old nature in control) cannot please God." We are to be changed from the old nature, and carnal mind, to Christ, that we might have His mind and His spirit.

B. The body, then, is the only thing which we can present to Christ for service. Paul said to "present your *bodies* a living sacrifice." He did not say to present the spirit.

C. We are sanctified through the offering of the *body* of Jesus Christ (Heb. 10:10), for God was not satisfied with burnt offerings and sacrifices, but rather prepared a body for Christ to offer (Heb. 10:5). This, too, is to be our offering to the Father. The only thing which many Christians have offered to the Lord is a set of excuses. As C. T. Studd said, "We are among the 'I pray Thee have excused' Apostles."

II. THE BODY AS A VESSEL:

A. God shows His nature to the world when we glorify Him in our bodies as we are commanded in I Cor. 6:19-20.

387

B. II Cor. 4:7 . . . "We have this treasure (meaning the Gospel of Christ) in earthen vessels, that the excellency of the power may be of God and not us." The showcase of the Gospel is the body of a Christian.

C. Every vessel should be clean, empty of self and filled with Christ.

III. STEWARDSHIP OF THE BODY:

A. Does your thought life meet the standard of Phil. 4:8? Compare this with Psalm 1:1-3.

B. Are there things in our lives that Christ might not love?
1. Prov. 4:23.
2. Mark 7:20-23.
3. John 13:34-35—What is God's standard of love? Are there those whom you know, but do not truly love?

C. How do our eyes compare with the stewardship Christ demands?
1. Matt. 5:27-28 . . . Christ warns of lustful looks.
2. II Pet. 2:14 . . . Peter warns of the same.
3. Heb. 12:2 . . . Our needed standard.

D. For what is the mouth used? Compare the following:
1. Romans 3:14 . . . cursing and bitterness.
   Prov. 19:5 . . . false witnesses which speak lies.
2. Mark 16:15 . . . spreading the gospel.
   Psa. 146:1-2 . . . praising the Lord.

E. Testimony of what we hear and listen to is important.
1. Prov. 21:13 . . . depicts lack of mercy.
2. II Tim. 4:3-4 . . . the refusal to hear sound doctrine and truth.
3. Rom. 10:17 . . . hearing the Word to gain faith.
4. Prov. 23:12 . . . hear the words of knowledge.

F. Our feet should walk the paths of righteousness.
1. Prov. 6:18 . . . not running into mischief.
2. Eph. 6:15 . . . feet should be walking about sharing Christ.

IV. STEWARDSHIP OF TIME:

A. Are our activities really counting for the work of the Lord (I Cor. 10:31)?

B. Is our time being redeemed according to Eph. 5:15-16?

V. NECESSITY OF STEWARDSHIP:

A. What must one do before he can be made a fisher of men (Matt. 4:19)?

B. What must one do before he can bear much fruit (John 15:5)?

VI. SUMMARY:

Christians waste their power because of sin which separates them from fellowship with their Lord (I John 1:6-7), costs them power in prayer (Psalm 66:18; Isaiah 59:1-2), and makes them unfit for their Master's use (II Timothy 2:19-21).

Others are willing to pay the price to get their message before the people. A student at an eastern university recently went to Mexico, where in the process of time he discovered true dedication to some cause in Communist workers. He became a Communist. Shortly afterward, he wrote to his fiancee, breaking off their engagement. This letter was given to Billy Graham by a Presbyterian minister in Montreat, North Carolina. This is what it says:

"We Communists have a high casualty rate. We're the ones who get shot and hung and lynched and tarred and feathered and jailed and slandered and ridiculed and fired from our jobs, and in every other way made as uncomfortable as possible. A certain percentage of us get killed or imprisoned. We live in virtual poverty. We turn back to the party every penny we make above what is absolutely necessary to keep us alive.

"We Communists don't have the time or the money for many movies or concerts or T-bone steaks or decent homes or new cars. We've been described as fanatics. We are fanatics. Our lives are dominated by one great overshadowing factor—*the struggle for world Communism*. We Communists have a philosophy of life, which no amount of money could buy. We have a cause to fight for, a definite purpose in life. We subordinate our petty, personal selves into a great movement of humanity, and if our personal lives seem hard or our egos appear to suffer through subordination to the Party, then we are adequately compensated by the thought that each of us in his small way is contributing to something new and true and better for mankind.

"There is one thing in which I am dead in earnest about and that is the Communist cause. It is my life, my business, my religion, my hobby, my sweetheart, my wife and my mistress, my bread and meat. I work at it in the day time and dream of it at night. Its hold grows on me, not lessens, as time goes on. Therefore I cannot carry on a friendship, a love affair, or even a conversation without relating it to this force which both drives and guides my life. I evaluate people, books, ideas, and actions according to how they affect the Communist cause and by their attitude toward it. I've already been in jail because of my ideas and, if necessary, I'm ready to go before a firing squad."

(Graham, Billy, *Call to Commitment*, Billy Graham Evangelistic Association, 1960, pp. 1-2.)

"Dost thou love life?" asked Benjamin Franklin. "Then do not waste time, for that is the stuff it is made of." The Lord and the lost cry, "Redeem the time" to redeem the lost.

THE STEWARDSHIP OF OUR GIFTS

LESSON FIVE   STEP EIGHT

OBJECTIVE: To encourage each Christian to be in such condition that the Holy Spirit can use him.

I.   OPEN WITH PRAYER: "Father, cause us to desire to be led daily and momentarily by the Holy Spirit."

II. MEMORY VERSE: Philippians 2:13. (Ask students to explain the following phrases: worketh, to will, to do, His good pleasure.)

III. MOTIVATION:

Pass out copies of *Traits of the Self-Life* (see the Lesson Amplification) and ask each individual to underline those portions which apply to him. Ask what effect they believe these sins have on their lives.

IV. BIBLE STUDY: (See the Lesson Amplification.)

The Word and prayer are two channels through which the Holy Spirit works in our lives. Divide the group in two sections, asking them to write answers to the following:

Group I—Why is the word of God such an important instrument to the Holy Spirit? (Give references.)

Group II—Why is prayer such an important instrument to the Holy Spirit? (Give references.)

Allow ten minutes for discussion.

V.   PARALLEL PASSAGES:

A. Why did the Holy Spirit come? (To give us the Gospel through the New Testament Scriptures and to enable us to carry it to all the world.)

1. To convey the Scriptures: John 14:26; 16:12-14.

2. To confess the Saviour: John 15:26-27.

3. To convince the sinner: John 16:7-11.

4. To capacitate the saints: Luke 24:32; Acts 1:8.

B. What hinders Him (Ezekiel 22:30; Proverbs 20:6; II Chronicles 16:9a)?

C. What should be our response (I Cor. 15:34; Matt. 5:16; Isa. 6:8)?

VI. SUMMARY:

God is looking for men who will serve as living and verbal advertisements for the Lord Jesus. Will you be such a person?

VII. CLOSE IN PRAYER.

THE STEWARDSHIP OF OUR GIFTS

LESSON FIVE   STEP EIGHT

INTRODUCTION:

As normal human beings, we are so filled with traits that stem from self that we are often hindered in even recognizing types of sin existing in our lives. A short Biblical review of the various forms which sin takes will help us see ourselves as we really are, and then immediately see how we stand positionally perfect before God, because we have met Jesus Christ, the only true righteousness.

A. Types of sin which hinder the work of the Spirit in a Christian.

1. Missing the mark—Romans 5:12-6:1, 15.

2. Trespasses—Romans 2:2-3; Gal. 3:19; I Tim. 2:14 (willful disobedience).

3. Falling away or deviation from truth—Rom. 5:15, 17-18.

4. Disregard of truth; unwillingness to hear—Rom. 5:19; II Cor. 10:6.

5. Unrighteousness—Rom. 1:18; Col. 3:25.

6. Ungodliness—Rom. 1:18; Titus 2:12.

7. Lawlessness—II Thes. 2:3; Titus 2:14.

8. Ignorance—Eph. 4:18.

9. Defeat or loss—Rom. 11:12; I Cor. 6:7.

10. Grievous wickedness—Rom. 1:29-31; I Cor. 5:8.

B. As you read over "Traits of the Self-Life," try to notice in which category these various sins fall.

TRAITS OF THE SELF-LIFE (Psalm 139:23-24)

The following are some of the features and manifestations of the self-life. The Spirit alone can interpret and apply this to your individual case. As you read, examine yourself as if in the presence of God.

Are you conscious of: A secret spirit of pride—an exalted feeling, in view of your success or position, because of your good training and appearance, because of your natural gifts and abilities? An important, independent spirit? Stiffness and preciseness?

Love of human praise; a secret fondness to be noticed; love of supremacy, drawing attention to self in conversation; a swelling out of self when
you have had a free time in speaking or praying?

The stirrings of anger or impatience, which, worst of all, you call
nervousness or holy indignation; a touchy, sensitive spirit; a disposition to
resent and retaliate when disapproved of or contradicted; a desire to throw
sharp, heated retorts at another?

Self-will; a stubborn, unteachable spirit; harsh, sarcastic expressions;
an arguing, talkative spirit; an unyielding, headstrong disposition; a com-
manding, driving spirit; a disposition to criticize and pick flaws when set
aside and unnoticed; a peevish, fretful spirit; a disposition that loves to be
coaxed and humored?

Carnal fear; a men-fearing spirit; a shrinking from reproach and duty;
a shrinking from doing your whole duty; a fear that someone will offend
and drive some prominent person away; a compromising spirit?

A jealous disposition, a secret spirit of envy shut in your heart; an un-
pleasant sensation in view of the great prosperity and success of another;
a disposition to speak of the faults and failings, rather than the gifts and
virtues of those more talented and appreciated than yourself?

A dishonest, deceitful disposition, the evading and covering of the truth,
the covering up of your real faults; the leaving of a better impression of yourself than is strictly true; false humility; exaggeration; straining
the truth?

Unbelief; a spirit of discouragement in times of pressure and opposition; lack of quietness and confidence in God; a disposition to worry and
complain in the midst of pain, poverty, or at the dispensations of Divine
Providence; an over-anxious feeling whether everything will come out all
right?

Formality and deadness; lack of concern for lost souls; dryness and indifference; lack of power with God?

Selfishness; love of ease; love of money?

These are some of the traits which generally indicate a carnal heart.

By prayer, hold your heart open to the searchlight of God until you
see the groundwork thereof. The Holy Spirit will enable you, by confession
and faith, to bring your "self-life" to the death. Do not patch over, but go
to the bottom. It will pay.

> Oh to be saved from myself, dear Lord,
> Oh, to be lost in Thee;
> Oh, that it might be no more I,
> But Christ that lives in me.

—A.A.F.

This description comes from Victory Tract League, Asheville, North Carolina—not to defeat us, but to cause us to more fully understand the price our sin cost Christ on the cross.

I.   THE WORD AS THE SPIRIT'S INSTRUMENT:

A. The word of God is said to be:

   1. "The sword of the Spirit . . ."—Eph. 6:17.

   2. "Alive and powerful, and sharper than any two-edged sword . . ."

   3. "Piercing"—so as to divide what is humanly impossible, i.e., soul and spirit; joints and marrow.

   4. "A discerner (critic or judge) of thoughts and intents (motivations) of the heart" (Heb. 4:12).

B. A sword of this kind cuts with both edges, but must he handled if it is to cut. The word of God also must be used and handled correctly if it is to cut the heart.

C. Since the Word must be used by the Spirit and not forced by a personality, the believer must be controlled by the Spirit when he reads it or gives it out. Otherwise, it will not prosper whereunto the Lord sent it.

D. Other descriptions of the Word.

   1. Fire—Jeremiah 20:9; 23:29 (fire and hammer); a hammer can be used for construction or destruction—so the Word!

   2. Truth—James 1:18.

   3. Seed—Mark 4:14; Matt. 13-19.

II.   THE MINISTRY OF THE SPIRIT IN PRAYER:

A. Romans 8:26-27—What the Spirit does as our indwelling intercessor:

   1. Helps our infirmities.

   2. Makes intercession for us and reveals what we should ask for in prayer.

   3. Helps us pray in and for the will of God.

B. Some "hows" of intercession.

   1. Enlightens our minds and makes the truth take hold of our souls.

   2. Spirit teaches us the value of a soul and guilt and danger of sinners without Christ.

3. Leads believers to understand and apply promises of the word of God.

4. Leads believers to pray for things not specifically mentioned in the Word.

5. The Spirit gives us a spiritual discernment concerning Providence, so as to expect and pray in faith for certain coming events or situations.

III. SUMMARY: Training to be God's Steward (amplification of question 3, page 18):

Men and women of many generations have gone through vigorous, diligent and sacrificial training for many occupations. Lawyers and doctors, for example, must spend several years in consistent study and preparation, usually spending great sums of money on technical books and training manuals. They undergo heavy periods of university and board examinations, all for the purpose of accomplishing their desire to be a lawyer or a doctor. Nothing costs us too much if we want it badly enough. In the Christian life, we have the high calling of God for which to prepare, but the personnel of God's firm are often the most lax in their willingness to prepare for His call in their life. However, since God's word shall stand forever, His standards for His work have not changed. Every work of God must be accomplished in the power of the Holy Spirit and should be examined in light of the following Scriptural principles:

A. The Lord must prepare our hearts and provide our answers—Prov. 16:1.

B. We should, however, appreciate God's use of others for our partial instruction—Prov. 12:1; 1:5-6.

C. We should apply ourselves and be diligent—Prov. 13:4; 23:12.

D. We should study from the heart—a willing attitude—Prov. 15:28.

E. If our work is committed, our thoughts will be—Prov. 16:3.

F. Intense study and application of the Word—Psa. 119:41-42, 133; II Tim. 2:15.

G. Be consistent in life and testimony—II Tim. 4:2, 5.

H. God's attitude toward slothfulness—Prov. 10:26; 19:15.

I. Careful choice of companions—Prov. 1:10; 13:20.

J. Endure hardness—II Tim. 2:3-4.

THE STEWARDSHIP OF OUR POSSESSIONS

LESSON SIX   STEP EIGHT

OBJECTIVE: To get students to begin giving faithfully to God's work throughout the world.

I.   OPEN WITH PRAYER: "Lord, impart to each one of us a vision of the needs of the world, then give us the desire to help meet those needs."

II. MEMORY VERSE: Luke 16:13.

III. MOTIVATION:

Ask each individual to think for a moment and estimate how much of his material wealth is given over to God for His use. Show the results of poor stewardship according to Luke 6:38. Ask if this might be a reason for lack of power and victory and provision of needs in his life.

IV. BIBLE STUDY: (Discuss these questions—see the Lesson Amplification for the answers.)

A. Define stewardship. Of what are we to be stewards?

B. What should one give before he gives his money to Christ?

C. What is tithing?

D. Is tithing necessary today?

E. Why is giving a privilege?

V.   PARALLEL PASSAGES:

A. I Tim. 6:6-11; Heb. 13:5—Be content with what you have. Don't seek to be rich.

B. Matt. 6:19-21—Don't lay up treasures on earth (big bank account); but have treasures in heaven. Earthly treasures are temporal; heavenly treasures are eternal.

C. Luke 6:38; II Cor. 9:6; Prov. 11:24-25; Matt. 7:7-11—God promises to meet the needs of the giver.

D. Mark 10:23-25—The warning Jesus gave to the rich.

VI. SUMMARY:

According to Revelation 4:10-11 everything was created for the Lord's pleasure. This includes our material possessions. Are they at His disposal?

"Wealth is no harm, but the inability to give it up is deadly."

"The Christian abuses the Jew for his stinginess, and yet is meaner than the Jew in his gifts to God."

VII. CLOSE IN PRAYER.

LESSON AMPLIFICATION

THE STEWARDSHIP OF OUR POSSESSIONS

LESSON SIX   STEP EIGHT

I. DEFINE STEWARDSHIP.

Of what are we to be stewards? A steward is, "a manager or superintendent of another's household." We are stewards of all that God possesses, and His possessions include our money, our talents, our minds, our bodies and the time we live in this world.

God owns everything. He is the creator and sustainer of the universe. "Christ, who is the image of the invisible God, the firstborn of every creature; for by Him were all things created that are in heaven and that are in earth, visible and invisible, whether they be thrones, or dominions, or principalities, or powers: all things were created by Him and for Him; and He is before all things and by Him all things consist" (Col. 1:15-17).

There is just one thing that God does not, strictly speaking, own—that is, you and me. In creating the human being He allowed us to have the moral choice of whether we would subject ourselves to Him. All of us have made the wrong choice. "All have sinned and come short of the glory of God" (Rom. 3:23). By this choice we have forfeited our love relationship with God. But, praise be to God, we who have accepted Christ "are not our own, but are bought with a price." The price is God's Son.

So we see that God owns everything, and therefore we own nothing and are only stewards of what He gives us. God holds the key to every material and spiritual thing, and the only reason that we have had any· thing, or have it now, or will have it, is that God loves us enough to give it to us.

II. WHAT SHOULD ONE GIVE BEFORE HE GIVES HIS MONEY TO CHRIST?

"With eyes wide open to the mercies of God, I beg you, my brothers, as an act of intelligent worship, to give Him your bodies, as a living sacrifice, consecrated to Him and acceptable by Him. Don't let the world around you squeeze you into its own mold, but let God remold your minds from within, so that you may prove in practice that the plan of God for you is good, meets all His demands, and moves towards the goal of true maturity" (Rom. 12:1-2—Phillips N. T.).

"Now, my brothers, we must tell you about the grace that God has

398

given to the Macedonian churches. Somehow, in most difficult circumstances, their joy and the fact of being down to their last penny themselves, produced a magnificent concern for other people. I can guarantee that they were willing to give to the limit of their means, yes and beyond their means, without the slightest urging from me or anyone else. In fact they simply begged us to accept their gifts and so let them share the honors of supporting their brothers in Christ. Nor was their gift, as I must confess I had expected, a mere cash payment. Instead *they made a complete dedication of themselves first to the Lord* and then to us, as God's appointed ministers" (II Cor. 8:1-5 —Phillips N. T.).

III. WHAT IS TITHING?

In the Old Testament the tenth of all produce, flocks and cattle was declared to be sacred to Jehovah. These tithes were a symbol of the people's recognition and acknowledgment that the whole land belonged to God.

Illustration: "And he blessed him and said, Blessed be Abram of the most high God, possessor of heaven and earth: And blessed be the most high God, which hath delivered thine enemies into thy hand. And he gave him tithes of all" (Gen. 14:19-20).

IV. IS TITHING NECESSARY TODAY?

Today we are under grace, not law. We are to give "not grudgingly or of necessity, for God loves a cheerful giver" (II Cor. 9:7). "Moreover, it is required in stewards, that a man be found faithful" (I Cor. 4:2).

Illustration: Bob Pierce, president of World Vision, tells this story of an outstanding physician—"When he was in his early twenties the Lord called him to be a missionary. He thought about it at length and finally came to this decision, 'Instead of being a missionary, I'll stay here in the homeland and build up the finest practice I can. Then I'll take on the financial support of several missionaries. Instead of going I'll send others.' Do you know the result? Well, last year he contributed $4,000 to missions. That's a lot of money—a big donation. Do you know what he kept for himself? $36,000! In other words his contribution to sending missionaries in his place was exactly ten per cent of his income. I say that this physician has failed miserably in fulfilling God's purpose for His life. It hasn't cost him anything. He had $36,000 for comfort and ease last year. He gave precisely ten per cent. Of all the missionaries I know, I am sure that all of them give at least ten per cent of their missionary allowance, do you not think that thousands of people here in the homeland should give 20 per cent, 30 per cent, or even 50 per cent of their big salaries to this challenge?" (Savage, Robert, *At Your Orders, Lord!* Grand Rapids: Zondervan, pages 52, 55.)

Illustration: William Borden was a dedicated young Christian. As a student at Yale University he was extremely active in Christian service. It was said of him by a European visitor that what impressed him the most about America was: "The sight of that young millionaire kneeling with his arms around a 'bum' in the Yale Hope Mission."

While a missionary in Egypt at the age of 25, Borden died of cerebral meningitis. Two remarkable wills were probated within a few days after Borden's death. One was his own, and the other was that of J. Pierpont Morgan, who died possessing almost a hundred million dollars. Mr. Morgan at the age of seventy-five left little more than half as much to the work of God as William Borden left at twenty-five! (Taylor, Mrs. Howard, *Borden of Yale*, Moody Press, pp. 202, 205.)

Who was the faithful steward—the physician, J. Pierpont Morgan, or William Borden? What about you?

V. WHY IS GIVING A PRIVILEGE?

Giving is one of the greatest privileges that we as believers in Christ enjoy. Think of it, God has need of nothing, yet we have the privilege of giving *things* to the God of the Universe. How can we resist giving in gladness?

At the most we only enjoy this privilege for 75 years. Compare this with the immeasurable treasure that we will inherit with Christ in heaven. "The Spirit itself beareth witness with our spirit that we are the children of God: and if children then heirs; heirs of God and joint heirs with Christ" (Rom. 8:16-17). For all of eternity we will enjoy riches that we do not deserve to enjoy, that were given to us, that were paid for by the death of the very Son of the Everlasting God. In heaven we will not have this priceless privilege of giving.

God is pleased like a father is when his small son comes to him and says, "Daddy, I love you. I want to mind you and obey you because you always want me to do the best thing. Here is all I have." Imagine the father's reaction. The father would be so pleased and overcome that he would take the little that his son brought and cause it to multiply into an abundant life for his son even at the cost of his own.

How can we hold back from giving all we are and have to the One who took the five loaves and fishes, broke them, and multiplied them and fed five thousand people? We have entrusted to Him our eternal salvation. Surely He can keep our earthly lives secure and cause our little to be multiplied in order to feed many.

LESSON PLAN

STEWARDSHIP ACCOUNTING TO OUR MASTER

LESSON SEVEN   STEP EIGHT

OBJECTIVE: To motivate students to be faithful stewards by bringing
home the fact that Christ will hold them accountable for
what He has given them and commanded them to do.

I.   OPEN WITH PRAYER: "Lord Jesus, help us to invest and spend
our lives wisely so we will not be ashamed to give an account to You
when You come again to claim us for Your own."

II. MEMORY VERSE: Review and check verse with person on your
right.

III. MOTIVATION:

Imagine that Jesus Christ were to return to earth and walk into this
room and ask you: "How have you used the time, treasure and talents
I have given you?" How would you feel? How would you answer?

IV. BIBLE STUDY:

A. When will Christ come?

B. Will Christians be judged?

C. What should we, His stewards, be doing?

D. For what do Christians receive rewards?

V.   PARALLEL PASSAGES:

A. At Christ's second coming, what will happen to the material universe (II Pet. 3:10-13)?

B. What conclusion does this lead to (II Cor. 4:18)?

C. How should one invest his life in the face of this (I John 2:15-17)?

VI. SUMMARY:

The Bible encourages faithfulness because Christ will return unexpect-
edly to punish the unfaithful and reward the faithful steward.

VII. CLOSE IN PRAYER.

STEWARDSHIP ACCOUNTING TO OUR MASTER

LESSON SEVEN   STEP EIGHT

HIS PLAN FOR ME

"When I stand at the judgment seat of Christ,
And He shows me His plan for me,
The plan of my life as it might have been
Had He had His way, and I see how
I blocked Him here and checked Him there,
And I would not yield my will,
Will there be grief in my Saviour's eyes,
Grief though He loves me still?
He would have me rich, but I stand there poor
Stripped of all but His grace,
While memory runs like a hunted thing,
Down the paths I cannot retrace.
Then my desolate heart will well-nigh
Break with the tears I cannot shed.
I shall cover my face with my empty hands,
And bow my uncrowned head.
Lord, of the years that are left to me,
I give them to Thy hand.
Take me and break me, mold me,
To the pattern Thou hast planned."

—Author Unknown.

I. WHEN WILL CHRIST COME?

A. Luke 12:40—We know not; we are to be ready.

B. I Thess. 5:2-4—Illustration: He will come as a thief in the night.

II. WHEN CHRIST COMES, WILL CHRISTIANS BE JUDGED?

A. II Cor. 5:10—All Christians must appear before the judgment seat of Christ.

B. Rom. 14:12—"So then every one of us shall give an account of himself to God."

C. For what will Christians be judged?

I Cor. 3:12-15—for their works.
Verse 15: "If any man's work shall be burned, he shall suffer loss: but he himself shall be saved; yet so as by fire."

D. How will some Christians feel?
I John 2:28—ashamed.

III. WHEN CHRIST COMES, WHAT SHOULD WE, HIS
STEWARDS, BE DOING? (See the Lesson Amplification.)

A. Matt. 24:42—be watching.

B. Matt. 24:44—be ready.

C. Matt. 25:14-29—the parable of the servants (also I Cor. 4:2).

The first servant is given five talents, the second servant is given
two talents, and the third servant is given one talent. The first two
servants double the number of talents they have and when their
master returns he praises them and calls them good and faithful
servants. This third servant hid his one talent, and his master, upon
returning, calls him wicked and slothful.

D. Are you a faithful steward, ready for your Master's return?

IV. FOR WHAT DO CHRISTIANS RECEIVE REWARDS?

A. II Tim. 4:8—A crown of righteousness, granted for loving the appearing of Christ.

B. I Thess. 2:19—A crown of rejoicing, granted for souls won to
Christ.

C. James 1:12—A crown of life, granted for loving Christ and enduring temptation.

D. I Pet. 5:4—A crown of glory, granted for being an example to
the flock of God.

What should we be doing when Christ returns?

Christ will come again, but not as a meek child in a manger. He
shall come in all His glory (Rev. 19-20). Light exposes darkness
and reveals it. In the same way, the radiance of the risen Christ
will reveal the sinfulness of man and will expose to us what kind
of life we have been living. He came the first time to die. This
time He comes to judge. We do not know when He will come but
we are admonished to watch.

James says, "Our life is a vapour." Life is too short to be wasted;
in fact, the most precious possession we have is time. God wants
our lives available to Him, that He might use us to do His will.
It has been said that in times of peril such as just before an accident, a person sees his life pass before him. Would we be pleased
with our lives as we are now living if we knew that we had only

a few minutes or hours left to live? The urgency of the hour demands Christian discipleship. We know not when Christ will come; so we must live every day as if it were our last. Can you say with the writer of Revelation, "Even so, *come* Lord Jesus?"

Dr. J. Sidlow Baxter gave this illustration of the second coming of Christ: A Scotchman and his two sons were returning from a fishing trip. The younger son said: "I can see her now, my precious wife, waiting at home for me—oh yes, she is indeed a faithful one." The elder son said; "My wife will not only be waiting, but she will be perched on the window sill watching for me to come home. That is what I call faithfulness." The father Scotchman said, "Sons, I can show you where your mother, bless her dear heart, excels them both. She will not only be waiting and watching for me to come home, but she will be fixing my dinner as well!"

We should be watching, waiting and working until our Lord comes.

How about you?

HIGHLIGHTS OF THE OLD TESTAMENT

STEP NINE

OBJECTIVE: To illustrate to the students the main message of the Old Testament—the sin and failure of man; the grace and mercy of God.

I.   OPEN WITH PRAYER: Lord, thank You for the examples of the fear and failure of Your people. Thank You also for the examples of faith and courage. We ask that we might *learn* from their experiences.

II.   MEMORY VERSE: Choose one or two from all the ones given in the lesson.

III.   MOTIVATION: "Every day in every way man is getting better and better." Evaluate this statement. Is it true or untrue? Why?

The Old Testament is a perfect illustration of the fact that man is *not* improving.

IV.   BIBLE STUDY: (See the Lesson Amplification.)

A. The Pentateuch.

1. What is the Pentateuch?

2. How would you summarize its major events?

3. How does it illustrate man's failure and God's grace?

B. The Historical Books.

1. Which books are these? Why are they called history?

2. Summarize some of the important happenings which these books record.

3. Give some specific incidents which show God's grace reaching out to sinful man.

C. The Poetical Books.

1. Why are these books considered poetry?

2. What do these books depict?

D. The Prophetical Books.

1. Why are they divided into the major and the minor prophets?

2. Give a general review of the main theme of the prophets.

3. Give some specific examples of how they illustrate the grace of God and sinfulness of man.

V. PARALLEL PASSAGES:

A. Pentateuch.

Illustrations of man's failure and God's Grace.

God's promise	Man's failure	God's grace
Genesis 12:1-3	Genesis 3:6-7	Genesis 3:15,21
Exodus 6:6-8	Genesis 16:1-3	Genesis 21:1-3
	Exodus 6:9	Numbers 14:30-34

B. Historical Books.

Illustrations of man's failure and God's grace.

God's promise	Man's failure	God's grace
II Samuel 7:8-13	Judges 2:11-13	I Kings 11:9-13
	Judges 21:25	I Kings 15:3-4
	II Samuel 2	

VI. SUMMARY:

Many people feel that the Old Testament is a book of fables and myths with very little value. How would you describe its value to the world? What impact has it had on history? The leader should note that its impact has been immense, only superseded, perhaps, by the New Testament. In the pages of the Old Testament are some of the greatest dramas, greatest poems, greatest speeches and greatest truths ever recorded. We should be diligent students of it as Christ was. Note that one of its main themes is the total depravity of all men and the infinite grace of God.

VII. CLOSE IN PRAYER.

LESSON AMPLIFICATION

HIGHLIGHTS OF THE OLD TESTAMENT

SUMMARY LESSON   STEP NINE

The Old Testament is an account of a Nation.

The New Testament is an account of a Man.

The Nation was founded and nurtured of God to bring the Man into the world.

Structure of the Old Testament:

I.   THE PENTATEUCH is the Greek word for the first five books of the Old Testament. They were written by Moses. The Pentateuch is also called "the Law."

    A. **Genesis** means "book of beginnings." It contains the story of the creation of the world, the fall of man, the flood, the calling out of Abraham and the formation of the Hebrew nation. The main characters are Adam, Noah, Abraham, Isaac, Jacob and Joseph.

    B. **Exodus** means "going out." It contains the Egyptian bondage of the Hebrews, their deliverance through Moses, the giving of the Law and the building of the tabernacle.

    C. **Leviticus** means "pertaining to Levites." That is, the book contains the System of Laws administered by the Levitical Priesthood under which the Hebrew nation lived. It is a book full of rules and regulations.

    D. **Numbers** means "numbering," and it contains the numbering of the Hebrews (about two million people). They were placed into tribes and were given specific tasks. It also contains the story of their wanderings in the wilderness (for 40 years) because of their unbelief that God would cast out the heathen people so that they could enter the "promised land."

    E. **Deuteronomy** means "this is the copy (or repetition) of the law." It consists of the parting counsels of Moses delivered to the Jews in view of their impending entrance upon their covenanted possession, the promised land. During the 40 years of wilderness wanderings, a new generation of people had arisen. They, along with Joshua and Caleb (of the past generation), were the only ones allowed to enter the land (Deut. 1:21-39).

II. HISTORICAL BOOKS: They tell of the rise and fall of the Commonwealth of Israel.

A. **Joshua** means "Jehovah saves." It contains the conquest of Canaan (the promised land), the crossing of the Jordan, the fall of Jericho, the victories over the Canaanites, the sun made to stand still and the tribes settled in the land.

B. **Judges** contains the theme "every man did that which was right in his own eyes." There was no king, no system of government, no monarchy. The Israelites were to live in the land and serve God, but they failed. The country was infiltrated with heathen people and idolatry abounded.

C. **Ruth** is the story of the faithfulness and love of a woman. Its purpose: 1) to show that during times of apostasy (time of the judges) there were individuals serving God; 2) to show the founding of the Messianic family; 3) to illustrate the principle of redemption.

D. **I Samuel** presents the personal history of Samuel, last of the Judges. It also contains the establishment of a monarchy under Saul, the failure of Saul and the introduction of David.

E. **II Samuel** marks the restoration of order through the enthroning of God's king, David. God established the great Davidic Covenant out of which the eternal kingdom of the Messiah was to come.

F. **I Kings** contains the reign of Solomon, the building of the temple and the division of the kingdom under Rehoboam and Jeroboam. (Rehoboam was head of the Southern Kingdom, commonly called Judah, and its main center was Jerusalem. Jeroboam was head of the Northern Kingdom, commonly called Israel, and its main center was Samaria.)

G. **II Kings** contains the story of the two kingdoms and their final captivity. The Southern Kingdom (Judah) was conquered and brought into captivity by Babylon. The Northern Kingdom (Israel) was conquered and brought into captivity by Assyria.

H. **I Chronicles** contains the reign of David. It is told from a religious point of view.

I. **II Chronicles** contains the reign of Solomon, and the reigns of Rehoboam, Jeroboam and other kings who followed. It is told from a religious point of view.

J. **Ezra** is the story of the return of a Jewish remnant to Jerusalem, the restoration of law and ritual, and the rebuilding of the temple.

K. **Nehemiah** is the story of the rebuilding of the walls of Jerusalem and the restoration of civil authority.

L. **Esther** was a Jewess who became queen of Persia. Though a remnant had returned to Jerusalem, the majority of the nation had preferred to remain under the Persian rule. This book is the story of how Esther, the queen (through the providence of God), kept the Jewish nation from being exterminated.

III. POETICAL BOOKS: They are the books of the human experiences of the people of God under the various exercises of earthly life.

A. **Job** is in the form of a dramatic poem. It is probably the oldest of the books of the Old Testament and deals with the problem: "Why do the godly suffer?"

B. **Psalms** is the Hebrew hymnbook. The great themes of the Psalms are: The Messiah, Jehovah, the Law, Creation, the future of Israel and the exercises of the renewed heart in suffering, in joy, in perplexity. It was to be used in private and public worship.

C. **Proverbs** consists of wise sayings about life, especially emphasizing righteousness and the fear of God.

D. **Ecclesiastes** is the book of man's reasonings about life and the vanity of it without God.

E. **Song of Solomon** is the story of the love of a bride and a bridegroom, symbolic of the love of Christ for the Church.

IV. PROPHETICAL BOOKS: Prophets were men raised up of God in times of apostasy. They were primarily revivalists and patriots, speaking on behalf of God to the heart and conscience of the nation. The prophetic messages have a twofold character: first, that which was local and for the prophet's time; second, that which was predictive of the divine purpose in the future.

A. Major Prophets—so called because of the size of the books.

1. **Isaiah** is considered to be "the Prince of the Old Testament prophets." He was thoroughly imbued with the idea that his nation was to be a Messianic Nation to the world. He prophesied to Judah, the Southern Kingdom.

2. **Jeremiah's** ministry extended over the last forty years of the kingdom of Judah to the destruction of Jerusalem and the deportation of its inhabitants to Babylon. His orders constitute a stern warning to Judah to abandon idolatry and apostasy to escape the inevitable consequence of Babylonian captivity.

3. **Lamentations** consists of five poems lamenting the destruction of Jerusalem at the time of Babylonian captivity. It was written by Jeremiah.

4. **Ezekiel** prophesied during the Babylonian captivity. His mission was to instruct the Israelites that God was just in permitting the captivity of His people, and that eventually the nation would be restored.

5. **Daniel** prophesied during the Babylonian captivity. His book is is indispensable to New Testament prophecy, the themes of which are: the apostasy of the Church, the great tribulation, the return of Christ, the resurrections, and the judgments. His vision sweeps the whole course of Gentile world-rule to its end in catastrophe, and to the setting up of the Messianic kingdom.

B. Minor Prophets—so called because the books are shorter.

1. **Hosea** was a prophet to the Northern Kingdom (Israel) at the same time Isaiah was prophesying to the Southern Kingdom. His book is the prophecy of God's unchanging love for Israel; and Israel is pictured as an adulterous wife, shortly to be put away, but eventually to be purified and restored.

2. **Joel** was a prophet to the Southern Kingdom. He warns the nation to repent in the light of approaching judgment. He also stirs up the faithful among the people to believe the promises of God involving coming salvation and destruction of the enemies of God's Kingdom.

3. **Amos** prophesied to the Northern Kingdom when it was at its height. Fiery denunciation of luxurious living and the idolatry and moral depravity of Israel were the subjects of his messages.

4. **Obadiah** is a denunciation of the Edomites (bitter enemies of the Jews), predicting their forthcoming decimation.

5. **Jonah** was a prophet called of God to testify to Nineveh, the capital of the Assyrian Empire. The book teaches that God's grace goes beyond His chosen people, and that it reaches out to embrace the heathen nations.

6. **Micah** was a message to both Israel and Judah, stressing their sins, their destruction and their restoration.

7. **Nahum** was a message of judgment to Nineveh, predicting its destruction. Jonah's was a message of mercy; Nahum's, a message of doom. Together they illustrate God's way of dealing with nations; extending grace, but punishing continued sin by judgment.

8. **Habakkuk** was a prophet who was more concerned that the holiness of Jehovah should be vindicated than that Israel should escape judgment. It is written on the eve of the Babylonian captivity.

410

9. **Zephaniah** prophesied right before the Babylonian captivity. He told of the judgments which were to come: captivity for Israel and eventually the judgment of nations, followed by the blessings of the kingdom and the Messiah.

10. **Haggai** prophesied when the remnant of Jews returned to Jerusalem after 70 years of captivity. The theme of his message is the building of the unfinished temple.

11. **Zechariah** was a prophet to the remnant which returned after the 70 years. Much of his message deals with the first and second comings of the Messiah.

12. **Malachi** is the last of the prophets to the restored remnant. He also predicts both comings of the Messiah and the love of God for his disobedient people.

"The Old Testament was written to create an anticipation of, and pave the way for the coming of Christ. It is the story of the Hebrew nation, largely dealing with events and exigencies of its own time. But all through the story there runs unceasing expectance of the coming of ONE MAJESTIC PERSON, who will rule and do a great and wonderful work in the whole world. This person, long before He arrived, came to be known as the MESSIAH. The predictions of His coming constitute the Messianic strain of the Old Testament. They form the golden thread extending through, and binding together, its many and diverse books into one amazing unity" (*Bible Handbook,* Halley, Henry H., page 346).

THE DRAMA BEGINS

LESSON ONE   STEP NINE

OBJECTIVE: To teach the relevance of Genesis to today's living.

I.   OPEN WITH PRAYER: "Father, we pray that our lives will be changed as the result of seeing how You do things. Open our hearts to let You begin a new work in them today."

II. MEMORY VERSE: Rom. 5:12.

Review verses, Romans 5:12; I John 2:15-17, by having several in the group quote them.

III. MOTIVATION (Use one of the following):

Where do we find these doctrines in Genesis, chapters 1-3?

Doctrine	*Answer*
Creation by God	Gen. 1:1.
Sin	Gen. 3:6-7.
Salvation by Christ	Gen. 3:15.
Satan	Gen. 3:1; Rev. 12:9; 20:2.
Sin Nature	Gen. 2:17; Rom. 5:12.
Death, Suffering and Toil	Gen. 3:16-19.
Satanic Persecution of God's People	Gen. 3:15.
Virgin Birth	Gen. 3:15.
Subordination of Wife to Husband	Gen. 3:16.

IV. BIBLE STUDY:

V.   PARALLEL PASSAGES:

A. Salvation by Christ—Isa. 7:14; Gal. 3:16; 4:4.

B. Fall of Man and Creation—Rom. 5:12-21; Rom. 8:18-23.

C. Creation and Re-creation—Rev. 21:1-4; Rev. 22:2-3.

D. Satan—I Pet. 5:8; Eph. 6:11.

E. Vicarious Sacrifice—Lev. 17:11; Gen. 22; Hebrews 9:22.

VI. SUMMARY:

We have seen from Genesis the great spiritual events which have shaped the world since. List as many ways as possible in which these truths have practical application today. Here are some suggested ones for the leader:

A. We learn here that God is the creator and ruler of all things. This makes us realize our responsibility to Him as creator, and gives us a glimpse of His omnipotent power. Anyone who denies God as creator automatically is faced with an empty, purposeless existence.

B. We learn here how sin came into the world and what it is. Sin is the greatest single problem of mankind. In Christ, the Christian alone faces it with a realistic solution.

C. We learn that man was created to have fellowship with God. We see how the fellowship was broken, and how it can be restored. Christianity has revealed that man is not just a species of protoplasm, but that he is God's special creation.

VII. CLOSE IN PRAYER.

413

THE DRAMA BEGINS

LESSON ONE   STEP NINE

INTRODUCTION:

Of the thirty-nine books of the Old Testament, Genesis is perhaps one of the most important. It answers one of the greatest mysteries of all time, the mystery of how things came into existence. This book deals with the origins of the world, man, woman, sin, marriage (and its sanctity) and nations.

The Bible has been written over a period of 2,000 years in three languages, on three continents, by a score of authors, and is composed of sixty-four books. Its symmetry, fulfilled prophecy, types and anti-types, unity of symbolism and its teaching about God demonstrate Divine superintendence during composition. One would not, for instance, expect to find this unity and symmetry in a book of medical thought collected over 2,000 years, etc. You may wish to see the symmetry by comparing Genesis 1-3 with Revelation 21:1-4 and 22:1-5. You will discover that both deal with creation or re-creation (Genesis 1-2, Rev. 21:1-8); a river (Gen. 2:10, Rev. 22:1); the tree of life (Gen. 3:24, Rev. 22:2); God's presence among men (Gen. 3:8-20, Rev. 21:3-4); the curse and its removal (Gen. 3:14-19, Rev. 22:3). Why would Genesis be significant to the twentieth century? And why would Genesis 1-3 be important for this Bible study group? Of course, you remember, we stated that it answers one of the greatest mysteries of all time, namely, how things came to be. But, secondly, this book is important because it tells us of God's acts of redemption in our behalf. This world is cursed and at odds with itself (Romans 8:19-25) and we are a considerable portion of its problem. In Genesis, the "Fall" is followed by the promise of a Redeemer (3:15). Furthermore, we see God choosing a people (12:1-3) and guiding them to a land where He could give them a spiritual education and a Messiah, even the Son of God. Later portions of the Old Testament announce that the Messiah would come from the tribe of Judah and even specify a certain family of that tribe, that of David, their great king (Micah 5:2, II Sam. 7:16, Matt. 1:1). An outline of the book is as follows:

A. Primeval History, chaps. 1-11.

   1. The Creation-Hymn, 1:1-2:3.

   2. "The Generations of the Heavens and Earth," 2:4-4:26.

   3. (Adam) "The Book of the Generations of Adam," 5:1-6:8.

4. (Noah) "The Generations of Noah," 6:9-9:28.

5. (Noah's Sons) "The Generations of the Sons of Noah," 10:1-11:9.

B. The History of God's People, chaps. 12-50.

1. (Shem) "The Generations of Shem," 11:10-26.

2. (Abraham) "The Generations of Terah," 11:27-25:11.

3. (Ishmael) "The Generations of Ishmael," 25:12-18.

4. (Isaac) "The Generations of Isaac," 25:19-35:29.

5. (Esau) "The Generations of Esau," 36:1-43.

6. (Jacob) "The Generations of Jacob," 37:2-50:26.

The opening sentence of Genesis, "In the beginning God . . . ," places God-the-Creator at the center of the stage. One scholar notes that this is a doctrine of the Creator, more than a doctrine of creation. As one reads the next three chapters, he then realizes that Man is at the climax of creation. Throughout the Bible, God and Man are great Bible themes.

Of course, questions about Genesis may arise. Is the Creation account scientific? Are the "days" referred to in the Genesis account twenty-four hour days? Did Moses write or is this authorship attributed to him merely by later scribes? Perhaps it would be helpful to note what Dr. E. F. Kevan, well-known scholar and principal of the London Bible College, says:

"Running the obvious risk of being dogmatic, it is here taken for granted that Moses was the writer of the book. No reason has yet been produced which categorically requires that the belief in the Mosaic authorship should be abandoned. This is the considered judgment of the present writer. But his view that Moses was the writer does not by any means deny the fact that Moses employed sources of some kind. What were these sources? It is thought by some, and with considerable probability, that the recurring phrase 'toledoth', 'these are the generations of', may be an indication of the historical sources which were available to him . . . There is the amazing likelihood, however, that Moses may have possessed original writings, possibly on clay tablets, and that these may have come from the hands of men like Noah, Shem, Terah and others (p. 75).

"Is this account to be regarded as science, as myth, or as revelation? If by science is meant the systematic arrangement of the contents of knowledge, and the expression of that knowledge in formal statements, then the creation account does not claim to be 'scientific'. There is every advantage in this, for had the record been written in the scientific terminology of the twentieth century it would have remained unintelligible to everybody until the present time, and even then would have been understood only by those with a scientific training. Further, if it had been written in accordance with the scientific ideas of the present day it would most certainly be outdated and inaccurate in a century's time . . . The question may be further pressed, however, as to whether, even though not scientific in its language, it is scientific in its substance. The complete answer to this is that no errors have yet been proved . . . Before the enquiry regarding the supposed mythical character of the Genesis account be pursued, it is necessary to be clear as to the meaning of myth . . . In its classical sense a myth is a story constructed with a view to enshrining certain abstract truths which otherwise would be incapable of being communicated. The biblical record of creation is not a myth in this sense. It is rather to be regarded as a picturesque narrative, affording a graphic representation of those things which could not be understood if described with the formal precision of science. It is in this pictorial style that the divine wisdom in the inspiration of the writing is so signally exhibited. Only a record presented in this way could have met the needs of all time. The facts are given in pregnant language which is capable of containing within it all the established results of scientific research (p. 76).

"What was the 'day' which marked the divine stages of the work of creation? It is contended by some that this is an ordinary day of twenty-four hours. In support of this it is pointed out that the periods of evening and morning are specifically mentioned, but there are serious difficulties in the way of accepting this interpretation. Others conceive of these days as days of dramatic vision, the story being presented to Moses in a series of revelations spread over six days. This is an intensely interesting suggestion, but can scarcely be regarded as more than a conjecture. A third view is held by many at the present time. This is that each 'day' represents, not a period of twenty-four hours, but a geological age . . . The chief difficulty attaching to this last interpretation is the mention of 'evening' and 'morning,' but this may perhaps be but a purely figurative way of saying that the creation was characterized by clearly defined epochs" (The New Bible Commentary, Eerdmans, Grand Rapids, Michigan, 1954, p. 77).

Some may wonder if Genesis 2 is another account of Creation. Several scholars point out that parallel repetition is involved. A most illuminating discussion is given by J. Laurence Eason in his recent book, The New Bible Survey, Zondervan, Grand Rapids, Michigan, 1963:

"Hebrew literature has its peculiarities of style. One of these is repetition. This characteristic in its simplest form may be seen in the parallelism of Hebrew poetry. Examples of repetition are to be found in Hebrew literature as early as the Song of Moses, which the people sang after they escaped from the hand of Pharaoh across the Red Sea:

'I will sing to the Lord, for he has triumphed gloriously; The horse and his rider he has thrown into the sea. (Exodus 15)'

"Every Bible reader is familiar with this type of repetition also in the book of Psalms.

"But here is another form of repetition which is not so readily understood. In the Creation, for example, some readers and scholars have thought that the narratives of chapter one, and of chapter two, were two separate stories of Creation, originating from two different sources, and brought together here in sequence by the author or compiler.

"A closer examination of the two chapters, however, will show their purposes to be different. In chapter one, the writer reveals the creative work of God the Creator as an accomplished fact. In chapter two, he is giving a brief history of the world as created, with special emphasis on man as the climax of earthly creation. In short, we have here an example of parallel repetition, and not two separate accounts of Creation" (p. 73).

Is it important who wrote Genesis? Why it is a significant consideration? For one thing, the New Testament considers Moses the author of the Pentateuch. That is, Jesus Christ said much about this (Mk. 7:10, 12:26, Lk. 16:31, 20:37, 24:44, Jn. 5:46-47), as well as Paul (Ro. 10:5, I Cor. 9:9) and John (Jn. 1:45, Rev. 15:3). The Pentateuch lays claim to Mosaic authorship (Ex. 24:4, 34:27; Dt. 31:9, 24). Should this claim be in error, Christ and the New Testament promote it. (Extended discussion of this is undertaken by Merrill Unger, Professor of Old Testament at Dallas Seminary, in his book, *Introductory Guide to the Old Testament,* pp. 213-275, a prize-winning book.)

According to Genesis 1:26, God made man in His own image. What is the image of God? The image of God is: 1) What each man now possesses which makes him different from any other created being (Gen. 9:6, I Cor. 11:7, Jas. 3:9), and 2) "Original" righteousness, or a true knowledge, righteousness and holiness (Gen. 1:31, Ecc. 7:29). This was *lost* through sin and is restored in Christ by means of progressive sanctification, i.e., true knowledge (Col. 3:10), righteousness and holiness (Eph. 4:24). The qualities which make man different from any created being are the natural capacities of morality, rationality, spirituality, immortality and dominion over lower creation. When we speak of spirituality we mean that life principle breathed into him by God in Genesis 2:7, a "living soul" which exists apart from the body. For the Redeemed, the soul will, in the future, have a perfect spiritual body (Phil. 3:21, I John 3:2), governed by the Holy Spirit and become a perfect instrument for the soul's expression. The reference to immortality applies to the soul. Originally the body was immortal, but this immortality was lost through sin (Rom. 5:12, 6:23, I Cor. 15:20-21). The Christian looks forward to receiving an immortal body fashioned in the image of Christ.

Marriage and its sanctity are presented in Genesis 2:18, 21-25, wherein man received "a helper fit for him" (Gen. 2:20 RSV). As one scholar noted, "Let us notice that God did not take the woman from man's *feet*, to be trampled upon and enslaved; nor from his *head* that she should dominate him; but from his *side* to be his companion; from beneath his *arm* to receive his protection; and from near his *heart* to have his love and affection" (Johnson, S. L., Jr., "Bibliotheca Sacra," V. 121, #482, Apr.-June, 1964, p. 110). Though wives are to be subject to their husbands (Eph. 5:22, Col. 3:18), what wife would not wish to obey a husband who loved her as Christ loved the church (Eph. 5:25)?

An interesting picture to bring to your Bible study group for this lesson involves the two Babylonian seals—the Temptation Seal and the Adam and Eve Seal, *Halley's Bible Handbook,* p. 67-68. The beliefs in the "Fall" are contained in perverted creation epics of Babylon. Many striking parallels with Genesis, the preserved Creation form, are to be found in the Babylonian, Assyrian and other creation epics. These parallels are listed in the Handbook. (Halley, *Pocket Bible Handbook,* Box 774, Chicago 90, Illinois, pp. 67-68.)

Genesis 3:1 introduces Satan as a Serpent. He indwells a serpent for his attack upon Creation. The book of Revelation pictures his punishment and interestingly enough uses the name serpent:

> "And the great dragon was thrown down, that ancient serpent, who is called the Devil and Satan, the deceiver of the whole world—he was thrown down to the earth, and his angels were thrown down with him" (Rev. 12:9 RSV).

Concerning the work of Satan a helpful statement is concisely made by H. C. Thiessen, formerly head of the faculty of the Graduate School of Wheaton College:

> "There are indications of Satan's work in the various names given to him, for each name expresses a quality of character, or a method of operation, or both; e.g., as Satan he opposes, as devil he slanders and accuses, while as tempter he seeks to lure men to commit sin.

> "In addition the Scriptures reveal the nature of his work directly. Generally speaking, Satan's object is expressed in Isaiah 14:14: "I will make myself like the Most High." . . . In order to achieve his avowed purpose he sought to kill the child Jesus (Matt. 2:16, Rev. 12:4) and when that effort failed, to induce Him to worship him (Luke 4:6-7).

> "Satan employs various methods for the realization of his purpose. Since he cannot attack God directly, he attacks God's master-creation, man. The Scriptures mention the following methods used by Satan: (1) lying (John 8:44; 2 Cor. 11:3), (2) tempting (Matt. 4:1), (3) robbing (Matt. 13:19), (4) harassing (2 Cor. 12:7; Job 1 and 2), (5) hindering (Zech 3:1; I Thess. 2:18; Eph. 6:12), (6) sifting (Luke

22:31), (7) imitating (2 Cor. 11:14-15; Matt. 13:25), (8) accusing (Rev. 12:9-10), (9) smiting with disease (Luke 13:16, cf. I Cor. 5:5), (10) possessing (John 13:27), and (11) killing and devouring (John 8:44, I Pet. 5:8). The believer must not let Satan gain an advantage over him by remaining ignorant of his devices (2 Cor. 2:11), but should be sober and vigilant and resist him (I Pet. 5:8; Eph. 4:27; Jas. 4:7). He should not speak lightly of him (2 Pet. 2:10; Jude 8-9), but put on the whole armor of God and take his stand against him (Eph. 6:11)" (Thiessen, H. C., *Lectures in Systematic Theology,* Eerdmans, Grand Rapids, Michigan, 1956, pp. 210-211).

The following is recommended reading in the event a more intense study of Genesis is desired:

Aalders, G. C., "The Historical Literature of the Old Testament," *The New Bible Commentary,* Eerdmans,, Grand Rapids, Michigan, 1954.

Bacon, B. W., *The Genesis of Genesis,* Hartford, 1892.

Eason, J. L., *New Bible Survey,* Zondervan, Grand Rapids, Michigan, 1963.

Green, W. H., *The Unity of the Book of Genesis,* N. Y., 1910.

Halley, H. H., *Pocket Bible Handbook,* Box 774, Chicago, Ill., pp. 31-105.

Ryle, H. E., *The Early Narratives of Genesis,* London, 1892.

Unger, Merrill F., *Introductory Guide to the Old Testament,* Zondervan, Grand Rapids, Mich., 1951, pp. 183-195, 213-275.

Wilson, R. D., *A Scientific Examination of the Old Testament,* Moody Press, 1959. Revised Edition by E. J. Young.

Young, Edward J., *An Introduction to the Old Testament,* Eerdmans, Grand Rapids. Revised edition, 1958, pp. 43-164.

I.   EXPLAIN OBJECTIVE: "This lesson is to teach the significance of Genesis to today's living."

II. QUESTIONS AND LEADER'S COMMENTARY

A. A short quiz is to be given in which the members write answers to the following questions and hand in the papers. They are mixed and returned for reading of the differing answers.

1. Quiz:

a. How did matter originate?

b. What good do you find about the world?

c. What evil do you find about the world?

d. Where did evil originate?

B. Do the Bible Study. (If the answers have not been written into the blanks, assign the questions one to an individual for an answer.) Inquire as to the answers they gave to the questions.

C. Ask for the Biblical answers to the quiz (when they finish the lesson material).

D. If there is time, have them look into some parallel references given in the Lesson Plan. Or, share some material from the Lesson Amplification, or the pictures from Halley's Handbook on the Temptation and Adam and Eve Seal, etc.

E. Close with the summary from the Lesson Plan.

III. SUMMARY

A thought provoking statement is made concerning the account of creation by Merrill Unger, Professor of Old Testament at Dallas Seminary, as he quotes America's outstanding archaeologist, W. F. Albright, under whom he studied:

> "The account of the origin of the cosmos in Genesis, moreover, is not only incomparably superior in every respect to ancient cosmogonies and creation accounts, but what is all the more amazing in the light of the utterly unscientific age in which it was produced, is its scientific precision even when judged by the standards of our modern scientific age. Commenting on the account of creation which we find in Chapter I of Genesis, W. F. Albright calls the 'sequence of creative phases' which it outlines 'so rational that modern science cannot improve on it, given the same language and the same range of ideas in which to state its conclusions. In fact, modern scientific cosmogonies show such a disconcerting tendency to be short-lived that it may be seriously doubted whether science has yet caught up with the Biblical story' " (Unger, M. F., *Introductory Guide to the Old Testament*, Zondervan's, Grand Rapids, Michigan, 1951, p. 186).

LESSON PLAN

FROM ADAM THROUGH ABRAHAM

LESSON TWO   STEP NINE

OBJECTIVE: To promote obedience to the word of God by demonstrating successful living as a result of obedience and failure as a result of disobedience.

I.   OPEN WITH PRAYER.

II. MEMORY VERSE: Romans 4:20-21.

III. MOTIVATION:

Ask a person in the group to share how God was faithful in fulfilling a promise. Have him mention the exercise of will involved in committing his problem to the Lord. (If there is not an able person in the group, then leader should share.)

IV. BIBLE STUDY: (Halley's *Bible Handbook* can be supplementary.)

V.   PARALLEL PASSAGES: Assign some verses to students letting them explain their significance whenever possible.

A. Famous expressions of trust in God's promises—GOOD MOTTOES FOR LIFE.

1. Moses, Exodus 14:13, "Stand still and see the salvation of the Lord."

2. David, I Sam. 17:47, "The battle is the Lord's."

B. Illustrations of God and Christ in Abraham and Isaac in Genesis 22.

1. Isaac.

a. Phil. 2:5-8, Obedient unto death.

b. Heb. 11:17-19; James 2:21-23, Illustration of resurrection.

2. Abraham, John 3:16; Rom. 8:32, Spared not His own Son *for us!*

3. Matt. 1:1 is an outline of Matthew. Christ is Son of David in chapters 1-25 but Christ is Son of Abraham in chapters 26-28 because He is a sacrifice for sin.

C. Chastisement for disobedience is unavoidable.
Famine in Israel was God's discipline for disobedience and sin.

1. Deut. 28:23-25, famine, one of the judgments for sinfulness.

2. II Sam. 24:13, David given choice of famine by God.

3. II Chronicles 6:26-31, Solomon's prayer recognizes famine as a discipline of God.

VI. SUMMARY: (Use either of two.)

A. Why won't we trust Christ to be our Saviour? Why won't we trust God's word? Are the same reasons given for both?

B. Can you name any great Christian leader who did not trust the Bible? Why is it necessary for leadership?

VII. CLOSE IN PRAYER.

FROM ADAM THROUGH ABRAHAM

LESSON TWO   STEP NINF

INTRODUCTION

One can trust the promises of God because, "God is not a man, that he should lie; neither the son of man, that he should repent: hath he said, and shall he not do it? or hath he spoken, and shall he not make it good" (Numbers 23:19)?

All spiritual problems arise from a problem in our relationship to the Bible. Either we do not trust God's promises, so we worry; or we are ignorant of God's promises. We refuse to make God's word a part of our lives. When we get out of fellowship we refuse to use I John 1:9 and confess and be restored. A very famous Chinese missionary, for these very reasons, said that ministers and missionaries have nervous breakdowns, emotional problems, etc., because of their relationship to the Bible, or lack of relationship to the Bible. Do you worry, fret, complain to God, want to give up Christian living?

Satan is supremely interested in undermining confidence in the word of God. Perhaps, for example, you have been informed of "contradictions" and "superstitions" in the Bible by destructive literary critics. You feel you cannot trust the Bible, though you are a Christian. I Cor. 10:13 tells us that we are not tempted above our capacity, that we are given a way to escape, that if we fall it is our fault. God's way of escape is to affirm your trust in the Bible, ask God to show you His answer, redouble your Bible study. We have always found that "contradictions" lead to great blessings and insights into the inspiration of the Bible.

In the event you do trust your Bible, Satan is interested in keeping you ignorant of God's word. Are you unstable, undynamic, fearful, worried and loaded with spiritual problems? You say that you read your Bible every day and even memorize sometimes. Fine. But, are you out to conquer for Christ—standing on promises, not sitting on premises? The Bible is not operating in your life; it really does not mean anything at all—a bore to read? Reading and studying are joys when we are using the word of God in our lives. Lack of study, lack of understanding of the word of God, the Bible, make us fail God's tests for spiritual living. The book and the battle are bound inseparably. Study as a soldier. Learn it as a tactical manual.

It takes a choice of will to act on a promise. That is the crux of many a spiritual problem. The "flesh" does not desire to launch out. Abraham and Isaac went to Egypt for food when the word of God told them that they should confess sin and God would supply food. Abraham begat Ishmael when the promise of God was that he would have an heir without resorting to the "flesh." For them and us, repercussions of faithless behavior are so great! Determine that you will not allow Satan's lies, lack of study and unwillingness to keep you from applying the promises to your experience.

I. EXPLAIN OBJECTIVE: "This lesson is to inspire us to be obedient to the Bible."

II. QUESTIONS AND LEADER'S COMMENTARY:

A. Question 1. Have students look up some of the parallel passages that follow on the sacrifice of Cain and Abel. Assign one to a student.

1. Cain—I John 3:12; Isaiah 64:6; Eph. 2:8-10; Titus 3:5.

2. Abel—Heb. 9:22; Lev. 17:11; Heb. 11:4.

3. Make sure they understand Cain had no sense of sin or need for atonement. Abel's sacrifice involved confession of sin and expression of faith in God's substitute.

B. Question 2. Ask students to describe a present day Cain and Abel incident as it pertains to good works, church, ignoring the blood of Christ, etc.

C. Question 3. Assign each Scripture reference to a different person to look up and read to the group: Gen. 12:2-3; 16:4, 15; and 17:19.

1. Emphasize that Abraham's lack of faith in the promise resulted in the birth of Ishmael and Moslem persecution of Jews, for Abraham is the forbear of the Moslem people through Ishmael.

2. Emphasize that Abraham is father of the believing Jews, not the unbelieving; the father of the Judaism which pointed to Christ (Rom. 2:17-29; Rom. 3:4). At Christ's death the veil of the Holy of Holies was rent. True Judaism no longer exists—no Temple, no Blood, no Holy of Holies, etc.

D. Question 4.

1. Assign student to read Gen. 12:2-3 and another to read Gal. 3: 13-14.

2. Ask group to tell how Gen. 12:3 was fulfilled in Christ.

E. Question 5.

1. Ask, "What are the elements in these two believers that show spirituality or carnality?"

2. Ask, "Why does spiritual living profit more than carnal living?" Assign Gal. 6:7-8; I Cor. 11:30-32; Heb. 12:5-13 which speak of God's discipline, and Romans 8:32 which speaks of God's bounty for spiritual Christians.

3. Ask, "How are we carnal in our choices?"

F. Question 6.

1. Before discussion of this question have them read Gen. 17:16 and Gen. 22:8. Ask, "What discipline of faith must have transspired in Abraham?"

2. Note that Isaac was a sacrifice of his father just as Christ was. Turn to Matt. 1:1 and read it aloud. Note that this is an outline of Matthew. In chapters 1-25 Christ is Son of David, the king. In chapters 26-28 he is Son of Abraham, sacrifice of His Father.

III. SUMMARY:

Successful living demands obedience to the Bible. Many men have said this in so many words.

"If I am asked to name the one comfort in sorrow, the safe rule of conduct, the true guide of life, I must point to what, in the words of a popular hymn, is called 'the old, old story' told in an old Book, God's best and richest gift to mankind " — Gladstone.

"The promises of the Bible have behind them God's knowledge and power" — John Wanamaker.

"If I were to have my way, I would take the torch out of the hand of the Statue of Liberty and in its stead, place an open Bible " — Marshall, Vice-President of the United States.

"It is hard to see how a great man can be an atheist. Doubters do not achieve. Skeptics do not contribute. Cynics do not create. Faith is the great motive power and no man realizes his full possibilities unless he has the deep conviction that life is eternally important and that his work, well done, is a part of an unending plan"—Calvin Coolidge (Brooks, K. L., *The Cream Book,* American Prophetic League, Inc., Los Angeles, 1938, pp. 11-12).

LESSON PLAN

MOSES: THE PASSOVER AND THE LAW

LESSON THREE   STEP NINE

OBJECTIVE: To illustrate the faith-rest life. Israel symbolizes the Christian in his failure to achieve it by faith.

I.   OPEN WITH PRAYER: "Oh, Father, may we realize today, that the Christian life is a life of faith. May we launch out by faith to live by the promises which You have supplied for us."

II. MEMORY VERSE: I Corinthians 10:13.

     Have several explain the verse after others quote it from memory. (Optional—Use I Corinthians 10:11 as additional memory verse. Discuss its meaning and importance in understanding the purpose of the Old Testament.)

III. MOTIVATION:

     Susan has come to her last year at Nursing School. A fine Christian fellow has proposed to her. She loves him and would like to marry him. The problem is that she felt God called her to Africa as a nurse when she was sixteen. What should she do?

IV. BIBLE STUDY:

     A. Explain lesson objective: "This lesson aims to illustrate that we can trust Christ to take care of us now. In this lesson, Israel illustrates the Christian who will not trust God now. For instance, Israel came out of Egypt (sin and the world), but will not enter Canaan (a life of victory and rest)."

     B. Assign questions 1-7 around the circle, one to a person. Each individual will read the question, the reference and his answer. Allow a few minutes at first for looking up answers.

     C. Read responsively Ex. 12:21-36. Ask group to note correlations to Christ's death as our passover; also, note the role of faith in saving the life of the eldest sons.

     D. Have silent reading of Ex. 14:1-31 and then assign questions 12-14 to be read and answered.

426

E. Read I Cor. 10:1-15 silently and assign questions 15-16 to be read and answered.

V. PARALLEL PASSAGES:

   A. Wilderness wanderings—Deut. 1:2-3; Num. 14:20-35.

   B. Christ our passover—John 1:29; 19:31; I Cor. 5:7, I Pet. 1:18-20.

   C. Christ's death in Old Testament—types:
      Brass serpent—Num. 21:6-9, John 3:14-15.
      Abraham offering his son—Gen. 22.

   D. Law brought us to Christ—Gal. 3:24-25.

VI. SUMMARY:

   A. What are the motives that keep us from trusting Christ as Saviour? (Doubt about the Bible, desire to live for self, fear that life will become negative and meaningless.)

   B. Why do we try to handle our own problems? Why not let Christ handle them?

VII. CLOSE IN PRAYER.

LESSON AMPLIFICATION

MOSES: THE PASSOVER AND THE LAW

I. MOSES:

This incident in Moses' life illustrates the blessing of trusting God. Note these facts about Moses:

He was supremely a man of faith. Though this lesson reveals his unbelief and shows his faith growing, still what Moses accomplished, he accomplished by faith. The "hall of fame" listed in Hebrews 11 contains all men made great, not by inherent talent, not by their own greatness, but by trust in a God of greatness. No man *ever* counted for God without faith (Heb. 11:6). Note the change which faith made in Moses' life:

Before faith	*After faith*
Had great opportunities, lost them, Ex. 2:11-15.	Had nothing but closed doors, accomplished tremendous feats, (performed miracles, led Israel out of Egypt, gave Law, wrote first five books of Bible).
Spent forty wasted years, Acts 7:23, 30.	Became one of history's greatest men, after he was eighty years old.
Fled as a coward, Ex. 2:15.	Defied the greatest empire of his day.

The simple act of trusting God completely transforms a life. Note what God called Moses to do—defy the greatest ruler of his day, with no backing but the promise of God. God usually calls us to do far greater things than we have ever imagined. Compare the calls of Abraham in Gen. 12:1-3 and David, I Sam. 16. Is God calling you to do more than you are doing? In questions 3 and 4, note how well God had things planned—does He have all things planned for us, also? God does the planning, He only expects us to fit into His plans. How much of his success did Abraham plan? How much of his success did Peter plan? On question seven, note that if we do not hesitate too long, we can still fit in God's plan, *if* we believe and follow Him. Moses could have disobeyed God's call, with the result that he would have faded into oblivion. When we deny God's program for our lives, we are the losers. Note some of the ways we can do this: we can refuse His call into full time service; we can disobey Him by marrying the wrong person; we can be in an occupation, school, or place where He will not use us.

II. THE PASSOVER:

Note these correlations between Christ's death and the Passover:

A. Christ called the lamb of God, John 1:29.

B. The lamb without blemish, Ex. 12:5-6; Christ sinless, I Pet. 2:22.

C. The lamb was slain, Ex. 12:6; Christ sacrificed for us, I Cor. 5:7.

D. The blood must be applied. The placing of the blood on each side of the door and on the top pictures a cross, cf. John 3:18.

Note how clear this makes the issue of salvation. Salvation is based *solely* on what one does with Christ. Many of our friends, cultured, educated, polite, pleasing in personality and a pleasure to be around, are just as lost as the most heathen savages of Africa, or as Adolf Hitler. A man is either saved or lost. There is no in-between or second chance for "nice" people, just as there was no in-between for those who, whatever their social status and personality, refused to apply the blood.

In I Cor. 10:6-10, list the mistakes made by Israel, and remember this was all in light of the fact that they had witnessed tremendous miracles by God on their behalf. They committed idolatry (v. 7), fornication (v. 8), they tempted Christ (v. 9), and they complained against God (v.10). For all of these things God sent judgment upon them. Apply Gal. 5:7-8 here. According to verse 12, is it possible for us to fall into the same types of sins despite our present maturity as Christians?

Once again, the failure of Israel was a lack of *faith*. Likewise, those who escaped judgment by applying passover blood did so by faith (Heb. 11:28). Faith has been the key word of this lesson. We are saved only by faith (Gal. 3:3). We must ask ourselves whether we are trusting God for salvation only, or for everything in life: finances, studies, marriage, etc. The little child is a picture of trust. He does not worry about his future, what he will do, whom he will marry, etc. He does not wonder about whether he will some day get a serious illness, he does not doubt that there will be food to eat and clothes to wear; he lives a happy life of simple faith. Jesus had immense responsibilities, as did Paul and Peter. Yet, do you picture them as worried and frenzied, having nervous breakdowns, taking tranquilizers?

III. LAW AND GRACE:

Because of the length of the lesson, there is not room for the final part, on the Law, in the Bible study. The leader would do well to have a separate Bible study on this most important subject. Below is a suggested outline:

A. OPEN WITH PRAYER: "Lord, make clear to us the difference between law and grace that we might know better how to serve Thee."

B. MEMORY VERSE: Gal. 3:10-13.

C. MOTIVATION: Ask the group "What is law?" "What is grace?" "What is the difference between the two?" Let them express their answers without giving the answer yourself, and then move into the lesson.

D. BIBLE STUDY:

1. What is law?

   a. "A rule of conduct or action prescribed by the supreme governing authority and enforced by a sanction" (Webster). Law always means two things: (1) a specific standard which differentiates right from wrong: (2) an impartially administered penalty inflicted upon those disobedient to the law.

   b. In the New Testament, there are two important uses of the term "law" which concern us: (1) law describes the legal method of approach to God –in other words, seeking to be justified before Him by obeying His righteous standards; (2) the law of Moses, which is the highest and best representative of the legal approach to God. All religions and moral systems, which take God into account, approach God legally, *except* true Christianity. Of these legal systems, the law of Moses is the highest, truest and best, and the only one ordained of God. All who seek salvation or blessing on the basis of *obedience,* even if it be obedience to the Ten Commandments or Sermon on the Mount, are approaching God by *law.*

   c. Two examples of the legal system:

      1) The speed law — a definite standard which sets a definite limit on speed, differentiating between right and wrong. An impartially administered fine is given to all who break the law, regardless of what good qualities they have.

      2) The law of the Sabbath, Ex. 31:15.– no work was to be done on the Sabbath. This was a definite standard. The penalty impartially administered was death (Num. 15:32-36). Law always means a *standard* and a *penalty.*

2. What is grace?

   a. Rom. 6:14. Grace is an entirely different way of approaching God. Law and grace are two different systems ordained for two different purposes, and are never to be mingled. Each is complete in itself. We are either under one system or the other, not both. Rom. 6:14 states that all Christians, whether or not they enjoy the privilege are under the grace system.

b. Grace defined: Grace is the kindness and love of God expressed toward us entirely apart from what we deserve (Tit. 3:5-6; Eph. 2:8-9; Rom. 4:4-5). Under the law, we earn whatever we get. Under grace, whatever we get is a free gift.

c. The scope of grace: Since grace depends only on our accepting it, and not on what we deserve, it is in no way dependent on how good we are, and can *never* be limited by how bad we are (Rom. 5:8). God did the most for us when we deserved the least from Him.

3. What is the purpose of each?

a. The purpose of the law is to condemn and expose sin (I Tim. 1:8-10). Its purpose is *never* to save, to encourage, to comfort, to enable. The purpose of your bathroom mirror is to show you what you really are like. If you have dirt on your face, your mirror does not remove it, it only shows you it is there. The law shows us our need of grace.

b. The purpose of grace is to save, to comfort, to encourage, to enable (Eph. 2:8-9; Rom. 6:1-2; Tit. 3:5-6). The purpose of grace is not to condemn, to discourage, to judge. Just as the mirror exposes the dirt on my face, so the soap and water wash it off. I do not look into the soap to see the dirt, or wash my face with a mirror.

4. What is the practical application of being under grace?

Romans 6:14, Eph. 2:8-9, Galatians, Acts, and practically the whole New Testament repeat over and over that the Christian is under the grace system, and is delivered from the law system. No truth of the Bible is so clear, yet so misunderstood. These applications follow:

a. The burden of guilt is now removed from life. All my sins have been (not will be) forgiven by Christ (I John 2:2). Although I have not obeyed all of God's laws, or because I have sinned, I do not labor under a burden of guilt. God has forgiven forever all sin. Christians who labor under a burden of guilt, who look at God as an awful judge, who feel perplexed because they never seem to please Him, have put themselves under law. In Rom. 8:1, R.S.V., there is no condemnation to the Christian. Do you feel God is your judge, or justifier?

b. The burden of a false motive for living the Christian life is now removed. I do not live the Christian life to earn God's approval. He sees only my life in Christ. He looks on Christ instead of me. Nothing I ever have done or ever will do has the slightest effect on whether I will go to heaven. Only the cross justifies me—not witnessing, Bible study, etc. Thus what I do for God I do freely, out of love, because I want to, not because of fear or threat. Many Christians have surrounded their lives with laws of their own which they obey not out of love, but out of a desire to earn God's approval. They witness once a day, they read the Bible early in the morning for a set period of time, they rigorously use a prayer list, and when they fail to obey these laws they have set up, they live under a load of guilt. Some of these habits may be good, but they should never be followed from any motive other than love. Further, we must be careful that we do not set laws on ourselves and make them moral issues. Murder is a moral issue according to the Bible. Witnessing once a day, or reading the Bible in the morning is *not* a moral issue. Our standards are the New Testament standards alone, without the additions of well-meaning men.

c. The burden of weakness is now removed (Rom. 8:2-3). The law set us a standard, but gave no enablement. Grace gives the Holy Spirit to enable us to follow its standards. Grace is liberty. But liberty is not license. My life is not worse under grace, but better:

> " 'This do and live,' the law commands,
> But gives neither feet nor hands,
> A better word the Gospel brings,
> It bids me fly, and gives me wings."

Thus, under grace, I have a higher standard, the life of Christ, but also His life within me to aid in fulfillment. And even though I never fulfill the standards completely, I approach them and am forgiven freely and instantly where I fall short.

IV. SUMMARY:

There are thousands, tens of thousands of Christians today who have all that they have by God's free grace. Yet, because of their own weakness, they labor in misery, defeat, plagued with guilt and feelings of condemnation because they wish to live under law. God is to them a very hard, exacting, and scrupulous taskmaster. They spend all their lives trying to make up for sins, trying to earn His love and acceptance, trying to lift themselves toward heaven with their good works. But the God of grace is one whom Jesus called a loving Father, one who forgave freely, one who gave bountifully, one who was a joy to know. Are you living under the God of law or the God of grace?

V. CLOSING QUOTATION:

"God is willing to do for you all His grace and power will allow Him to do."

432

LESSON PLAN

JOSHUA AND DELIVERANCE—
DAVID AND FORGIVENESS

LESSONS FOUR AND FIVE   STEP NINE

OBJECTIVE: To teach the Christian how to rest by faith in the promises of God, and keep an unhindered fellowship with the Lord by confession of sin.

I.   OPEN WITH PRAYER: "Father, we pray that You would apply these principles of faith-rest and confessing sin to each of our lives."

II. MEMORY VERSES: Leader should quote verses, having students explain the meaning of each phrase in the verses (Josh. 1:9; Psa. 32:5).

III. MOTIVATION:

Compare and contrast the characters of Joshua and David. What were their strengths? What were their weaknesses?

IV. BIBLE STUDY:

A. Joshua and deliverance.

B. David and forgiveness.

C. Results of faith and obedience.

D. Modern application.

V.   PARALLEL PASSAGES:

A. Lesson 4 on Joshua:

1. Rest in activity—Heb. 4:1-10; I Cor. 10:13; I Pet. 5:7.

2. Failure due to self-activity.

a) Elijah—Kings 19:2-3, 15-16, 18 (Carnal solution to spiritual problem).

b) Saul—I Sam. 9:1-2, 15-16, 21-22; 13:7-9; 15:13-23 (Carnal capacities substituted for spiritual).

c) Paul—Gal. 2:7-9; Phil. 3:4-6 (Health forced him to depend upon the Spirit).

B. Lesson 5 on David:

   1. Chastening is in the plan of God for man—Heb. 12:5-11.

   2. Suffering for Christ's sake brings glory to God—I Pet. 2:19.

   3. Privilege of confession is based on priesthood of every believer as seen in the Old Testament. Examples:

      a. Priest by birth—Ex. 28:1; John 3:3.

      b. Priest bathed by another upon entering priesthood—Ex. 29:4; Col. 2:13; Titus 3:5.

      c. Priesthood for life—Heb. 7:23.

      d. Priestly functions of New Testament believers.

         1) Access to God—Heb. 10:19-22.

         2) Sacrifice—Rom. 12:1; Phil. 2:17; Heb. 13:15-16.

         3) Intercessory prayer—I Tim. 2:1; Col. 1:9-12.

VI. SUMMARY:

Shall we expect a greater path of ease than the Saviour walked? His word to us is, "The servant is not greater than his Lord. If they have persecuted me, they will also persecute you." Though He was a Son, yet He learned obedience by the things which He suffered. Paul probably suffered more than any other disciple for the sake of the Lord Jesus, yet his attitude was, "For our light affliction, which is but for a moment (he actually suffered many years, but counted them nothing!), worketh for us a far more exceeding and eternal weight of glory!"

VII. CLOSE WITH PRAYER:

"Lord, we sincerely praise You for every hardship which You graciously bring into our lives to draw us closer to Thyself. May we forever be grateful that You alone know what is best and do only that for Your own redeemed children."

JOSHUA AND DELIVERANCE—
DAVID AND FORGIVENESS

LESSONS FOUR AND FIVE   STEP NINE

I. JOSHUA AND DELIVERANCE—Josh. 1.

   A. God's choice of Joshua.

      1. God's command—v.2.

      2. Promise—v.3.

      3. Comfort—v.5.

      4. Exhortation—v.6-7.

      5. God's promised result—1:8-9.

   B. Question: How much of chapter 1:1-9 depended on Joshua?

      Answer: 1:2—God's promised blessing depended upon only one thing: Joshua's willingness to "arise and go!"

      1. How much of our Christian life depends on us?

         a. I Thess. 5:24—"Faithful is He that calleth you, who also will do it!"

         b. II Tim. 2:13—"If we believe not, yet He abideth faithful; He cannot deny Himself!"

      2. See Abraham's example of believing God—Rom. 4:20-21.

   C. When God gives a command, He also must open the way of our ability to obey. God was faithful to Joshua as previously to Moses —He is no respecter of persons (Josh. 4:23).

      1. To what lengths did God go in order to complete His will and promise to Joshua? (Josh. 10:13-14).

      2. Has God changed? Heb. 13:8—"Jesus Christ, the same yesterday, and today, and forever."

II. DAVID AND FORGIVENESS—II Samuel 11.

   A. David's position: God had graciously chosen this young man, brought him out from feeding sheep and anointed him King of Israel.

   Background: Sheepherder.
   Occupation: King.
   Ministry: Feeding the flock of God.

B. God's dealing with David.

    1. The Jewish new year ended with March, and it was customary for kings to go to battle at this time; however, David sent Joab (v.1) and disobeyed the Lord. Result of disobedience: loss of fellowship with God.

    2. Disobedience . . . doubt . . . dallying.

        a. Ps. 5:3; 63:1, 143:8, all reveal that David was faithful in meeting God daily and seeking guidance early.

        b. 11:2, shows David arising at eventide instead of early morning, walking on his balcony, and overwhelmed by the temptation of a beautiful woman. One who walks away from God always walks into trouble.

        c. David's sins:

            (1) Committed adultery—v.4.

            (2) Murder—v.15.

            (3) Hypocrisy—v.25.

    3. Price of sin:

        a. Child of adultery died—12:18.

        b. One son committed adultery—13:14.

        c. One son committed murder—13:28-29.

        d. Absalom rebelled and died—Chs. 14-18.

    4. The Bible says that man can only enjoy sin for a season, and Psalms 32, 38 and 51 all reveal David's distress and misery during this year's period out of fellowship with God.

C. Confession and complete forgiveness and restoration.

    1. David admitted his guilt—12:13; Ps. 51:3.

    2. Prayed for the joy of his salvation to be returned—Ps. 51:12.

    3. Realized he must have a clean heart in order to be used of God —Ps. 51:13.

    4. Key New Testament passage on confession: I John 1:9.

        a. It is our responsibility to confess.

        b. God is responsible for forgiveness and cleansing.

        c. God also blots out and forgets sins that are confessed— Ps. 103:12; Isa. 43:25.

III. RESULTS OF THE LIFE OF FAITH AND OBEDIENCE AS SET FORTH BY JOSHUA.

A. Reproach of Egypt was rolled away—Josh. 5:9. (Egypt represented nothing but a land of misery and hardship, one of burden and stress. What a great burden was lifted when God took away the guilt of 40 years of wandering in the wilderness and opened up the gates of Canaan.)

B. New food for a new place—5:11. The children of Israel began to enjoy the fruit of the land instead of the manna they had indulged in so long. They were finally possessing their promise of long ago—a land flowing with milk and honey. No one can ever possess wilderness; one only wanders in the wilderness.

C. God conquered as He had promised—6:20. The walls of Jericho fell flat and Israel took possession.

D. Each tribe received its own personal inheritance of promised land —Chapters 13-19; 21:43.

E. Joshua chose obedience and eternal reward—24:15.

F. Summary of God's goodness—24:13.

"And I have given you a land for which ye did not labour, and cities which ye built not, and ye dwell in them; of the vineyards and oliveyards which ye planted not do ye eat." Now, SERVE YE THE LORD!

IV. MODERN APPLICATION:

A. The blood of Jesus Christ rolls away the reproach of sin and all its defeats; we become perfectly clean (Eph. 1:7).

B. There is a new fruit of love, joy, peace, etc., to thrive upon when we abide in Christ and allow His Spirit to live out through us (Gal. 5:22-23).

C. God fights our battles while we rest in Him (Ps. 108:13).

D. Each believer has a particular place in the body of Christ and a service to perform (I Cor. 12:18-31).

E. When we choose for God, we lay up eternal rewards, and are said to be building upon gold, silver and precious stones (I Cor. 3:12, 14; Matt. 6:20).

F. Is there anything which the Lord will not supply if and when we need it (Matt. 6:31-33)?

V. SUMMARY:

The reality of Christian experience depends upon obedience to Christ. Confession of disobedience restores the sense of right standing, or joy of our salvation. In this, one must not wait for feelings of restoration, but simply believe it, just as the Bible teaches in Prov. 28:13, "He that covereth his sins shall not prosper; but whoso confesseth and forsaketh them shall have mercy."

LESSON PLAN

ELIJAH: THE POWER OF THE SPIRIT-LED MAN

LESSON SIX

STEP NINE

OBJECTIVE: To demonstrate and promote spiritually powerful service; to promote a spirit of fearlessness.

I. OPENING PRAYER.

II. MEMORY VERSE: I Kings 18:21.

Have each person share the verse with the person on his left. Have two students share what this verse has meant to them.

III. MOTIVATION: Two Christians have the same background. However, one is fearless in his witness and the other is not. Instead, he is a spiritual "Milquetoast." Why?

IV. BIBLE STUDY:

A. Explain the objective: "The aim of this lesson is to examine the powerful service of Elijah with the purpose of inspiring us to live the same way."

B. Note the question in parentheses in question 2.

C. Discuss similar experiences in our lives according to 3-5.

D. Even if we think God tells us to do something humiliating or ridiculous, why should we do it (Questions 6-7)?

E. For whom was Ahab not concerned (Question 10)?

F. Have group read aloud the verses, I Kings 18:36, 42.

G. Call attention to page 18 and have points read silently.

V. PARALLEL PASSAGES:

A. God's power to work miracles for those who fearlessly stand for Him:

438

David and Goliath—I Sam. 17:32-54.
Jehoshaphat—II Chron. 20:1-13, 20-25.
Hezekiah's prayer—II Kings 19:10-19, 35.
Elisha—II Kings 6:13-23.
Daniel—Dan. 6:16-24.
Esther—Esther 6:1-14; 7:10; 8:1-11.

B. Spirit-filled ministry—I Kings 17:1; Heb. 11:6; Lk. 1:17.

C. Instant obedience—Acts 8:26-39.

D. Answers to prayers—John 15:7; I John 3:22; 5:14-15.

VI. SUMMARY:

A. Why is it true to say, "In any size group of non-Christians you and God are a majority?"

B. Inquire if the group remembers the miracles involved in the lives of Daniel, Hezekiah, Esther and Elijah. Ask, "Has God changed, or is it we who have changed?"

VII. CLOSE IN PRAYER.

ELIJAH: THE POWER OF THE SPIRIT-LED MAN

LESSON SIX   **STEP NINE**

Review of the two chapters in I Kings (17-18):

I. THE IMPACT OF ELIJAH'S MINISTRY.

"To understand the history of Elijah, let us briefly consider the condition of affairs when Elijah made his appearance. Ahab had taken for wife, Jezebel, a Canaanite woman, daughter of Eth-baal. Of a weak and yielding character, he allowed Jezebel to establish the Phoenician worship on a grand scale—priests and prophets of Baal were appointed in crowds—the prophets of Jehovah were persecuted and slain, or only escaped by hiding in caves. It seemed as if the last remnants of true religion were about to perish. Jezebel had also induced Ahab to issue orders for the violent death of all the prophets of Jehovah who, since the expulsion of the Levites, had been the only firm support of the ancient religion.

"Elijah suddenly appeared before Ahab and proclaims the vengeance of Jehovah for the apostasy of the king. 'As the Lord God of Israel liveth, before whom I stand, whose constant servant I am, there shall not be dew nor rain these years, but according to my word.' This was probably the conclusion of a warning, given to the king, of the consequences of his iniquitous course.

"Elijah was named by God, and went to hide by a brook where he was supported by ravens until the brook dried up. Then another refuge was provided for him.

"He went to the city where he met the woman who was to sustain him, herself on the verge of starvation. Obedient to his request to prepare him food, she was rewarded by the miracle of the prolonging of the meal and oil, and the restoration of her son to life after his sudden death.

"For three years and six months, there had been no rain. At last the full horrors of famine, caused by the failure of the crops, descended on Samaria. Elijah, returning to Israel, found Ahab yet alive and unreformed, Jezebel still occupied with her idols, and the prophets of Baal still deceiving the people. Elijah first presented himself to Obadiah, the principal servant of Ahab and a true servant of God. He requested him to announce his return to Ahab; and Obadiah, his fears having been removed by the prophet, consented. The conversation between Ahab and Elijah, when they met soon after, began with the question of the king, 'Art thou he that troubleth Israel?' Elijah answered, unhesitatingly, 'I have not troubled Israel, but thou and thy father's house, in that ye have forsaken the commandments of the Lord, and thou hast followed Baalim.' He then challenged him to exercise his authority in summoning an assembly to Mount Carmel that the controversy between them might be decided.

"Whatever were his secret purposes, Ahab accepted this proposal, and the people also consented. Fire was the element over which Baal was supposed to preside. Elijah proposed (wishing to give them every advantage) that two bullocks be slain and laid each upon a separate altar, the one for Baal, the other for Jehovah; whichever should be consumed by fire would be He whom it was their duty to serve. There are few more sublime stories in history than this. On the one hand is the servant of Jehovah with calm dignity and the minutest regularity of procedure. On the other hand are the prophets of Baal with the wild din of their 'vain repetitions' and the maddened fury of their disappointed hopes . . . and the silent people surrounding all. These form a picture which brightens into fresh distinctness every time we consider it. The Baalites were allowed to make trial first. All day long these false prophets cried to Baal, leaped upon the altar, and mingled their blood with that of the sacrifice; but all was in vain, for at the time of the evening sacrifice the altar was still cold and the bullock lay stark thereon—'there was neither voice, nor any to answer, nor any that regarded.' Then Elijah repaired the broken altar of Jehovah, and having laid thereon his bullock and drenched both altar and sacrifice with water until the trench about it was filled, he prayed, 'Lord God of Abraham, Isaac, and of Israel, let it be known this day that thou art God in Israel, and that I am thy servant, and that I have done all these things at thy word.' The answer was all that could be desired for 'the fire of the Lord fell, and consumed the burnt sacrifice, and the wood and the stones, and the dust, and licked up the water that was in the trench.' The people acknowledged the presence of God, exclaiming with one voice, 'The Lord, he is God; the Lord, he is God.' By Elijah's direction the juggling priests were slain, and Ahab informed that he might take refreshment, for God would send the desired rain.

"Elijah prayed, God heard and answered; a little cloud arose and, diffusing itself gradually over the entire face of the heavens, emptied its refreshing waters upon the whole land of Israel. Ahab rode to Jezreel, a distance of at least sixteen miles, the prophet ran before the chariot, but going no farther than 'the entrance' of the city.

II. THE CHARACTER OF ELIJAH:

"Elijah's character is one of moral sublimity. His faith in God seemed to know no limit nor questions. His zeal for Jehovah was an all-absorbing motive of his life, so that he justly said, 'I have been very jealous for the Lord God of hosts.' No danger nor duty was too severe to shake his confidence—no labor too great for his Lord. His courage was undaunted, even in the presence of royalty or famine. His obedience was simple and as unquestioning as a child's. Tender of soul, he could sympathize with the widow when she lost her child, or weep over the sad condition of his deluded countrymen. Stern in principle, he was, in his opposition to sin, as fierce as the fire that more than once answered his command. He was by nature a recluse, only appearing before men to deliver his message from God, and enforce it by a miracle, and then disappearing from sight again."

Unger's Bible Dictionary, Moody Press, pp. 302-03, 305-06.

III. SUMMARY:

Aim to inspire the students and end in a good season of prayer. The object is to have them close the time with a sense of fearlessness, unlimited confidence in God and absolute desire to serve Him.

A dynamic Christian is one whose morale is high. He or she is abandoned to God enthusiastically, positively God-involved in everything done. The fearful Christian has his eyes upon self, situations, people; and sinks, as Peter when he took his eyes from Christ to look at the wind and waves. The Spirit-filled man or woman is the difference between the "Milquetoast" Christian and the Christian conqueror. Faith in the promises, abandonment to God, knowledge of the Bible and a good devotional life all enter in to produce a Christian leader.

Elijah was later guilty of turning his eyes upon self and the situation. Read I Kings 19. It merely demonstrates that failure can come on the heels of victory as we take our eyes from God and put them upon ourselves and situations.

The question of maintaining spiritual vigor is in order, i.e., "How may I maintain my enthusiasm?" The Ten Basic Steps answer it by the word, GROWTH:

A. Go to God in prayer.

B. Read your Bible every day.

C. Obey God.

D. Witness.

E. Treasury (our Stewardship).

F. Holy Spirit.

Mere zealous feelings are not what we propose, but faithfulness expressed in abandonment and service. The word GROWTH gives us handles for keeping God and Christ central in our lives, being controlled by the Holy Spirit so that Christ can live the CHRISTian life through us.

442

JEREMIAH: A WITNESS WHO STOOD ALONE

LESSON SEVEN   STEP NINE

OBJECTIVE: To produce faithfulness in the face of discouragements.

I. OPEN WITH PRAYER:

"Lord, we pray that You might teach us the joyous privilege of sharing Your sufferings in order that we might be conformed to Your
image."

II. MEMORY VERSE:

Jeremiah 23:29. Discuss the words *fire, hammer* and *rock* as they
apply to the word of God. Have one student give the verse from memory.

III. MOTIVATION:

The discipline of standing alone is found in the following reflection:

"I thank God for the bitter things; they've been a 'friend to grace';
They've driven me from the paths of ease to storm the secret place.
I thank Him for the friends who failed to fill my heart's deep need;
They've driven me to the Saviour's feet upon His love to feed.
I'm grateful too, through all life's way no one could satisfy,
And so I've found in God alone my rich, my full supply!"

—Author unknown

IV. BIBLE STUDY:

A. Questions 1-6, 10, 14, 15 with comments (Lesson Amplification).

B. Details of history concerning Jeremiah's position are included in
the Lesson Amplification.

V. PARALLEL PASSAGES: (See the Lesson Amplification.)

A. How to deal with inferiority complexes.

B. Dealing with discouragement and fearfulness.

443

C. The discipline and training of open and closed doors.

VI. SUMMARY:

    A. What are some practical lessons gained from standing alone with the Lord? Have several suggest applications to life.

    B. Leader may point out the following:

        1. God's faithfulness—Lamentations 3:22-23.

        2. His mercy overcoming our distress—Psalms 103:17-18.

        3. Grace during human weakness—II Corinthians 12:9-10.

        4. Confidence in God rather than men—Hebrews 10:35-36.

        5. Communion of knowing and loving the Lord—Jeremiah 24:7.

VII. CLOSE IN PRAYER.

JEREMIAH: A WITNESS WHO STOOD ALONE

LESSON SEVEN   STEP NINE

I.   QUESTIONS AND COMMENTS:

A. Question 1.

Use this for discussion of specific illustrations from the experiences of your group in dealing with people who need Christ. Have they felt incapable?

B. Question 2.

If we have hidden God's word in our hearts and are controlled by the Holy Spirit, then the Spirit will call to mind the words to answer every man in every situation (John 14:26; Col. 4:5-6).

C. Question 3.

Get a clear answer from the Scripture about denying our fear and counting on God to make us invincible.

1. Then ask, "This is unusual. Have any of us come to a place of exercising such deep trust?"

2. Ask a mature Christian: "Why not?" (One answer would be, because of compromise with sin, failing to have a soldier outlook, not enough prayer, Bible study, or claiming promises.)

Discuss, reviewing points from previous lessons, then conclude with: "By the time we end chapter twenty in Jeremiah we shall have some answers that have not been mentioned."

D. Question 4.

What was Paul's testimony regarding persecution (II Tim. 3:10-12)?

E. Question 5.

What is the promise of God for a life of service to the Lord (Luke 18:29-30)?

F. Question 6.

The point of this question is, was Jeremiah really fearless, after

445

all? His prayer indicates that though he was a strong witness, inner doubts and fears had to be dealt with in prayer. The reason he was fearless in public was that he dealt with and removed these fears by his prayer life (see Phil. 4:6-7; I Pet. 5:7). We should put the prophet's prayer methods into practice and then we can know his strength of character. Note his understanding of the total inadequacy of the flesh and the capability of God to meet the situation. Note how fully he unloads his burdens and hardships on his Lord. He is completely open in the presence of God, hiding nothing. He is abiding in Christ, letting Him bear every weight, just as the branch allows the trunk of the tree to support it in storm (John 15:4-5).

G. Question 10.

Have you had similar experiences? Has the Bible caused you to reprove unfruitful works in yourself and others (Eph. 5:8-11) when, in the flesh, you would have remained silent? Share these with one another in order to understand what the text means.

H. Question 14.

Here is the source of true peace and happiness, being true to God and conscience. Complete dedication to the Lord does not eliminate all our problems, but we have peace in the midst of problems. What mental and even physical state would Jeremiah have suffered if he had given in to pressures? How will you fare if you give in to the pressure? In Christ, we are designed for pressure, as a submarine. We are in the world, but not of it. Christianity is a way through trouble, not out of it. The three were delivered in the furnace, not out of it.

I. Question 15.

God has given us the "ministry of reconciliation" (II Cor. 5:18). It is our privilege to share the gospel frankly, as did Jeremiah. Ours, however, is a message of life and freedom, not one of condemnation and captivity.

II. DETAILS CONCERNING JEREMIAH'S POSITION:

In the thirteenth year of Josiah, King of Judah, Jeremiah began his ministry (626 B.C.). A three-way struggle for power between declining Assyria, rising Babylon and aspiring Egypt had begun. Jeremiah knew that God had selected Babylon as his potential instrument to thresh Judah for her sinfulness. He knew Egypt would fall before Babylon.

Early in his prophetic career two encouraging situations prevailed. They were:

1. In 621 B.C., Josiah began his religious reform involving the return to pure worship, removing impurity and idolatry. Nationwide revival was occurring, though it was not as yet a deep moving in the majority of hearts. Jeremiah preached genuine repentance as the only means of averting Babylonian destruction.

2. Other prophets were early contemporaries of Jeremiah with their ministries overlapping his: Zephaniah (640-621 B.C.); Habakkuk (625-608 B.C.) backed up his proclamation that Babylon would demolish Judah unless there was repentance; Nahum prophesied the fall of the Assyrian capital, Nineveh; while Obadiah prophesied judgment for Edom's attacks (before and during Jeremiah's ministry) on Judah.

In the forty years that followed, 626-586 B.C., Jeremiah ministered faithfully. Sixty years before, Isaiah had been God's man in Jerusalem. The Assyrian conqueror, Sennacherib, was turned from siege by the angel of the Lord, who struck down 185,000 in one night (II Kings 19:35). The year was 701 B.C., but now in 626-586 B.C. Jeremiah was God's man in this doomed city. Babylon loomed over it in judgment. By the time of Jeremiah, the Northern Kingdom had fallen to Assyria in two major deportations. Judah followed the same idolatrous, sinful path as Israel. In 597 B.C. Jehoiachin surrendered to Nebuchadnezzar with resistance. Many were removed to Babylon along with Jehoiachin. In 586 B.C. Nebuchadnezzar laid siege and decimated Jerusalem because Zedekiah, whom he had put in power after Jehoiachin, made league with the Egyptians to revolt. All but the poorest were removed as captives (Jer. 39:4-10).

The question arises, if Jeremiah began his ministry in national revival and auspicious circumstance, how could the country deteriorate so rapidly? This should be a lesson to us. Let us return to Josiah, the last spiritual king. In II Kings 23:28-30 and II Chronicles 35:20-27 we read of what may have been the cause. Josiah went to attack Pharaoh Necho contrary to God's will (II Chronicles 35:22) and lost his life. The war highway by which the kings of Egypt, Assyria and Babylon went to meet each other was east of Jordan. Pharaoh Necho was on his way north to meet Babylonian forces at Carchemish (605 B.C.). In this battle God gave Babylon ascendancy. Josiah was interfering with God's planning. He attempted to attack and defeat the Pharaoh himself. As a result of his death, the great revival crumbled without the backing of the throne. In fact, wicked kings followed who resisted Jeremiah's message. This is a lesson to us in the midst of spiritual success to remain in close fellowship with God. Jeremiah is called the weeping prophet for obvious reasons (Jer. 9:1, 10; 14:17). He was the model of a weeping soul-winner in Jeremiah 2-20. His messages were constantly unheeded, even after Jerusalem had fallen and he prophesied to the remnant. He called for repentance before the siege, surrender to Babylon during the siege, for the remnant to remain in Judah after the siege. All his advice went unheeded. Yet, he was faithful in proclaiming the truth.

The people not only made him weep because of their spiritual choices, but for their political choices, as well. The political problems were due to the fact that Egypt, since Carchemish, would not risk all-out war with Babylon. Instead, she offered military assistance for those who would revolt. Jeremiah fought the pro-Egyptian court element. Hananiah (Jer. 28:1-17) was a false prophet who proclaimed that revolt was under God's blessing. Jeremiah came to court wearing a yoke as a symbol of what would happen (Jer. 27:1-22). The co-conspirators were there with Zedekiah from Edom, Moab, Tyre and Zidon. Zedekiah respected Jeremiah but did not have the courage to obey him. How sad Jeremiah must have felt. Not only was Judah's sin bringing God's judgment from Babylon, but they were bringing on war intentionally! No wonder he wept.

Since the country did not repent, as Jeremiah requested, Babylon fell upon them in judgment. Let us look at the history of Israel from 626 B.C. to 586 B.C. more closely. Josiah was killed. JEHOAHAZ, his wicked son, followed in 608 B.C. Three months later, his brother, JEHOIAKIM, was put on the throne by the Pharaoh while Jehoahaz was carried to Egypt. In time, Jehoiakim died and his son JEHOIACHIN took the throne (597 B.C.). Three months later Nebuchadnezzar laid siege to Jerusalem, probably because Jehoiachin was pro-Egyptian. Jehoiachin surrendered and was carried with many others to Babylon. ZEDEKIAH was put on the throne by Nebuchadnezzar under oath to remain dutiful. Approximately eight years later he began to revolt, making league with Egypt (Ezekiel 17:12-20; Jeremiah 37:5-11; 34:21). The Egyptian army came to their rescue when Nebuchadnezzar attacked, but withdrew later (Jeremiah 37:4-8). As the Egyptian armies came, the siege was lifted temporarily, and Jeremiah tried to leave the doomed city, but was discovered at the gate and falsely accused of deserting to Babylonian forces and cast into a miry dungeon (Jeremiah 37:11-16). At this point the full siege began again and Jerusalem fell, Zedekiah was severely punished (Jeremiah 39:4-8) and the city was destroyed (586 B.C.). All but the poorest were deported and GEDALIAH was made governor over the remnant by Nebuchadnezzar. Jeremiah was given his freedom by the Babylonians (Jeremiah 40:1-6) and he chose to remain in Judah under Gedaliah.

Jeremiah was still faithful under new discouragements as this new chapter opened in his life. Ishmael murdered Gedaliah through Ammonite prompting (Jeremiah 40:13-14; 41:1ff) and terror struck Jewish hearts. They expected Babylonian reprisal (Jeremiah 41:17-19). They took their way toward Egypt but asked Jeremiah for his opinion. In Jeremiah 42:18-23 and 43:7 he pleaded with them to remain. Inasmuch as his former prophecies came to fruition, one would have believed the Jews would have accepted his word. However, they chose flight to Egypt. He followed. In faithfulness he suffered with them till, according to one tradition, five years later they stoned him to death in Tahpenes, Egypt. How much this parallels Christ who did not cling to equality with God, but humbled Himself, became a servant, and was obedient unto death (Philippians 2:5-11). This parallels Paul's experience in II Timothy 4:16-18. Jeremiah forms the prophetic bridge between the prophets of Judah and the prophets of the Exile (Daniel and Ezekiel). He inspired Daniel. Jeremiah prophesied the restoration after seventy years of Babylonian Captivity (Jer. 25:11, 29:10). Daniel, as he read it, began to pray (Dan. 9:2). As he prayed he received the famous vision of Seventy Weeks (Dan. 9:20-27) which describes Christ and the millenial restoration of Israel, one of the most famous prophecies of the whole Old Testament. We would be remiss if we did not point out that Jeremiah speaks of this restoration in chapters 30:3-10 and 23:6, but because Jeremiah stood for God when there was no other prophet, no encouragement and no fellowship, God used him to inspire Daniel, others and ourselves. You may be as inclined to despondency as Jeremiah (20:7-9, 14-18) as you look at circumstances. Instead of allowing this dubious luxury of despondency you should read and apply I Cor. 15:58; Matt. 14:30-31; and II Tim. 4:17-18. Put your attention on Christ and keep "abounding in the work of the Lord."

A. Historical narration, Jeremiah's experiences, Chs. 1, 25-26, 35-44, 52.

B. Jeremiah's prison experiences.

    1. Cast into the dungeon on treason charge, 37:11-16 (he is released later).

    2. Malchiah places him back in dungeon, 38:1-6.

    3. Ebed-melech releases him, 38:13-28.

    4. Babylonians give freedom, 40:1-4.

C. Jeremiah's persecution, 19:14-20:18; 32:2-3.

D. Israel's restoration with Christ, 23:6; 30:3-10.

III. OUTLINE OF JEREMIAH:

A. Prophet's call—1.

B. Prophecies concerning Judah—2-45.

    1. Six sermons during the reigns of Josiah to Jehoiakim—2-20 (repent or perish).

2. During the siege—21-29 (surrender to save life—Babylon will win).

3. A future and a hope—30-34.

4. The reign of Jehoiakim and Zedekiah—35-39.

5. After the Fall—40-45 (destruction if you go to Egypt).

C. Prophecies against nations—46-51.

D. Historical appendix on Jerusalem's fall and Jehoiachin in Babylon—52.

IV. PARALLEL PASSAGES:

A. Dealing with our inferiority complex.

1. Great men have cured this through their prayer life.

   a. Moses—Exodus 4:10-16.

   b. Isaiah—Isaiah 6:4-7.

   c. Solomon—I Kings 3:7-13.

   d. Jeremiah—Jeremiah 1:5-10.

2. We are formed by God and it is blasphemy to claim imperfect construction for the task for which we were created, Jeremiah 1:5-7.

B. Dealing with discouragement and fearfulness.

1. Results of failure in dealing with discouragement.

   a. Elijah lost his power (I Kings 19:9-18).

   b. Peter denied Christ with profanity because he habitually had his eyes on circumstances (John 21:3; Matt. 14:22-23; 27:69-75).

2. How to deal with discouragement and fearfulness.

   a. I Cor. 15:58—abounding in the work of the Lord, not stopping.

   b. I Peter 4:1-2, 19—suffering disregarded.

   c. Romans 8:28-29—knowing experiences are conforming us to Christ.

   d. I Cor. 10:13—it is our fault if we fall.

   e. II Tim. 1:7—God does not give us fear.

f. Romans 6:1-13; Ps. 37:1-5 —know, reckon, yield, obey; fret not, trust, delight, commit, rest, wait.

g. Matt. 11:25-26; Phil. 4:6-7; I Thess. 5:18; Heb. 13:15; Job 1:21; Acts 16:25-26 —praise, thank and bless God for the circumstances.

C. Open and closed doors.

1. Rev. 3:8, faithfulness and little strength mean NO MAN can close the door, only God.

2. I Cor. 16:8-9, adversaries are always at any open door.

3. II Cor. 2:12-17, in going through an open door we are caused to triumph *in* Christ (II Cor. 4:7-12), not our flesh.

V. SUMMARY:

One is faithful, like Jeremiah, not because he shall see a favorable resolution of the difficulties, but because "The love of Christ constraineth us . . ." (I Cor. 5:14). What he received was far more than success. Jeremiah had a personal relationship with God and, though he could become despondent, he conducted his life not by feelings but by the principle of obedience to the One whom he loved. Suffering adds deep quality to our lives:

"Millions of human beings but for suffering would never develop an atom of affection. The man who would spare due suffering is not wise. It is folly to conclude a thing ought not to be because it hurts. There are powers to be born, creations to be perfected, sinners to be redeemed through the ministry of pain, that could be born, perfected, redeemed, in no other way"—George Macdonald (Robertson, J. D., *Handbook of Preaching Resources from English Literature,* Macmillan, 1962, p. 222).

HIGHLIGHTS OF THE NEW TESTAMENT

STEP TEN

OBJECTIVE: To help the student gain insight into the basic teaching of the New Testament, with emphasis upon each individual book.

I.   OPENING PRAYER: Have one of the group open in prayer.

II. MEMORY VERSE:

Check one verse from each lesson. Emphasize John 20:31; Matthew 28:18-20; Acts 1:8.

III. MOTIVATION:

Have the group answer and discuss the following questions:

A. Why has God given us the New Testament?

B. What is the basic difference between the New and Old Testaments?

C. How do we know it is the word of God?

IV. BIBLE STUDY:

Ask the following questions, giving answers and teaching the lesson from the Lesson Amplification.

A. List on paper as many of the New Testament books as you can remember.

B. Put each of the books into a category or group—Gospels, Acts, Pauline Epistles, other Epistles, Revelation.

C. Discuss the purpose of each group and, briefly, the theme of each book.

V.   PARALLEL PASSAGES:

A. The benefit of the Old Testament for New Testament believers— II Tim. 3:16-17.

1. The benefit of Old Testament prophecy—I Pet. 1:10-12.

2. The benefit of Old Testament history—I Cor. 10:11.

3. The benefit of Old Testament worship—Heb. 8:5; 9:23-24.

4. The benefit of Old Testament law—Galatians 3:24-25.

B. The superiority of the New Testament.

1. The superiority of grace—John 1:17.

2. The superiority of revelation—Heb. 1:1-2.

3. The superiority of the New Covenant—Heb. 8:6.

VI. SUMMARY:

We might compare the New Testament to a bank building that has a tower on top which forecasts the weather. The building is complete with foundation, superstructure, internal furnishings, and weather forecaster. The four Gospels are the foundation of the New Testament. They present the person and work of Jesus Christ, the central figure of history. Christ and His work are the foundation upon which the rest of the New Testament rests. Without this we could not have the rest of the New Testament. The Book of Acts represents the superstructure of the building. It presents the historical framework of the New Testament Church. It relates the story of the spread of the gospel and the growth of the Church. The epistles represent the internal furnishings of the building. Here we see the heart of the Church. We see the life, the motivation and the spirit of the early Christians. We see what they believed and how this belief affected their lives. We see Christ alive in them. The Book of Revelations stands like a weather tower, forecasting what is to come—good and bad—and pointing to the climactic return and reign of the King of Kings and Lord of Lords.

VII. CLOSE IN PRAYER.

HIGHLIGHTS OF THE NEW TESTAMENT

SUMMARY LESSON   STEP TEN

I.   FORMATION OF THE NEW TESTAMENT CANON:

The word "canon" literally means "cane," or "rod of measurement."
In Christian use it came to mean the "written rule of faith," that is,
the list of original and authoritative books that composed God's inspired word. The "canonical" New Testament books are those which
came to be generally recognized by the churches as the genuine and
authentic writings of apostolic authority.

In the days of Christ there was in the literature of the Jewish nation
a group of writings called "The Scriptures," now called the "Old
Testament," which the people commonly regarded as having come
from God. They called it THE WORD OF GOD. Jesus himself so
recognized it. It was read publicly and taught regularly in their
synagogues. Christ read from this Scripture in Luke 4:16-19.

Even while certain New Testament apostles were still living, collec-
tions of their writings began to be made for the churches and placed
alongside the Old Testament as the inspired word of God.

A. Paul claimed inspiration—Galatians 1:11-12; I Thess. 2:13.

B. John claimed the same—Rev. 1:2.

C. Both Peter and Paul stated that their writing should be read and
   kept in the churches after they were gone—Col. 4:16; I Thess.
   5:27; II Pet. 1:15; 3:1-2.

D. Peter classes Paul's epistles with "other Scriptures"—II Pet.
   3:15-16.

The Council of Carthage, 397 A.D., gave its formal ratification to
the 27 books of the New Testament as we know them. It did not
make the New Testament Canon, but merely expressed what had
already become the unanimous judgment of the churches, and accepted for itself THE BOOK that was destined by God to become
man's most precious heritage. Concerning the attack of time which
some have declared to be a reason for doubting the authenticity of
our present Scripture, if God so protected the first inspiration and
declaration of his own precious thought and plan for man, can we

not also trust that He will take whatever precaution necessary in order that this word to men remain pure and untouched by human hands? Matthew 24:35—"My words shall not pass away!"

Some have taught that certain writings of men of God were selected and voted on as authentic Scripture and the books so chosen became the word of God. The true Scriptural authority is quite contrary to that view. Rather, the writings *already proved* to be the inspired word of God and accepted by the Church were bound into 27 books as stated above.

II. CONCERNING THE WRITTEN WORD—II Pet. 1:21, "For the prophecy came not in old time by the will of man; but holy men of God spake as they were moved (or carried along) by the Holy Ghost."

    A. Amazing composition—66 books, 40 authors, written over a 2000-year period in 3 languages on 3 continents; yet, it is one book with one theme, Jesus Christ.

    B. Miraculous preservation—most books are forgotten in fifty years; yet the New Testament has survived the tests of more than 19 centuries!

        1. The Bible has survived time and attack; Diocletion (303 A.D.) tried to burn all Bibles; 100 years later Constantine made Christianity the state religion.

        2. Today, Bibles are printed in over 1,000 languages.

        3. Voltaire predicted the end of Christianity; the house he lived in was later used to publish Bibles.

    C. Internal evidence reveals the authority of the Scriptures.

        1. Matthew 5:18—all the law will be fulfilled.

        2. Luke 24:25-27—Christ taught them about Himself, beginning at Moses and including the prophets and Psalms.

        3. John 16:13—the Holy Spirit will teach us things to come.

        4. II Pet. 1:16-21—the disciples were eye witnesses of the majesty of Christ, yet they proclaimed the written Word a more sure word of truth.

    D. Incarnate Word—Heb. 1:1-2; John 1:14.

III. THE FOUR GOSPELS—MATTHEW, MARK, LUKE AND JOHN: The four Gospels record the eternal being, human ancestry, birth, death, resurrection and ascension of Jesus the Christ, Son of God, and Son of Man. They reveal incidents of His life and incidents from

456

His words and works. Taken together, they set forth, not a biography, but a personality. These Gospels, though designedly incomplete as a story, are divinely perfect as a revelation from God, and as such their greatest importance is to set forth a person, Jesus Christ, that the world may trust in Him. These narratives can be compared to the evangelist, who seldom seeks to describe Christ, but rather to make Him known.

Although God Himself inspired every word, He permitted the personality of each human writer to be reflected. They told the same story, but each in his own way. That accounts for the variation in certain incidents recorded. There is no cause for the accusation of contradictions, but rather many writers giving testimony provide much more authority to what is written and prove beyond doubt that there was never any collusion among them.

Why written? The Gospel of Matthew, written by Matthew, a Jew of Galilee and a hated tax-collector under the Roman government, was written for the Jews to prove that Christ was their promised King and the fulfillment of Old Testament prophecies of a coming Messiah. *The Gospel of Mark,* written by John Mark (called either name), who was an associate of the apostles and mentioned in the writings of Paul and Luke. This Gospel sets forth Jesus as the mighty worker, records many miracles He performed and seems directed to the Gentile reader. The emphasis here is on what Christ did rather than the things he said, and shows Jesus as the great Conqueror, as well as Servant of the Lord. *The Gospel of Luke* depicts Him as the Son of Man as well as the divine Saviour. The style is orderly and classical, appealing to the Greek love for beauty, culture and philosophy. Luke, called the "beloved physician" by Paul, is the author. *The Gospel of John,* written by the most intimate personal friend of Jesus, the Apostle John, places great emphasis on Christ as the Son of God, co-equal with the Father and Holy Spirit as deity. The content is chiefly Jesus' discourses and conversations. The principal words are "believe" and "life".

IV.   THE ACTS OF THE APOSTLES:

This is one of the most important books in the whole New Testament, because God makes it clear to man how His work is to be carried forth in the power of the Holy Spirit. With the promised coming of Pentecost and the fulfillment of God's word to men, the apostles and every phase of their ministry are transformed by a new authority and boldness. As Christ had said, "And I will pray the Father, and he shall give you another Comforter, that he may abide with you forever" (John 14:16). Meek, fearful men, whose own handicaps often marred the work of God, are transformed into true disciples, full of wisdom and power given at the coming of the Holy Spirit.

In addition to the descent of the Holy Spirit at Pentecost (Acts 2), other major themes include the ascension and promised return of the Lord Jesus; Peter's use of the keys to the kingdom; the conversion and powerful ministry of the Apostle Paul; the beginnings of the true Church as the body of Christ and the calling out of a people for the Lord; the taking of the gospel to the Gentiles in the house of Cornelius and their reception of the Holy Spirit; and the conversion of thousands to Christ and their careful establishment in the faith—all accomplished in the power of the Spirit.

The writer does not name himself, but this book, along with the Gospel of Luke, is accepted as the work of Luke.

V.   THE EPISTLES OF PAUL:

Key thoughts of the Epistles.

A. *Romans*—the nature of Christ's work, the whole body of redemptive truth and full doctrines of grace.

B. *I and II Corinthians*—Christian conduct and answers to disorders in the churches; Paul's vindication of his apostleship.

C. *Galatians*—the complete gospel and salvation by grace alone, not dependent upon human obedience to the law. Pure grace!

D. *Ephesians*—the unity of the Church; the believer's position; the truth concerning the body of Christ and the walk according to one's position in Christ.

E. *Philippians*—a missionary epistle and Christian experience within the believer.

F. *Colossians*—deity of Jesus Christ and Paul's answer to two major problems: legalism and false mysticism.

G. *I and II Thessalonians*—the second coming of Christ and the confirmation of young disciples.

H. *I and II Timothy*—church order, sound faith and discipline; personal walk and testimony of the believer.

I. *Titus*—the divine order of the local churches, especially dealing with the churches of Crete.

J. *Philemon*—the conversion of a runaway slave, Onesimus, and the teaching of practical righteousness, brotherhood and love.

VI.   OTHER EPISTLES:

Key thoughts of these Epistles.

A. *Hebrews*—Christ, the Mediator of a New Covenant; contrasting the good things of Judaism and the better things of Christ, thus confirming Jewish Christians; a great book of doctrine.

458

B. *James*—the necessity of good works to show forth a living faith; some patterns of Christian conduct.

C. *I and II Peter*—the foundation of the Christian faith with emphasis on the atonement; encouragements for a persecuted Church; prediction of apostasy.

D. *I, II, III John*—love, caution against false teachers and those who reject John's authority.

E. *Jude*—imminent apostasy and how to detect and deal with it.

VII. *Revelation*—the final triumph of Jesus Christ as the complete fulfillment to every individual and nation; the close of the age and the coming glory of God in its full revelation; the seven churches, the tribulation, the second advent, the doom of those who reject Christ and the ultimate reward for those who do receive Him: heaven and eternity with God.

VIII. REVIEW OF THE TESTAMENTS:

A. OLD TESTAMENT: 39 books.

    1. 17 Historical books.

    2. 5 Poetical books.

    3. 17 Prophetic books.

B. NEW TESTAMENT: 27 books.

    1. 4 Gospels.

    2. Acts.

    3. 21 Epistles.

    4. Revelation.

Historical—Rise and fall of the Hebrew Nation.
Poetical—Literature of the Nation's Golden Age.
Prophetic—Literature of the Nation's Dark Days.
Gospels—The MAN whom the Nation produced.
Acts—His reign among all nations begins.
Epistles—His teaching and principles.
Revelation—Forecast of His universal dominion.

MATTHEW AND MARK

LESSON ONE   STEP TEN

OBJECTIVE: To let the student see how the life and teachings of Christ
relate to prophecy and the moral teachings of the Old
Testament. To show the basic distinction between Matthew's and Mark's presentation of the life of Christ. Example: Matthew contains what Jesus said and particularly
emphasizes prophecy; Mark contains what Jesus did and
emphasizes miracles. Each book presents a different facet
of the life of Jesus.

I.   OPEN WITH PRAYER: Lord Jesus, thank You for Yourself. May
we love You more as we see You revealed in these two Gospels.

II. MEMORY VERSE: Have each one quote the verse he has chosen.

III. MOTIVATION:

Distribute sheets of paper. Give the students an assignment to write
a portrait of Christ from their knowledge of Matthew's and Mark's
Gospels. Allow about five minutes. Have them give an example of
Christ as a servant and an example of Him performing a miracle
(from the book of Mark). Also have them give an example of Him
as the Messiah, pointing out a specific Scripture reference (from the
book of Matthew).

IV. BIBLE STUDY: (See the Lesson Amplification.)

A. Why are there four Gospels? What is the different emphasis of
each Gospel? Illustrate.

B. Why do we find prophecy relating to the life of Christ? Discuss
some of the fulfilled prophecy found in Matthew.

C. Why did Jesus perform miracles? Discuss some of the miracles
found in Mark.

D. What is the purpose of the Sermon on the Mount? To whom is it
addressed, and what is its application to us? In what way does the
Sermon on the Mount reflect Law? Grace?

V. PARALLEL PASSAGES:

Compare the content of Matthew and Mark.

A. Some parallel passages are very similar—Matthew 8:23-27; Mark 4:35-41.

B. In some parallel accounts there are marked differences—Matthew 20:29-34; Mark 10:46-52.

C. In some parallel accounts Matthew goes into greater detail, especially concerning what was said—Matthew 3:1-4:11; Mark 1:1-13.

D. Most of the material treated by Mark is found in Matthew. However there is much in Matthew, especially by way of discourse, that is not found in Mark.

VI. SUMMARY:

Three principal divisions offer a good summary for Matthew:

A. The manifestation to Israel and rejection of Jesus Christ, born King of the Jews.

B. The sacrifice and resurrection of Jesus Christ, the Son of Abraham.

C. The risen Lord in ministry to His own.

Mark manifests the servant character of the Incarnate Son. He emptied Himself of the "form of God" and being found in fashion as a man, gave Himself on the cross. The ministry of Jesus the Servant-Son is now exalted to all authority at the right hand of the Father, where He makes constant intercession for the saints.

The overcoming life of every Christian is always found in what *we are* because of what Christ *is*, rather than our own sinful natures manifesting what we were without Him. "We are more than conquerors through Him that loved us!"

VII. CLOSE IN PRAYER.

LESSON AMPLIFICATION

MATTHEW AND MARK

LESSON ONE   STEP TEN

I.   BIBLE STUDY:

    A. Why do we have four Gospels?

In the report of an accident, four witnesses give a clearer and more complete picture than one because of their different positions. So in the Gospels we have four accounts, each from a different point of view, but all in perfect harmony. They present a perfect portrait of Christ.

      1. Matthew—presents Jesus as King, the Jewish Messiah. It was written with the Jew in mind. Illustration: Matthew 5:17-19.

      2. Mark—presents Jesus as the great Conqueror—of storm, demons, disease and death. Also, He is presented as Servant, conquering, suffering and finally triumphant. Illustration: Mark 10:45 (Key Verse). Mark was probably written at Rome, and primarily for the Romans.

      3. Luke—presents Jesus as the perfect man, as well as the Divine Saviour. It was written with the Greek in mind. Illustration: Luke 2:11 and 19:10.

      4. John—presents Jesus as God. It was written with everyone in mind. Illustration: John 1:1-14.

"The one Jesus is King in Matthew, Servant in Mark, Man in Luke, and God in John. But not only so: for Matthew's King is also Servant, Man, and God; and Mark's Servant is also King, and Man, and God; Luke's Man is also King, and Servant, and God; and John's eternal Son is also King, and Servant, and Man" (Scofield, page 990).

    B. Prophecy.

This is the oral or written message of a prophet. The purpose of it is to demonstrate God's power and wisdom, and to disclose His plans and purposes for the future. As we see fulfilled prophecy throughout the book of Matthew, it strengthens our faith in Christ, the Messiah. Examples:

      1. That He was to be of David's family—Matthew 22:44; Isaiah 9:6-7.

2. That He would be born of a virgin—Matthew 1:23; Isaiah 7:14.

3. That He would be born in Bethlehem—Matthew 2:6; Micah 5:2.

4. That He would sojourn in Egypt—Matthew 2:15; Hosea 11:1.

5. That He would live in Galilee—Matthew 4:15; Isaiah 9:1-2.

6. That His coming would be announced by an Elijah-like herald —Matthew 3:1-11; Isaiah 40:3-5.

7. That His coming would be the occasion of weeping for Bethlehem's children—Matthew 2:18; Jer. 31:15.

8. That His mission would be to Gentiles—Matthew 12:18-21; Isaiah 42:1-4.

9. That His ministry would be one of healing—Matthew 8:17; Isaiah 53:4.

10. That He would teach by parables—Matthew 13:14; Isaiah 6:9-10.

11. That He would be disbelieved, hated and rejected by the rulers —Matthew 15:8-9; Isaiah 53:1.

12. That He would make a triumphal entry into Jerusalem—Matthew 21:5; Zechariah 9:9.

13. That He would be like a smitten shepherd—Matthew 26:31; Zechariah 13:7.

14. That He would be betrayed by a friend for 30 pieces of silver —Matthew 27:9-10; Psalm 41:9.

15. That He would be buried by a rich man—Matthew 27:57-60; Isaiah 53:9.

16. That His dying words would be foretold—Matthew 27:46; Psalm 22:1.

17. That He would rise the third day—Matthew 12:40; Psalm 16:10-11.

Here is an amazing thing: the complete story of Jesus' life, its main features, events and accompanying incidents, even to many of the minutest details, are plainly foretold in the Old Testament Scriptures. Is this not overwhelming evidence of the existence and working of a mind that transcends the human mind to a degree that awes us into wonderment and humility?

C. Miracles.

These are supernatural manifestations of divine power in the external world, in themselves special revelations of the presence and power of God. The purpose of miracles is to arrest the attention of men, and aid in winning their acceptance of revealed truth.

1. Examples:

    a. Bodily cures:

        (1) Peter's mother-in-law—Mark 1:29-31.

        (2) A leper—Mark 1:30-45.

        (3) A paralytic—Mark 2:3-12.

        (4) A man with a withered hand—Mark 3:1-16.

        (5) A deaf and dumb man—Mark 7:31-37.

        (6) A blind man—Mark 8:22-26.

        (7) A woman with a hemorrhage—Mark 5:25-34.

    b. Nature:

        (1) Tempest stilled—Mark 4:35-41.

        (2) 5,000 fed—Mark 6:34-44.

        (3) Jesus walked on the water—Mark 6:45-52.

        (4) 4,000 fed—Mark 8:1-9.

        (5) Fig tree withered—Mark 11:12-14.

    c. Cures of demoniacs:

        (1) A demoniac in the synagogue—Mark 1:21-28.

        (2) Gerasene demoniacs—Mark 5:1-21.

        (3) The Syro-phoenician's daughter—Mark 7:24-30.

        (4) The epileptic boy—Mark 9:14-29.

    d. Raised from the dead:

    Jairus' daughter—Mark 5:22-43.

The miracles were a part of God's way of authenticating Jesus' mission. Jesus said that if He had not done works that no other ever did, they would not have had sin (John 15:24), thus indicating that he regarded His miracles as proofs that He was from God. Christ's miracles were always:

    1. Profound.

    2. Helpful.

    3. Illustrative of an important truth.

    4. Majestic.

Legendary writings of miracles always exaggerate.

D. The Sermon on the Mount.

Since the Sermon on the Mount is part of this study, a brief word should be said about it. The Sermon on the Mount is probably the most well-known oration in history. Its influence has been simply immense. There are several views as to its purpose in the ministry of Jesus.

1. Some feel it was addressed to the Christian Church, giving it a standard righteousness. This could not be, however, because the Church, as we know it, did not come into existence until Pentecost, and great Church truths are not here presented. There is nothing about the Holy Spirit, our position in Christ, redemption through the blood of Christ in this sermon.

2. Some feel it was addressed to mankind in general.

3. Some feel it was meant for the kingdom which Jesus would establish. But verses 11 and 12 show that there is persecution and evil, which are not present in the kingdom. Besides, Jesus would have been giving a message which did not apply to his audience.

The best view is that Jesus was addressing the Jews of His time, showing them what would be required for entrance into His Kingdom, contrasting God's righteousness with that of the Scribes and Pharisees.

Does the Sermon on the Mount have a definite value for us today? As a way of salvation it is useless. No one has yet lived up to its standards. It is legal, not gracious in character, and is full of judgment and threats (Matthew 5:22-29). It offers no salvation to any man. The non-Christian world, which so admires this sermon, is condemned to hell by it. As a way of sanctification it is also useless. It gives a standard, but no enablement. The motive is fear, not love. It represents the law at its best, which condemns all and comforts none. The way of grace is not here. But as a revelation of the moral requirements of God, it is a mountain peak in Scripture. Here we see what a Holy God expects; here we see how shallow and external human morality is; here we see God at His purest. If we then take these requirements as a guide for personal living, put them in the context of grace, where all judgment, penalty and fear is removed, and supply the enablement of the Holy Spirit, we have made it of real value. The Sermon condemns the world, that the world might seek salvation in the cross. The Sermon guides the Christian, who, under the power of the Spirit alone, can approach its standards.

The background of the Sermon on the Mount is instructive. Jesus is addressing an audience living in the atmosphere of Pharisaism. The ruling religious party of Jesus' day had twisted the Old Testament Law from its true meaning with their perverted interpretations, as men also pervert the Bible today. They had made it an external, hypocritical, superficial thing. Jesus now comes to the fore to show what real godliness is.

The following suggestive outline presents the Sermon as a series of contrasts—Jesus contrasts His view of the Old Testament with that of the Pharisees:

1. SPIRITUAL REALITY TRANSCENDS MATERIAL SOCIETY—Matthew 5:1-16.

   Here Jesus gives the Beatitudes. The word "blessed" is the same as the word "happy." The truly satisfied person is described here. Blessedness is not here associated with material possessions or external righteousness, but with holy character, with real spirituality.

2. INTERNAL PURITY TRANSCENDS EXTERNAL PIETY—Matthew 5:17-6:18.

   Jesus now takes to task the Pharisees for their externalism. He shows that true belief is of the heart, and that God's laws reach inside a man.

3. GODLY FAITH TRANSCENDS WORLDLY ANXIETY —Matthew 6:19-34.

   The Pharisees were "lovers of money." Jesus rebukes materialism here, one of the great sins of America. Apply this to your financial problems.

4. BROTHERLY LOVE TRANSCENDS CRITICAL JUDGING—Matthew 7:1-12.

   Jesus sees through another sin of hypocrites—that of judging unjustly. He prescribes love (v. 12). Prayer produces this (v. 7-11).

5. TRUE DEVOTION TRANSCENDS FALSE DOCTRINE —Matthew 7:14-28.

   Jesus concludes by making a believer's responsibility clear and by warning of false prophets, whom we are to avoid.

LESSON PLAN

LUKE AND JOHN

LESSON TWO   STEP TEN

OBJECTIVE: To compare these two accounts of the life of Jesus so that
we might better understand His ministry and person.

I.   OPEN WITH PRAYER.

II. MEMORY VERSES:

Have three students quote the verses they chose to memorize and
give a reason for their particular choice.

III. MOTIVATION:

Have someone read aloud Luke 1:1-4; have another student read John
20:30-31. From these two passages what would you say is the specific
objective of each of these Gospels? Are there any similarities or contrasts?

IV. BIBLE STUDY:

A. The Gospel of Luke.

   1. The author.

   2. Early life of Christ.

   3. Genealogy of Christ.

B. The Gospel of John.

   1. Ask students to name as many miracles in the book of John as
      they can remember.

   2. Give the spiritual application demonstrated by Jesus' physical
      miracles.

   3. Ask students for their ideas and applications learned by the
      teaching of the miracles in light of John 20:30-31.

C. What is the meaning of "synoptic" as applied to the first three
   of the Gospels? Name the special emphasis of each Gospel and explain to students.

V. PARALLEL PASSAGES:

A. Discuss the different details concerning the Incarnation in the following passages:

1. Luke 1:26-38; 2:1-20.

2. John 6:1-14, 22-59.

B. Compare the treatments of the same miracle. Which author uses the miracle as a background for a discourse, rather than a self-evident event in the following passages:

1. Luke 9:10-17.

2. John 6:1-14; 22-59.

VI. SUMMARY:

A. Luke presents Christ as a perfect man. As a man He always reacted to every situation as a man should. In what way is Christ our example (I John 2:6)? In what way is He not our example?

B. Luke 20:19-26 is an illustration of His conduct under stress. How did He react? How do we react under stress? Is it possible to experience the same victory under fire that Jesus had? How?

C. The Lord Jesus was continually dependent on the Father and absolutely obedient (John 14:10). He was a perfect man walking in the power of the Holy Spirit throughout his life on earth. We, in turn, are dependent on the Son.

VII. CLOSE IN PRAYER.

LUKE AND JOHN

I.   THE GOSPEL OF LUKE:

A. About the author.

1. Although a physician, Luke was primarily a missionary and in this case an eyewitness with a good understanding of the Gospel of Christ (Luke 1:1-4).

2. Occasion of the Gospel—Luke wrote to Theophilus to assure him that the things which he had heard about Jesus Christ were factual (Luke 1:4).

3. What is one way of effective witnessing in light of Luke's example? God's best ways to carry out His work often take time and organization. How does this apply to the Gospel Luke wrote?

B. Early life of Christ.

The first thirty years of Jesus' life are often termed "the silent years". Scripture gives few details of these years, but the growth and development of the character of Christ are extremely important.

1. Have students read Luke 2:39-52 and name some qualities of Christ's early life as recorded in this passage.

2. Leader may present the following suggestions:

   a. Strong in spirit, filled with wisdom—2:40.

   b. Independent and desirous of learning.

   c. Able to talk and learn from doctors at only twelve years of age!—2:46.

   d. Astounded men by his understanding—2:47.

   e. Primarily concerned with the business of the Father, even more so than that of home and family—2:49.

   f. Obedient to parents, however—2:51.

   g. Pleased other men while honoring God—2:52.

C. Other areas of importance in the Gospel of Luke.

1. The genealogy of Christ traced through the line of Mary.

   a. Many Bible readers tend to "skip over" the passages listing the various generations recorded in Scripture, failing to realize that these passages prove the identity of Jesus Christ as the Messiah, and the fulfillment of the promises of God's word to the nation Israel.

b. In the past God chose one particular family, that of Abraham (and later the family of David within Abraham's line), to be the vehicle through which His Son would come into the world. The Hebrew nation was founded and protected of God through the ages in order to preserve the line of descent of His Son to come.

c. Matthew goes back to Abraham in its record of the genealogy; Luke goes back to Adam; neither contradicts the other but traces the line of Christ through two different lines—one is Joseph's, the other Mary's.

2. What is significant about Christ's triumphal entry into Jerusalem as set forth in Luke 19:37-44?

II. THE GOSPEL OF JOHN:

A. The significance of the miracles of Jesus.

1. John 2:1-11—the turning of the water into wine. Jesus commanded the servants to fill the waterpots (picture of thirsty human heart, empty without Christ, needing His fullness) and the servants obeyed His word. Salvation is always by the agency of the word of God. John 3:5—the water of the word of God is the means to salvation (I Peter 1:23). What Christ provided was better than a rich man's best (John 2:10).

2. John 4:46-54—the healing of the nobleman's son. The nobleman heard of Jesus; hearing is not enough for salvation. The nobleman besought him; that wasn't adequate. The man believed the word that Jesus had spoken and his son was healed. This is also a picture of our salvation—believing the word of God.

3. John 5:1-9—the healing of the sick man at the pool. This man, sick for thirty-eight years, was completely unable to help himself. He was unable to climb into the pool—a picture of man's inability to help himself or do anything to deserve salvation. The Lord chose this man and healed him. Salvation is obtained by grace!

4. John 6:1-14—the feeding of the five thousand. Whatever one may have of his own, whether five loaves and two fishes, or position, popularity and wealth, no one but Jesus Christ can ever supply the present need of men. Jesus took what the boy had and multiplied it into more than necessary for the present need. Christ broke the loaves to provide physical sustenance; he broke his own body on the cross to provide an eternal redemption for the whole human race. Spiritual feeding at the cross is the only food which eternally satisfies and presently blesses.

5. John 9:1-7, 25—healing of the blind man. To be blind from birth indicates total darkness. This is evident in the unbeliever so far as spiritual things are concerned; he is in total spiritual darkness, unable to see or react spiritually. After receiving Christ, one of the first miracles is that one begins to see spiritual truth, understand the Bible and take note of the guidance of the Lord in one's life. Spiritual light follows new birth, just as seeing physical light follows normal birth into this life.

6. John 11:38-44—raising Lazarus from the dead. Before one is born into the family of God and has experienced regeneration, he is said to be spiritually dead and without hope in this world or in the next. Christ's raising of Lazarus is a complete likeness of His miraculous work in the human heart when He brings a person out of spiritual death into spiritual life.

B. Overall key verse—John 20:31, "these are written that ye might believe that Jesus is the Christ . . . and that believing . . . have life through his name."

The first three Gospels are called the Synoptic Gospels. The word "synoptic" implies that the three writers look at the life of Christ from a similar point of view. We find that about one half of Matthew's material is found in Mark also. About one third of Luke is found in a similar form in Mark. All but fifty-five verses of Mark can be found in Matthew or Luke. About one fourth of Matthew's and Luke's Gospels is similar material that is not found in Mark. Each gives a sort of running account of the life and teaching of Christ but with a different slant.

Matthew was an eyewitness of many things in his Gospel. Mark, it is believed, wrote with the help of his eyewitness companion, Peter. Luke, a historian of first caliber, admittedly used various first-hand source material (Luke 1:1-4). The Fourth Gospel is radically different from the other three. It, too, is the testimony of an eyewitness (John 21:24). But it is not a rapid moving account of Christ's life and teachings. This had already been provided in the other three which were written a number of years before. John's account is more reflective, more philosophical, more subjective, more interpretative.

He largely brings out new material omitted by the other three writers. He takes a few events and enlarges and amplifies the treatment of them. The miracles he incorporates are chosen with special purpose (John 20:30-31).

III. SPECIAL EMPHASES OF LUKE AND JOHN:

A. LUKE.

The special emphasis of Luke is the humanity of Jesus. Like the other Gospel writers, he represents Jesus as the Son of God, but he features Jesus' sympathy for the weak, the suffering and the outcast.

Luke wrote to a particular person, Theophilus, probably a Greek. He therefore appeals to the thoughtful, cultured, philosophic Greek mind in an orderly and classical story which has been called, "the most beautiful book ever written." He depicts the beauty and perfection of the life of Jesus: the ideal, universal man. Luke is also the author of the Book of Acts.

Luke is called by Paul, "the beloved physician" (Col. 4:14) and "my fellow-labourer" (Philemon 24—"Lucas"). In the book of Acts he is seen as a frequent companion of Paul. He was with Paul just before Paul's death (II Tim. 4:11).

B. JOHN.

The special emphasis in John is the deity of Christ. The emphasis is on belief and faith. However, there is the strong counter theme of willful rejection and unbelief.

John himself was one of the inner circle of the disciples—Peter, James and John.

He speaks of himself as the "disciple whom Jesus loved" (John 13:23; 19:26; 20:2; 21:7, 20).

In John, many of the expressions used by Jesus about Himself can be predicated only by His deity:

"I am the truth"—John 14:6.

"I am the way"—John 14:6.

"I am the door; by me if any man enter in he shall be saved, and shall go in and out, and shall find pasture"—John 10:9.

"No man cometh unto the Father but by me"—John 14:6.

"I am the bread of life"—John 6:35,48.

"I am the life"—John 14:6; 11:25.

"I am the resurrection"—John 11:25.

"And whosoever liveth and believeth in me shall never die"—John 11:26a.

" I am the Messiah"—John 4:25-26.

"Before Abraham was, I am"—John 8:58.

". . . glorify thou me . . . with the glory which I had with thee before the world was"—John 17:5.

"He that hath seen me hath seen the Father "—John 14:9.

"I and my Father are one"—John 10:30.

THE ACTS OF THE APOSTLES

LESSON THREE   STEP TEN

OBJECTIVE: To trace the lives of Peter and Paul and their respective ministries as seen in the early New Testament Church.

I.   OPEN WITH PRAYER: "Lord, we thank You for Your chosen men in ages past, and we pray that You will teach us obedience and faithfulness to Your kingdom just as they learned it from You."

II. MEMORY VERSES:

Have a student quote Acts 1:8 and state its importance to his personal life and to the life of every believer. Ask for volunteers to share any other verses which they have memorized.

III. MOTIVATION:

Action is important in our daily life. Have students think of several examples of activities which would fit under the following three categories—give verses to back up examples suggested.

A. Acts for Christ.

   1. Being His ambassadors—II Cor. 5:20.

   2. Being obedient—Genesis 12:1,4.

B. Acts for others.

   1. Be an example to believers—II Tim. 4:12.

   2. Maintain a loving, long-suffering attitude toward other believers —Col. 3:12-14.

C. Acts for self.

   1. Profitable study—I Tim. 2:15.

   2. Proper attitude toward self—Romans 12:3.

IV. BIBLE STUDY:

A. Introduction to the Book of Acts.

B. Central personalities and their effective ministries.

C. The early Church under the power of the Spirit.

V. PARALLEL PASSAGES:

A. The work of the Holy Spirit.

    1. Before conversion: conviction—John 16:7-11.

    2. At conversion:

        a. Seals—Eph. 1:13.

        b. Baptizes—I Cor. 12:13.

        c. Regenerates—Titus 3:5.

        d. Indwells—I Cor. 3:16-17.

        e. Fills—Eph. 5:18. (Commanded; filling takes understanding and appropriation by faith; any known sin cancels filling.)

    3. Following conversion:

        a. Filling should occur—Eph. 5:18.

        b. Guides into all truth—John 16:13.

        c. Shows us things to come—John 16:13.

        d. Glorifies Christ—John 16:14.

B. Paul's ministry.

    1. Paul's motivation—Phil. 3:7-14.

    2. Paul's obligation—Romans 1:14-17.

    3. Paul's message—I Cor. 1:18-25.

    4. Paul's attitude—I Thess. 2:3-12; Acts 20:24.

    5. God's results—I Thess. 1:5-10.

        a. Paul's prayer in his early ministry—Acts 22:10.

        b. Assurance at end of life—II Tim. 4:7-8.

VI. SUMMARY:

The early Church was commissioned of Christ and empowered by the Spirit to take the message of Christ to every creature. In its generation the known world heard the claims of Christ. The commission has not changed. But only as the Church of today avails itself of the power of the Holy Spirit can we reach our entire generation with the message of life.

VII. CLOSE IN PRAYER of thanksgiving for the privilege of sharing in bringing others to the Lord.

THE ACTS OF THE APOSTLES

LESSON THREE   **STEP TEN**

INTRODUCTION:

A. Who is the author of the Book of Acts? (Luke 1:1-4; Acts 1:1-2.) Dr. F. F. Bruce—"The Book of Acts is the sequel to the Third Gospel and is written by the same author, Luke, the beloved physician, and companion of the Apostle Paul. The external evidence of various writers from the second century onward is unanimous and adequate on this point, and the internal evidence of the style, outlook and subject matter of the two books is equally satisfactory."

In much of the latter part of the book, Luke uses the personal pronoun *we,* indicating that he traveled with Paul and was an eyewitness of much that is recorded in Acts. He quite possibly kept a log or diary from which he could draw in writing this book.

B. Why is Acts 1:8 considered the key verse of the book?

The Book of Acts is a record of the early Church in action, getting the gospel to the Roman world. Acts 1:8 is a prophetic outline of what happens in the book in the spreading of the gospel. The gospel was first preached to the Jews in Jerusalem (Acts 2:6). Next, the gospel spread throughout the regions of Judea and Samaria (Acts 8:1-4). The Samaritans were a kind of half-breed Jew and Gentile. Their reception of the gospel was one step toward Gentile evangelism (Acts 8:14). By a vision to Peter, God arranged circumstances and saw to it that the gospel was taken to the Gentiles (Acts 10; especially verse 45). As the book continues, Gentile acceptance of the truth continues and Jewish rejection becomes more and more pronounced (Acts 13:46; 18:6; 28:25-29). What is our Jerusalem? Judea? Samaria? Uttermost part of the world? What are we doing about it?

II. CENTRAL PERSONALITIES:

A. Who are the two main characters of the book? Contrast their ministries.

1. In the first part of the book Peter is the prominent personage. Jerusalem is the center of his activities and his ministry is primarily to Jews.

His first major sermon—Acts 2:14-36.

a. What are the key thoughts (2:21, 36, 38, 41, 42)?

b. Name the characteristics of Peter (boldness, preparedness).

2. In the last part of the book Paul is prominent and his ministry is increasingly to the Gentiles (Gal. 2-7).

a. On his first major missionary journey, where did he preach (Acts 13:5)?

b. What significance does this have for us? (We should share Christ in key centers of learning as well as other places.)

B. What kind of man was Paul before he was converted (see question three)?

Gal. 1:13-14; Phil. 3:4-6. No man is too sinful to be saved— I Tim. 1:15-16.

C. What was the key to Paul's effective ministry?

1. Instantaneous obedience—Acts 9:6; 26:19.

2. Filling of the Spirit—Acts 13:4. (See parallel passages in Lesson Plan. Compare our lives to Paul's at various points.)

III. THE EARLY CHURCH, EMPOWERED BY THE HOLY SPIRIT:

A. What are some of the ways in which the Holy Spirit was the dynamic of the early church?

1. He gave power in witnessing—Acts 1:8.

2. He gave boldness in witnessing—Acts 4:31.

3. He gave power to speak other languages—Acts 2:4-8; 10:46; 19:6.

4. He gave peace and confidence in the face of danger and death— Acts 7:54-60.

5. He gave guidance to the early Church—Acts 10:19-20; 13:2-4; 16:6; 20:22-23.

6. He gave power to prophesy—Acts 11:28; 19:6; 21:10-13.

7. He gave insight into the motives of others—Acts 13:9.

8. He gave wisdom—Acts 15:28.

B. Why does the church today lack dynamic?

The early Church was enabled for tasks by the filling of the Holy Spirit (Acts 2:4; 4:8, 31; 6:3, 5, 8; 7:55; 9:17; 11:24; 13:9, 52). Today the Church needs the message of the filling of the Holy

Spirit. We cannot expect to do God's work by our own power. We need to be filled with the Holy Spirit. We need to know how to share with others the means of being filled with the Holy Spirit (John 14:16-17; 16:7-15).

C. What was Paul's strategy of evangelism?

1. He went to areas which had not heard the gospel before he arrived—Romans 15:20.

2. He concentrated on centers of culture, commerce and influ-ence. Examples: Antioch, Athens, Corinth, Ephesus, Jerusalem, Rome.

3. When he came to a city, he first went to the Jews, if possible. He built on their religious foundation of the Old Testament, showing that Jesus of Nazareth was the Messiah. He then pre-sented the message to the Gentiles (Acts 13:19-49).

4. When he went to Gentiles alone, he appealed to their innate knowledge of God, the creator and sustainer of the world. He, of course, explained Christ's relationship to making this true God known to man (Acts 17:22-34).

5. He built up the converts, establishing local organized groups of believers (Acts 14:21-23; 16:5).

6. He trained the believers to be witnesses for Christ (Acts 19:8-10; I Thess. 1:6-8).

D. What might be a good strategy for evangelism today?

I Peter 3:15; II Timothy 2:2,15; I Thessalonians 5:19. Let group use its imagination. What of Paul's strategy should we em-ploy? Should we wait for people to come to church meetings in order to tell them about Christ? Discuss failure in the Church to-day.

E. Who in the early Church proclaimed the gospel to the lost?

Everyone—Acts 8:1,4. It is not the duty of the pastors alone to win the lost. They are to build up the Christians so that they can evangelize as well (Eph. 4:11-13).

ROMANS, I AND II CORINTHIANS, GALATIANS

LESSON FOUR   **STEP TEN**

OBJECTIVE: To understand what the gospel is and how it is personally appropriated. To show the need of sharing the good news with others. (Note—this is a good evangelistic Bible Study.)

I.   OPEN WITH PRAYER.

II.   MEMORY VERSE: Have a student quote the memory verse.

III.   MOTIVATION:

Explain that word "gospel" means good news. Have students write on a sheet of paper four reasons why they feel that the Christian message is good news. Have each person read his answers.

IV.   BIBLE STUDY:

A. Romans.

B. I Corinthians.

C. II Corinthians.

D. Galatians.

V.   PARALLEL PASSAGES:

A. The source of the gospel—Gal. 1:11-12.

B. The basic content of the gospel—I Cor. 15:1-8.

C. Paul's attitude toward those who would proclaim a perverted gospel—Gal. 1:6-9.

D. Various reactions to the gospel—I Cor. 1:17-25.

E. The reason why people are blind to the gospel—II Cor. 4:3-4.

F. Paul's attitude toward proclaiming the gospel to others—Romans 1:14-17.

VI. SUMMARY:

Conclude with practical application.

A. The gospel is such good news that the non-Christian cannot afford rejection. It would be like a man with a fatal disease rejecting the only cure.

B. The Christian who has accepted it (the gospel) should not be ashamed of it. Failure to share it would be like knowing the cure for a fatal disease and refusing to share it with those whom you know are dying of the disease.

VII. CLOSE IN PRAYER.

ROMANS, I AND II CORINTHIANS, GALATIANS

LESSON FOUR   STEP TEN

I.   DEFINITIONS OF MAJOR THEMES:

A. Sin

With references from Romans, explain the condition of man before a Holy God (Romans 2:9-12; 3:23; 6:23). Sin (summary). Sin originated with Satan (Isa. 14:12-14); entered the world through Adam (Romans 5:12); was and is universal, Christ alone excepted (Romans 3:23); incurs the penalties of spiritual and physical death (Genesis 2:17; 3:19; Romans 6:23); and has no remedy but the sacrificial death of Christ (Heb. 9:26; Acts 4:12) accepted by faith (Acts 13:38-39). Sin may be summarized as: the violation of or lack of obedience to the revealed will of God; absence of righteousness; or a natural attitude of opposition or indifference toward God.

B. Reconciliation

What has God done for us to bring us into a right relationship with Himself?

1. Redeemed us—Romans 3:24; 5:6-8; Gal. 3:13.

Redemption means "to deliver by paying a price." The underlying thought is to be purchased out of a slave market, in this case, the slavery of sin. Only a free man can purchase the slave's freedom.

2. Justified us—Romans 3:26; 4:25-5:2; Gal. 2:16.

To be justified is the judicial act of God whereby He justly declares righteous one who believes on Jesus Christ. Literally, God imputes or credits to our account His righteousness, which is in reality the only righteousness.

Herein lies the gospel! God redeems us, justifies us and gives us His righteousness. He does it all because of His grace. This is certainly good news!

What has God done for us to give us the power to live for Him? He has given us the Holy Spirit—Romans 8:11, 15; 6:11-13; Gal. 5:16, 22-23.

C. Themes of Galatians and Corinthians

1. What is the main theme of Galatians? Illustrate.

The theme is that the gospel of God comes by grace and is sustained by grace. Law has nothing to do with it. We can do nothing to receive it or to keep it. All is of God and of His grace. Example: Gal. 3:1-3, 10-11; 4:9-10; 5:1-6.

2. What is the main theme of I Corinthians? Illustrate.

The theme is Christian conduct—I Cor. 10:13,31-33.

a. Morality—6:18-20.

b. Marriage—7:1-40.

c. Questionable practices—8:1-13.

d. Divisions among the Christians—1:10-17.

Conduct had to be stressed because these Christians were carnal (Christians who were walking "after the flesh"), thus remaining babes in Christ (I Cor. 3:1-4).

3. What is the main theme of II Corinthians? Illustrate.

The theme is the vindication of Paul's apostleship (II Cor. 4:1-7).

II. ROMANS:

The theme of Romans is the "gospel." What is the gospel? An outline of the book of Romans shows all that the gospel of Jesus Christ includes.

Chaps. 1-5	Provisions for forgiveness of sin.
Chaps. 6-8	Power to live a victorious life.
Chaps. 9-11	Program for the ages.
Chaps. 12-16	Precepts for Christian living.

Many think the gospel refers only to the fact that a Christian is saved from hell. But as this outline shows us, it is much more inclusive. The gospel guarantees that we shall go to heaven; but, because of our position in Christ (Chap. 6) and the Holy Spirit in our hearts (Chap. 8), it also guarantees we can live the life God wants us to live here on earth. Furthermore, the gospel includes the future salvation of the Jewish nation (Chaps. 9-11); and finally, it gives us practical instructions on how to live (Chaps. 12-16). As Paul contemplated all the gospel, he broke into an exclamation of praise: "O the depth of the riches both of the wisdom and knowledge of God! How unsearchable are his judgments, and his ways past finding out!" (11:33). The gospel of Jesus Christ is God's answer to every human dilemma. There is not one problem it will not solve, no need it cannot satisfy, no question it cannot answer. It is no wonder Paul was not ashamed of it and felt a debtor to preach it to every creature (1:14-16).

III. I CORINTHIANS:

Outline of I Corinthians:

A. Problem of their divisions (Chaps. 1:10-4:21).

B. Problem of their immorality (Chaps. 5-7).

C. Problem of food offered to idols (Chaps. 8:1-11:1).

D. Problem of public worship (Chaps. 11:2-14:40).

E. Doctrine of the resurrection (Chap. 15).

F. Practical concern of Paul (Chap. 16).

IV. II CORINTHIANS:

Outline of II Corinthians:

A. Ministry—Paul's defense (Chaps. 1:1-7:16).

B. Money—for the Christians at Jerusalem (Chaps. 8:1-9:15).

C. Ministry—Paul's defense (Chaps. 10:1-13:14).

V. GALATIANS:

The theme of Galatians is likewise the gospel, but more specifically Paul emphasizes here that it is a gospel of grace. What is grace? Grace is the unmerited love of God shown toward sinful men. Grace means that God has *given* us the gospel without any strings attached; we can do nothing to *earn* it. The gospel is a gift. To try to earn it is to deny God's love and generosity. If we cannot earn it, what then is our responsibility? We must simply receive it by faith, just as any gift is received. Faith is the only channel through which grace can operate. (See Ephesians 2:8-10.) The Galatians made the mistake of trying to impose the law of Moses on the gospel. They said it was necessary to do some work, such as circumcision, to be saved. Many Christians realize that they cannot do anything but receive God's gift to be saved, but they make the mistake of trying to earn their way in the Christian life. In Galatians 3:1-5, Paul also speaks against this heresy. This transforms Christian living from moralistic striving in our own effort, to an attitude of rest and faith, where we let Christ live in us and through us. Galatians 2:20 and 5:16 are two of the key passages of the book. These passages teach us that our only responsibility is to trust Jesus Christ to live through us by the Holy Spirit—"not I, but Christ liveth in me." Here is the secret to victory. Give up your own struggling and striving—your own efforts to please God—and by faith trust Him to live through you. "The life which I now live in the flesh I live by . . . faith . . ." (Gal. 2:20).

Outline of Galatians:

A. The gospel of grace—Paul's apostolic authority (Chaps. 1-2).

B. The gospel of grace—contrasted with the law (Chaps. 3-4).

C. The gospel of grace—results in practical living (Chaps. 5-6).

VI. SUMMARY:

A. Receiving the gospel:

It is not man's wisdom, religion, or good works that bring him salvation; it is the simple gospel of Christ received by faith (Romans 1:16).

B. Sharing the gospel with others:

Compare our lives with the three "I am's" of Paul:

1. "I am a debtor" (Romans 1:14). We need to realize the obligation that we have toward all men to tell them the good news. We gain a sense of obligation as we study the Bible and see man's desperate need and God's provision for this need through Jesus Christ.

2. "I am ready" (Romans 1:15). We need to be prepared to share the gospel with others. We need to know how to explain the gospel in terms that people can understand and respond to (Four laws).

3. "I am not ashamed" (Romans 1:16). If we are ashamed of the gospel of Christ, this means that we need the filling of the Holy Spirit to give us boldness (Acts 4:31).

THE PRISON, THESSALONIAN AND PASTORAL EPISTLES

LESSON FIVE   STEP TEN

OBJECTIVE: To present a brief survey of the Prison, Thessalonian and
Pastoral Epistles; particularly to note how they reflect the
character of Paul.

I.   OPEN WITH PRAYER: "Lord, teach us to be like Thy servant Paul."

II. MEMORY VERSE: Have each one quote the verse he has chosen.

III. MOTIVATION: See the illustration, "vacant pulpit," in the Lesson
Amplification.

IV. BIBLE STUDY:

   A. The prayer life of Paul as revealed in Ephesians.

      1. What were some of the things Paul prayed for in Eph. 1:15-21;
      3:13-21?

      2. Why did he pray for these things? Why does he not pray for
      material things?

   B. The prison life of Paul as revealed in Philippians.

      1. How would you describe Paul's attitude toward his affliction in
      1:12-21? What seems to be his main concern?

      2. List all the things which you think would ordinarily discourage
      one from witnessing when in a situation like that in which Paul
      was. Why, then, did he still witness?

   C. The personal life of Paul as revealed in Thessalonians.

      1. Note the astounding witness of the Thessalonians in I Thess.
      1:8-9. What do you see in the first chapter which would indi-
      cate the reason for this? (Leader should note vs. 5-6.) How
      much does the example of a soul winner influence the lives of
      his converts?

      2. In I Thess. 2:1-10, list all the strengths of Paul's ministry.

D. The pastor's life of Paul as revealed in the Pastoral Epistles.

   1. In I Timothy 6:6-10, find all the reasons you can why Paul should say that having food and clothing alone is sufficient. Is it wrong to have more than just the basic necessities? Why does Paul have so much to say about money in this chapter? What are some ways in which we are tempted by materialism today?

   2. According to Titus 2:7,14; 3:8,14, what was one thing Paul emphasized among his converts?

   Why? How would you relate Titus 3:5 to Titus 3:8?

V. PARALLEL PASSAGES:

A. Christ's teaching on prayer—Luke 11:11-13; John 15:7; 16:23-24.

B. Christ's teaching on suffering for the Gospel's sake—Matthew 5:11-12.

C. Christ's teaching on personal example—5:13-48.

D. Christ's teaching on money—Matthew 6:19-34.

E. Christ's teaching on good works—Matthew 5:16.

VI. SUMMARY:

Christ is our supreme example (I John 2:6), but lest we weary in well-doing, the Scriptures have given us the example of Paul, a man of the same passions as ours. He is proof that Christianity works. All we need is one case that works to refute the claims of those who would reject Christianity because of hypocrites in the church. Furthermore, the man with whom it worked was a murderer of Christians and "chief of sinners" (I Tim. 1:15). Observe Paul, and follow his example.

VII. CLOSE IN PRAYER.

THE PRISON, THESSALONIAN AND PASTORAL EPISTLES

LESSON FIVE   STEP TEN

INTRODUCTION:

A church was in need of a pastor. One of the elders was interested in knowing just what kind of a minister they desired. He therefore wrote the following letter, as if he had received it from the applicant and read the letter before the pulpit committee.

"Gentlemen: Understanding that your pulpit is vacant, I should like to apply for the position. I have many qualifications which I think you would appreciate. I have been able to preach with power and have had success as a writer. I have been told that I am a good organizer. I have been a leader in most places I've gone.

"Some folk, however, have things against me. I am over fifty years of age. I have never preached in one place for over three years at a time. In some places I have left town, after my work caused riots and disturbances. I have to admit that I have been in jail three times, but not because of any wrong doing. My health is not good, though I still get a good deal done. I have had to work at my trade to help pay my way. The churches I have preached in have been small though located in several large cities.

"I have not gotten along too well with the religious leaders in different towns where I have preached. In fact, some of them have threatened me, taken me to court, and even attacked me physically. I am not too good at keeping records. I have been known to forget whom I have baptized. If you can use me, however, I shall do my best for you, even if I have to work to help with my support."

The elder read this letter to the committee, asking for a reply. The committee said he would never do for that church. They were not interested in an unhealthy, contentious, troublemaking, absent-minded jail-bird. After inquiring about the name of the presumptuous applicant, the elder answered, "The Apostle Paul."

This illustrates how modern Christians are more often concerned with surface issues in a man's life, and how little they know of true spirituality. In Paul we have a man who is truly spiritual. The lesson gives us many interesting insights into his life.

I.   BIBLE STUDY:

A. The prayer life of Paul in Ephesians.

486

Paul gives us interesting pictures of his spiritual life in the epistles. His two recorded prayers in Ephesians are monumental. Notice that he prays, not for spiritual blessings, nor for material blessings, but that they should know of the spiritual blessings they already possessed. Eph. 1:18—"The eyes of your understanding being enlightened"; 3:18-19 — that they may "comprehend" and "know." This is in accord with Eph. 1:3. We already have all we need in Christ; we need only realize it and make use of it. It is not wrong to pray for things which are material, especially when they affect our spiritual well-being. But our concern should always be a spiritual one. The Christian life is not so ethereal that it is unrelated to the world. But though we find the physical provisions of the world necessary for our existence, we are to be "anxious" about spiritual things, the kingdom of God, and not money. Try patterning your prayers after Paul's.

B. The prison life of Paul in Philippians.

Paul was a prisoner in Rome. Not many prisoners are happy about it, even when justly punished. Paul was unjustly punished, yet rejoiced. Why? Because his great concern was Christ and his work. For him, "life" was Christ. What is life for most people, for you? Is it money, social life, grades? Everyone has a great driving passion to which other things are subordinated. For many, Christ is subordinate to girls, sports cars, top grades, fraternities, pleasing their friends, etc. When Paul has Christ first, his misfortunes do not overcome him. Our misfortunes often bring us to misery and defeat because we are so much attached to ourselves and our circumstances, and so little to Christ. Not, how does this benefit me, but how does it benefit Christ? Note reasons which would otherwise have discouraged Paul: (1) he was unjustly in prison; (2) he had been there some time (first jailed in Jerusalem); (3) he was opposed by others who claimed to be Christians; (4) he was rejected by his own race; (5) he was probably alone and inactive much of the time; (6) he was in a large, strange city; (7) he was uncertain about his future; (8) he had to take charity from others (Chap. 4). These reasons would tend to throw one into self pity and keep him from witnessing at all. Paul considered them an open door for spreading the gospel in a new place.

C. The personal life of Paul in Thessalonians.

There is a phrase, "like father, like son." We tend to copy the environment in which we live. We are often exhorted to win others to Christ. Some carry the importance of soul-winning so far, however, that they put no emphasis on Christian character. A person who witnesses all the time and has many so-called "results," yet whose life is un-Christlike, dishonors God and harms his converts. He gives them the wrong example to copy, and his children are unhealthy and spiritually malformed, just like their spiritual father. There is NO substitute for Christian character. This is why Paul was successful. Note some of his characteristics in I Thess. 2:1-10: (1) boldness; (2) sincerity; (3) ability to please God; (4) not seeking to please men (contrast the average college student with this); (5) gentleness (not harsh, argumentative, unkind); (6) love for converts; (7) hardworking; (8) holiness, righteousness, blamelessness.

D. The pastor's life of Paul in the Pastoral Epistles.

Paul here speaks much of material possessions. Why? Because in his day, as now, this was the consuming drive in the lives of many. Perhaps there were many wealthy people in Timothy's church. Money is like luggage on a trip. It is a necessity for the trip—we have to take luggage along—but it is not the main thing. We are concerned about where we are going, what we will see on the way, etc., not our luggage. Food and clothing are basic necessities. Without them we cannot live. Therefore we *must* have them. But suppose we are like Paul was as he wrote this epistle. We have food and clothing but nothing else!—no extra bank account, no credit card, no closetful of the latest clothes, no car, no secure job. WILL WE THEN BE CONTENT? Paul was. Christ was. Because materialism was not their main concern. The question is not whether I have a lot of money, but how concerned am I about it? You CANNOT serve God and money (mammon).

Note also the concern in Titus about "good works." It is important to understand Titus 3:5 and 3:8. Christians do good works. But we NEVER do them to earn God's approval or our salvation. Salvation is a free gift, received by faith alone (Eph. 2:8-9). This is contrary to the notion that most of us are good enough to "get by" with God. Good works are the result, not the cause, of becoming a Christian. If a man is sick, I do not tell him to play a game of tennis to get well. But if he is well, he can play without trouble. We do not tell people to be good to obtain salvation. We tell them to be good after God has given salvation to them and because he has given it to them.

LESSON PLAN

THE GENERAL EPISTLES

LESSON SIX   STEP TEN

OBJECTIVE: To understand and apply the implications of the gospel Jesus Christ taught, as it is amplified and defined in the General Epistles.

I.   OPEN WITH PRAYER.

II. MEMORY VERSE:

Have three students give one of the suggested verses; then compare the verses with one another, giving some applications to our personal life.

III. MOTIVATION:

Some years ago, the Chinese missionary, Watchman Nee, had taken a young convert by the name of Brother Wu on a preaching visit to an island just off the South China coast. Though laboring faithfully the two found little response from the people and began to wonder why. One morning while outside preaching, Brother Wu asked publicly: "Why will none of you believe?" Someone in the crowd replied: "We have a god—one god—Ta-wang, and he has never failed us." "How do you know he has never failed you?" asked Wu. "We have held his festival procession every January for 286 years, and every year without fail his day is a perfect day without rain or cloud," was the reply. Aftei learning that the festival was scheduled for January 11 at eight in the morning, Wu said impetuously, "I promise you that it will certainly rain on the 11th at eight this year." Responding with cries, the people said that if there were rain at that time this year, Wu's God would become their God. Watchman Nee and Brother Wu immediately committed themselves to prayer, claiming knowledge of "The God of Elijah"—a whole village's fate depended upon the faithfulness of God. At the breakfast table on the appointed morning as grace was offered for the food, there was also thanksgiving for the rain to come. Moments later, at eight on the dot, the rain came down. Shouts from the children were first heard, "There is God, there is no more Ta-wang!" Was this a miracle? Yes, the miracle of faith.

IV. BIBLE STUDY:

A. Hebrews—This epistle brings to great reality many various Old

Testament doctrines which in the past were mere "shadows" of truths to come in the person of Jesus Christ.

1. The position of faith—Heb. 10:19-21.

   a. We are placed in Christ, a position of perfection, acceptable to the Father ("into the holiest"—v. 9).

   b. Gives boldness rather than fear when approaching God ("a new and living way"—vs. 19-20).

   c. The blood cleanses and makes forgiveness possible (v. 19).

   d. Only our high priest can present an acceptable sacrifice.

2. The assurance of faith—Heb. 10:22-25.

   a. What types of obedience give one assurance before God, according to question 1? Is church attendance anywhere implied (v. 25)?

   b. What quality has promise of reward in Heb. 10:35 (question 3)?

3. In Heb. 11, find examples of men of faith whom God has used in the Old Testament past.

4. To whom should we look during periods of trial (Heb. 12:1-3)?

B. James—The theme of James is the necessity of outward willing service as true evidence of an inward faith.

   1. God must test faith to determine and build quality.

      a. Testing produces patience—1:3 (question 1).

      b. Have students give personal examples of how God has led and taught them during periods of testing.

   2. What emphasis on Christian conduct is brought out in the following passages:

      a. James 1:22, 26 (question 4—prove knowledge by action).

      b. James 2:1-4 (partiality).

      c. James 3:10-12 (conversation and the tongue).

      d. James 4:6, 17 (humility and obedience).

C. I and II Peter—The foundation of the faith, and warning to stand against coming apostasy—faithful unto death!

   1. In light of what God has proclaimed to us in I Pet. 2:9, what difference does Christ make in our lives (question 3)?

a. Dead to sin and alive unto righteousness—2:24.

b. Sanctified because of Christ within—3:15.

c. Alive in the will of God—4:2.

d. Relationships in the home—3:1-7. (Is this our experience?)

2. Methods of defending the faith.

a. Claiming the promises of God—II Pet. 1:4.

b. Allow the world to be an eyewitness of the love and truth of God as seen through our lives lived for Him. What knowledge should an eyewitness have?

c. How can we recognize those who are not true to the faith in our modern times? See characteristics—question 2.

D. I II, III John—Relationships of love in the family of God; the walk of the believer during apostasy; church policy.

1. General tests of discipleship.

a. Keeping His commandments—I John 2:3.

b. Walking in the light—1:7.

c. Victory over three major problem areas in living the Christian life—lust of flesh, of eyes, and pride—2:16; 4:4.

d. Loving—3:11, 14, 18; 4:7.

2. Can we be assured of eternal life while here on earth—5:13?

3. What was John's joy in II John 4? In III John 4?

4. If a person claims he believes in God, but not in Christ, what does the Word say about him—II John 9?

5. Where do we find the Christian attitude toward visiting believers? We should receive them—III John 8.

E. Jude.

Have students compare questions 1 and 3, with the great need today for men to stand for the faith.

1. Build—v.20.

2. Keep—v.21.

3. Save—vs.22-23.

V. PARALLEL PASSAGES:

A. Our position in Christ—Eph. 1:1-14.

1. Chosen in Him—v.4.

2. Predestinated to adoption—v.5.

3. Accepted in the beloved—v.6.

4. Redeemed—v.7.

5. Informed of His will—v.9.

6. Obtained an inheritance—v.11.

7. Sealed by the Spirit—v.13.

B. The reward of faith and obedience—story of Naaman—II Kings 5.

C. Outward testimony of willing death; supreme test of inward faith —account of death of Stephen—Acts 7:54-60; 8.

1. Characteristics of this man of God—Acts 6:8.

2. Result of his death and impression on the life of Paul—7:58.

D. Building a good foundation of faith — Matthew 7:24-27; I Cor. 3:11-15.

E. Evidences of present day apostasy—II Tim. 3:1-5,7; Rev. 3:14-18.

VI. SUMMARY:

We can praise God today that in His matchless grace He has given us everything which pertains to life and godliness. Nothing depends upon what we have been in the past, what we are at present, or what we shall become in the flesh in the future. When Christ said, "It is finished," on the cross, this was an eternal sign to man that He had completely accomplished everything it will ever take to make man acceptable before God. The only barrier remaining today, which can keep man from God, is the barrier of unbelief. In the light of these great Scriptural truths which we have reviewed today, let us come to the Lord Jesus and accept by faith His work for us and let us thank Him that He alone is worthy to be called the Son of God.

VII. CLOSE IN PRAYER.

THE GENERAL EPISTLES

LESSON SIX   STEP TEN

INTRODUCTION:

In Hebrews, James, I and II Peter, I, II, III John and Jude we have a group of inspired writings differing in important respects from Paul's Epistles. But this difference is in no sense one of conflict. All present the same Christ, the same salvation, the same morality. The difference is one of extension, of development. The Jewish-Christian writings deal with the elementary and foundational things of the gospel, while to Paul were given the revelations concerning the Church, her place in the counsels of God and the calling and hope of the believer, as vitally united to Christ in the one body.

The Judeo-Christian writers view the Church as a professing body in which, during this age, the wheat and tares are mingled (Matthew 13:24-30). These writings abound in warning to arouse mere professors of religious beliefs, who are sincere in their practices as far as they go, but do not completely embrace the true gospel of Jesus Christ and commit themselves to Him as Lord. In contrast to these truths, Paul writes in view of the body of true believers who are assuredly saved, a called-out priesthood, members of Christ's Church on earth.

A. Hebrews.

1. The first chapter of the Epistle of Hebrews has importance in fulfilling a declaration of Jesus Christ previously presented in Genesis 1:1 and John 1:1. Here Jesus—His deity and everlasting glory—is displayed more fully as the only true Son of God. By an eternal act of God, ONCE FOR ALL, Jesus paid the penalty for the sin of the world and provided everlasting salvation for the whole human race.

2. Christ is the fulfillment, rather than administrator, of the Mosaic system, thus the writer compares Jesus to angels through whom the law was given (Acts 7:53), and to the Levitical Priesthood through whom the law was administered.

3. Major points of doctrine include: Christ's unity with man (Chap. 2), the Christian's rest of faith (Chap. 4), the New Covenant as superior to the old law (Chaps. 8, 10), and great heroes of the Old Testament (Chap. 11).

B. James.

    1. The man: James was thought to be the blood brother of Jesus and a recognized holy man according to the law's standards. He was surnamed "the just" by his countrymen and chosen a "bishop of Jerusalem" where he was very influential in the church. He endorsed Paul's Gentile work, was a Jew and himself primarily concerned with Jews. His life-work was to win Jews and aid them in a smooth change-over to Christianity.

    2. Major doctrines and subjects include: the value of testing, discrimination, faith and works contrasted, the tongue, worldly-mindedness, difficulties with wealth, and a religion of deeds backed up by a faith in Christ.

C. I Peter.

    1. The man: from Jesus' words in John 21:28, we judge that Peter must have died a martyr's death. He was a leader of the twelve and probably visited all the leading church centers of the Roman world.

    2. Occasion of the writing, and brief content: I Peter was written to churches in the five provinces of Asia Minor. The Church as a whole was undergoing severe persecution. The example of the emperor encouraged the enemies of Christians to take advantage of his permission to persecute. This was the first world-trial for the Church and many Christians were burned nightly in Nero's gardens. Peter reminded the Church to "bear up under it all," recalling that Christ did His perfect work by suffering.

    3. Doctrine included: the Christian's incorruptible inheritance, the earthly pilgrimage of believers (attitudes toward the elect, government, family, etc.), and the fiery trial and reward of patience and endurance.

D. II Peter.

    1. This epistle was written by Simon Peter. It was Peter's second message to the same people and his objective was to warn them of coming apostasy.

    2. The principal doctrines include: the great and precious promises, false teachers, the destruction of the ungodly and the time of the Lord's coming.

E. I, II, III John.

    1. John's epistle (I John) is intensely personal and recognized as

a circular letter from John the Apostle to the churches around Ephesus to emphasize the main essentials of the Gospels and to warn against heresies.

2. Christianity had been in the world some sixty or seventy years, and in many parts of the Roman Empire it had become an important influence. Feeling the impact of the Church, false teachers arose, seeking to neutralize its power. These epistles were written to correct false doctrine, and to expound God's love and the Christian's righteousness.

3. Major doctrines include: how to walk in the light of God, true righteousness, love, false prophets and teachers, and the need for recognizing authority of the apostles and their chosen servants (III John).

F. Jude.

1. There were two Judes: Judas, brother of James, one of the Twelve (Luke 6:16); and Judas, the brother of Jesus (Matthew 13:55). The latter is commonly regarded as the author of this epistle. Jude also wrote to counteract a heresy.

2. Major doctrines and subjects include: warnings connected with the imminent apostasy, descriptions of false teachers (4-9), fallen angeles and their fate, Michael's contention with the Devil, and the prophecy of Enoch.

3. The entire tone of this book is that every Christian should contend for the faith once delivered to the saints—v.3.

LESSON PLAN

THE REVELATION OF JESUS CHRIST

LESSON SEVEN   STEP TEN

OBJECTIVE: To teach the student some fundamentals of God's prophetic
program.

I.   OPEN WITH PRAYER.

II.   MEMORY VERSE: Have each one quote the verse he has memorized.

III. MOTIVATION:

Name three major events in God's prophetic program. Can you think
of any reasons why it is important to be familiar with prophecy?

IV.   BIBLE STUDY: (See the Lesson Amplification for answers.)

A. What is the Tribulation? What are some of the events that happen
during this time?

B. What events accompany the Second Advent of Christ?

C. What is the condition of the world during the Millennium? Discuss.

D. What events happen after the Millennium?

E. What is the "eternal state?"

F. Have a student outline these major events and make sure that
everyone understands.

V.   PARALLEL PASSAGES:

These can be used in the Bible Study to throw more light on the
book of Revelation.

A. Concerning the Rapture of the Church — The Bride of Christ: I
Thess. 4:13-18, I Cor. 15:51-58; John 14:1-3; Titus 2:12-13.

B. Concerning the Great Tribulation: Daniel 9:20-27; 12:1-3; Matthew
24-25; II Thess. 2:1-12.

496

C. Concerning the Second Coming of Christ: Isa. 63:1-6; Zech. 14:1-7; Matthew 24:27-31; II Thess. 2:8; II Peter 3:1-11.

D. Concerning the Millennium: Isa. 61-66; Jer. 31-33-40; Ezek. 36-37; Zech. 14:8-21; Romans 8:19-21.

E. Concerning the Eternal State: Isa. 65:17; II Pet. 3:13.

VI. SUMMARY: Conclude with a practical application.

A. How should a knowledge of God's prophetic program affect our manner of living (II Peter 3:10-14)?

B. How should it affect our attitude toward the world and material possessions (I John 2:15-17)?

D. How should it affect our attitude toward the difficulties in life (John 14:1-3)?

E. How should it affect our attitude toward Christian work and soul winning (I Cor. 15:54-58)?

VII. CLOSE IN PRAYER.

THE REVELATION OF JESUS CHRIST

LESSON SEVEN   STEP TEN

I. SUMMARY OF THE BOOK:

The book is not correctly called the "Revelation of Saint John." It is precisely, "The Revelation of Jesus Christ" (Rev. 1:1). That is, it is an unveiling of His future plan for the earth and for His redeemed saints, both for time and eternity. It is necessary to view the book as in no sense sealed (Rev. 22:10). A distinct blessing is to be upon the person who reads and hears the words of this prophecy (Rev. 1:3). The figures and symbols of the book, which furnish the basis of its interpretation, are found elsewhere in divine revelation and can be understood only in the light of a coherent and connected study of all other lines of prophecy as they converge upon the book of Revelation. Interpretation of this book demands a thorough acquaintance with all the other great prophecies which merge here.

It is a book of optimism for God's people, assuring us again and again that we are under God's protection, with a life of everlasting blessedness ahead.

Alternating scenes between earth and heaven, it is also a book of the "wrath of God," ever contrasting the joys of the redeemed with the agonies of the lost. How we need to be reminded of that, amidst our careless and godless generation.

II. BACKGROUND OF THE BOOK:

These visions were given, and the book written, in the lurid light of burning martyrs. The Church had made enormous strides in growth, although it had suffered and was suffering terrific persecutions.

III. AUTHOR OF THE BOOK:

God Himself dictated it, through Christ, by an angel, to John, who wrote it down, and sent the completed book to the Seven Churches. John was called "the beloved disciple." He was the most intimate earthly friend of Jesus (John 21:20,24; Rev. 1:1). The book was written when he was on the Isle of Patmos, around 96 A.D.

IV. AN OUTLINE OF THE BOOK OF REVELATION:

There are several different ways of interpreting Revelation, but the best seems to follow the outline of Rev. 1:19.

A. "The things which thou hast seen"—i.e., the vision of a glorified Christ—are in the first chapter.

B. "The things which are"—i.e., the letters to the seven churches—are in the second and third chapters. These seven churches represent all facets of Christendom, good and bad, during the Church age.

C. "The things which shall be"—i.e., the unfolding of the prophetic events—are in the fourth through the twenty-second chapters. These chapters contain descriptions of the Great Tribulation, the Second Coming of Christ, and the Millennium.

WHAT THEN?

When the great plants of our cities
    Have turned out their last finished work;
When our merchants have sold their last yard of silk
    And dismissed the last tired clerk,
When our banks have raked in their last dollar
    And paid the last dividend;
When the Judge of the earth says, "Close for the night,"
    And asks for a balance—WHAT THEN?

When the choir has sung its last anthem,
    And the preacher has made his last prayer;
When the people have heard their last sermon
    And the sound has died out on the air;
When the Bible lies closed on the altar
    And the pews are all empty of men
And each one stands facing his record—
    And the great Book is opened—WHAT THEN?

When the actors have played their last drama
    And the mimic has made his last fun,
When the film has flashed its last picture
    And the billboard displayed its last run;
When the crowds seeking pleasure have vanished
    And gone out in the darkness again—
When the trumpet of ages is sounded,
    And we stand before Him—WHAT THEN?

—Author Unknown.

Jesus Christ will actually return to earth! All the material accomplishments of mankind will be destroyed. Christians will be judged on the basis of what they have done with Jesus Christ and what they have allowed Him to do with and through their lives.